PROBLEMS AND POLICY
IN PUBLIC ASSISTANCE

Harper's Social Science Series
F. STUART CHAPIN, *Editor*

Problems and Policy in Public Assistance

*A project submitted to the Faculty
of Teachers College, Columbia University,
in partial fulfillment of the requirement
for the Degree of Doctor of Education*

By the late Hilary M. Leyendecker

Harper & Brothers   Publishers   New York

HV
91
. L4

Blessed is he that understandeth concerning the needy and the poor: the Lord will deliver him in the evil day. Psalm 40

Contents

Foreword

Shortly after the death of Hilary Leyendecker on March 4, 1953, the dean of a school of social work wrote this about him:

Hilary was an original as well as a scholarly thinker. His drive to get public assistance placed in our scheme of things in a way to enable staff to function in an optimum manner is, in my opinion, a force which will be greatly missed.

During the 19 years of his working life Hilary was in social welfare and for half of that time in positions in which he taught social work subjects in academic institutions or was responsible for training programs in public and private agencies.

He first began to teach in the spring of 1939, when he participated in a civil service training course sponsored by the Centre Club of New York City, where he taught a course on "The Content of the Social Investigator's Job" to more than 400 workers of public and private agencies in New York City. He next obtained experience in training while director of personnel service for the United Seamen's Service. He was responsible for programs of social work orientation for nearly all members of the Service's overseas training pool and conducted a two-weeks training course for all trainees.

In the fall of 1945, Hilary became welfare training consultant of the New York State Department of Social Welfare and for the next five years he pioneered in the establishment and operation of a state-wide program to train, develop, and recruit staff in public welfare. Throughout this period he served intermittently as a member of the Rural Sociology faculty at Cornell University. Two going concerns in the establishment of which he played a major role are the Public Welfare Institute at Cornell University which has just completed its ninth annual session and the New

York State Conference on Pre-Professional Social Work Education.

In 1950–1951, while he was doing graduate work he served as lecturer on public welfare administration at the Adelphi College School of Social Work. His last position in social work was that of defense welfare training supervisor of the New York State Department of Social Welfare, a post he assumed in September, 1951, and held until his death.

His own educational background reflected his basic professional interests—social work and teaching. He received his bachelor's degree at Columbia University in 1933 and his master's degree at the New York School of Social Work of Columbia University ten years later. He received the doctor's degree in education from Teachers College, Columbia University, posthumously.

This book is an outgrowth of Hilary's activities in training public welfare personnel and teaching courses at the undergraduate and graduate level for young people planning to enter the field of social work. The following professional friends of Hilary have joined me in the sponsorship of its publication:

ALDEN E. BEVIER	Director, Defense Welfare Service, New York State Department of Social Welfare
DR. HERBERT A. BLOCH	Chairman, Department of Sociology and Anthropology, St. Lawrence University; and Lecturer, Brooklyn College
GEORGE J. CLARKE	Associate Executive Director, Goodwill Industries of New York, Inc
MARY L. GIBBONS	Formerly Technical Consultant on Welfare Problems, Catholic Charities, Archdiocese of New York
GORDON HAMILTON	Associate Dean and Professor of Social Work, The New York School of Social Work, Columbia University.

ALEXANDER F. HANDEL	Consultant in Community Planning, American Foundation for the Blind; formerly, Dean, School of Social Work, Adelphi College
JANE M. HOEY	Director of Social Research, National Tuberculosis Association; formerly, Director, Bureau of Public Assistance, U. S. Department of Health, Education, and Welfare
DR. EGON PLAGER	Professor of Sociology, Siena College; Chairman, New York State Conference on Pre-Professional Social Work Education
DR. PHILIP TAIETZ	Department of Rural Sociology, College of Agriculture, Cornell University
WAYNE VASEY	Dean, Graduate School of Social Work, Rutgers University, The State University of New Jersey
HON. MALCOLM WILSON	Member of New York State Assembly, First District, Westchester County.

ROBERT T. LANSDALE

Consultant, New York Commission on the Fiscal Affairs of State Government; formerly, New York State Commissioner of Social Welfare

October, 1954

Preface

Someone once said that the purpose of a preface is to provide an opportunity for the author to explain why he wrote what he did rather than that which the critics might have preferred. This author is keenly aware of the need for such explanation.

This book is an outgrowth of the writer's need as a teacher of public welfare in professional, preprofessional, and in-service training programs. As originally conceived, it was to have been an introductory text covering the whole range of public social services. As the work progressed, however, this plan was found to be impracticable—no one volume could deal adequately with so vast a subject. Accordingly, this book has been restricted to public assistance and its related income-maintenance programs.

The literature of public assistance is extensive. Much, however, lies buried in public documents, reports, pamphlets, and unpublished studies difficult of access. Moreover, most of the published material has been written by specialists more for the edification of their colleagues than for the enlightenment of the beginner. Edith Abbott's monumental work *Public Assistance* (published in 1940) has never progressed beyond the first volume, which deals with the poor law and unemployment relief programs. As valuable as is this book as a source book it does not deal with current programs and with many of the issues that are of concern to the present-day student of public assistance. The only other work that attempted to meet this need was the little volume *The Public Assistance Worker,* edited by Russell Kurtz and published in 1938.

The present volume has been written with the needs of the beginner in mind—the student, the worker-in-training, the newly elected or appointed public official or board member, and the ordinary citizen concerned about this increasingly important (and costly) function of government.

The writer is aware that he has given short shrift to many important aspects of public assistance and of related programs—notably administrative organization, medical and institutional care, and the veterans' programs. This has seemed necessary to keep the book within manageable size and to avoid overwhelming the beginner with details.

If the reader acquires an appreciation of the general characteristics of public assistance, its processes, and its organizational and human problems, the expectations of the author will have been fulfilled.

A few words are necessary concerning bibliography. The references in the text have been kept to a minimum and represent reading matter which should be studied for a richer understanding of the material covered in each chapter.

This project was undertaken under the direction of Professors Harold F. Clark and Edmund de Schweinitz Brunner of Teachers College and Professor Philip Klein of the New York School of Social Work. The writer is indebted to them for helpful guidance and friendly encouragement.

H. M. L.

January, 1953

PROBLEMS AND POLICY
IN PUBLIC ASSISTANCE

CHAPTER 1

Economic Dependency
and the State

Economic insecurity is a product of the modern highly developed industrial era. The agricultural pioneer, the medieval feudal serf, and
the slave all possessed economic security—at some level. But the free
and independent worker of the modern age has long been faced with
periodic loss of income in consequence of the fluctuations in the labor
market.
—HAROLD G. MOULTON, *Controlling Factors in Economic Development*

INTRODUCTION

What This Book Is About

This book deals with the way in which government discharges
its obligation to relieve economic want by means of money payments or assistance in kind to needy persons. It deals with the
problem of economic insecurity, society's understanding of that
problem, and the institutions and programs evolved to cope with
it. It treats in particular of that part of our social security system
known as "public assistance" and the factors which have shaped
its growth—economic, social, political, moral. It analyzes the
policies and structure on which public assistance is based, and
the legislative, financial, and human issues related to its administration. Its objective is to present a comprehensive view of the
way in which public assistance is administered, and to develop
understanding of how and why it has taken its present form. It
is an introduction to a highly complex professional service of
government.

What Is Public Assistance?

Public assistance is financial aid extended to needy people in their own homes or places of residence. It is "an affirmation of the community's responsibility for meeting the needs of persons who lack sufficient resources for maintenance." [1] In this country it is part of a developing system of social security designed to provide protection against distress caused by lack of income. Although social insurance will eventually become the main defense against income loss, public assistance, for the present, continues to be the major instrumentality of government for relieving want.

Economic assistance to the needy has been provided by government, in one form or another, since colonial times. Its basis is that sense of public responsibility which first found expression in the poor laws of sixteenth-century England. It has been only in recent years, however, that such assistance has become a major function of government.

Twenty-five years ago, that is, prior to the great economic depression of the 1930's, the average citizen knew little about this function—and cared less. He probably had glimpsed the "poorhouse" on his drives in the country; no doubt he was aware of a public official called "the overseer of the poor"; perhaps he had heard, vaguely, of the movement for "old-age pensions" and "widows' allowances." But these were matters of concern only to a few public officials, social workers (members of a new and relatively unrecognized profession), and a handful of zealous reformers.

Since that time the picture has changed. "Relief" has become a topic of public interest and concern. The millions of people brought to destitution as a result of the depression focused attention on the necessity for an extensive governmental program which would provide adequate relief from want and intelligent and humane guidance for those who found themselves in need. Although the assistance program which came into being as a consequence has expanded and contracted with fluctuating economic conditions, nevertheless, as contrasted with the pre-depression years, governmental activity in this sphere continues

[1] *Social Work Year Book,* Russell Kurtz, ed. (New York: Russell Sage, 1945), "Public Assistance," p. 316.

to be extensive. In the prosperous year of 1950, approximately six million individuals were supported in whole or in part from public assistance funds at a cost of roughly two and one-half billion dollars. Some thirty thousand public assistance workers, supervisors, and executives, in addition to clerical staff, administered the program.[2] The need for efficient and economical administration has led to the development of a career service in public assistance based upon a high degree of technical knowledge and skill.

The growth of public assistance has occasioned no little criticism. Many people find it hard to understand why, in a period of full employment and high wages, and in spite of a system of social insurance paying benefits for unemployment, for retirement due to age, and for survivors of deceased workers, the need for assistance should be so great.

Before beginning our examination of policies and practices in the administration of public assistance, it would be well for us to consider briefly some of its economic and social implications.

THE PROBLEM OF INADEQUATE INCOME

Poverty in the Midst of Plenty

In January, 1937, when the United States was still in the throes of an unprecedented depression, Franklin D. Roosevelt, in a memorable inaugural address, spoke these words: "I see millions lacking the means to buy the products of farm and factory and by their poverty denying work and productiveness to many other millions. I see one-third of a nation ill-housed, ill-nourished, ill-clad."

Curiously enough, eleven years later, although the nation was experiencing unparalleled prosperity, the proportion of the population in the depressed category had not changed. Thus, a Congressional committee investigating the problem of low-income families could say:

We have found about one-third of all the families and individuals in the United States had total money incomes of less than $2,000 in

[2] *Public Social Welfare Personnel,* U.S. Department of Health, Education and Welfare, Bureau of Public Assistance and Children's Bureau (Washington: 1953), Table 2.

1948. . . . A surprisingly large proportion of the Nation's families was underproducing and underconsuming in the generally prosperous full-employment year of 1948.[3]

There are several different causes of the poverty and in many cases, the dependency of these families. . . . The complex causes admit of no single prescription, no rapid cure.

> Studies of living standards based upon money income alone are not entirely satisfactory; to have meaning, data should be related to price levels, and when there are wide fluctuations this relationship may be difficult to measure. Money income, moreover, should be related to the size of the family unit. Money, however, does not reflect the total economic resources of the family. Farm produce and ownership of a home represent income. Since the boundary line between sufficiency and want is difficult to determine except by income and expenditure studies of individual families, we are not justified in assuming that an annual income of under $2000 is necessarily inadequate. But since ten million families have less income than this (four million of which had less than $1000), it is not unreasonable to conclude that the majority are faced with problems of insecurity and marginal living, if not actual dependency.

How do we account for this phenomenon? The staff report of the committee reveals characteristics of this low-income group which shed light on the nature of the problem:

First   Most of the families below the $2,000 income level are urban or nonfarm families, but farm poverty is also a most important problem. Of the nearly ten million families, about 3.3 million lived on farms. Of this number 1.7 million had incomes below $1,000 in 1948.

Second   The problem of impoverished old age is one of the most difficult and one of the most important facing our society. It is a problem which is becoming more and more serious as the proportion of older people increases. Of the total of 6.3 million nonfarm families with incomes below $2,000 in 1948, more than one-fourth, or 1.7 million were headed by persons over 65; they constitute one-half of all families in this age group.

Third   There will always remain in our form of society a sizable group of individuals who for one reason or another cannot be made producing members. These nonearners, however, are still consumers and their consumption is maintained, at least partially, through social insurance and public assistance programs.

[3] U.S. Congress, Senate, *Report of the Subcommittee on Low-Income Families of the Joint Committee on the Economic Report,* Senate Document No. 146, 81st Congress, 2nd Sess. (Washington: Government Printing Office, 1950), p. 1.

Fourth When nonfarm low-income families are classified by oc-cupation of the head of the family, the unskilled and the semi-skilled service workers, laborers, and operatives are found to make up the hard core of the urban low-income group. They number 2.2 million.

Fifth Nonwhite families make up a significant group of the low-income families. Of the nonfarm families with income below $2,000 about 800,000—or one-eighth—were headed by nonwhite males . . . considerably greater than the proportion of nonwhites in the general population.

Sixth Broken families, those headed by women because of widow-hood, desertion, or divorce, are found in large numbers in the non-farm low-income group. Of the total of 6.3 million urban families receiving incomes under $2,000, about 1.5 million were headed by women.

Seventh Low-income families are, as would be expected, headed by persons with little education. Sixty-four percent of the nonfarm families receiving incomes below $2,000 in 1946 had not progressed beyond the eighth grade. Only 6 percent had gone beyond high school.

Eighth Disabled persons in need of vocational rehabilitation

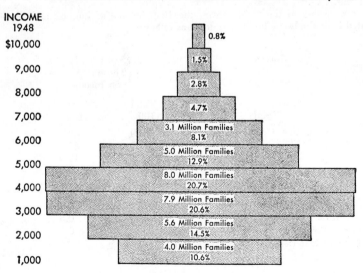

UNITED STATES BUREAU OF THE CENSUS
CURRENT CONSUMER'S INCOME

INCOME OF FAMILIES AND PERSONS IN UNITED STATES, 1948

INCOME
1948

$10,000 — 0.8%
9,000 — 1.5%
8,000 — 2.8%
7,000 — 4.7%
6,000 — 3.1 Million Families 8.1%
5,000 — 5.0 Million Families 12.9%
4,000 — 8.0 Million Families 20.7%
3,000 — 7.9 Million Families 20.6%
2,000 — 5.6 Million Families 14.5%
1,000 — 4.0 Million Families 10.6%

number about 1.5 million and they are found in the low-income group.[4]

The situation is considerably more optimistic than these data suggest at first glance. Thus, although the number of families with less than a minimum income is still large, there has been a substantial improvement in their income in recent years.[5] The fact remains, however, that in spite of national prosperity many Americans are living on marginal incomes—and many would have even less to live on were it not for public assistance.[6]

[4] U.S. Congress, Joint Committee Print, *Low-Income Families and Economic Stability* (Washington: Government Printing Office, 1949), pp. 3–5.

[5] Thus the New York *Times* (March 5, 1952) comments on a study of changes in distribution of income by Dr. Simon Kuznets for the National Bureau of Economic Research:

"The marginal worker, the first to lose his job in times of depression, and once regarded as the 'forgotten man' of American capitalism, has been the greatest beneficiary of recent gain in national output. . . .

"From published and unpublished estimates of the President's Council of Economic Advisers, family incomes can be segregated into classes roughly indicating what has happened at the very bottom and very top of the income scale. . . .

"Over the twelve year period covered by the estimates, families with substandard incomes declined from one in every two to one in ten. Families with minimum or better incomes rose from one in five to nearly three out of four. . . ."

[6] According to the 1950 census, the 1949 income of families and unrelated individuals can be broken down as follows:

Income	Percent Distribution for Those Reporting on Income	
Total	Total 100	Nonwhite 100
Under $1,000	22.9	43.3
$ 1,000 to $1,999	16.2	27.3
2,000 to 2,999	17.7	17.0
3,000 to 3,999	17.0	7.4
4,000 to 4,999	10.1	2.4
5,000 to 5,999	6.5	1.3
6,000 to 6,999	3.5	0.7
7,000 to 9,999	3.8	0.5
10,000 and over	2.4	0.1

SOURCE: 1950 Census of Population Series PC-7, No. 2.

Remedies for low income and methods for strengthening our economic institutions lie outside the scope of this book. The existence of the problem, however, is germane because low-income families are either currently receiving assistance or else constitute a great reservoir of economically marginal people from which the assistance recipients of the future will largely be drawn.

The Threat of Insecurity

Poverty and insecurity are not coextensive terms. As serious as is the problem of low income, the threat of insecurity is even more widespread. Low-income families are, to be sure, insecure; they cannot purchase many of the things that are considered part of the American standard of living; a slight decline in income, a slight rise in the price level may bring them below the subsistence level; they can make no provision against the future—for their old age, for the education of their children, or against the day when sickness or unemployment cuts off their income or requires some unusual expenditure. But insecurity is not a threat to the poor alone. A low-income subsistence farmer may be relatively more secure than a highly paid white-collar worker, even though his standard of living is lower, because he has greater assurance of the continuance of his income.

While it is undoubtedly true that in depressions the low-income family is likely to be the first to suffer, nevertheless, families at all income levels may be affected. In the great depression of the 1930's many skilled workers, executives, and professional people were thrown out of work on short notice. Bank savings were wiped out overnight, investments became worthless, homes in which there was substantial equity were lost. The poor, perhaps, are more conscious of the ever present threat of insecurity, but depressions affect all sectors of the economy, and as Professor Moulton points out, between 1819 and 1938 American business was depressed one-third of the time: [7]

[7] Harold G. Moulton, *Controlling Factors in Economic Development* (Washington: Brookings, 1949), p. 40.

1819–21	24 months	1882–85	36 months
1825–26	12 "	1890–91	9 "
1833–34	9 "	1893–97	48 "
1837–43	72 "	1907–08	12 "
1857–59	18 "	1913–14	20 "
1866–67	18 "	1920–21	18 "
1873–78	66 "	1929–33	42 "
		1937–38	10 "

The paradox of the modern age is that in spite of our vast wealth, our great productive capacity, our tremendous technological advances, the average person is probably less secure than his counterpart in the Middle Ages. "Security," of course, is a term subject to widely differing interpretations. It is used here to mean assurance of the continuance of cash income or its equivalent, without reference to· any particular standard of living—except that basic needs are met. Actually, the standard of living in the Middle Ages was low compared to our own. Even the nobility (aside from power, privilege, and prestige) were not much better off than the serf; indeed, their standard of living would compare unfavorably even with the standards of the low-income groups we have been discussing. But what they had they could depend on.

As part of the general scheme of ordered town and country life, with its regulated industry and "just" price, wages were as a matter of course socially controlled. The town through the medium of the guild fixed the price and the amount of the commodities to be sold. The reward of labor in the agricultural community of feudal times, whether expressed in terms of wheat or pence, was just as established as was the order of plowing, the rotation of crops, and the apportioning of the meadow land.

Certainty, conformity, and uniformity were the order of the medieval day. The preservation of the social unit was the chief end in view both in the agricultural village and in the industrial town. A dull dish perhaps, but judged by the hectic standards of the age of adventuring that followed, one that spelled to the individual a fair economic security according to the standards of the day.

The serf bound to the soil with a copper ring around his neck at least had his place in the village life and a share of the village wheat. Except in rare periods of actual famine when everyone suffered, the lowly apprentice was sure of bed and board, and the able-bodied journeyman's wage was a fact, not a hazardous possibility. The medieval scheme of things "insured the essentials" to its members far better than does its modern prototype.[8]

It would, of course, be absurd, simply for the sake of economic security, to advocate a return to a social pattern such as this— however well it may have been suited to a feudal agricultural society. Industrialization is necessary if productive work is to be available to a rapidly increasing population. The poverty of much of Asia attests the fact that a simple, nontechnical agricultural economy cannot support a large population at even a bare subsistence level.

To flourish, however, an industrial society requires a social structure of many intricate relationships. "It is the organization rather than the individual which is productive in an industrial system."[9] To obtain the benefits of industrial production it has seemed necessary to sacrifice simplicity and stability and to expose the individual to the risk of insecurity. Thus, although our standard of living has risen rapidly, it has become increasingly difficult to protect oneself against income loss because income is dependent not so much upon individual ability and effort as it is upon the smooth functioning of the whole economic system.

Unfortunately, when the medieval economy was replaced, there went with it a social philosophy which had stressed individual rights and duties, social relationships and obligations. This was replaced by a philosophy of individualism which equated material prosperity with godliness and looked upon poverty as a disgrace rather than as a misfortune. Only in recent years, and largely as a result of the great depression, has America begun to recognize the fact of economic interdependence and the need for social protection against income loss.

[8] Barbara Nachtrieb Armstrong, *Insuring the Essentials* (New York: Macmillan, 1932), pp. 17–18.
[9] Peter Drucker, *The New Society* (New York: Harper, 1949), p. 6.

Who Are the Needy?

Who are those persons, so unfortunate, who even in a time of general prosperity must be supported by the state? Statistics are not available on the exact number of individuals so aided, owing to variations in methods of reporting. The following data for the past two years, however, indicate the scope and magnitude of the problem:

Recipients of Public Assistance, December, 1951 and 1952

	1951	1952
Persons 65 years of age or older in receipt of Old-Age Assistance	2,701,080	2,634,662
Children under 16 years of age, or between 16 and 18 if still in school, in receipt of Aid to Dependent Children	1,522,930	1,494,563
Relatives of the above children (usually the mother, aunt, grandmother)	591,844	496,256
Visually handicapped persons in receipt of Aid to the Blind	97,179	98,461
Other handicapped persons in receipt of Aid to the Permanently and Totally Disabled (a new program established October, 1950)	124,419	161,441
Cases in receipt of General Assistance because of unemployment, sickness, inadequate income, etc.	323,000	280,000

Data from *Social Security Bulletin,* Annual Statistical Supplement, September, 1951, *Social Security Bulletin,* September, 1952, Table 38; and May, 1953, Table 7, p. 24.

These figures by no means represent the total number of persons supported by government. To them should be added inmates of public homes for the aged, patients cared for at public expense in general and special hospitals, and dependent children cared for at public expense in foster homes and institutions.

Many hundreds of thousands more are not dependent (in the strict sense of the word) solely because they are the beneficiaries of social insurance or of veterans' pensions.

No detailed analysis is needed to show that the overwhelming majority of assistance recipients are either aged or children and that the remainder are predominantly sick or handicapped or are caring for children.

Neither old age, childhood, sickness, nor unemployment is *necessarily* a cause of public dependency; but all of them are predisposing factors that warrant further examination.

PREDISPOSING FACTORS IN DEPENDENCY

Old Age

The American people are growing older. Recent census reports indicate that persons sixty-five years of age and over have increased 36 percent between 1940 and 1950. In contrast, persons between the ages of forty-five and sixty-four and between twenty-five and forty-four increased only 16.7 and 13.3 percent respectively. These changes conform to a long-term trend. In 1870, persons sixty-five years of age and over comprised 3 percent of the population; by 1900, they had increased to 4 percent; by 1910, to 4.3 percent; by 1920, to 4.6 percent; by 1930, to 5.3 percent; by 1940, to 6.9 percent; and by 1950 to approximately 9.4 percent. It has been estimated that by the year 2000 they will constitute 13 percent of the population.

These shifts in the age distribution of the American people are primarily the result of decreases in the birth rate, death rate, and immigration.

The life span of older people is increasing. The present life expectancy of persons reaching their sixty-fifth year is now thirteen years; not so long ago it was only three years. More persons are thus living to an age when physical and social disabilities make self-support difficult if not impossible.

Although proportionately there are many more persons in the older age groups than there were a century ago, it is a moot point whether they are any more healthy and vigorous as a group. Medicine, sanitation, and improved nutrition have promoted the health and well-being of the population generally and have made it possible for more persons to live longer because of the prevention, cure, or arrest of disease; but life has often been prolonged *in spite of* degenerative illness and other ailments impairing productivity and the ability to be self-supporting.

Dependency among older people is increasing, not only because their numbers are increasing but also because of lessened opportunities for gainful work:

> In countries most affected by population aging there has also been a tendency over a long period of time to lower the age at which workers retire from active employment. . . . In 1890, about 68 percent of the men 65 years old in this country were still following gainful occupations. During the following half-century this proportion decreased steadily and sharply until in 1940 it was only about 42 percent. There was also some decrease in the proportion gainfully occupied among men 55 to 64 years old, which dropped from 89 to less than 85 percent.
>
> This tendency to cease working at an earlier age can be explained partly as a result of improvements in economic well-being which have made it possible for larger numbers of men to retire voluntarily and live on life savings or pensions. Mainly, however, it is the result of deep changes in economic structure which have made it increasingly difficult for men to hold their places in the labor force after passing middle age. Most important in this connection is the transition from an agrarian to an industrial economy. As independent farmers, aged and partially disabled men have an opportunity to continue working at least part time, perhaps with the help of their sons or of hired hands. As industrial wage earners they may be forced to retire when they can no longer meet the competition of others.[10]

The necessity for older persons to seek support from the state has also come about because of social and economic changes in the family. With smaller-sized families there are fewer adult offspring among whom the burden of maintaining an aged father or mother can be spread. The shift in the population from rural to urban living, with the consequent dependence upon wages or salary, and the increasing use of rented dwellings have also made

[10] John D. Durand, "Age Distribution of the Population," *Birthdays Don't Count* (New York State Joint Legislative Committee on the Aging, Leg. Doc. No. 61, 1948), p. 63.

it difficult for children to provide either funds or living space for dependent parents.

Old Age Retirement benefits under the Social Security Act have not yet had any marked influence on the volume of public assistance. They have, however, prevented even more widespread dependency among the aged. The maximum retirement benefit at the present time is only $85.00 a month. Although coverage in the retirement system has been extended and the eligibility requirements have been eased for older persons, many are still unprotected. It is interesting to note that the volume of assistance to the aged is greatest in those low per capita income agricultural states where insurance coverage is limited because of the exclusion of farmers.

Dependent Childhood

In spite of decreases in the birth rate the proportion of children in the population has risen markedly. Between 1900 and 1950 the number of children under eighteen years of age jumped from 31,000,000 to 47,000,000—an increase of 52 percent. In the most recent census the rate of increase of children under ten years of age was even greater than that of the elderly—39.3 percent.

The death or physical incapacitation of the male parent is, of course, a major factor in dependency of children. But to an increasing degree dependency is arising from family breakdown —by separation or divorce, by desertion of one or both parents, by unmarried parenthood.

The difficulty faced by the remaining parent (or parent substitute), especially when that person is the mother, grandmother, or aunt, is accentuated by rising living costs and by the lengthening time span during which young people must be supported. It is no longer considered desirable or even possible for children of fourteen to begin earning their living.

The fact that dependency in childhood is frequently the result of the inadequacy, if not actual delinquency, of one or both parents makes the necessity of relieving that need no less urgent. We cannot permit children to be the victims of our disapproval of parental shortcomings. We have learned, moreover, that in the long run it is usually better for the child—and less costly to society—to assist the remaining parent to maintain a home. Except in cases of extreme neglect or abuse, the child's own home is a better place in which to provide for his needs than is an institution or foster home.

As in the case of the aged, social insurance has not yet made any noticeable reduction in the need for assistance. The maximum benefit under any circumstance is only $168.75 a month. While these benefits are by no means insignificant, it is obvious that fatherless families, with no other outside resources, may not be able to provide adequately for their needs. Again, as in the case of the aged, the volume of assistance to children is highest in those low per capita income agricultural states where social insurance coverage is limited because of the exclusion of farmers.

Sickness and Disability

As factors contributing to dependency, sickness and disability need no detailed analysis. Even when the person affected is not the primary income producer in the family, the cost of treatment and maintenance is frequently more than the family can pay out of current earnings and from savings. In growing numbers, persons who are normally self-supporting must seek governmental assistance in paying for hospitalization for themselves and for members of their family.

Unemployment

Relatively few assistance recipients are in need because they are "unemployed" in the strict sense of the term. The aged, the sick, the handicapped, the mothers with young children to care for at home are not considered to be in the labor market. Of the remainder, either the great majority have never been attached to the labor market (e.g., the recently widowed woman of sixty-three who has never worked outside the home) or else their attachment to the labor market has been sporadic owing to lack of education or training, or because of limited intelligence or personality defect which militates against regular employment.

Of course, even though employment conditions are good at the present time, every month finds thousands of able-bodied workers without jobs because of seasonal or cyclical conditions in business and agriculture, because of labor disputes, or for a variety of other reasons. There is relatively little prolonged unemployment, however, and that is why few persons who are able-bodied and possess skills that are in demand require public assistance.

We have no guarantee, however, that conditions of full employment will continue indefinitely. Should shifting economic, political, or social forces bring about an economic recession, many thousands of persons would lose their jobs, unemployment compensation benefits would be exhausted, and there would be a great increase in the need for assistance.

In these days of high wages it must be recalled that not all forms of employment have benefited. Some workers are caught between static, or relatively static, wages and rising prices. If they have family responsibilities they may have great difficulty in making ends meet. Frequently they must seek supplementary assistance. It is a serious matter when the state must supplement the earnings of fully employed workers because their income is insufficient to meet their family obligations. Except in cases where a family is unusually large, it represents a subsidy to the employer. If need exists, however, it must be met, however distasteful is the idea of such indirect subsidy.

PUBLIC ASSISTANCE AND THE WELFARE FUNCTION OF GOVERNMENT

The Role of the State in Relieving Want

There has never been a society so ordered that none of its members were ever in need. There have always been some people who for one reason or another have been economically unproductive and who have had to be helped. In simpler societies the family or the clan saw that its needy members were cared for. In more complex societies other institutions assumed this responsibility or new institutions were created for that purpose. The church has played a leading role in providing relief to the poor. As religious dissensions weakened its fabric, or as society became secularized, the burden of relieving poverty became too great for the church. The state then emerged as the chief agent for meeting economic need.

Originally, the state assumed responsibility for two reasons: (1) The public conscience could not tolerate the reproach that people in the community were suffering pangs of cold and hunger; and (2) the existence of such needy persons was a threat to the well-being of those more comfortably circumstanced— since desperate persons might be driven to violence. It is a moot point which of the two reasons carried greater weight. At any rate, the extent to which the community was willing to help the needy was limited by the extent to which guilt was overshadowed by reluctance to pay taxes for this purpose.

The myth was cultivated that the poor, for the most part, were poor through their own fault; consequently not only had they no "right" to assistance but most of them did not even deserve it. Poor relief, therefore, was considered a benevolence; and lest its beneficiaries be corrupted, it was limited in amount and administered in a manner to deter all but those in the most exigent circumstances. Thus society rationalized its hardness of heart.

In recent years the state's role in relieving want has undergone a change. This has come about partly through a revival of the sense of social justice—and even of charity [11]—and partly through increased understanding of economic relationships, of the nature of poverty, and of human needs. Thus, as societies have become more democratic they have come to recognize that government is not merely an instrument for preserving order and securing legal justice but an instrument for promoting the well-being of everyone.

Some Fundamental Assumptions

Underlying the administration of public assistance in a democratic society are certain basic assumptions concerning the indi-

[11] I.e., in its pristine sense, namely, love or regard for one's neighbor, as contrasted with a begrudging and niggardly dole to the poor.

vidual, his place in society, and the responsibility of society for helping him achieve certain minimum goals. These assumptions are implicit in all that is to follow. They are stated here because an appreciation of the scope and nature of public assistance depends in large measure upon their acceptance:

1. A democratic society, imbued with the great tradition of Christian and Jewish thought concerning the essential worth and dignity of the individual, has an obligation to help everyone attain a minimum but decent level of living.

2. To the extent that misery, deprivation, and want exist, such a society is thereby weakened.

3. To function effectively a democratic society must strive to create conditions such that everyone, in so far as it is possible, can contribute to the general welfare and share in its benefits.

4. Inability to attain a minimum but decent level of living through individual initiative may be the result of one or of several interrelated causes—physical, psychological, emotional— or of economic or social consequences beyond the control or understanding of the individual.

5. Persons who cannot or will not participate in productive effort should not be cast aside as useless. Though it is essential for society to help its members be economically productive, an individual's worth to society is not to be measured in monetary terms alone; he is a human being and not a machine whose value is based solely on economic utility.

6. Where economic need exists, regardless of cause, it should be relieved—with adequate safeguards so that dependency is neither encouraged nor prolonged.

Why Public Assistance?

Obviously, under ideal conditions everyone who can work should have work which in return for the labor, skill, and risk invested will provide an income adequate at least for the minimum needs of the worker and his natural dependents. Furthermore, this income should be sufficient to allow for savings to meet continuing needs should sickness, old age, or other vicissitudes of life interrupt or terminate employment. It is doubtful if such conditions will ever prevail.

Granted, then, that need will always exist, is public assistance the best or the only means for coping with it?

Modern societies are characterized by the tremendous growth in social and economic legislation designed to stimulate the economy and to assure the individual a fair share of the wealth produced. Laws in the areas of tariffs, taxes, land grants, conservation of resources, business monopoly, wages and hours, trade unionism, discrimination, and price controls are but a few of the efforts toward this end.

Modern democratic societies have recognized, however, that even under optimum conditions it is not possible to guarantee income from continued employment. Social insurance thus came into being to assure the continuance of at least some income to those who are unable to work.

To the extent that social insurance can prevent need by maintaining income, it is clearly an improvement over public assistance. But the extent to which social insurance can do this is subject to dispute. There are many informed persons who, though warmly approving social insurance, believe that its role is limited. They fear that efforts to protect the bulk of the population by means of social insurance paying benefits sufficient to prevent need would be too costly and would jeopardize the finances of the country. There are others who would question even the desirability of any social insurance. Thus, Lewis Meriam of the Brookings Institution rejects most of the insurance features of the Social Security Act. He would replace them by a greatly liberalized and expanded system of public assistance—one which would pay higher grants under less restrictive conditions than as at present. The U.S. Chamber of Commerce, in contrast, favors a wide extension of social insurance (except in the field of health) and a gradual withdrawal of federal participation in public assistance.[12] While neither of these opposite views is likely

[12] Referendum No. 93, Proposed Policy Declaration, *Federal Social Security Program for the Aged*, Chamber of Commerce for the U.S. (Washington: Government Printing Office, 1953), p. 2.

to prevail, they are indicative of the differences among important elements in the country.

Although the extent to which social insurance will eventually reduce the demand for public assistance is by no means clear, we can be reasonably certain that some public assistance will always be needed in the foreseeable future. Public assistance is essential because it is the last defense against want and because it is sufficiently flexible to cope with need as it arises. The limitations of social insurance in this regard are pointed out by Professor Eveline Burns, who says: "But social insurance deals with *presumptive* rather than *demonstrated* need, and is a social institution dominated by the concept of *average* rather than *individual* need." [13] This characteristic of social insurance limits the extent to which this form of social security can deal with the total problem of family economic insecurity.

SELECTED REFERENCES

Altmeyer, Arthur J., "Issues Facing Social Welfare Today," *Social Work Journal*, January, 1952.

Burns, Eveline M., *The American Social Security System*, Boston: Houghton Mifflin, 1949, Part One, pp. 3–62.

Burns, Eveline M., "How Much Social Welfare Can America Afford?" *Proceedings of the National Conference of Social Work*, New York: Columbia University, 1949.

Burns, Eveline M., "Trends in Our National Economy and Their Effect on Public Welfare Planning," *Public Welfare*, February, 1950.

Corson, John J., "The Place of Public Welfare in Our Present Society," *Public Welfare*, July, 1947.

Haber, William, and Cohen, Wilber J., *Readings in Social Security*, New York: Prentice-Hall, 1948, esp. "Why Social Security?" by Mary Ross, p. 4; "Income Cycle in the Life of Families and Individuals," by W. S. Woytinsky, p. 22; "The Catastrophe That Is Unemployment," by Abraham Epstein, p. 145; "The Trend Toward an Older Population," by John D. Durand, p. 221; "Emerging Problems of the Aged," by P. H. Landis, p. 228; "The Problem of Medical Care," by the National Health Assembly, p. 328; and "Disability Among Gainfully Occupied Persons," by I. S. Falk, Sanders

---

[13] Eveline M. Burns, *The American Social Security System* (Boston: Houghton Mifflin, 1949), p. 36.

S. Barkev, and David Federman.

Hoey, Jane, "Human Rights and Social Work," *Proceedings of the National Conference of Social Work*, New York: Columbia University, 1949.

Rubinow, I. M., *The Quest for Security*, New York: Henry Holt, 1934.

Smith, A. Delafield, "Community Prerogative and the Rights and Freedom of the Individual," *Social Security Bulletin*, August, 1948.

"Social Security Progress and Problems: Report for the Fiscal Year 1951," *Social Security Bulletin*, March, 1952.

CHAPTER 2

The Poor Law
in England and America

The word "poorhouse" has become the threatening symbol of one of humanity's great degradations. To many a despairing heart it comes with a sound like the crack of doom. It is a word of hate and loathing for it includes the composite horrors of poverty, disgrace, loneliness, humiliation, abandonment, and degradation.

—HARRY C. EVANS, *The American Poor Farm*

THE ELIZABETHAN POOR LAW

As in so many other facets of our culture, we are heirs of the British tradition with regard to the care of the poor. If we would understand our present elaborate system of public assistance, and why it has taken its present form rather than one that might seem more reasonable, we must view it in the perspective provided by history. It is only through an appreciation of the social, economic, and moral forces that have shaped the growth of institutions in this field that we can deal intelligently with the problems they present.

Since there are many excellent histories of poor relief, it will be sufficient for our purpose to consider in this and the following chapter only the highlights in the development of public assistance, and in its poor-law antecedents.

Governmental concern with destitution can be traced to the Middle Ages—to the reigns of Edward III and Richard II. This early concern, however, manifested itself entirely in the discouragement, or at least the regulation, of begging and in the control of the movement of the laboring classes—in order to maintain an adequate supply of agricultural labor for feudal land-owners.

The Black Death, which had swept over Europe in the middle of the fourteenth century, had reduced the population by at least a third. The resulting shortage of man power, accentuated in England by the growth of commerce and industry, began to change the economic position of labor. Landowners had to compete with one another to secure farm workers. Wages had come into use. In growing numbers, agricultural workers began to leave the feudal manors and make their way to the towns, some by begging, others by thieving, attracted by the offer of wages and by a new sense of freedom, but without reckoning the loss of the security which the manor had provided. As De Schweinitz points out: "The king and his lords saw begging, movement, and vagrancy, and the labor shortage as essentially the same problem to be dealt with in one law." [1] That law was the Statute of Laborers, first enacted in 1349 and followed by similar measures.

These early developments need not concern us since they made no provision for meeting need—other than the need of the landowners for an adequate supply of labor. The poor law, which had its beginnings in the reign of Henry VIII, is, however, of great importance, because it established a pattern of dealing with the poor that has survived to this day. The Poor Relief Act of 1601, the so-called "Elizabethan poor law," was a recodification of early legislation, and it included provisions which influenced the administration of relief to the poor for the next 350 years.

Major Provisions of the Elizabethan Poor Law

1. Recognition of governmental responsibility for the care of the poor.
2. Establishment of administrative agencies.
3. Use of tax funds.
4. Distinction between the able-bodied and the impotent poor.
5. Recognition that not all able-bodied poor could get work.
6. Care of dependent children.
7. Use of the workhouse and the almshouse.

[1] Karl de Schweinitz, *England's Road to Social Security* (Philadelphia: University of Pennsylvania, 1943), p. 6.

8. Responsibility of relatives to provide help.
9. Return of beggars.

Recognition of Governmental Responsibility for the Care of the Poor, and Establishment of Administrative Agencies

We have seen that during the Middle Ages the social structure was relatively stable and secure. As De Schweinitz observes: "Under feudalism there could, at least in theory, be no uncared for distress. The people who today would be in greatest economic danger were, in the Middle Ages, presumably protected by their master from the most acute suffering." [2]

The system naturally could not provide security for everyone under all circumstances, and where it failed, an extensive though unintegrated program of charities filled the gap. During the most vital period of medievalism the income of the parish church was divided into three parts—one-third each for the maintenance of the church property, the living of the parish priest, and the care of the poor. The great monasteries extended hospitality as an ancillary function; food and temporary shelter were available to anyone who came to their doors—pilgrims, scholars, farm laborers traveling to and from the harvests, merchants, the aged, lame, and halt, people of means as well as the poor. No questions were asked; anyone was eligible to enjoy the hospitality of the monks, though, doubtless, wealthy guests left a donation. In later years many of the monasteries maintained a few aged or handicapped pensioners on a more permanent basis.

The strong emphasis upon charity led to the foundation of many institutions specifically for the care of the sick and the poor. Hospitals, lazar houses, almshouses were established through charitable bequests, and placed in charge of religious orders or lay brotherhoods. The guilds, though their primary function was the mutual protection of their members, often set aside funds for the care of the poor.

Over and above these charitable institutions, the poor were supported by individual almsgiving. Class distinctions, though strong, were based on rank rather than wealth; poverty itself was

[2] *Ibid.*, p. 2.

not a disgrace; indeed the poor, in the light of the gospel injunctions concerning charity, had an important function in medieval society in that they provided an opportunity for the exercise of the virtue of charity. Voluntary poverty for religious motives was highly regarded. Men and women of high estate often renounced worldly pomp. Embracing poverty and living on alms, they devoted their lives to the care of the sick and the poor, to the ransoming of prisoners, to fasting, prayer, and other religious works. Begging, moreover, was an acceptable means whereby poor pilgrims and scholars could travel throughout the medieval world.

The Black Death undermined the foundations of medieval society, and by the time Henry VIII broke with the Roman Catholic Church, charitable institutions had lost much of their vitality and efficiency. The quality of personnel in the orders and brotherhoods had deteriorated. The great wealth of the monasteries and foundations had aroused the cupidity of influential persons. Royal favorites were awarded the titular headship of various institutions and, of course, the rights to their revenues, while subordinates were left to manage them with whatever scanty sums the superior was willing to let slip through his fingers. Morale declined; there were corruption and indifference.

On the other hand, it must be remembered that the Church had been striving since the Council of Vienne (1311) to reform her charitable institutions. In many places she had been successful, and in general, a Catholic reform movement, based upon the principle that poor-relief was a social obligation, and thus to be shared by the civil authorities, was inaugurated. During the 14th and 15th centuries this movement prospered, especially in the towns and cities of Italy, the Netherlands and Spain, and to a lesser degree in Germany and England. The basic principle that the Christian community was responsible for the relief of its own poor members was worked out usually by turning the management of temporal affairs of the charity system over to the local civil authorities; the spiritual authority of the Church remained supreme, and the local Bishop was the highest judge in settling disputes which occurred in the administration of relief or in determining new policies.[3]

[3] Carl R. Steinbicker, *Poor Relief in the 16th Century* (Washington: Catholic University of America, 1937), p. xxx. See also De Schweinitz, *op. cit.*, chap. 4.

But in England political and religious issues, extraneous to the problem of poor relief, made any lasting reform under church auspices impossible. Henry VIII, in his greed and his rage at the church, decided to suppress the religious foundations entirely, thereby enriching his coffers and rewarding the supporters of his policy. Thus, in 1539, in one fell swoop, all monastic institutions were seized. They totaled 186 greater and 374 lesser institutions, in addition to 48 houses of the Knights Templars, making a grand total of 608, of which at least 460 were institutions providing some form of poor relief.[4] Their lands, buildings, and endowments went to the crown or were parceled out to the king's supporters.

Inadequate as these institutions may have been for coping with poverty in a period of rapid economic and social change, they were all that Britain had for this purpose. The problem of distribution and dependency created by their suppression was magnified since thousands of priests, nuns, and lay brothers were cast adrift without means of support (that is, those who had not been martyred in the process), as were the aged, sick, and crippled pensioners whom these institutions had maintained.

During the fifteenth and sixteenth centuries poverty and economic dislocation were aggravated by the policy of "enclosure," that is, the conversion of farm land into pasture for sheep. The great landowners found that raising sheep was more profitable than raising grain because there was less need for agricultural labor, and because the growing woolen industry provided an attractive market. Enclosure meant unemployment for farm laborers and dispossession for tenants. Thus many people were uprooted from the land and left without any certain means of making a living. Eventually, many were absorbed into the growing commercial and industrial life of the cities, but the process of readjustment resulted in much misery. Ironically enough, the fact that the sixteenth century was relatively peaceful for England resulted in unemployment for soldiers, who took to the road begging and robbing for want of a more suitable way to make a living.

Definite measures were called for to relieve all this distress.

[4] Steinbicker, *op. cit.*, p. 40 n.

With the elimination of the church as an instrument for the relief of want, the state had no alternative but to assume responsibility. Beginning in 1536, a series of statutes were enacted which eventually led to the poor law as enunciated in the Act of 1601. In brief, responsibility for the care of the poor was placed back on the parish, which in England had civil as well as ecclesiastical functions. It was the smallest unit of local government, roughly equivalent to the American township. The officials responsible for discharging this new function were known as "overseers of the poor"; they consisted of the parish churchwardens and from two to four "substantial householders" nominated by the justices of the peace. They served without pay.

Use of Tax Funds

Although responsibility for the care of the poor was placed in the hands of public officials, it was not the intention of the crown to permit them to tax for this purpose; neither did it propose to let the parishes share in the great wealth that had been seized from the church, though much of this wealth represented endowments precisely for that purpose. It was believed that the poor could be cared for by the old method of charity, and the overseers were charged with the duty of collecting and disbursing alms.

But affairs did not work out that way. The changes that had swept away so much of the old order seemed also to have swept away the strong impulse to charity that had characterized the Middle Ages. At any rate, there was marked reluctance to contribute the necessary funds. Pressure began to be applied. When men of property were found delinquent in their contributions, they were exhorted, reprimanded, and warned, by the overseers, the justices, and even the bishop—all to no avail. As Sir George Nichols put it: "It would appear, however, that hitherto the gentle askings of the collectors and the exhortations of the clergy and the churchwardens and the charitable 'ways and means' of the Bishop had all failed to induce the people to contribute 'according to their means' and the time seems to have arrived where, voluntary charity having failed, compulsion of some kind must be resorted to, in order to provide means of relief for the 'impotent, feeble, and lame' which are the poor in very deed." [5]

Reluctance to resort to outright taxation is reflected in continued efforts at persuasion, but, to quote the statute, ". . . if he will not be persuaded therein by the said justices they may sesse, tax, and limit upon every such obstinate person so refusing, according to their good discretion, what sum the said obstinate shall pay." [6] British obstinacy must have reached great heights, because by the time the Act of 1601 had been passed the pretense of voluntary contributions had been discarded and a regular tax rate instituted.

Distinction Between Able-Bodied and Impotent Poor, Recognition That Not All Able-Bodied Poor Could Get Work, and Care of Dependent Children

By fixing administrative and fiscal responsibility upon the smallest unit of local government, the poor law established, in theory at least, a comprehensive and uniform method for meeting need. There was considerable variation, of course, in the willingness and ability of the parishes to deal with the problem, but there was at least one agency in each community whose duty it was to discover and relieve want. In placing responsibility on the parishes, Parliament reasoned quite rightly that the overseers of so small a district would be in the best position to understand what needed to be done. At a time when England was still largely agricultural, when transportation and communication were primitive, and when the administrative arts were poorly developed, a larger unit of administration might well have proved unmanageable.[7] It must be remembered, moreover, that at the time when the parish was first decided upon, it was anticipated that charity, influenced by close association with one's place of worship, would be the source of relief funds.

---

[5] Sir George Nichols, *History of the English Poor Laws* (New York: Putnam, 1898), p. 152.

[6] *Ibid.*, p. 27.

[7] A rudimentary "rate in aid" clause in the legislation of 1601 permitted parishes to secure help from other parishes and even the county if they were unable to raise sufficient taxes to maintain their poor. In later years, moreover, parishes could combine to form "unions" for the more efficient administration of poor relief.

The overseers were responsible for preparing a register of the parish poor, and with providing them with appropriate care. Every unmarried person, and every married person under thirty years of age, not being employed and not having forty shillings a year, could be compelled to serve as a yearly servant in the trade to which he was brought up. If such employment could not be found for needy able-bodied persons, especially if they lacked a trade, they could be placed in a workhouse or house of correction established by the parish for the purpose of engaging them in some useful occupation in return for their keep. Unemployable persons could be maintained in an almshouse or receive assistance in their own homes.

Children whose parents were dead, or who were unable to support them, or who had abandoned them could be bound out by the overseers to householders who would teach them a trade, provide a rudimentary education, feed and clothe them in return for their services from the time they were old enough to work (usually an early age) until they reached maturity.

Use of the Workhouse and the Almshouse

Institutional care of the poor in these early days was not mandatory, nor did it achieve popularity until some years later; but from the beginning of poor relief it was a recognized instrument for the relief and correction of the poor. De Schweinitz, commenting upon the mixture of purpose that characterized the use of work in connection with relief, says, "The Elizabethan lawmaker proposes work as training for the youth, as prevention of roguery, as a test of good intent, and as a means of providing employment for the needy. In the background is the House of Correction with its threat of punishment. How ancient is the confusion about work and how deep-rooted is our conflict of feeling concerning it." [8]

Responsibility of Relatives to Provide Help

Because of the importance of this provision for present-day public assistance administration, the topic will be considered in detail in Chapter 9.

[8] De Schweinitz, *op. cit.*, p. 27.

The Return of Beggars

The parochial system of poor relief administration soon bred an equally parochial attitude toward those in need of such relief. Fears were aroused lest parish resources be drained by needy persons who were not natives of the parish—vagabonds, transients, even needy families smuggled in by the overseers of neighboring parishes. Legislation was soon forthcoming making it possible to remove nonresidents to their place of origin.

Concern lest the poor who belonged elsewhere might swarm into parishes more richly endowed culminated in the Law of Settlement enacted in 1662. This law had two major objectives: first, to determine, in cases of need, the district which had responsibility, and second, to set up barriers to the acquisition of settlement so that people of small means, who might possibly become public charges at some future date, would not become a burden upon a parish to which they were not native. Thus, any newcomers to a parish, renting property valued at less than ten pounds a year, could be returned to the places they had come from if, in the judgment of the overseers, this seemed desirable.

This oppressive piece of legislation touched the lives of most poor persons—even those who never sought relief. In short order a vast body of legal doctrine and precedent developed concerning the acquisition and loss of settlement. The parishes involved themselves in extensive and expensive litigation, and the poor were shipped back and forth like so many pieces of furniture. Amidst all this litigation there was no one to inquire whether or not it was necessary. No studies were made to determine whether the poor actually betook themselves from one parish to another simply for the purpose of securing more generous relief. Possibly this occurred; but more probably people tried to change their residence primarily to improve their chances for a decent livelihood through work. In all likelihood, the time, money, and effort (not to mention the discomfort of those who were directly affected) that went into the determination of settlement far outweighed the cost of caring for the occasional transient or newcomer.

During the four centuries of its existence, the poor law was investigated and modified frequently, but rarely with benefit to those whom it was designed to help. Throughout its history it was administered and financed locally; institutional care was favored over assistance in the home; and the standards were low. While it is undoubtedly a sad commentary that this antiquated instrument survived for so long, the fact is that its specific provisions would not have been nearly so hard on the poor had it not been for the spirit in which it was administered—something we shall consider in a later chapter.

The first serious challenge to the supremacy of the poor law occurred in 1908, when England introduced categorical assistance programs. Finally, in 1948, the last vestiges of the British poor law were eliminated, and replaced by a national system of insurance, assistance, pensions, and public medical care.

THE POOR LAW IN AMERICA

Hardly had the Atlantic seaboard become dotted with the settlements of the early colonists when the problem of providing for the care of the poor arose. As early as 1642 we find the statutes of Plymouth colony stipulating that "Every township shall make competent provision for the maintenance of their poor according as they shall find most convenient and suitable for themselves by an order and general agreement in public town meeting. And notwithstanding the permission that all such person and persons as are now resident and inhabitant and within the said towns shall be maintained and provided for by them." [9]

In casting about for a method to deal with this problem, it was natural for the English colonists, regardless of their political or religious persuasion, to turn to the English poor law. Accordingly, the principles, structure, and philosophy of the Act of 1601 were soon transplanted to these shores; in some instances, in fact, the exact wording was copied.

The situation in America, however, differed in many respects from that in the mother country. There was no unemployment such as existed even in preindustrial England. There was work

[9] Robert Kelso, *History of Public Poor Relief in Massachusetts* (Boston: Houghton Mifflin, 1922), p. 92, quoting *Plymouth Colony Records,* "Pulsifer 'laws,' " Vol. XI, p. 41.

for all who had bodily energy, initiative, and a modicum of skill and resourcefulness. But not all those who thronged to the colonies were adapted to the back-breaking labor, the privations and dangers attendant upon the opening up of a new land. The provincial governments, in consequence, were faced with the necessity of relieving the distress not only of established settlers but also of newcomers who were unable to adjust to pioneer life—or, for that matter, to the rigid, puritanical mode of life which was the ideal in theocratic New England. The necessity of coming to terms with these problems led, in short order, to that almost inextricable intermingling of poor relief with enforcement of public order and morality, and with the promulgation of rules regarding the conditions under which persons could enter, move about in, or become established members of the community.

Marcus Jernegan, writing on "The Development of Poor Relief in Colonial Virginia," comments that "These elements of Virginia society that made a system of poor relief necessary may be described as follows. The chief dependence for a supply of labor in the seventeenth century was this large body of unemployed in England—the paupers, vagabonds, and convicts who were transported to Virginia mainly through the agency of the indentured servant system." [10] Shipmasters provided passage for destitute immigrants in return for their signing of articles of indenture, which could then be transferred, for a consideration, to colonial landowners. The indentured person was obligated to serve without pay, but in exchange for his keep, for a term of years—often seven or more.

Doubtless the majority of impecunious persons who were thereby enabled to reach America eventually established themselves and contributed to the growth of the country; but there were many who were unsuited to the life of a bond servant, even though they could adapt themselves to the other hardships. Since this traffic was highly profitable to shipmasters, they were not inclined to look closely to the qualifications of those whom they sought to indenture. Many were old, sickly, or otherwise incapacitated; others were lazy, rebellious, the off-scourings of British

[10] *Social Service Review,* March, 1929, p. 4.

gaols, only waiting the chance to resume their former way of life, begging, pilfering, or engaged in such dubious occupations as fortunetelling, juggling, fiddling, and the like, which the sober colonists, especially in New England, thought scandalous. The wretched conditions of passage were such, moreover, that many who were hale and hearty on leaving the old country arrived here weak and diseased. Those of whom the shipmaster could not dispose would ordinarily be left behind with little more than the clothes on their backs, to save the expense of their keep on the return trip. It is understandable, then, that the colonies became fearful lest they be saddled with a great horde of dependent persons.

The Elizabethan poor law which the colonies had adopted contained the great principle of public responsibility for the care of the needy but placed this responsibility upon local government, which in this country usually meant the township or county. Inasmuch as this obligation extended only to persons who were established members of the community, elaborate precautions were taken to prevent anyone who was likely to become a public charge from acquiring this status. The precautions are reflected in the statutes relating to the acquisition of "legal settlement." A review of treatises on the poor laws of the several colonies reveals a preoccupation with problems of settlement almost to the exclusion of such matters as adequacy of assistance, methods of determining eligibility, and the like.

While it is unnecessary for us to delve into the intricacies of the law of settlement, the provisions of a Massachusetts law, enacted in 1794 are illuminating:

1. A married woman has the settlement of her husband if he has any; if not, she retains her own settlement at the time of marriage.

2. If the unsettled husband of a settled wife requires aid from the state, he shall receive it in the place of her settlement, the state reimbursing.

3. Legitimate children follow and have the settlement of their father, if he has any, until they gain one for themselves; if he has none, then they follow the mother in like manner.

4. Illegitimate children follow the mother's settlement at the time

of their birth if she had any; but no child gains settlement by birth if neither parent had a settlement in the place of birth.

5. Any citizen twenty-one years of age or over who has an estate inheritance of three pounds yearly net income, taking the rents and profits three years in succession, is settled in the town where he has such estate and so dwells.

6. Any citizen, as above, who has an estate or freehold of sixty pounds value and pays taxes on the same for five years in succession is settled where he has such an estate.

7. Any town officer is settled ipso facto.

8. Any ordained minister is settled in the place of his pastorate.

9. Any minor who serves four years' apprenticeship and actually sets up in business in the town where he has served within one year after his term, being twenty-one years old and who continues such trade for five years, is settled in that place.

10. Any citizen twenty-one years or over who resides in any town for ten years and pays all taxes assessed for any five years within that time is settled in that town.

11. Every settlement when gained continues till lost or defeated by the gaining of another elsewhere.[11]

While requirements differed, among the colonies (and later the states) the following were characteristic principles. (1) Settlement could be gained only after a term of residence, perhaps of from five to ten years, during which time the person who sought to establish settlement had to be self-supporting. (2) Not all persons could gain settlement in their own right. Children took the settlement of their parents; wives derived theirs from that of their husbands. (3) There were many impediments to the acquisition of settlement. Thus a man could not gain a new settlement if, during the period in which he sought to qualify, any person naturally dependent upon him was in receipt of relief elsewhere.

As if these requirements were not sufficient, further precautions were taken. There were stringent regulations regarding the entertainment of strangers. Householders were forbidden to extend hospitality to persons who were not residents of the community unless with express permission of the authorities. If this permission were not secured, and the stranger subsequently had to be

[11] Kelso, *op. cit.*, p. 60.

helped by the town, his erstwhile host was responsible for the charges.

Perhaps the most effective barrier to the acquisition of settlement was the practice of "warning out," used extensively in New England and New York. "Until formally admitted as an inhabitant of a town, a newcomer might at any time be warned by the authorities to depart as an 'undesirable.' " [12] There was frequent resort to this device. It was used not only to prevent needy people from becoming a burden on the town but also to rid the community of persons whose way of life was considered offensive.

Poor relief was administered by overseers, usually town officials although sometimes (as in Pennsylvania) they were appointed by and responsible to the county judges. In some jurisdictions needy persons were obliged to secure orders from the justices of the peace before their names could be entered on the relief rolls. In the light of the way relief was administred, there was an ironic appropriateness in this requirement. Thus, in the words of the late Commissioner William Ellis of New Jersey: "Slowly an application for relief began to take on the color of a criminal prosecution in which an adult, if found guilty of requiring aid, would be given grudging assistance but would be segregated from the general population by the severance of civil rights and by the wearing of pauper badges." [13]

Kelso sums up the functions of the overseers of the poor thus: "The efforts of the Massachusetts overseers of the poor have been from the outset directed toward avoiding or unloading the financial burden of supporting the poor. Consequently the records of these hundred years are replete with ordinances and warnings and votes embodying shrewd Yankee bargaining aimed at ridding the town of the family which through sickness or death or other misfortune, had come to want." [14]

How, then, was relief administered; and what was the standard of assistance? The poor were rarely aided in their own homes, and

[12] David Schneider and Albert Deutsch, *History of Public Welfare in New York* (Chicago: University of Chicago, 1938), Vol. I, p. 40.
[13] William J. Ellis, *Public Welfare in New Jersey* (New York: Lewis Historical Publishing Company, 1945), p. 5.
[14] Kelso, *op. cit.*, p. 94.

then usually only in cases of emergency or where dependency was likely to be of short duration. A common practice in the northern colonies was to "farm out" the poor; that is, the town fathers would contract with a householder to care for one or more needy persons in his own home. This was often accomplished by "auctioning off" the poor at public town meetings. Early records reveal that the expenses of such auctions might include an item for hard cider or other strong drink, presumably for the purpose of helping the meetings run more smoothly. One needs no vivid imagination to appreciate the plight of Granny Jones, old, feeble, and friendless, when left to the tender ministrations of some farmer who has awakened the next morning to the realization that he has contracted for her care in the coming year for a sum half that he had intended to ask. The poor were usually farmed out to various householders for extended periods, although Kelso reports that one Th. Elgar was boarded with thirty-two different families in the sixty-five-week period to January, 1685.

Dependent children were apprenticed or bound out until they reached maturity. When help was extended to the needy in their own homes it was usually of a supplemental nature. Old records reveal that it took various forms such as the remission of taxes, the building of an extra room so that a family could care for aged parents; even the building of a house and the provision of a cow and additional pasture land are recorded. When help of this nature was provided, we can be sure that a return to self-maintenance looked particularly promising.

Frequent reference was made to the need for almshouses, but they were never used to the same extent as in contemporary England. It was not for any lack of desire, however, but rather because such institutions were impracticable in a rural and sparsely settled country. Boston erected its first almshouse in 1660, but it was not until 1734 that New York established an institution with the all-embracing title of "House of Correction, Workhouse, and Poorhouse." In 1727 Connecticut opened a "colony workhouse." Criminals and the poor as such were excluded, but it was for

. . . all vagabonds and idle persons going about in town or country begging or persons using any subtil craft, juggling or unlawful games or plays or feigning themselves to have knowledge on physiognomy, palmistry or pretending they can tell destinies, fortunes or discover where lost goods may be found, common pipers, fiddlers, runaways, stubborn servants or children, common drunkards, common night-walkers, pilferers, wanton and lascivious persons either in speech or behavior, common railers or brawlers such as neglect their callings, misspend what they earn, and do not provide for themselves or the support of their families . . . as also persons under distraction and unfit to go at large, whose friends do not care for their safe confinement.[15]

The cities naturally were in a better position to establish alms-houses, and, indeed, they had the greater need. The practice of "warning out" prevalent in the rural towns tended to force unsettled persons back to the ports where they had had entry. Great emphasis was placed upon making these institutions self-supporting, but, as in England, this was doomed to failure.

The pattern of poor relief based upon the English poor law survived almost unchanged from the colonial period until the present era. It is astonishing that in spite of political, economic, and social changes that took place during that period an institution presumably geared to the needs of the people could have shown so little development. But perhaps it was because the attention and energy of the American people were focused on progress in so many other areas that they had little time to consider the problem of human wastage and misery.

Because of the prevailing opinion that poverty was usually the result of one's personal shortcomings, little effort was made to understand its causes, and the need for variation in treatment. "Poverty was not differentiated from chronic pauperism and pauperism was akin to crime. The sturdy beggar, the idiot, the drunkard and the widow who was only poor were herded together under the same roof, the chief source of anxiety being the net cost of the establishment." [16] There was perennial conflict between advocates of "indoor" and "outdoor" relief. With the increase in population, the number of almshouses increased, and

[15] Edward W. Capen, *Historical Development of the Poor Law in Connecticut* (New York: Columbia University, 1905), p. 61.

[16] Kelso, *op. cit.*, p. 101.

efforts were made to have them become the dominant, if not exclusive, method of caring for the poor. In 1824 New York's Secretary of State, John V. N. Yates, made an extensive study of the problem. The scandalous abuses in the care of the poor revealed by his investigation, especially the practice of "farming out," prompted him to recommend that the townships be relieved of this function and that it be taken over by the county. He believed that care in an almshouse would be more humane than the barbaric "farming out" method; that it would provide work for the able-bodied poor; that it would provide more suitable care for dependent children; and finally, it would cut costs by almost 50 percent. Mr. Yates's enthusiastic advocacy of the almshouse antedated by ten years the similar proposals in the celebrated English poor law reform of 1834. The Yates proposals were embodied in legislation, but so many counties were excepted from its provisions (thirty-eight out of fifty-four) as to nullify its objectives. By 1835, fifty counties had poorhouses, and county responsibility prevailed in forty of them; yet by 1849 a reaction had set in and new legislation permitted the counties to adopt whatever system they preferred—town relief, county relief, or a combination of both. Actually, of course, the evils of the poorhouse were no less than the methods it replaced.

In New England the town maintained its supremacy in matters of poor relief, but there was an increase in almshouses. Capen reports that in Connecticut in 1886, of the 168 towns, 67 had public almshouses while 16 used private almshouses.[17] County almshouses were permitted in Pennsylvania as early as 1798 and soon became the required method of poor relief although, as in New York, there was considerable shifting back and forth.

A fair estimate of poor relief, prior to the depression of 1929–1939, was that congregate care was the usual method in rural areas and small communities, while outdoor relief was used more extensively in the cities, where the rapid increase in population made it difficult to expand institutional facilities to accommodate all the needy.

Regardless of the method, care was uniformly inadequate. In

[17] Capen, *op. cit.*, p. 336.

1890, in Pennsylvania, a poor law investigating committee was appalled to find that the needy were still being auctioned off in some places. Haffner, writing in 1913, complained that "many counties are administering poor relief under laws that were passed between seventy-five and one hundred years ago and whose changes were so inconsequential as to leave them practically unaltered." [18] The situation in Pennsylvania could have been duplicated in most other states.

Poorhouses were the repository of misery in its most varied and abject form. The abandoned child, the aged respectable widow, the unemployed farm hand, the unmarried mother and her infant shared quarters with the prostitute, the senile, and the feeble-minded—misfits of all kinds, whose personal problems, though of long standing, were understood neither by themselves nor by those who were responsible for their care. Filth, squalor, inadequate food and clothing, lack of privacy, and exposure to the most degrading influences characterized the poorhouse. The following is a report on a poorhouse of the 1920's:

Poor farm located 13 miles south of Manassas (Va.) way back on poor, cutover land, off any traveled road in a woods. Very few know that such a place exists. The poorhouse is an old frame shack, one-storey, about 14x84 with six rooms, some without doors, windows boarded up. Fertilizer sacks filled with straw and old buggy cushions for mattresses on broken down beds. Bed covers are rags, parts of old blankets or quilts very filthy. An old man, clothes ragged and filthy, asleep on a pile of dirty rags, in a vile room swarming with flies and vermin. Poor and insufficient food; poor and filthy clothing; no music, amusements, or religious services. No medical attention whatsoever; no screens, the place reeking with bedbugs and body lice. Well water, filthy outside privies used by both sexes. No sewerage, slop and garbage just thrown through the doors. Contaminating diseased inmates use the same bedrooms and toilets as do other inmates, and their clothes go into a common wash. Men's and women's bedrooms adjoin. The superintendent's salary is $13.33 a month with an additional $13. per month per pauper for their keep.[19]

[18] William C. Haffner, *Poor Relief Legislation in Pennsylvania* (Cleona, Pa.: Holzopfel Publishing Company, 1913), p. 136.
[19] Harry Evans, *The American Poor Farm and Its Inmates* (Moosehart, Ill.: Loyal Order of Moose, 1926), p. 13.

The inadequacy of public provisions for the poor during most of our history had its immediate cause in the fact that relief was administered and financed by the smallest units of local government, the function being discharged by officials who had neither the interest, aptitude nor authority to provide adequate care. A more fundamental cause, however, lay in the indifference of the public to the plight of those who were economically dependent. Karl de Schweinitz summarizes the problem vividly:

The official, perhaps most often cited as an illustration of incompetence, was the overseer of the poor. Everybody knew him as the man who managed the almshouse and supplied outdoor relief, as assistance money or goods was called, to the people who could not support themselves. The inefficiency of his administration was notorious, a combination of neglect and petty despotism.

While his treatment of the persons entrusted to him was usually all that the public thought it to be, and worse, he himself was largely the victim of a society that did not know what it wanted. Its feelings were divided. On the one hand the necessity of providing for the poor was recognized; that implied humane administration.

On the other hand, people did not like to be bothered by beggars and they wanted their property protected. From this point of view stern measures were required and public relief before the Twentieth Century was administered as a function of the police power of the state.

Always present as a major complication was the fact that not everyone in need was sick and feeble. Some people were able-bodied but did not have jobs. The duties of the overseer included the provision of employment but at no time did he succeed in doing this for all those who sought help. The difficulty of the problem did not cause the community to be any more willing to maintain the person for whom there was no work. Such individuals were immediately suspect and the suspicion extended to the official responsible for determining and relieving their necessity. The community expressed its frustration in contempt for the overseer. He in turn vented his exasperation upon his charges representing government at its punitive and repressive worst.

With this most despised of public officials, the community deposited its central social problem. It turned over to him its human wastage, the people it wanted to forget, the least appealing among the miser-

able in body and mind and those whom it disposed of by calling
unworthy and undeserving.[20]

SPECIALIZED INSTITUTIONAL CARE AND
THE RISE OF STATE AGENCIES

Public dissatisfaction with the poor law first manifested itself
in connection with the inadequate care it provided for certain dependent groups—children; the deaf, dumb, and blind; the feeble-
minded and insane. This dissatisfaction was expressed first
through the establishment of private institutional facilities for
children—the so-called "orphan asylums," and later, in the second
and third quarters of the nineteenth century, by institutions for
the other groups mentioned. Although the child-caring institutions were largely private, other institutions were usually operated under public auspices—generally by the state. Thus the first
challenge to the poor law resulted not in efforts to reform or replace it but rather in removing certain groups from its jurisdiction.

Prior to 1800 there were only eight institutions for children, all
but one being private. After that, the number increased rapidly.
In New York, for example, between 1825 and 1866 the number
increased from two to more than sixty. Although their primary
purpose was to secure the removal of children from almshouses,
they never succeeded in achieving this objective. Thus, in New
York the number of children in almshouses continued to grow
until in 1866 they numbered more than 26,000. In 1875 it was
necessary to change the poor law so as to prohibit the admission
or retention of healthy children over three years of age in public
almshouses. Finally, in 1929, the new Social Welfare Law of the
state prohibited almshouses from admitting such children entirely, except for children under the age of two who are in the
care of their mothers. The continued increase in the number of
children in institutions had been due in part to the rapid growth
in the nation's population, and to the effects of the Civil War. It
must be remembered, moreover, that institutional care was not

[20] Karl de Schweinitz, "The Development of Governmental Responsibility
for Human Welfare," *Public Welfare*, August, 1948, p. 147.

restricted to orphaned or abandoned children; many children were institutionalized simply because their parents lacked the means to provide for them at home.

Almost from the beginning, private child-caring institutions received financial aid from government. In campaigning for funds, it was only natural for the groups managing such institutions to appeal to the city fathers, and even to the state legislatures for help. The aid that was promptly forthcoming was in the nature of a contribution to a worthy cause rather than payments to private agents for the discharge of a public responsibility. Appropriations were made with little or no reference to the needs of a given institution; nor was any effort made to ascertain whether such subsidies were wisely used. This haphazard subsidy system led to abuses. Well-run institutions could not be distinguished from those that were poorly run; institutions were placed in a position in which they competed with one another for public funds; and they tended to become ends in themselves rather than one of several methods of caring for dependent children according to their various needs. The failure of the state to provide adequate "outdoor" relief to parents who could not support their children, combined with its willingness to subsidize child-caring institutions, naturally led to their increase in size and number.

The problems created by this new relationship between government and private organizations were worked out in a variety of ways. Some states took over the function of caring for dependent children, operating public institutions for that purpose; other states assumed responsibility for child care but continued to use private agencies on a payment-for-service basis and exercised supervisory powers over institutions in receipt of public funds to insure adequacy of service.

The rapid growth in the number of children in institutions eventually led to a reëxamination of the role of the institution in child care. Various programs of foster home care developed, based on the conviction that long-time congregate care is not conducive to wholesome development in children. It was not until the early years of this century, however, that forces were set in motion which resulted in a radically different approach to the problem. The White House Conference on Dependent Children, called by President Theodore Roosevelt in 1909, had enunciated the principle that no child should be removed from its home by reason of poverty alone. One of the most tangible results of this conference was its influence on the establishment of programs of "mothers' aid" designed to enable widows, or women whose husbands were in hospitals or prisons, to remain at home to care for their children rather than to work, leaving their children unsupervised at home or on the streets or placing them in foster homes or institutions.

The care and treatment of persons suffering from physical or mental disabilities is outside the scope of this text. The significance of these programs for public assistance lies in the fact that their establishment marked the entry of the state (as distinguished from local government) into the field of social welfare. Institutions for the care of the insane, the feeble-minded, etc., were too costly to be operated as private philanthropic ventures, and only the most populous cities and counties had the fiscal capacity to operate them publicly; hence the state had to assume this responsibility.

Prior thereto, the state's responsibility in the field of social welfare had been confined to the enactment of a poor law which defined certain obligations of local government. A few states, moreover, reimbursed the counties and townships for the cost of care given to the poor who lacked local settlement. Now, however, state government became involved in the administration of a direct service to certain dependent groups.

As these institutions were established it was customary to place them in charge of boards of managers responsible to the governor and legislature. As the number of state institutions increased, it became apparent that there was need for some integration. Massachusetts led the way by creating a state Board of Charities in 1863.

For centuries the Commonwealth had assumed financial responsibility for the care of the "unsettled poor." In 1851, as a result of the influx of immigrants from Europe, a Board of Commissioners had been created to superintend the execution of state laws pertaining to aliens. This board was given the power to appoint officials to inspect almshouses and other institutions in which the state poor were lodged. The following year, upon the recommendation of the board, legislation was enacted transferring the responsibility for providing care for the state poor from the localities to the state. Three state almshouses were erected, and the inspectors in each state almshouse district were given the same powers with regard to the state poor as the local overseers had with respect to the settled poor.

By 1863 there were nine state institutions with welfare functions: the three state almshouses, a hospital for the alien poor, three hospitals for the insane, a reform school for boys, and one for girls. In addition, there were four private institutions which were in receipt of public funds: the Perkins Institution and Massachusetts Asylum for the Blind, the Massachusetts Eye and Ear Infirmary, the School for Idiotic and Feeble Minded Youth, and the American Asylum for the Deaf and Dumb.

The state Board of Charities, composed of seven unpaid members and a salaried secretary, was responsible for administering the program for the care of the state poor. It had supervision, but not control, over state and local institutions; the latter continued under the management of their separate boards. For the first time, however, a state had a central body concerned with the problems of social welfare. In Massachusetts, it pioneered in developing state leadership and in making studies, reports, and recommendations with respect to the welfare needs of the state.

New York followed suit, and in 1867 established a Board of State Commissioners of Public Charities. Unlike the Massachusetts board, it was strictly advisory and inspectional. Its reason for being was well expressed by Governor Reuben E. Fenton in his annual message to the legislature on January 2, 1867:

For some years past the State has made large annual appropriations to the aid in the support of Orphan Asylums, Hospitals, Homes for the Friendless, and other charitable institutions. No adequate provisions, however, has been made by law for the inspection of these and other institutions of a like character holding their charters under the State, or for any effectual inquiry into their operations and management. There are a great number of these institutions, and the amount contributed for their support by public authorities and by public benevolence is large, and so many persons—the aged, the helpless, the infirm and the young—fall under their care that I deem it expedient that the State should exercise a reasonable degree of supervision over them.[21]

The New York board was granted extensive powers to inquire into the management, finances, and physical conditions of all institutions in receipt of public funds—that is, all eleemosynary, correctional, and reformatory institutions except prisons, whether receiving state aid or maintained by municipalities. In 1873 a salaried state Commissioner in Lunacy was appointed. He was responsible to the Board of Charities and was an ex officio member thereof. Institutions for the mentally ill had to be licensed by the board.

In 1873 the board was given responsibility for the "state poor." It was empowered to return such persons to their homes or to friends or relatives in other states, or to provide for their care in almshouses through contract with certain counties and cities. In 1875 a constitutional amendment prohibited state aid to private agencies except those for the blind, the deaf, and juvenile delinquents. This amendment did not, however, deny local governments the right to reimburse private institutions for the cost of care to public charges.

In 1873 ten states had established state boards of charity. By 1931 only five states were without some central state agency concerned with matters of social welfare. These agencies differed widely in function; some were advisory, some supervisory, while a few were administrative in nature.

Where state agencies had direct service functions, these usually pertained to institutional care. Other welfare services were usually administered locally. Even where the state participated financially in programs of categorical assistance it was customary to operate through administrative agencies that were branches of local government.

[21] Schneider and Deutsch, *op. cit.*, Vol. II, p. 14.

THE ROLE OF THE VOLUNTARY AGENCY IN RELIEF GIVING

For several centuries after the enactment of the poor law, organized private philanthropy played a minor role in relief of the poor in England; in America it was practically nonexistent. The nineteenth century, however, witnessed a remarkable revival of private charity which at one point came close to superseding public outdoor relief.

The revival of private charity was largely a protest against the inadequacy of the poor law. To understand the nature of this protest, we must first consider the prevailing attitude toward the poor, and toward the kind of help that should be extended to them. There was general agreement that public relief to the needy should be restricted to institutional care. The practice of farming out the poor was recognized as being barbarous by people who were concerned with the plight of the destitute, but they also believed that public relief to the poor in their own homes was dangerous. The poor, it was thought, were poor mainly through their own fault; they were lazy, improvident, and addicted to vice of one sort or another. If the conditions under which relief was received were in any way palatable, they would soon prefer it to supporting themselves by their own labor. Outdoor relief, therefore, was a two-edged sword; it tended to create the very need it was designed to alleviate.

Public outdoor relief was considered particularly objectionable because its administration was believed to be necessarily either corrupt (in that it afforded opportunities for graft and peculation) or, at best, merely ineffective (in that public officials did not know how to distinguish between those who were worthy and those who were unworthy of such help). The very fact that outdoor relief was "public," moreover, suggested that poor persons might have a right to such help, and the idea that everyone might think they had a claim to largess from the public purse was repugnant and considered demoralizing to those who were its beneficiaries. The attitude that prevailed until relatively recently was neatly expressed by a speaker at the National Conference on Charities and Corrections in 1891:

The system [outdoor relief] tends to excite hostility to the state itself. First, relief educates a large class to look to government for help; and when this is received the feeling of dependence increases. The poor man has become a pauper, a beggar. A willing pauper is near to being a thief. As the State excites hope which it cannot fulfil, a time comes when the pauper is a public enemy. It is in this class that the worst foes of order are found, the only real proletariat we have. As the State cannot distribute its funds fairly, discontent is aroused in the neighborhood where aid is given. One poor man cannot see why he is not aided as much as his next-door neighbor, since he is quite as poor and has more children. Having been educated by the State to be a beggar, he turns upon the State because it does not recognize his demand for support to be based on "natural rights." None of these considerations weighs against personal and voluntary charity, which is a favor and not a legal obligation, and which may be suspended when the demand is made in the name of right.[22]

While the poor as a class were, thus, generally distrusted, it was recognized that some poor persons were "worthy" in that their poverty was "no fault of their own," or because there seemed to be evidence that they had the capacity for "moral regeneration." It was this group of "worthy poor" that private philanthropy was disposed to help with outdoor relief; the almshouse with its deterrent and punitive features would be the only recourse of all others who professed to be in need.[23]

This emphasis upon almshouse care was the occasion of conflict among many charitably inclined persons. While public indoor relief was accepted as the rule, it was seen that such care was clearly inadequate, especially during periods of widespread economic distress. From time to time, therefore, there was an upswing in public outdoor relief, either because institutional facilities were inadequate to meet the demand or because institutional care was so obviously inappropriate for many of the needy people who requested help. Since the socioeconomic nature of need was unrecognized, such upswings became a cause for

[22] Josephine Brown, *Public Relief, 1929–1939* (New York: Henry Holt, 1940), p. 43, quoting C. R. Henderson.

[23] Karl de Schweinitz relates how one large private family agency used to classify families turning to self-support under the heading of "redeemed." See Chapter 6 for further discussion of attitudes toward the needy.

alarm and were followed by renewed efforts to suppress outdoor relief entirely.

Organized private charity came into being for two reasons: to supplement the efforts of the public authorities during depression periods and to ease the conscience of many charitably disposed persons who were distressed to see so many "worthy" poor persons shunted to the workhouse or almshouse because of the established principle that public outdoor relief was dangerous. Thus, a "Society for the Relief of Widows with Small Children" was founded in New York City toward the end of the eighteenth century; by the middle of the next century there were thirty or forty private relief-giving societies in that city alone. For the most part they were sponsored by individual churches, by groups identified with particular denominations, by groups with a common national origin, or by small groups of well-to-do, altruistically inclined persons. They were small and staffed by volunteers. Agencies of this kind were to be found in most large American cities.

In spite of the principle that private outdoor relief should be restricted to the worthy poor, these agencies soon found themselves engaged in relief-giving practices as indiscriminate as those for which they had criticized the public authorities. The poor law was not an instrument adapted to cope with widespread economic depressions, nor could it deal with the influx of poverty-stricken immigrants fleeing famine and political persecution, who created a serious problem for the large coastal cities. Private groups responded to this misery by instituting a variety of relief measures—soup kitchens, wood yards, second-hand clothing depots, and so on—to supplement the generally inadequate municipal appropriations for emergency public works and outdoor relief. These private programs often continued to operate even after the acute phase of the depression had passed because even in "prosperous" periods there were thousands of persons still in dire need. Unfortunately these efforts were sporadic and uncoördinated, and there was no real investigation of need, so that often those whose need was greatest were overlooked to the advantage of the professional beggar who "went the rounds" of the various societies. If people were "pauperized" (and undoubtedly many were), it was not the relief that was responsible but the way in which it was administered. This fact, unhappily, has only begun to be recognized in our own times.

Toward the end of the depression of 1837–1843 a new movement got under way in New York City when a group of citizens formed an "Association for Improving the Conditions of the Poor." The objective of this association was the elimination of indiscriminate relief giving by substituting methods that would reform character as well as alleviate wretchedness. Material relief was to be granted when absolutely necessary, but great reliance was placed on "moral means"—personal advice, encouragement, and sympathy. Among the most significant aspects of this new organization was that it was city-wide and employed a salaried director assisted by a staff of male volunteers, each of whom assumed responsibility for a particular district. The AICP method of approach, while condescending, lacked the callousness, indifference, and cynicism which typified the administration of public relief. The emphasis it placed upon friendly visiting in the homes of the poor and on the collection of accurate factual data paved the way for a more realistic grasp of the cause and meaning of poverty.

Another phase in the development of private relief giving was the Charity Organization movement. The first Charity Organization Society was established in London in 1869 and similar societies were soon founded in this country. The Charity Organization movement came into being in response to the acute economic distress in England during the 1860's. As was true in America, there was much perplexity in England as to how to meet the problem of want. There were those who thought the poor law too harsh; others believed that it was not strict enough. Many voluntary societies were founded to give aid and comfort to the poor. But a reaction set in; many sincere persons concluded that most material aid was futile since it did not help its recipients become self-supporting; rather it encouraged them to continue their dependency. These persons sought a means whereby the poor could be helped to help themselves—through education, job referrals, assistance from relatives, and, of course, good advice and moral support. Relief should be reduced to a minimum.

The London Charity Organization was established to carry out these objectives. Its purpose, as its name implied, was to organize, or rather to coördinate, the numerous independent charitable agencies in the city by constituting itself a clearing house on all phases of charitable work; by setting up a central registry for all requests for help, so as to eliminate duplication; by providing skilled staff to investigate such requests so that the agencies would have the assurance that their aid would go only to the "worthy" poor; and, in general, to study the problem of poverty and of unmet needs.

Although the first COS was not established in this country until 1877, in Buffalo, a private "Bureau of Charities" was founded in New York City in 1873. Its establishment proved to be premature, but its statement of purpose reflects the COS idea:

1. To obtain authoritative information regarding the objects and resources of the various benevolent societies of the city.
2. To secure a system of registration of the persons receiving aid from the societies and to arrange for such inter-communication of the officers as will prevent imposition.
3. To ascertain whether existing organizations are adapted to meeting existing wants, and whether special and extraordinary provision is required during the winter and to report the same to the public.
4. To ascertain and report to the public the most simple methods of testing and verifying applications for aid, and of directing claimants to the agency adapted to their respective cases.
5. To ascertain and report to the public the state of the law regarding charitable societies, and also regarding street begging and other forms of pauperism.[24]

The COS movement gave impetus, and a sense of purpose and direction, to private charitable agencies. They saw the philosophy and method being evolved by the movement as the answer to the vexing problem of outdoor relief. Charity Organization societies or similar agencies were established in most large cities, absorbing many of the smaller agencies. They soon ceased

[24] Schneider and Deutsch, *op. cit.*, Vol. II, p. 37.

to be coördinating bodies and instead became the chief private relief-giving agencies in their communities. Although nonsectarian, the Charity Organizations had their greatest support, financial and otherwise, from Protestant sources. The Jewish and Catholic communions, which were growing rapidly, established their own agencies. This action was due in part to their still vital traditions concerning the close association of charity and religion; in part to the possible proselytizing implications of relief; and in part to the fear that secular agencies, which made eligibility for relief conditional upon the recipient's conforming to agency demands, might fail to respect or encourage the religious sensibilities of dependent persons.

The leading private agencies in large American cities became confident that they could furnish all necessary outdoor relief from private funds. The corruption in municipal administration, particularly as revealed in the "Tweed ring" scandal in New York City, was another reason for their desire to reduce public appropriations for this purpose. There appeared to be precedents to justify this move. For example, all public outdoor relief had been suspended by the New York City authorities between July, 1874, and January, 1875, with no observable hardships to the poor. Early in 1879, Kings County (the city of Brooklyn) abruptly abolished all outdoor relief. Josephine Shaw Lowell, one of the most distinguished leaders of the American COS movement, could say with equanimity that "the result was—nothing." [25]

In other words, there had been no increase in requests for help made to private agencies. This strengthened the conviction among social workers that the existence of public outdoor relief was an inducement to pauperism.

The private agencies were successful—at least in many large cities—in their campaign to abolish public outdoor relief. Thus Feder could write:

The struggle between adherents of public and private relief that characterized earlier depressions was not conspicuous during the nineties. Generally speaking the private had outstripped the public

[25] Josephine Shaw Lowell, *Public Relief and Private Charities* (New York: Putnam, 1884), p. 60.

in the interval since the last depression and in most communities had secured a position of leadership. Philadelphia was a leader among the cities which had already abolished outdoor relief as inefficient and corrupt, placing responsibility for financial assistance entirely upon private agencies.[26]

New York City, Baltimore, Washington, St. Louis, Kansas City, and San Francisco followed suit. Taking the nation as a whole, however, the poor law remained the major resource against want; in rural communities it was the only resource. Except for emergency outdoor public relief, the poorhouse reigned almost supreme.

SELECTED REFERENCES

Abbott, Edith, *Public Assistance,* Chicago: University of Chicago, 1940, esp. Introduction to Parts One, Two, and Three.

Breckinridge, S. P., *Public Welfare Administration in the United States,* Select Documents, Chicago: University of Chicago, 1938.

De Schweinitz, Karl, *England's Road to Social Security,* Philadelphia: University of Pennsylvania, 1943.

Feder, Leah, *Unemployment Relief in Periods of Depression,* New York: Russell Sage, 1936.

Jernegan, Marcus, "The Development of Poor Relief in Colonial Virginia," *Social Service Review,* March, 1929.

Jernegan, Marcus, "The Development of Poor Relief in Colonial New England," *ibid.,* June, 1931.

Kelso, Robert, *History of Public Poor Relief in Massachusetts,* Boston: Houghton Mifflin, 1922.

Miles, Arthur P., *An Introduction to Public Welfare,* Boston: D. C. Heath, 1949, esp. chaps. 2, 3, and 4.

Schneider, David, and Deutsch, Albert, *History of Public Welfare in New York,* 2 vols., Chicago: University of Chicago, 1938.

Witmer, Helen L., *Social Work,* New York: Farrar & Rinehart, 1942, chap. 7.

[26] Leah Feder, *Unemployment Relief in Periods of Depression* (New York: Russell Sage, 1936), p. 126.

CHAPTER 3

The Emergence of Public Assistance

The primary function of public assistance is to provide cash income to individuals who do not have sufficient resources to maintain themselves. Helping people in need takes on the characteristics of public assistance as contrasted with "poor law" philosophy to the extent that financial need is recognized as not necessarily related to personal inadequacy but primarily to economic factors beyond the control of the individual. Assistance must be furnished according to standards becoming the dignity of man as a human being, assuring adequate maintenance and reasonable and equitable treatment.

—JANE HOEY and ROSE MCHUGH, "Public Assistance," *Social Work Year Book.*

THE MOVEMENT FOR PREFERENTIAL ASSISTANCE

Not long after the private agencies had begun their campaign to eliminate public outdoor relief, a new and diametrically opposed movement was initiated—pensions for certain categories of needy persons: the blind, the aged, and widows with minor children. Although as far back as 1840 a few states had experimented with legislation providing grants to the needy blind, these laws were short lived. The new movement seems to have been inspired by European developments in social insurance and pension programs. Various special interest groups (which were not necessarily in accord regarding the categories of persons in whose interest they were lobbying) generated the driving force behind the movement. Thus, with respect to old-age pensions, the American Association for Labor Legislation and the Fraternal Order of Eagles were notably active.

The advocates of "pension" programs were in agreement that they should be noncontributory; that is, eligibility should not depend on any prior contributions. The programs should be financed entirely out of public funds. The "pensions" should consist of a monthly or semimonthly cash grant based on need. Need, however, was to be interpreted much more liberally than under the poor law. Applicants did not have to be destitute; they might own their own homes, retain sufficient life insurance for burial, and even have a small amount of cash. The standard of assistance should be substantially higher than poor relief. Grants, moreover, should be awarded in supplementation of outside income. There was some divergence of opinion as to whether eligibility should be based merely on insufficiency of income, or on insufficiency of total resources. With respect to the aged, at least, there was strong support for the idea that children of pensioners should be freed from the legal obligation of providing support. The preferential character of the proposed programs was reflected in provisions that pensions should be restricted to "worthy" persons, that is, widows who were of "good moral character," aged persons who had not been tramps or failed to support their families. Ex-criminals and beggars were to be excluded.

At first social workers were opposed to this movement. In spite of the more attractive name of "pension," they saw quite correctly that these programs would be nothing more than a liberalized form of poor relief. They were convinced that no matter what safeguards were instituted, the programs would be affected by the same abuses as those that had discredited outdoor relief under the poor law. Doubtless, part of this resistance could be attributed to the fact that private agencies had been preoccupied with the personal causes of dependency, were out of touch with nation-wide industrial conditions, and hence tended to overlook the underlying economic factors which justified programs of this kind.

In spite of the well-intentioned objections of many leading

social workers and the opposition of influential people in business and public life, small beginnings were made. In 1903 Illinois enacted the first program of financial aid to the needy blind; in 1911 Missouri passed the first "mothers' aid" legislation—applicable only to Jackson County (Kansas City); in 1923 Montana's old-age assistance law was the first to survive the challenge of constitutionality.

Social workers soon recognized their mistake in opposing this movement. While still adhering to their conviction about the undesirability of public outdoor relief for the great mass of the needy, they saw that the blind, the aged, and widowed mothers were clearly not in the labor market and, therefore, were not likely to be pauperized or made "work shy" by this form of public aid. In spite of the fact that some of the earlier programs were poorly conceived, the spirit in which most of them were administered did much to allay their fears of corruption and inefficiency. They even began to advocate more liberal measures and to take part in administering the programs.

Unfortunately, progress was slow. By 1934 (just prior to the enactment of the Social Security Act) only twenty-four states had programs of aid to the blind; only twenty-eight states had old-age assistance; and while forty-two states had some form of "mothers' aid," it was effective in only about half of the counties. In these states programs tended to be restrictive in respect to both eligibility requirements and the size of the grant.

Categorical assistance is now so well established in this country that persons unacquainted with its history might well be puzzled at its slow growth. In spite of superficial resemblances to the poor law, categorical assistance involved a radical departure from traditional relief methods. With respect to philosophy, structure, standards, and finance it operated within an entirely new frame of reference and required a fundamental revision in established habits of thought regarding public responsibility for the care of the needy. The translation of these proposals into effective legislation also involved important constitutional issues so that it is not surprising that progress was slow, and that the resulting legislation was based on many compromises.

Categorical assistance required greater expenditures than most cities and counties were either able or willing to finance, and hence there was great reluctance to enact legislation that would make such programs mandatory on civil subdivisions. Such legislation was possible only if it was permissive, or if the state used its wider taxing powers and financial resources to under-write a substantial part of the cost. But this committed state government to a new function, and many people thought it an unwise precedent to permit local government to shift even part of its traditional responsibility to the state.

The major constitutional difficulties resulted from the existence in some state constitutions of provisions which prohibited the use of state funds in behalf of individuals. These prohibitions were of long standing and had been adopted to prevent unscrupulous legislators from rewarding themselves or their friends out of the public treasury. Now these prohibitions were invoked against aid to the needy. A further constitutional difficulty arose from the preferential nature of the programs. They were challenged on the grounds that they were unconstitutional because they involved the payment of public funds to persons who were not in need— need, that is, as measured in terms of the poor law. This, it was claimed, violated the constitutional guarantee of equal protection under the laws because money would be taken from one group, by means of taxes, and given to another group that was not destitute.

The states responded in various ways. Some, of course, took no action; others passed permissive legislation to enable civil sub-divisions to establish programs if they were so disposed; other states enacted legislation which was declared unconstitutional, and it was necessary to undertake the long process of amendment that would permit such legislation. The realization that legislation would not stand the test of constitutionality discouraged some states from attempting to establish categorical programs.

The effectiveness of categorical assistance legislation depended to a great extent on whether or not the statutes provided for state financial participation. In 1934, of the twenty-four states with blind assistance programs, only seventeen had state aid; of the twenty-eight states with old-age assistance programs, only sixteen had state aid (six were financed entirely by the state). Some of the early programs were barely distinguishable from poor relief. Thus *Survey* magazine, in commenting on Montana's old-age assistance law, complained that it "is not a pension for the aged, it is a possible pension for aged paupers. It fails to carry with it the dignity of foreign old-age pensions which are usually administered by an experienced bureau of the federal government." [1]

Epstein describes the Montana program thus:

The Montana law sets up old age pensions commissions composed of the boards of county commissioners who are generally also in charge of the county poor relief, with no central state supervision whatsoever. That this in practice is merely an extension of the principle of outdoor relief, and fails even to remove one of the main objectionable features—the stigma of pauperism—is evident from the fact that the state auditors' report for 1924 shows an average allowance per applicant of $151.21, as against the maximum of $300 allowed under the law. Obviously these grants are not based on the principle of adequate pensions and are hardly more than the accustomed poor relief given prior to the enactment of the so-called pension law. A canvas recently made of those commissioners revealed that the great majority continue to look on these grants as merely poor relief.[2]

Social workers in Pennsylvania believed that the old-age pension law (later declared unconstitutional) exemplified all the dangers inherent in public outdoor relief. The New York law, passed in 1930, represented a vast improvement in old-age assistance legislation. Although it was locally administered, it provided for state supervision and reimbursement of 50 percent of the grant.

Many states disassociated the administration of the categorical programs from poor relief. The "widow's pension" was often administered by county children's courts; in New York there were separate county boards of child welfare. Some states ad-

[1] Editorial comment, *Survey*, March 15, 1923.
[2] Abraham Epstein, *Proceedings of the National Conference of Social Work* (Chicago: University of Chicago, 1925), p. 333.

ministered old-age assistance directly; and where it was locally administered it was usually administered by a separate division within the local welfare agency.

Opposition to the idea of state-financed assistance outside the terms of the poor law continued to be strong even after the passage of the Social Security Act. Walter Gifford, President of the Charity Organization of New York City, writing in the *Atlantic Monthly* for February, 1930, just prior to the passage of New York's old-age assistance law and only a few months prior to his assumption of the chairmanship of the President's Organization on Unemployment Relief, reflects the reservations entertained by many influential people: "The agitation for state old-age pensions brings in concrete form the question whether the people of the United States wish to solve the old-age problem along the lines of their own development or to abandon this field to governmental action which must of necessity confine itself to the dispensing of funds on a nondiscriminating basis."

THE GREAT DEPRESSION: THE EARLY PHASE

The great depression of 1929–1939 burst upon a nation which had neither the administrative machinery to cope with the misery that it produced nor the psychological readiness to adopt prompt and appropriate measures for its alleviation. The "depression decade" has great significance for the student of public welfare because it was a period during which the nation as a whole was forced to grapple with a problem that was unique in its magnitude. Poverty and insecurity, and their attendant suffering, were not new; the nation had experienced many depressions in the past. But now, pressure of circumstances demanded a reëxamination of the traditional attitudes toward the poor, and of the manner in which their needs were met. Although the historic explanation of the causes of deprivation and dependency continued to exert a strong emotional hold, it could offer no satisfactory reason why, during the period 1933–1938, the number of persons who were obliged to accept some form of public aid ranged from eighteen to twenty-eight million. Nor could it account for the swift declines in fortune, the almost overnight change from affluence to poverty, the fact that thrift and industry availed for naught.

Out of the bitter experience of this decade new forms of assistance have emerged, new administrative arrangements and relationships have been worked out, and a new approach to the problem of economic security has been adopted.

Although it is convenient to date the onset of the depression from the stock market crash in the fall of 1929, actually, economic conditions prior thereto were far from sound despite a superficial appearance of prosperity. In the spring of 1929 the unemployed numbered 2,860,000; agriculture, moreover, had never recovered from the depression beginning in 1920–1921. In 1929 almost half the nation's farms produced gross annual incomes of less than $1000; almost eight million persons lived on farms that produced gross incomes of less than $600 a year.

The events that followed the Wall Street crash left no doubt as to the gravity of the situation. Production declined, banking and business houses failed, and unemployment mounted rapidly—four million in January, 1930, five million in September, seven million in December, and by spring, 1933, an estimated thirteen to seventeen million.[3] At first the American people seemed too stunned to appreciate the full import of what had happened; there was a reluctance to recognize that the "slump" was anything but temporary. A rather self-conscious optimism prompted many to believe that things would work themselves out in short order. "Prosperity," in other words, was "just around the corner."

Meanwhile, relief agencies, both public and private, were deluged with requests for help which they were unable to furnish. Except in some of the larger cities, the poor-relief authorities bore the brunt of this demand; and they had neither the organization nor the financial resources to cope with it. Poor relief was financed by a tax on real property; to increase these taxes would only have aggravated an already serious situation. Homeowners were having a difficult enough time meeting the existing taxes and interest charges on their property; and land-

[3] Josephine Brown, *Public Relief, 1929–1939* (New York: Henry Holt, 1940), p. 64.

lords were particularly hard pressed because of their tenants' inability to pay rent. The shortage of relief funds, moreover, obliged public and private agencies to omit rental allowances in their relief grants. The financing of relief through loans (which could be repaid at a future date when economic conditions had improved) would have been preferable to an increase in the real-property tax, but most communities were handicapped in this regard, either because their credit was exhausted or because of statutory or constitutional limitations on the amount of debt they could contract. There was, moreover, strong resistance to the incurring of debt for this purpose. To add to these difficulties the question was raised as to whether relief could be extended to the unemployed unless they qualified for it under the poor law, i.e., unless they were destitute. Many genuinely needy people were denied assistance because they had an equity in their home. To become eligible for help they were obliged to liquidate their holdings—in a greatly deflated market.

During 1930–1932 the private agencies made valiant efforts to fulfill the high hopes that had been placed in them, but, although through regular community chest drives and extraordinary appeals they raised sums greater than ever before, these were insufficient to meet the demand. In communities where there was no public outdoor relief, local government made grants of public funds to private agencies to meet the emergency, but these too were insufficient.

For many years prior to the depression the role of the private agencies in relief giving had been overestimated. Their vigorous campaigns against public outdoor relief, marked with such striking success in many large cities, and their reiterated conviction that private philanthropy could take care of all those who were "worthy" of such help had given the public the impression that they were capable of meeting this challenge. The fact was, however, that they had never been able to do so even before this unprecedented demand for assistance. According to a study made by the Bureau of the Census in 1931, the breakdown between public and private expenditures for relief for the first quarter of 1929 and of 1931 was as follows:

Source	1929	%	1931	%
Public funds	$13,973,349	70.6	$43,249,743	65.8
Private funds	5,819,239	29.4	22,468,161	34.2

Edith Abbott, in commenting upon this study, calls attention to a significant point: ". . . The total relief expenditures reported by the census for private organizations represented merely the funds expended by those organizations, whether those funds came from the taxpayer or from private charitable gifts. That is, what is called 'private relief' in the census report is an exaggerated figure, since it includes an undetermined percentage of public as well as private relief funds." [4]

The first two years of the depression were times of soul searching among social workers, during which the great principles of the COS movement were jettisoned one by one. The change in thinking is illustrated by the contrasting comments of Linton Swift, Director of the Family Welfare Association of America, in papers presented at the National Conference of Social Work in 1930 and 1931. In 1930, Mr. Swift spoke in the following guarded terms:

. . . And finally, I wonder whether in making use of the wholesale appeal for relief, we have not been merely fostering a community relief psychology which has already gone beyond our control, is "spilling over" into pressure for development of public agencies and into community demands for new types of government relief such as old-age pensions? And may not all of this gradually result in a great governmental relief system the more dangerous because it is not consistently planned but created category by category? . . .

If we are not careful, a continued use of the wholesale appeal for relief is likely to lead us into a situation where a real individualization of human needs will be impossible, and in which we and later government will become the almoners of industry and society. [5]

[4] Edith Abbott, *Public Assistance* (Chicago: University of Chicago, 1940), pp. 662–663. Even prior to the depression it was not uncommon for private social agencies to act as agents of a municipality in providing outdoor relief—a service for which public funds were appropriated. Wendell Johnson reported at the National Conference of Social Work in 1931 that, of thirty-three private agencies responding to a questionnaire, fifteen were receiving public funds.

[5] Linton Swift, "The Community Fund and Relief Giving," *Proceedings of the National Conference of Social Work* (1930), p. 242.

In 1931, Mr. Swift saw public relief in a somewhat more positive light:

Perhaps as good a cue for discussion as any, is the statement, reiterated several times by President Hoover during the past winter, to the effect that the American method of assisting the unemployed is through private charity. Many of us sharply disagree with this statement, not merely because it is not true, but because of its implications. If the President had said that our American philosophy favors local or state action in preference to federal action wherever possible, in relief as well as in other problems he might have found wide agreement. Many of us are convinced that responsibility should be continued as much as possible in local and state governments where the people may be more continuously aware of its implications.[6]

At the same conference, Harry Lurie commented ruefully:

How uncomfortable many of us must have been during the present year to find these ancestral beliefs of social workers (i.e., regarding public outdoor relief, the "worthy" and "unworthy" poor, etc.) repeated by President Hoover and other governmental and industrial leaders as a justification for thwarting emergency public measures for the relief of the unemployed.[7]

The criticism of President Hoover in the above statement relates to his unwillingness to bring the financial resources of the federal government to bear upon the problem of unemployment, which was now very great. In repeated utterances he maintained his conviction that the American people could, should, and would respond to the needs of their neighbors through voluntary effort. Where public funds were absolutely necessary, they should come from state and local government. He was adamant against granting what he considered would be a federal "dole."

In 1930, economic distress was intensified by a severe drought affecting many agricultural states, especially in the South and West. In August of that year the President called a meeting of the governors and appointed a committee to study the problems

[6] Swift, "The Future of Public Social Work in America from the Point of View of the Private Agency," *ibid.* (1931), p. 451.

[7] Harry L. Lurie, "The Drift to Public Relief," *ibid.*, p. 213.

created by the drought. The American Red Cross was asked to use its disaster relief fund to help the poverty-stricken people in the rural areas affected by the drought.

In October, 1930, the President organized an "Emergency Committee for Employment." This committee was little more than a clearing house for the dissemination of information and of suggestions as to ways in which communities could handle the task of creating employment opportunities. Emphasis was placed on slogans such as "Give a job," and "Spread the work," as if it were possible to advertise the nation out of its predicament.

In December the President, in his annual message to Congress, requested $150,000,000 to provide additional employment in various federal departments. He made no other reference to relief except as it applied to conditions arising from the drought.

In January, 1931, Congress, appalled by the reports of hardship in the drought areas and by the meagerness of Red Cross relief grants, considered the possibility of appropriating $25,000,000 to be given to the Red Cross for relief purposes. Officials of the Red Cross, however, were opposed to such a subsidy. During the hearings on the bill under consideration, Judge John Barton Payne, chairman of the board, distinguished between unemployment, which he considered an urban and industrial problem, and the situation in the drought areas. It was the latter problem for which the Red Cross had accepted responsibility because of its role in disaster relief.

Judge Payne took exception to the terms of the bill because it did not distinguish between these two problems but would have made the Red Cross responsible for the distribution of federal funds "for the purpose of supplying food, medicine, medical aid, and other essentials to afford adequate relief in the present national emergency to persons otherwise unable to procure the same." [8] He pointed out that the distribution of such relief would require the establishment of a nation-wide organization with paid staff, and that it would, in a sense, be competing with local public and private relief agencies that were already engaged in providing assistance in urban areas. Even $25,000,000, moreover,

[8] Quoted in Abbott, *op. cit.*, p. 721.

would not go far in meeting the needs of the unemployed, who were estimated to number at this time 5,700,000. For these reasons, and also because the receipt of public funds would "to a large extent destroy voluntary giving," the central committee of the Red Cross adopted a resolution to the effect that it could not accept responsibility for the administration of funds for general relief purposes.

In the spring of 1931 the Red Cross was aided in its work by some $10,000,000 collected from public employees who contributed a day's pay. Late in 1931 Congress transferred to the Red Cross government-owned surpluses of wheat and cotton for food, clothing, and feed for livestock. In the meantime, the Friends Service Committee had been called upon to help feed children in the poverty-stricken mining communities of West Virginia, Kentucky, Pennsylvania, and Illinois.

In August, 1931, the Emergency Committee for Employment was replaced by the "President's Organization on Unemployment Relief." This organization, headed by Walter Gifford, directed its efforts toward coördinating and improving local unemployment relief activities. Practical help was confined to a national campaign to promote increased contributions to community relief drives. The similarity of Mr. Gifford's philosophy and that of the President is revealed in his comment on local responsibility:

Should such community and state responsibility be lessened by federal aid, the sincere and whole-hearted efforts of hundreds of thousands of volunteers engaged in raising and administering relief funds would doubtless be materially lessened. Individuals would tend to withdraw much of the invisible aid (i.e. cash, board and lodging extended by relatives and friends) they are now giving; private funds raised by popular subscription would become less, efforts to spread work and to provide work that would not be done except for the emergency would be lessened; business organizations would tend to do less for their employees. Communities, counties, and states undoubtedly would appropriate less public monies. The net result might well be that the unemployed who are in need would be worse instead of better off.[9]

[9] "Relief Needs, Relief Sources," *Survey Graphic*, February, 1932, p. 446.

In December, 1931, Senator Costigan introduced a bill to provide federal aid to the states for unemployment relief. The bill would have appropriated $125,000,000 for the current fiscal year and $250,000,000 for the following year. The funds were to be administered by the federal Children's Bureau through a "Federal Board for Unemployment Relief." Forty percent of the funds would have been allocated to the states on a population basis and the remainder distributed in accordance with need. Senator La Follette introduced a similar measure, and the two were subsequently combined. The hearings on the bills revealed in unmistakable terms the extent of unemployment and its shocking consequences. The bill, however, failed to pass the Senate.

In January, 1932, the Reconstruction Finance Corporation was created by Congress to aid financial institutions, commerce, industry, and agriculture. Thus when federal loans were extended to banks and railroads, it was said that they were the first recipients of federal relief.

From the beginning of the depression the inability of local public and private agencies to meet need had resulted in appeals to state governments for aid. The states, it will be recalled, had little in the way of precedent for the use of state funds in behalf of individuals. Many states were still handicapped by constitutional limitations that either prohibited direct aid to individuals or limited the borrowing power of the state. Nevertheless, during the first two years of the depression a few states were able to make appropriations for disaster relief and unemployment relief. These appropriations, which were not large, were turned over to the localities, and there was no continuity of either financing or supervision.

Pennsylvania affords an interesting example of the problems confronting some states in helping local government to meet its responsibilities. In the latter part of 1931 the legislature had appropriated $10,000,000 to be distributed among the counties for unemployment relief. The constitutionality of the appropriation act was challenged on the grounds that this was an appropriation for a "charitable purpose" and thus conflicted with Article III, Section 8, of the state constitution, which stipulated:

"No appropriation, except for pensions or gratuities for military services, shall be made for charitable, educational or benevolent purposes, to any person or community, nor to any denominational institution, corporation or association."

The state supreme court, in reversing an adverse decision of an inferior court, upheld the constitutionality of this act, declaring that "unemployment relief" according to the act was relief to the *needy* unemployed; that such persons were eligible for assistance under the poor law; and finally, that the care of such persons was not a charitable undertaking any more than the performance of other public functions is a charity, and hence the appropriation was not for a charitable purpose but rather to enable local governmental units to carry out the duties with which they were charged.

New York was the first state to adopt a relatively long-range plan of financial assistance to local government for unemployment relief. In August, 1931, Governor Franklin D. Roosevelt called a special session of the legislature to consider measures to meet the emergency in the state. On August 28, he delivered a message to the Senate and Assembly in which he discussed the function of the state with particular reference to the immediate crisis. His message included the following outline of a program of emergency assistance:

1. I suggest that the administration of unemployment and distress relief within the State be placed in the hands of a temporary emergency commission of three persons to be appointed by the Governor to serve without pay. The Commission, to be known as the "Temporary Emergency Relief Administration," should be empowered to recommend to the Governor the appointment of local subsidiary commissions of three or more men and women in cities and counties as it deems advisable. The sum of twenty million dollars, which I am reliably informed is the estimated amount required to meet the needs of the coming year, should be appropriated and should be apportioned by this commission among the various counties and cities of the State. The distribution should be based in amount on several factors, such as: (1) The number of people and families unemployed in the locality, requiring assistance; and (2) the amount of local effort and initiative as shown by the money raised in the municipality by public

and private means, consistent with the financial abilty of the municipality and its people.

Based on the theory that the distribution of relief of the poor is essentially a local function, I believe that the State in supplementing the amount locally raised should seek so far as possible to encourage local initiative by matching local effort; so that the larger the amount raised locally, the larger the contribution of the State.

The actual disbursement of this money should be in the hands of the local welfare officer of the municipality, subject however to the approval of the local Temporary Emergency Relief Commission, if one be appointed. . . .

It should be provided by statute that the money be expended as follows: If any form of employment can be found for the public use, the prevailing rate of wages should be paid for such work; if, however, it is impossible to locate or provide work of this kind, then the local welfare officer may purchase and give to the unemployed within his jurisdiction necessary food, clothing, fuel and shelter for them and their families. Certain definite restrictions should be embodied within the statute, viz.:

1. That under no circumstance shall any actual money be paid in the form of a dole or in any other form by the local welfare officer to any unemployed or his family.

2. That this relief should be restricted to persons who have resided in New York State for at least two years prior to the enactment of the statute.

3. That no employment or relief be undertaken except in accordance with the rules and regulations laid down by the Temporary Emergency Relief Administration.

. . . There is another requirement for a scientific and proper system of relief which experience has shown us has not been hitherto properly recognized or organized. Experience has shown that many of the most deserving cases not only refuse to apply for relief until actual starvation has set in, but allow the future health of their children to become permanently undermined by undernourishment rather than seek community help. Any proper relief system must have a thoroughly organized, enthusiastic and tireless department of investigation, constantly seeking out those individuals or families who will not of their own accord come forward. . . .

2. The necessary money for this unemployment and distress relief should be raised by a tax on personal incomes. It seems logical that

those of our residents who are fortunate enough to have a taxable income should bear the burden of supplementing the local government and private philanthropic work of assistance. I believe that the tax should fall proportionately on all incomes over and above existing exemptions. . . .

3. Legislation should be enacted giving to the various cities and counties of the State authority to borrow money and expend it for the employment of its residents on public works. . . .[10]

On September 23, 1931, a bill (the "Wicks Act") was passed which incorporated Governor Roosevelt's recommendations. The TERA was established for a period of eight months; subsequent legislation extended it for "temporary" periods until July 1, 1937, when its functions were transferred to the state Department of Social Welfare. The TERA was the first state emergency relief agency, and because of its sound philosophy, methods, and pattern of organization its influence extended far beyond the borders of the state. Its contribution to the development of public assistance as we know it today is reflected in the precedents it set in such vital matters as standards of assistance; definition of eligibility; nondiscrimination with respect to political affiliation, creed, race, or lack of citizenship; work relief for the able-bodied; the employment of trained social service personnel; accurate and prompt reports and statistical data on expenditure of funds, verification of need, case loads, etc.

Other states were not far behind New York. New Jersey appropriated $10,000,000 for unemployment relief on September 21; Pennsylvania appropriated a similar amount in November (only to run into the constitutional issue mentioned above); Wisconsin, Rhode Island, Illinois, and Ohio also appropriated funds and established some form of state organization for unemployment relief prior to April, 1932. By the end of 1932 a majority of the states had followed suit, but there were some that did nothing, either because they were too poor or because of constitutional difficulties and the lack of resourceful and progressive leadership.

Josephine Brown comments: "Never before in the history of

[10] *New York State Assembly Journal,* 1931, III (extraordinary session), pp. 21–29.

the United States had state governments invested so heavily in relief for any purpose. These unprecedented appropriations established once and for all the responsibility of state government for relief of persons in need, not only in *this* unemployment emergency, but in any emergency; not only in any emergency, but for permanent programs of public assistance." [11]

In spite of state intervention in the problem of unemployment, the situation worsened. Production, wage rates, and tax revenues continued to decline, while unemployment and dependency mounted. President Hoover remained unshaken in his conviction that since federal aid would be "paternalistic," and could be provided only at the expense of a "balanced budget," it would aggravate an already desperate situation. He was, of course, not alone in this position; rather he was the most influential exponent for a point of view which was shared by many persons in industrial and public life, who feared that an increase in federal expenditures, either through increased taxes or loans, would bankrupt the nation.

Finally, however, the pressure on Congress became unbearable, and in the late spring of 1932 the Wagner-Rainey bill was passed by both houses, authorizing the Reconstruction Finance Corporation to provide loans for public works and to make loans and advances to the states for unemployment relief. The bill was vetoed by President Hoover, but on July 11 an almost identical bill was passed which the President signed with reluctance and misgivings.

Although the "Emergency Relief and Reconstruction Act" was inadequate, being a compromise worked out in the face of bitter opposition, it represented the first break with the "hands-off" policy of the national government. It authorized loans up to $300,000,000, carrying an interest rate of 3 percent to states, as advances on future federal grants for highway construction. Advances were to be made to the several states on certification by their governors that the resources of the state were insufficient to meet the demand for relief. No more than 15 percent of the total sum could be advanced to any one state. The basis on which the

[11] Brown, *op. cit.*, p. 96.

loans were made was designed to maintain the fiction that the federal government was not directly involved in the problem of relief; nevertheless, to receive these loans the states were required to take what amounted to a "pauper's oath." Since the RFC made the loans in its capacity as a banking institution, no real effort was made to provide either supervision or leadership to the states.

THE GREAT DEPRESSION: THE LATER PHASE

The presidential election of 1932 presaged a radical change in the role of the national government in the economic crisis; nevertheless, President Roosevelt was inaugurated in an "atmosphere of gloom and uncertainty" because in March, 1933, the depression was at its worst and the people were beginning to doubt whether the economic structure could survive the blows it had received.

The next few months witnessed the passage of a series of legislative measures designed to attack the problem on two fronts: by stimulating business activity and by relieving the acute distress of poverty and unemployment. Although the extent to which "New Deal" legislation actually stimulated economic recovery is still debated, it seems clear that, in the area of relief, federal activity was of inestimable value in improving the living conditions of millions of people who hitherto had been existing at a level little above starvation.

The "New Deal" program was largely extemporized, and was characterized by experimentation, compromise, and frequent shifts in policy. It is hard to conceive, however, how any program could have been otherwise in view of the unprecedented nature of the problem. In May, 1933, when the Federal Emergency Relief Act was passed, some eighteen million persons (four million families) were receiving emergency aid of one kind or another. In some states 40 percent of the population was on relief; in some counties the rate was as high as 90 percent. The low standard of assistance resulting from inadequate funds, moreover, denied assistance to many people whose need was acute.[12]

[12] *Ibid.*, p. 145.

The calendar of major federal legislation in the area of relief during 1933 was as follows:

March 31. The Civilian Conservation Corps was established to place unemployed young men from the cities in woodland camps where they could perform useful work in reforestation and flood control. They received maintenance and an allotment of $30 a month, of which they had to agree to send $25 to their families. Within three months 300,000 young men (including 25,000 veterans) were placed in some 1500 CCC camps throughout the country. The initial period of enrollment was for six months, and this could be extended under certain circumstances.

May 12. The Federal Emergency Relief Administration was established.

June 16. The Federal Emergency Administration of Public Works (PWA) was established and placed in the Department of the Interior. Its objective was to stimulate business by creating employment in construction trades and heavy industry by making loans and advances to federal, state, and local agencies for public works that ordinarily would not have been undertaken. These were not "relief" projects but were carried on by the regular agencies of government through the normal procedure of requesting bids and letting contracts.

November 11. The Civil Works Administration was created. This short-lived agency was established to put large numbers of unemployed persons to work on projects similar to work relief but without requiring a "needs test." It was planned to fill half of the four million jobs with employables from the relief rolls and the remainder from the ranks of the unemployed who were not on relief. It was hoped that CWA could bring about a more rapid increase in purchasing power than was possible under PWA, and reduce the number of persons in receipt of direct relief. The program was found to be impracticable and was discontinued after four and one-half months.[13]

October 4. The Federal Surplus Relief Corporation (later the Federal Surplus Commodity Corporation) was established. Its purpose was: ". . . (1) . . . to assist in relieving the existing national emergency by purchasing, processing, and distribution for

[13] See Chapter 13 for further discussion of work relief and public works.

consumption of agricultural and other products as a means to remove surpluses and improve prices; (2) to apply these surplus
agricultural and other products in the form of foodstuffs, clothing,
fuel and otherwise to the relief of hardship and suffering caused
by unemployment." [14]

The Federal Emergency Relief Administration

Under the terms of the Federal Emergency Relief Act of 1933,
Congress appropriated $500,000,000 for unemployment relief to
the states. The aid was to take the form of grants rather than
loans, and a "Federal Emergency Relief Administration" was
created to supervise the disbursement of federal funds by the
states. The new agency was patterned closely after the TERA in
New York, and the latter's director, Harry Hopkins, became its
chief. Unlike the TERA, no provisions were made for a citizen
policy-making board; the director was responsible only to the
President.

Mr. Hopkins set to work vigorously to implement the new program. Since Congress had enacted no substantive legislation concerning the structure, powers, and scope of the new agency, he
had practically a free hand. Each state was required to establish
an emergency relief authority to receive and disburse federal
funds. Rules and regulations were promulgated setting forth the
conditions of relief administration with which the states had to
conform to be eligible for grants. These included most of the for-
ward-looking measures that had originally been put into practice
in New York: relief could be disbursed only by public agencies,
and granted on a budget deficit basis; rent was to be paid, and
medical care provided; discrimination was to be avoided; [15] state
administrators were encouraged to use trained personnel in supervisory positions and to replace the incompetent and inhumane approach of the poormaster with the philosophy and method of
social work; sound work relief projects were encouraged, and
project workers were required to receive cash compensation.

[14] *Monthly Report, Federal Emergency Relief Administration* (Washington: December, 1933), p. 39.
[15] Nevertheless Negro and Mexican families in certain states did not fare
as well as their neighbors.

Allocation of Funds

Perhaps the greatest problem faced by FERA was in the allocation of funds to the states. The original appropriation act stipulated that one-half of the $500,000,000 was to be distributed on a matching basis, one dollar of federal money for every three dollars of state and local funds, the remainder to be distributed by the federal administrator according to his discretion and the requirements of the several states. Both the President and Mr. Hopkins believed that unemployment relief was primarily a local or at most a state problem, and that federal grants were to aid the states in discharging their responsibilities. Although the states and their local subdivisions were expected to carry "their share" of the cost, at no time did the FERA work out a definite formula by which this "share" could be computed—in spite of the fact that by the time FERA was liquidated in 1936 it had disbursed three billion dollars to the states. The reason for this failure to develop a formula lay in the fact that the states differed greatly with respect to their needs and resources. A uniform matching formula, applicable to all states, would have been unsatisfactory because there was no direct relation between the degree of need and the ability to raise funds. Thus, if the national government had matched state and local appropriations, the state that could raise the most money would receive the largest federal grant, even though its dependency rate might be much less than that of other states.

The FERA attempted to solve the problem created by the fact that states with the least fiscal ability tended to have the greatest need. Experts in taxation and public finance were consulted regarding the development of accurate measures of fiscal ability, but FERA was liquidated before suitable measures were forthcoming. In the meantime, FERA continued to exhort, cajole, and threaten states that were not contributing the "fair share" of the cost, while the funds that were actually allocated seemed to bear no relation to any objective standard. As Edith Abbott pointed out:

In 1934, the New Jersey authorities were able to persuade the administrator to make grants to that state which cared for 86 percent of the relief bill in that year, when 13 percent of the families of the state were on relief, whereas in Illinois, in the same year, with the same percentage of the families on relief, the authorities were not able to persuade the administrator to grant more than 68 percent of the relief expenditures. Illinois, of course, could not understand why her representatives were being admonished about not providing their "share" of the relief expenditures, when a state like New Jersey was providing much less. In North Carolina, with 10 percent of the population on relief in 1935, the FERA made grants that covered 100 percent of the relief bills while to drought-stricken North Dakota, with 25 percent of the families of the state on relief, the FERA granted not 100 percent but 86 percent of the funds needed for relief.[16]

The Southeastern states had the highest percentage of federal payments for relief; the New England states, the lowest. The administrator had the authority to bring recalcitrant states into line by withholding all grants, but, as he said, "Our dislike of falling back upon this means of pressure was that it victimized not the state official or the legislature, but the suffering fell upon the unemployed." [17] In the absence of a statutory formula, or even of an advisory board which might have shared the responsibility, the administrator would have had to bear the onus of so drastic a measure. It seems likely that Mr. Hopkins tried to get as large a financial commitment as possible from each state, and let it go at that.[18] Even so friendly a critic as Edith Abbott felt constrained to point out that "such a policy inevitably caused dissatisfaction and created a suspicion of favoritism and lack of fair dealing." [19]

Even had FERA been able to develop an accurate measure of fiscal ability, the problem would have been far from solved. Antiquated tax structures and constitutional limitations hindered many states from tapping potential sources of revenue. Obstructionist tactics on the part of small but influential elements within a state effectively blocked progressive legislation, so that the task

[16] Abbott, *op. cit.*, p. 683.
[17] Harry Hopkins, *Spending to Save* (New York: Norton, 1936), pp. 97–98.
[18] At one point in 1933 federal grants to Colorado and Missouri were held up because of their failure to participate.
[19] Abbott, *op. cit.*, p. 679.

of distinguishing between states that could not and states that would not achieve a specified goal was extremely difficult.

According to Professor Abbott: "The experience under the FERA makes it impossible to believe that 'variable grants' on a large scale can be satisfactorily administered." She favored a uniform rate of reimbursement, one that would be high, but not as high as the rates received by some states under FERA. If, for example, all states were reimbursed at the rate of 90 percent, rather than having North Carolina get 100 percent and New York 56 percent, federal expenditures would have been increased but the burden on the individual taxpayer would not have been increased because wealthy states like New York, while having to pay more in federal taxes, would have had to raise less for their share of relief costs.[20] Professor Abbott presumably does not reckon as undesirable the large measure of federal control over state relief policies that would be inevitable under such arrangements.

The American Association of Social Workers, through its Division on Government and Social Work, recommended an approach directly opposite to that of Miss Abbott, as follows:

(a) Initial basic grants to all states, fixed either at a small proportion (perhaps 25 percent) of their total expenditures for relief, or upon some simple basis such as per capita of population.
(b) Equalization grants designed to balance the disparity between states in wealth and income on the one hand and needs and liabilities on the other hand.[21]

The problem of the equitable distribution of grants-in-aid has yet to be solved, as we shall see in Chapter 5 when we consider the financing of public assistance.

Work vs. Direct Relief

Throughout the depression the provision of work rather than direct relief was considered an important objective. Even during the critical period prior to federal intervention public and private relief agencies had sponsored work projects for the unemployed.

[20] *Ibid.*, p. 687.
[21] American Association of Social Workers, *This Business of Relief* (New York: AASW), Appendix, p. 66.

Because of the volume of need, and the difficulties involved in the rapid development of suitable work projects, direct relief played a more important role in the FERA program. We have noted that the Civil Works Administration proved to be unsatisfactory, and after its dissolution the responsibility for work projects was turned back to the states.

The President, however, believed that the national government should make greater efforts to put the unemployed to work and that it "must and shall quit this business of relief." Accordingly, in his annual message to Congress on January 4, 1935, he outlined a program involving the dissolution of FERA and the creation of a new agency which would assume full administrative and financial responsibility for the development of work projects for substantially all employable persons currently in need. All other needy persons would be cared for entirely at state and local expense.[22]

In response to this message Congress passed the Emergency Relief Appropriation Act of 1935, on April 8. Under the terms of the act between four and five billion dollars were made available until June 30, 1937, for the purpose of increasing employment and providing useful work projects for the needy unemployed. Almost unlimited power was granted to the President in the matter of expenditures, development of basic policy, and creation of an administrative organization. The only major restriction related to the amounts that could be spent for certain classes of projects (i.e., highways, roads, streets, and grade crossings—$800,000,000; housing—$450,000,000; etc.). These restrictions covered only 80 percent of the total appropriation; the balance could be allocated as the President thought fit. This legislation prompted Lewis Meriam to comment: "Rarely, if ever, in our history have more important determinations of basic fundamental policy been embodied in an appropriation act without any substantive legislation authorizing it and without consideration by any committee of Congress other than the appropriation committee." [23]

[22] Plans were under way, however, for a comprehensive social security program which would include federal grants for certain categories of unemployable persons.

[23] Lewis Meriam, *Relief and Social Security* (Washington: Brookings, 1946), p. 352.

During the spring of 1935 the program which the appropriation act had made possible got under way. In April a Rural Resettlement Administration was established by executive order. Its functions were described by the President as follows:

(a) To administer approved projects involving resettlement of destitute or low-income families from rural and urban areas, including the establishment, maintenance and operation, in such connection, of communities in rural and suburban areas.

(b) To initiate and administer a program of approved projects with respect to soil erosion, stream pollution, seacoast erosion, reforestation, forestation, and flood control.

(c) To make loans as authorized under the said Emergency Relief Appropriation Act of 1935 to finance, in whole or in part, the purchase of farm lands and necessary equipment by farmers, farm tenants, croppers, or farm laborers.[24]

At the end of 1936 the Resettlement Administration ceased to exist as an independent agency, and its functions were transferred to the "Farm Security Administration" within the Department of Agriculture. A Rural Electrification Administration was created in May, 1935.

The major portion of the appropriation was divided between two agencies: the Public Works Administration, headed by Harold Ickes, Secretary of the Interior, and the newly established Works Progress Administration, headed by Harry Hopkins of the defunct FERA. The first agency, as has already been noted, was primarily a financial institution. It made loans and grants to various public bodies for public works activities that ordinarily might not have been undertaken. The grants, however, did not exceed from 30 to 40 percent of the cost of such projects. The second agency was essentially a work relief agency. Its objective was to remove all employable persons from the direct relief rolls, assigning them to projects in a vast federally administered and financed work program. State and local governmental bodies "sponsoring" these projects were required to put up a contribution of from 10 to 25 percent.

The fundamental differences between "public works" and

[24] *Ibid.,* p. 286.

"work relief" will be considered in Chapter 13; it is sufficient here to point out that because of these differences, and in the absence of any statutory allocation of funds between the two agencies, the administrators soon clashed. Hopkins and Ickes were both capable, conscientious, socially-minded public servants but they became competitors, as it were, for what they considered to be their fair share of the funds which Congress had turned over to the President to be dispensed at his discretion.

Perhaps the greatest problem arising out of the shift in federal policy was the withdrawal of grants-in-aid to the states for direct relief. The purpose of these grants had been to relieve the need of individuals and families whose income had been cut off by unemployment. It was administratively impracticable to separate this group from those persons who were unemployable and for whom the state and its civil subdivisions were responsible under the poor law. Many unemployable persons, moreover, were in need because of conditions arising out of the depression, notably the wiping out of bank accounts and investments, and the loss of help from relatives because of the latter's reduced income. It was recognized that those states that managed to secure grants-in-aid covering a very high percentage of their relief costs were using federal funds for a purpose which, strictly speaking, did not come under the terms of the federal appropriation bill. This discrepancy was tolerated because of the great difficulties that would have arisen in trying to distinguish between persons in need because of the depression and those in need for other reasons. Some states were thereby able to relieve themselves of most, if not all, of the financial burden of what was still technically poor relief. They did not anticipate the problems that would arise and the distress that would be entailed when federal participation in direct relief was discontinued.

In theory, a case might have been made for discontinuance, had the federal government been able to provide work for all employable persons. Since this group constituted by far the largest number of needy persons, it was not unreasonable to expect the states to care for the balance—those that were unemployable, most of whom, after all, would have been eligible for help under the poor law. FERA grants, however, had made possible a standard of assistance far superior to that customarily provided under the local poor law; hence, the withdrawal of federal aid meant that these improved standards could not be maintained even with substantial increases in state and local funds. The states that had relied almost entirely on federal grants found themselves in the greatest difficulties; but a problem affecting all the states was the fact that at no time was WPA able to provide work for all employable persons; hence the states had to care for many persons for whom the federal government had agreed to assume responsibility.

The rather arbitrary distinction between employables and unemployables gave rise to other complications. The direct relief burden in a given state depended upon the extent to which work relief was available; but whereas under FERA it was the state that assumed the initiative in developing work projects, now under WPA it was the federal government. State X might conclude that it was being treated unfairly because the volume of WPA activity in relation to need was less than the volume of WPA activity in state Y. This conclusion, however, was difficult to prove because of the lack of comparable statistical data. The WPA had no information on the number of employable persons on the relief rolls in a given state—nor, of course, on the number of needy employable persons who were denied direct relief because of low standards and lack of funds. The volume of work relief in a given area, moreover, depended upon many factors other than need, such as the availability of suitable projects. It is understandable that urban districts would have greater opportunities for work projects than rural areas; on the other hand, a relatively low rate of WPA activity in rural areas was often offset by the activity of the Farm Security Agency. In spite of the clear-cut division between federal and state responsibility, the federal government could not make good on its commitments; consequently no state could tell in advance what part of the burden of need it would have to be prepared to meet.

The WPA lasted until 1942, and it expended approximately 8.2 billion dollars. While it was extremely important in relieving economic distress, it is questionable whether it was an improvement over FERA, which, in spite of its defects, at least sought to maintain the sound policy of state-federal coöperation.

The Social Security Act

As the depression continued, the need for a long-range plan of care for the needy became increasingly evident. The public conscience was awakened not only to the great misery to which so many people had been exposed because the nation had been unprepared for the calamity that had come upon it but also to the miserable conditions to which dependent people had been subject even in "normal" times. Moreover, so many people had been impoverished, or brought to the brink of poverty, that the great gulf that hitherto had seemed to separate the economically dependent from the economically independent no longer seemed so wide. In all probability it was the thought that "it could have happened to me" rather than any true feeling of justice and charity that made the public more receptive to adequate and humane forms of assistance. At any rate the time was propitious for a new approach to the problem of insecurity and want. President Roosevelt, sensitive to this new ferment, sent a special message to Congress on June 8, 1934, in which he outlined his ideas regarding methods for achieving economic security. Later in the month he created the Committee on Economic Security, composed of the Secretaries of Labor, Agriculture, the Treasury, the Attorney General, and the Federal Emergency Relief Administrator, to study the subject. The committee secured the help of experts in various fields and submitted its report to the President on January 17, 1935. The President made recommendations to Congress based on these findings, and these were embodied in the Social Security Act, which was passed by Congress in August, 1935.

The Social Security Act has undergone various modifications in the years since its passage, but its essential features are unaltered. Its major provisions may be grouped into three areas: public assistance, social insurance, and children's services. Under the *public assistance* titles of the act, grants-in-aid on a matching basis are made to states adopting approved plans for old-age assistance, aid to the blind, aid to dependent children, and, as of 1950, aid to the totally and permanently disabled. Under the *social insurance* titles, the act provides for a federally administered program of old-age and survivors' insurance and, through the imposition of a pay-roll tax on employers of eight or more persons, has induced the states to enact unemployment compensation legislation. Under the *children's services* titles, lump sum grants are made to states for the extension of aid for maternal and child health, services to crippled children, and child welfare services in rural areas and areas of special need.

The act, moreover, is a substantive law establishing a permanent agency of government with clearly defined functions. At the present time the Social Security Administration is a branch of the Federal Security Agency, the other branches being the Office of Education, the Office of Special Services, and the Public Health Service. The Social Security Administration is charged with carrying out the federal responsibilities under the act except with respect to unemployment compensation. The Bureau of Employment Security, which supervises state unemployment insurance programs, has been transferred to the Department of Labor. The Bureau of Public Assistance of the Social Security Administration is the agency responsible for approving state public assistance plans, for studying their operations, for providing leadership, and for making grants-in-aid.

On April 11, 1953, under Public Law 13, the Federal Security Agency became the Department of Health, Education and Welfare. Under Section 4 of Reorganization Plan No. 1 of 1953, there shall be in the department a Commissioner of Social Security who shall be appointed by the President by and with the advice and consent of the Senate.

SELECTED REFERENCES

Abbott, Edith, *Public Assistance,* Chicago: University of Chicago, 1940, esp. Introductions to Parts Four and Five.
Breckinridge, S. P., *Public Welfare Administration in the United States,* Select Documents, Chicago: University of Chicago, 1938.

Brown, Josephine, *Public Relief, 1929–1939*, New York: Henry Holt, 1940.

"Constitutionality of Pennsylvania's Relief Act," *Social Service Review*, December, 1932.

Dunham, Arthur, "Pennsylvania and Unemployment Relief," *Social Service Review*, June, 1934.

Hoover, Herbert, *The Memoirs of Herbert Hoover—The Great Depression 1929–1941*, New York: Macmillan, 1952.

Miles, Arthur P., *An Introduction to Public Welfare*, Boston: D. C. Heath, 1949, esp. chaps. 11 and 12.

Mitchell, Broadus, *The Depression Decade*, New York: Rinehart, 1947.

Schneider, David, and Deutsch, Albert, *History of Public Welfare in New York*, 2 vols., Chicago: University of Chicago, 1938.

Security Work and Relief Policies, National Resources Planning Board, Washington: Government Printing Office, Washington, 1943.

CHAPTER 4

The Legislative Framework of Public Assistance

The aid, care and support of the needy are public concerns and shall be provided by that state and such of its subdivisions in such a manner and by such means as the legislature may from time to time determine.

—Article XVII, *Constitution of the State of New York*

It is hereby declared to be the legislative intent that the purpose of this act is to promote the welfare and happiness of all the people of the Commonwealth by providing public assistance to all of its needy and distressed; that assistance shall be administered promptly and humanely with due regard for the preservation of family life and without discrimination on account of race, religion, or political affiliation; and that assistance shall be administered in such a way and manner as to encourage self-respect, self-dependency, and the desire to be a good citizen and useful to society.

—Public Assistance Law, Commonwealth of Pennsylvania, Legislative Intent

INTRODUCTION

Public assistance comprises five separate programs or categories: Old-age assistance, aid to dependent children, aid to the blind, aid to the permanently and totally disabled, and general assistance. The first four categories are administered by the several states with the help of substantial financial aid from the federal government, and in accordance with rules and regulations of the Federal Social Security Administration. The last category, general assistance, is that form of aid available to needy persons ineligible for the other forms of public assistance. Wide as are the variations in standards of service among the first four categories—between the different categories, and within the same category from state to state—the variations in general assistance are still greater. In some states general assistance is on a par with the federally assisted categories, but in other states the term "general assistance" is merely a polite name for poor relief administered with the same spirit and with the same standards as those of half a century ago. General assistance is, in a sense, a residual category because it assists those needy persons for whom no special provision has been made.

The provision of medical care for those who cannot afford to pay for it is closely related to public assistance. Medical diagnosis and treatment are, of course, distinct professional services, but payment for this service and the determination of eligibility for free medical care are usually the responsibility of the public assistance agency. Medical care will be discussed more fully in the next chapter.

Public assistance, like its predecessor poor relief, is a function constitutionally reserved to the states, and it is in the statutes of the several states that we find the governmental mandate as well as the framework of the programs that have been authorized. It is necessary to emphasize this fact because the influence of the federal government, through the public assistance titles of the Social Security Act, is enormous. It has made possible a vast expansion of the categorical programs; it has exercised leadership in improving the quality of the service; and it has set the broad pattern of public assistance administration throughout the nation.

The federal government, however, can impose no legal obligation upon the states; in this respect the latter operate under their respective laws. If the latter conform to the requirements of the Social Security Act, it is only because that act offers a powerful financial inducement to such conformity. Several states have only recently become eligible for federal reimbursement on their programs of aid to the blind, not because these states have modified their laws so as to conform to the federal act but because the federal act has been changed to make such reimbursement possible.

The public assistance provisions of the Social Security Act did not emerge fully developed from the mind of Congress, nor from the Committee on Economic Security or its technical advisers; rather, they represent a pooling of the best thinking on this subject by specialists in many fields: social work, economics, public administration, etc. Planning was based upon the experience of various states with earlier forms of preferential assistance, and they have been modified from time to time to meet changing conditions and to improve their effectiveness. While differences of opinion are still to be found among state and federal officials regarding the various features of the act and the interpretation thereof, there is substantial agreement regarding the basic character of public assistance—its structure, philosophy, and future development.

We have noted that the objective of the public assistance titles of the Social Security Act is to enable the wider financial resources of the federal government to be applied to the extension and strengthening of categorical assistance programs in the states. This aid is predicated on the fulfillment of certain conditions by the states, and the acceptance of these conditions is reflected in state compliance legislation.

Prior to the passage of the Social Security Act the pattern of public assistance administration had been initiated by those wealthy and progressive states that had established sound programs of preferential assistance. The federal act has introduced some significant new concepts, but perhaps its greatest contribution has been its requirement that sound policy and practice, already in effect in some parts of the country, be extended and embodied in the substantive legislation of all states—if they are to receive federal funds.

The variations in structure, policy, and standards of administration in the several jurisdictions make it impossible to study the administration of public assistance in the light of the policies and procedures of any given operating agency. Fortunately, in spite of these variations, there are more likenesses than differences among the various assistance agencies, at least with respect to essential elements. A consideration of the major requirements of the Social Security Act and the implications thereof will reveal to us the basic pattern of public assistance administration.

SPECIFIC ELIGIBILITY REQUIREMENTS

Need

Need is the essential component in public assistance. If the beneficiaries of a program of financial aid are not required to establish their need, the program, whatever else it might be, is not public assistance. The Social Security Act does not define need but merely states that "the State agency shall, in determining need, take into consideration any other income and resources"[1] of individuals claiming assistance. Quite aside from the fact that Congress would probably have been unwilling to enact legislation empowering a federal agency to set specific standards with respect to need, there are other sound reasons why this responsibility should be left to the states. Inasmuch as the federal government is paying only part of the cost of such assistance (although an increasingly significant part), it would be administratively, as well as politically, unwise to seek to commit the states, with their varying financial resources, to make assistance payments in accordance with a federally defined scale—even though due allowance were made for regional variations in living costs. The underlying philosophy of the act, moreover—the philosophy which has given it such a wide degree of acceptance—is predicated on the idea that its purpose is to enable the states to develop their own programs subject only to minimum controls from Washington. The Social Security Administration insists, however, upon a realistic and equitable interpretation of the need requirement. Without this insistence, it is not at all unlikely that some states, with a high incidence of aged persons and powerful organizations to lobby for their demands, might be high-pressured into so liberalizing old-age assistance programs that they

---

[1] A 1950 amendment to the Social Security Act requires, however, that after July 1, 1952, the first $50 of monthly income must be disregarded in determining need for blind persons.

would lose their essential character and become more like pension programs. This would mean that more state funds would have to be diverted to such pension schemes to the detriment of the other assistance programs. The Social Security Administration, moreover, is becoming increasingly concerned about the variations in standards of assistance and in methods of determining need that prevail in different sections of the same state. It is placing pressure on such states to adopt uniform standards and methods so that persons in substantially similar circumstances will receive equal treatment regardless of the section of the state in which they reside.[2]

Citizenship

There is no federal requirement regarding citizenship. The act, however, does stipulate that no state plan can be approved which has "any citizenship requirement which excludes any citizen of the United States." This clause was introduced to prevent states from denying categorical assistance to citizens who are not native born, or whose citizenship is of recent origin. Many states have now eliminated all citizenship requirements, but as of January, 1953, fourteen states still retain them for OAA, five for AB, one for ADC, and two for AD. Five additional states require a lengthy period of residence in the United States for persons who are not citizens.[3]

Citizenship requirements are a holdover from the pre-Social Security Act forms of preferential assistance. Eligibility for such assistance had been predicated on "worthiness," and a person who had made his home in this country but had not thought enough of it to become a citizen was considered "unworthy" of receiving this aid from the community. Now, however, we are beginning to recognize that regardless of the reasons why a person is or is not a citizen, if he is in need and adequate provision is not made for his care, it is a detriment to the community of which he

---

[2] See Eveline M. Burns, *The American Social Security System* (Boston: Houghton Mifflin, 1949), chap. 12, for further discussion of this point.

[3] *Characteristics of State Public Assistance Plans,* Public Assistance Report No. 21 (Washington: Federal Security Agency, 1953). Item 2 on states' schedule.

is a member. Substantial federal participation in categorical assistance, moreover, has enabled states to become more generous in their attitude toward non-citizenship. It is less expensive than to care for a needy person through general assistance.

Residence

A person's place of residence is where he is actually residing and what he considers his permanent home. His place of settlement, however, is that civil subdivision responsible for the cost of his care should he become a public charge. The complexity of settlement law is such that it is quite possible for a person to reside in one community and have settlement in another. While it would be difficult to defend the concept of settlement under any circumstances, the excessive localism in the administration and financing of poor relief offered some rationale for its use. As state and federal governments, with their wider geographic areas and taxing powers, have entered the public assistance scene, even that rationale loses whatever reasonableness it once had.

As in the case of citizenship, the Social Security Act has no residence or settlement requirements. It does, however, set limits to the kind of residence requirement that can be in effect. In OAA there can be no residence requirement which excludes any resident of the state who has resided therein five out of nine years immediately preceding the application for assistance, and has resided therein continuously for one year immediately preceding the application. For aid to the blind and aid to the totally and permanently disabled, there can be no residence requirement which excludes anyone who has resided in the state for more than one continuous year before filing the application for aid. In ADC there can be no residence requirement which excludes any child who has resided in the state for one year immediately preceding the application for such aid, or who was born within the state within one year immediately preceding the application, or whose mother resided in the state for one year immediately preceding the birth. The federal maximum residence requirement is higher in OAA than in the other categories, but about one-half the states have adopted more liberal provisions—usually one year of continuous residence immediately preceding the application.

Settlement, therefore, remains a factor only in general assistance and in care for the medically indigent. Even here, however, this requirement is beginning to be discarded. In 1946 Rhode Island led the way by eliminating settlement entirely. She was followed by New York, and there are now a number of states that have either abolished settlement or entered into reciprocal agreements with other states to provide care for persons who lack settlement.

Categorical Eligibility Requirements

Each category (with the exception of the "catchall" general assistance category) has certain distinguishing eligibility requirements which mark it off from the other categories.

Age is, of course, the distinguishing characteristic in old-age assistance. No state plan for OAA can be approved if it denies assistance to an otherwise eligible person sixty-five years of age. States may choose to grant OAA to persons of a lower age, but in such cases there can be no federal reimbursement until age sixty-five is reached.

Although blindness is the basic requirement in aid to the blind, the states are allowed to develop their own criteria as to the degree of blindness constituting eligibility for this category. The states may also set an age limit; thus nineteen states have a lower age limit, ranging from sixteen to twenty-one, presumably based on the fact that children under these ages are usually resident pupils in state schools for the visually handicapped. One state has a maximum age limit of sixty-five, older persons presumably being transferred to OAA.

In ADC the requirements are somewhat more complicated. Section 406 of the Social Security Act reads as follows:

(a) The term "dependent child" means a needy child under the age of sixteen, or under the age of eighteen if found by the State agency to be regularly attending school, who has been deprived of parental support or care by reason of the death, continued absence from the home or physical or mental incapacity of a parent, and who is living with his father, mother, grandfather, grandmother, brother, sister, stepfather, stepmother, stepbrother, stepsister, uncle or aunt in a place of residence maintained by one or more of such relatives as his or their own home.

The Bureau of Public Assistance of the Social Security Administration is charged with interpreting these provisions. In recent years it has placed an increasingly liberal construction on such terms as "continued absence from the home" and "physical or mental incapacity," and it has recommended a more flexible approach to the problem of nonsupport in desertion cases. To protect the child during periods of adjustment, it has even approved ADC grants which are continued for temporary periods after changing circumstances make the family technically ineligible, e.g., when the father, after a period of desertion, returns home but has not had a chance to secure work to support his family.[4] These liberal interpretations have made it possible for states to add to the ADC rolls many children who, in fact, are dependent but who, up to this point, could not fulfill the eligibility requirements. A compelling reason for the liberalization has been the fact that in many states general assistance, the only other resource for needy children, has extremely low standards and many genuinely needy children were consequently deprived of assistance.[5]

The new category of aid to the permanently and totally disabled (usually called "aid to the disabled" because of the unfortunate psychological connotations of the full title) also involves complex eligibility requirements. It was not the intent of Congress to restrict this category to the completely helpless; consequently the Bureau of Public Assistance has developed the following interpretation:

"Permanently and totally disabled" means that the individual has some physical or mental impairment, disease, or loss that substantially

[4] A 1950 amendment requires that appropriate law enforcement agencies be notified in cases where ADC is granted in behalf of children abandoned or deserted by one or both parents.

[5] In states with comprehensive public assistance programs including general assistance with adequate standards this policy is meaningless since recipients receive substantially the same treatment regardless of the category through which they are helped.

precludes him from engaging in useful occupations within his competence, such as holding a job or homemaking. It has been suggested that the disability factor be considered as consisting of two parts—one dependent on medical findings and one on a social study of the individual and his ability to carry out his responsibilities, as for example, wage earner or home maker.[6]

The words "permanent" and "totally" have a qualified construction. They do not mean that the persons receiving this form of assistance can never engage in gainful work. Vocational rehabilitation is an important service within this program. The determination of eligibility for this category, since it must be based on competent medical, psychiatric, and social findings, requires far greater skill on the part of the assistance agency's personnel than determination of eligibility for the other categories.

Tests of Character or "Fitness"

Although the federal act requires no tests of character as a condition of eligibility, neither does it specifically prohibit them. Since tests of this nature have had a long history, and since they are still required in some states, either by law or by policy, they cannot be ignored.

Although during the period when the preferential programs were first being instituted society was beginning to question its assumption that the poor were usually poor through their own fault, nevertheless it did not want this assistance, so much more generous than poor relief, to be received by anyone who could not prove by his past life that he was "deserving" of it. Accordingly, persons who had been tramps or beggars, or who had criminal records, or who had failed to support their families were excluded. Widows of dubious reputation were denied "mothers' aid," as were unmarried mothers who *ipso facto* were not sufficiently respectable. The unfortunate part of these tests is that mistakes and weaknesses of the past can be resurrected to serve as a barrier to the receipt of a modest subsistence, even though what a person has done or has failed to do in the past might have

[6] Phyllis Hill, "Aid to the Permanently and Totally Disabled," *Social Security Bulletin*, December, 1950, pp. 12–13.

been the result of insufficient income or inadequate opportunity.

In this connection certain questions arise. What is "fitness," and who shall sit in judgment upon a person's character? What are the social objectives of public assistance, and what happens to needy people who are denied categorical assistance because they are "unfit"? Should we demand of recipients a standard of behavior higher than that we demand of the general community?

If people are unable to handle money, if their behavior results in the neglect of children or contributes to their delinquency, or if their behavior constitutes a threat to the health and morals of the community or to their own welfare, is the denial of categorical assistance a solution? It seems inconsistent with the objectives of public assistance, which is to relieve the distress caused by lack of income, to deny aid on this score, unless a person is so "unfit" as to be incapable of living in the community. And if such is the case, the further question arises as to whether the community should assume responsibility for seeing that such persons receive some form of protective or custodial care. What social good can come from denying categorical assistance to aged persons or to mothers with dependent children on the grounds that they are "unfit," if they are thereby required to shift for themselves or to rely on sporadic and inadequate general assistance? Policies of this kind can be based only on the mistaken belief that we can secure conformity in behavior by regulating the amount of money we will provide for needy people. Denial of adequate assistance is likely to aggravate the behavior we deplore, while in the case of denial of ADC the assistance agency exposes itself to the charge of grossly neglecting the interests of dependent children.

Fortunately, tests of fitness are declining, partly because of deeper insight into behavior, partly because it is less costly to maintain needy people on programs in which there is substantial federal reimbursement than to maintain them on general assistance.

In decrying tests of fitness there is no intent to disregard or minimize the very real problem which arises when the behavior of needy people runs counter to the norms of the community.

This is one of the most difficult and delicate problems in public assistance administration.[7] The question we raise here is whether the public assistance agency, in addition to its major function, should be saddled with the responsibility for regulating behavior. To be sure, it must be concerned with problems of management and adjustment faced by recipients, but should it use its authority to withdraw aid if recipients misuse public funds, or outside income makes assistance no longer necessary? Receipt of assistance does not deprive the needy of membership in the community; they are not the sole responsibility of the assistance agency; consequently, when their behavior contravenes the morals, customs, or laws of the community, other agencies should be concerned—the church, the school, the police, the courts, family and children's welfare agencies—who are (or should be) better equipped to deal with such problems.

GENERAL ADMINISTRATIVE REQUIREMENTS

A state plan for categorical assistance must either provide for the establishment or designation of a single state agency to administer the plan or provide for the establishment or designation of a single state agency to supervise the administration of the plan.

To secure federal reimbursement for public assistance, the states must develop plans of administration for each assistance category, which are embodied in legislation and which conform to the requirements of the Social Security Act. The act allows considerable leeway to the states and, as we shall see, there are wide variations in administrative structure and in the degree to which responsibility for providing direct service to individuals is retained by the state government or is delegated to civil subdivisions. The state, however, is responsible for the execution of each categorical program even though it may be administered locally. The Social Security Act requires that there be a single state agency which, if it does not administer the program, has sufficient authority to supervise local administration. There may be a separate state agency for each category, or there may be

[7] See Burns, *op. cit.*, chap. 11, for further discussion of this topic.

state agencies that administer or supervise one or more of the categories. The Social Security Administration will deal only with these state agencies and not with local units (which in locally administered programs may run into the hundreds) in connection with problems concerning the operation of the programs, submission of reports, and requests for reimbursement, etc.

A state plan must provide that it shall be in effect in all political subdivisions of the state and, if administered by them, be mandatory upon them.

Prior to the Social Security Act, state programs of categorical assistance were often based on permissive legislation. In those states which assumed no financial responsibility for such programs the statutes by which they were authorized did not require that they be established in all political subdivisions of the state. They merely permitted those counties and cities that were able and willing to do so to set up programs of assistance outside the poor law. Thus, in New York, where the "mothers' pension" program was locally financed, ten counties never appropriated any funds for this purpose; old-age assistance, however, which was financed in part by the state, was mandatory on all local units. In Wisconsin, where old-age assistance was locally financed, only eleven out of the seventy-two counties established the program.

Under the terms of the Social Security Act, public funds, derived directly or indirectly from taxes on all the people of the nation, are made available to aid certain classes of needy persons. The framers of the act wished to make sure that no needy person would be denied the benefits of the act simply because certain civil subdivisions of a state were unwilling to participate. If a state wishes to receive any federal reimbursement under a particular public assistance title of the act, it has to guarantee, therefore, that the program will be in effect in all parts of the state.

A state plan must provide for financial participation by the state.

The traditional method of financing poor relief was through local taxation—never a very satisfactory method, and particularly unsatisfactory under present economic and social conditions. In the first place, the smaller the taxing unit, the greater is the likelihood of disparity between its relief needs and its fiscal resources. This makes for wide variations among the cities, counties, and townships in a given state in their capacity to provide adequate assistance. Secondly, local governmental units are restricted in the kinds of taxes they can impose. To a great extent they must rely upon the real-property tax. Changes in our economy have made this tax increasingly inequitable as a method of raising revenue. In a simple agricultural society where most wealth was invested in land this tax was adequate, but today real property holders are no longer necessarily the element in the community best able to bear this burden. Although landlords may be able to shift at least part of the burden to their tenants, farmers and other householders must absorb these charges, which may have little relation to the income from their property. Income rather than property is a better index of ability to pay taxes. The state, with its wider taxing area, and especially its power to levy taxes on personal incomes, on profits, on estates, etc., is in a much better position to tap the real sources of wealth.[8]

The federal government cannot force the states to adopt more equitable forms of local public assistance financing, but, by making grants-in-aid conditional upon some state financial aid, it offers a strong inducement to the states to equalize the burden somewhat. Although the act does not specify the extent to which the state must participate, it is interesting to note that as of January, 1953, thirty-three out of fifty-three states and territories no longer require any local financial participation in OAA; fifteen out of fifty-two require local participation in AB, twenty-four out of fifty-two in ADC, and seventeen out of thirty-nine in AD.[9]

The state plan must provide for granting an opportunity for a fair hearing before the state agency to any individual whose claim is denied or is not acted upon with reasonable promptness.

From the beginning, it has been a major tenet of the Social Security Administration that assistance to needy people under

---

[8] This is not to suggest that every state does so.

[9] *Characteristics of State Public Assistance Plans,* Public Assistance Report No. 21 (Washington: Federal Security Agency, 1953). Item 15 on states' schedule.

the terms of the act is to be granted as a matter of right. Although there are differences of opinion as to just what the word "right" means in this connection, the Social Security Administration can point to the above requirement as an indication of Congressional intent. Although the "fair hearing" is administrative in nature rather than a court process, it is a long step forward in protecting needy people, or those who consider themselves to be needy, from arbitrary or erroneous decisions on the part of the assistance agency. It is important for us to examine this question of the "right" to assistance in some detail.

The need for the device of a "fair hearing" is inseparable from the question of the "right to assistance." A reading of the poor relief history might well prompt us to ask, "What rights, if any, do needy people have?" The reader will recall that the characteristic mode of providing assistance was to oblige the needy person to enter an institution which, from the point of view of greater comforts and freedom of action, differed little from a penal institution. Loss of the right of suffrage frequently attended the receipt of relief, while eligibility for help was hedged about with so many restrictions having little or no bearing upon need that it made a mockery of the principle of public responsibility for the care of the poor. A shocking illustration of callousness and of disregard for the most elementary of human rights is cited by Edith Abbott:

A poor farmer and his wife, both ill, asked for help from the county one winter, following a period of drought. The county responded to this appeal by sending the couple and their two children to the poor farm. In the Spring, the farmer, now recovered, obtained a job but was obliged to leave his family at the poor farm until he could earn enough money to send for them. While he was away, the poormaster bound out his son, aged eight, until the age of eighteen. The unfortunate parents, being deprived of their child, began legal proceedings. The case dragged on and two years later (1881) finally reached the State Supreme Court. The court acknowledged that the parents had had no knowledge or notice and had given no consent to the binding out of the child but that it was not necessary for the superintendent of the poor farm to notify the parents or to secure their consent, such safeguards not being provided by the Kansas poor law.

The statute, said the court, "contemplates independent action by the superintendent of the poor-house whenever any child becomes a county charge and the validity of the court's action in such a case in no manner depends upon the wishes or knowledge of the parents."

In the words of Professor Abbott:

The court granted that it was true that the little boy was only a temporary county charge due to the drought and that proper care had perhaps not been shown by the superintendent of the county poor-house and by the probate court to guard against the binding out of a child who only temporarily needed public assistance; nevertheless the court held that the absence of such care did not render the proceedings void.[10]

Although the administration of the poor law was usually characterized by a profound contempt for the people it was designed to aid, nevertheless, almost from the time when government first assumed this obligation, the question had been debated as to whether the obligation conferred a legal right to assistance. Professor Abbott suggests that American opinion has been influenced by British legal thinking. In England it was maintained that while government had a clear duty to provide poor relief, this duty was owed to the public in general and not to the needy person; for the latter it was merely a gratuity. Here is a clear expression of the belief that poor relief is an exercise of the police power—a power necessary to protect the community from the disorders that might ensue if no provision were made for the starving and homeless.

Despite this view, Professor Abbott believes that our early American statutes undoubtedly conveyed a right to assistance and that it is an obligation mandatory upon government. This right, however, remains a theoretical one unless it can be enforced, and here Professor Abbott is obliged to conclude, "in the language of wise lawyers," that the answer to the question of whether there is a right to assistance is "yes—and no."

Among the many cases cited by Professor Abbott, two in

[10] Edith Abbott, "Our Un-American Poor Laws," *Public Assistance* (Chicago: University of Chicago, 1940), Part II, p. 128. Much of the material in this section is drawn from Professor Abbott's monumental study.

particular reflect the negative opinion. The first involves a decision of the New Jersey Supreme Court.[11] Two justices of the peace, who were responsible for poor relief in their township, had given an order to the overseer of the poor to pay a poor man "the sum of one dollar a week." The overseer failed to comply and arrears of eight dollars accumulated. The poor man brought an action in debt against the overseer and the controversy eventually reached the Supreme Court. The court found that the poor man was not entitled to the arrears and that the only way the order could be enforced was by way of criminal action against the overseer for breach of public duty.

In the second case, the Iowa Supreme Court decided that damages could not be collected from the county even though the plaintiff had suffered the loss of both feet through the negligence of the county relief authorities. The facts were these: The plaintiff, while examining timber in anticipation of a contract to cut it, had fallen through the ice on the river and, being unable to find lodging, had spent the night in a straw stack. In the morning, both of his feet being frozen, he appealed to the county for help. The latter provided him with "emergency care" and, in the manner approved for dealing with transients in many communities, "passed him on" to the next county. This process was repeated so that by the time he reached Cerro Gordo County it was necessary to amputate both feet. The court ruled that this unfortunate victim of neglect could not recover damages because neither the county nor its agent, the overseer of the poor, was liable for the negligent performance of its duty.

A poor district is an instrumentality of government and the furnishing of aid to the poor is a governmental function. It is a general rule that where a governmental duty rests on a state or any of its instrumentalities, there is absolute immunity in respect to all acts or agencies and consequently there can be no liability of a district to a pauper for failure to furnish relief no matter how grievous the consequences, or for the negligence of its officers in furnishing relief.[12]

[11] Van Nuis v. McCollister, 3 N.J. law (2 Pennington) 805 (1811), quoted in *ibid.*, p. 20.

[12] Wood v. Boone Co., 153 Iowa, 92 (1911); 133 N.W. 377; 39, quoted in Abbott, *op. cit.*, p. 20.

A sequel to this decision was that when Cerro Gordo County, which had provided decent treatment and medical care, attempted to collect from Boone County for the cost of such care, which the latter county's heartless conduct had occasioned, the court denied the claim.

The courts, however, seem to have taken a much more liberal view on the matter of the right to assistance in cases where third parties have brought action for reimbursement for assistance furnished a presumptively needy person, when the poor relief authorities were unwilling to provide care or were unaware that the person was in need. According to the cases cited by Professor Abbott, the courts have tended to favor the "Good Samaritan" who provided emergency care.

The difficulty of finding consistent judicial guiding principles is illustrated by two relatively recent decisions: In 1936, unemployment relief in Douglas County (Omaha), Nebraska, was drastically curtailed as a result of the liquidation of the FERA, which had been paying a large part of the state's relief bill. An action was brought against the relief authorities for failure to provide funds for this purpose. The state supreme court, though taking cognizance of the dire need, ruled that the county could not be compelled to provide funds since there were certain statutory provisions which prevented it from collecting taxes to provide sufficient funds for this purpose.[13]

Four years earlier, however, the Washington State supreme court had rendered a diametrically opposite verdict. During the early days of the depression the county commissioners of King County (Seattle) had issued warrants for some $200,000 beyond the statutory debt limit in order to have sufficient funds to relieve the acute distress of the unemployed and their families. Certain residents of the county who disapproved of this measure sought to have it set aside by the courts. The supreme court ruled, however, that despite the statutory debt limit "it is the absolute duty of a county to provide for poor persons in need of assistance therein." In view of the "appalling and exigent" situation, the county commissioners were sustained.[14]

[13] Abbott, *op. cit.*, p. 31.
[14] *Ibid.*, p. 33.

We can see from the above record that, statutory provisions to the contrary, a needy person's claim to assistance from his government was at best an uncertain one. It was undoubtedly with this fact in mind that the framers of the Social Security Act introduced the "fair hearing" requirement, as a means whereby a needy person's rights might be safeguarded. This requirement, if it does nothing else, at least assures the presumptively needy person of a legal right to a fair hearing. Furthermore, his position before the courts is greatly strengthened, in that he has a legal right to a court determination as to whether he has been given a hearing, and whether it has, in fact, been a fair one. Thus, although the federal government cannot force a state to grant assistance, it requires the state to justify itself where such assistance is denied. Should a state fail to provide opportunities for fair hearings, or should the hearing decisions reveal a disregard of the rights of needy persons, the state agency condemns itself as having violated state legislation, and it runs the risk of losing all federal aid for the particular program. Important as these points may be, the main objective of the fair hearing requirement is to sustain the right of needy persons by reducing the necessity for court action, and even for fair hearings.

A recent article on this subject expresses the philosophy and purpose of the fair hearing procedure:

The provisions of the Social Security Act for Federal participation in public assistance are based on the concept that the claimant who meets the requirements established in state law has a right to the benefits and has a right to a fair hearing when he is denied these benefits.

Hearings in public assistance are not an appeals process in which the state agency merely reviews the record of the action taken by the local unit and either confirms that action or sends the case back for further consideration. Instead the state agency proceeds as if there had been no previous local action and the case had come to the agency for an original determination.

Fundamentally the administrative hearing is a very simple process. Reduced to basic terms it requires that an opportunity be provided for the claimant to tell his story to those who represent the highest authority in the state agency; to question those who took the action to which he objects; to have an objective review of the facts thus brought out; to get a decision which is the agency's final word, which is applicable to all other similar cases and which the applicant can take to court for review if he is still dissatisfied with the agency action resulting from it.[15]

Thus, the very machinery that is set up to provide for an orderly and equitable review of disputed points should go far in eliminating the need for further action, while the experience gained through such hearings should result in a growing body of precedent and guiding principles helpful to local administrative agencies in dealing with similar situations.

The process, as has already been pointed out, is a simple one; the hearing is presided over by an official sufficiently removed from responsibility for the case to be able to conduct the hearing objectively. The hearing is unlike court action, in which the principals seek to justify their position; rather it is a situation in which a difficult issue is reëxamined with the help of an impartial referee for the purpose of determining what is the appropriate course of action under the law.

The following excerpt from a bulletin of a state welfare agency describes the procedure:

4. Conduct of the hearing

The referee conducts the hearing. Every effort shall be made by the referee to keep the process impartial and informal, yet not disorganized. The applicant shall be permitted to tell his story in his own way. In turn, the agency concerned in the appeal shall be permitted a similar opportunity.

The applicant and the agency shall have an opportunity to examine all documents and records presented at the hearing; the applicant has the option to present his case in person or be represented; each party has the opportunity to bring witnesses to establish all pertinent facts and the circumstances, to advance any arguments without undue interference and to question or refute any testimony or evidence. Technical rules of evidence do not apply but the referee obtains the most credible evidence available for any fact.

Only information directly pertinent to the question under review may properly be introduced from agency records. The hearing will

---

[15] Bernard W. Scholz, "Hearings in Public Assistance," *Social Security Bulletin,* July, 1948, p. 14.

not be closed until the referee is satisfied that all facts have been as-
sembled which will be needed for a decision. If it develops that insufficient data are available at the hearing upon which to make a
decision the referee will either (a) adjourn the hearing and direct the
agency and/or request the client to produce additional data at a re-
convened hearing or (b) close the hearing and direct the agency to
submit specified additional pertinent material by a certain date, inform
the client he may submit additional pertinent material by a certain
date, all of which material is to be made available for examination
and comment by the other party, and is to be taken into consideration in rendering a decision.

During the hearing it may become evident that the issue actually
involved is different from the one on which the hearing was requested. In such instances the referee has discretion to conduct the
hearing on the new issue if it, too, constitutes a legal basis for appeal
and/or to adjourn the hearing in order to enable either the client or
the agency to prepare additional evidence for a hearing on a changed
basis.[16]

Before concluding this discussion, reference should be made to
those well-intentioned people who fight shy of the term "right
to assistance," not because they begrudge aid to the needy, but
because the term suggests that the needy have a vested interest
in the public treasury, which, after all, represents the earnings
of other people in the community. Underlying this attitude are
remnants, at least, of the old belief that people don't like to
work, that they prefer to get something for nothing, that relief is
habit-forming. To suggest that anyone has a "right" to money
that he has not acquired by his own labor, by shrewd or lucky
investments, or by the death of a wealthy relative smacks of
socialism to them. And yet, to say that a needy person has a
"right" to help from his government is no more socialistic than to
say that children of school age have a "right" to a free education.
This, too, was challenged in its day, thus:

One chief cause of poverty is that too much is done for those who
make no proper effort to help themselves and thus improvidence in its
various forms is encouraged. . . .

[16] New York State Department of Social Welfare, "Inquiries, Complaints,
Appeals and Fair Hearings" (mimeographed release), May 5, 1952, p. 12.

Additions are constantly being made to the list of those things which people ought to do for themselves but which they desire others to do for them. One of the latest examples is the demand which so many of the working-classes are now making, that the parents should not be required to pay for their children's education, but that all schools should be free. It will be found that these demands simply show how many there are who will always try to escape from the responsibility of their own acts. The extent to which they are permitted to do this will in no small degree determine the amount of poverty and misery which will exist in a country.[17]

Sometimes the argument for the "right" to assistance is carried too far. Consider the following:

All measures, statutory as well as those of individual discretion, which aim at enforcing a higher standard of behavior for the persons receiving assistance than for the rest of the community are incompatible with the idea that assistance is paid as a right. If it is truly a right the money is the recipient's own without qualification and the only controls to which he should be subject are those which govern the whole community.[18]

While there is a great deal of truth in the above paragraph, the phrase "the money is the recipient's own *without qualification*" is a little strong. Unemployment insurance benefits paid under the Social Security Act are subject to the qualification that the beneficiary be willing to accept suitable work; to be eligible for aid to the disabled, a person must be willing to undergo treatment that will make him employable, so long as that treatment does not involve serious risks. Were general assistance subject to federal reimbursement, we can be sure that the Social Security Act would not require states to eliminate requirements that employable recipients accept suitable work. Should recipients of federally reimbursed assistance misuse their grants, it might be necessary for their own welfare, as well as in the public interest, to withdraw the money payment and substitute assistance by

[17] Karl de Schweinitz, *England's Road to Social Security* (Philadelphia: University of Pennsylvania, 1943), p. 142, quoting Henry Fawcett, *Pauperism: Its Causes and Remedies.*

[18] Robert Ball, "Social Insurance and the Right to Assistance," *Social Service Review*, September, 1947, p. 333.

voucher—even though that would mean loss of federal reimbursement.

The state plan must provide safeguards which restrict the use or disclosure of information concerning applicants and recipients to purposes directly connected with the administration of assistance.

This provision was adopted by Congress in 1939. In 1951, however, the express purpose of the provision was obviated by the following section of the "Revenue Act of 1951":

Sec. 618. Prohibition Upon Denial of Social Security Funds.

No State or any agency or political subdivision thereof shall be deprived of any grant-in-aid or other payment to which it otherwise is or has become entitled pursuant to title I, IV, X, or XIV of the Social Security Act, as amended, by reason of the enactment or enforcement by such State of any legislation prescribing any conditions under which public access may be had to records of the disbursement of any such funds or payments within such State, if such legislation prohibits the use of any lists or names obtained through such access to such records for commercial or political purposes.

What this means in simple language is that, in spite of the foregoing provision of the Social Security Act concerning confidentiality of records, should states adopt legislation permitting public access to such records, federal reimbursement cannot be withheld, provided that the legislation prohibits the use of information obtained from such records for business or political purposes. What lies behind this reversal of policy concerning confidentiality?

Clauses regarding the confidentiality of records were added to the various public assistance titles of the Social Security Act following the 1938 elections, when it was brought to light that there had been widespread political misuse of the names of recipients of old-age assistance. For example, in Ohio (a notable offender), form letters were sent to aged recipients, actively soliciting votes for the governor in the primary campaign. These letters extolled the governor and intimated that if he were not reëlected old-age assistance grants would be cut off or reduced. Arrangements had been worked out whereby the names and addresses of recipients getting increases or first grants were routed to the governor's office. State public assistance employees electioneered actively among aged recipients.

It became apparent that unless controls were introduced immediately there would be even more blatant attempts to play upon the hopes and fears of recipients in the federally reimbursed categories for the attainment of political ends—hence the amendments to the Social Security Act mentioned above.

But even apart from the necessity for preventing political manipulation, there are strong reasons why public assistance records should be confidential: to spare recipients and their relatives from humiliation and commercial exploitation. Through the centuries, it had been a matter of policy to expose recipients of poor relief to the pitiless glare of publicity. They were a group set apart—herded into public institutions, auctioned off at public meetings, forced to wear badges proclaiming their dependent status. Decisions regarding their welfare were matters for public debate at town meetings. Even within recent years it was not uncommon to publish names and addresses of recipients in public reports and in newspapers. Publicity was one of the penalties for receiving help—imposed because of the conviction that the poor could not be trusted, and that the meager funds allotted for their care could best be conserved if the names of those who were assisted were a matter of common knowledge.

The emerging art of social investigation, and more enlightened thinking concerning the social objectives of public assistance led many public welfare agencies to protect their records from unnecessary publicity. Prior to the amendments to the Social Security Act, however, these safeguards were usually a matter of policy rather than law.

Following the end of World War II, however, there began a concerted attempt to vitiate the intent of the "confidentiality" clauses in the Social Security Act. It would be difficult to state the precise reasons for this effort. In part, it is probably due to concern over the mounting cost of public assistance (actually caused by the increase in population and the decrease in the value of the dollar, rather than by an increase in the volume of assistance), in part by exasperation at the inefficiency of assistance administration revealed by numerous public investigations, and in part to the mistaken belief that the "problem" cases revealed by public investigations indicate that a substantial part of the assistance load consists of persons who, if they are in need, are needy because of their delinquencies.

During its last session a number of states memorialized Congress to permit public access to assistance records. Indiana went farther than this and amended its public welfare law, over the governor's veto, to make this possible. Oscar Ewing, the Federal Security Agency Administrator, acted promptly, declaring Indiana's legislation out of conformity with the Social Security Act and suspending all payments to that state. Indiana appealed to the courts, but before any decision could be reached Congress succumbed to pressure from certain states and modified the law accordingly.

Public access to assistance records can be justified only on the basis of two related premises: (1) that large numbers of ineligible people are receiving assistance *and* (2) that the *only* way to correct this abuse is to allow public pressure to shame ineligible recipients into withdrawing from the assistance rolls, and to encourage the public to report information about ineligible recipients which would lead to the closing of their cases.

Even if the first premise were true, the second is not. Obviously, the logical way to correct whatever abuses there are is to improve the quality of administration. But this requires employment of more and better-trained staff and, consequently, increased outlays for administration. It is, of course, less expensive in the short run to expose recipients to the humiliation of publicity than to pay for governmental efficiency. Many states have found, however, that publicizing assistance disbursements does not achieve the purpose for which it was intended. Thus, one state reports: "Most of our counties have chosen not to publish the names of recipients since they feel that such publication does not have a deterrent effect on applications for assistance. If it has any effect at all it probably deters the most deserving from making application. It certainly doesn't deter the applicant who is usually the subject of public criticism."[19] Another state reports: "Our experience would indicate that the most careful readers of published rolls are the recipients themselves. After every publication a heavy demand is made on administration time to explain to individual recipients why other grants exceed their own and why their grants should not be increased to the maximum shown on the published schedule."

Fortunately, Section 618 of the 1951 Revenue Act is permissive rather than mandatory. Its wording, however, admits many loopholes. Although access to records for commercial or political purposes is prohibited, this section includes no penalty for violations. If there should be widespread access to such records it would be almost impossible to prevent abuse. One county welfare board in Indiana has already reported that enterprising individuals posing as "government" physicians and fire inspectors have been visiting old-age assistance recipients and securing small payments from them on one pretext or another.

The Social Security Commissioner has ruled that the confidentiality provisions of the Social Security Act remain in full force and effect, except as states choose to take advantage of the specific provisions of Section 618. These provisions have been interpreted strictly. Thus, the states may give "access" only to those who seek out this information. They may not publish such data or give them general distribution. Penalties and machinery for prosecution, moreover, must be provided for those who misuse this information.

According to a survey by the Associated Press after the 1953 legislative season, twenty-one states had opened the welfare rolls to public inspection: Indiana, Illinois, Kansas, Tennessee, Alabama, Utah, South Carolina, South Dakota, Oregon, Iowa, North Carolina, Arkansas, Florida, Oklahoma, Wisconsin, Montana, Georgia, Mississippi, Virginia, Louisiana, and Michigan. Two other states, New York and Washington, authorized limited public access to the relief rolls.[20]

[19] Indiana State Department of Public Welfare, "Concerning Senate Bill 86 Introduced by Bontrager and Malone and Passed by the Senate on February 13, 1951" (mimeographed statement).

[20] Published in the New York *Times*, July 20, 1953, p. 15.

Sometimes the supporters of confidentiality of records are criticized because they wish to throw a "veil of secrecy" around those who are being supported by the taxpayer. Actually, there is a wide distinction between confidentiality and secrecy. Although a few persons would extend the concept of confidentiality to extremes, most social workers and welfare officials merely advocate that access to assistance rolls and records be restricted to individuals and agencies directly concerned with the administration of assistance and care. Medical records of patients treated at public expense are not open to the public, nor are the records of children appearing in juvenile court; neither are the social insurance records or individual income tax returns.

To secure assistance, needy people usually must reveal intimate details of their life—past successes and failures, marital discord, illness, past indiscretions, and the like. Usually case records contain information on economic and social circumstances or persons other than the applicant or recipient—for example, relatives and friends who may have helped in the past. Painful as it is to reveal this information to the assistance worker, it becomes much more so when what has been revealed is likely to become public knowledge. One of the most constructive elements in the relationship between the public assistance worker and the people he is helping is lost.

The Social Welfare Law of the State of New York contains an excellent statement of the nature and intent of confidentiality:

Section 136. Protection of public welfare records.

1. The names or addresses of persons receiving public assistance and care shall not be included in any published report or printed in any newspaper or reported at any public meeting except meetings of the legislative body.

2. All communications and information relating to a person receiving public assistance or care obtained by any public welfare official, service officer, or employee in the course of his work shall be considered confidential and shall be disclosed only to the board or its authorized representative, a legislative body, or, by authority of a county or city public welfare official, to a person or agency considered entitled to such information.

3. Nothing in this section shall be construed to prevent registra-

tion in a central index or social service exchange for the purpose of preventing duplication and of coordinating the work of public and private agencies.

Assistance shall be provided in the form of money payments to, or medical care in behalf of, needy individuals.

This topic will be discussed in Chapter 7.

The plan must provide such methods of administration (including methods relating to the establishment and maintenance of personnel standards on a merit basis) as are found by the Social Security Administration to be necessary for the proper and efficient operation of the plan; and the state agency will make reports, in such form and containing such information, as the Administration may from time to time find necessary to assure their correctness.

See Chapter 12 for discussion of this topic.

The plan must provide that all individuals wishing to make application for public assistance shall have an opportunity to do so, and that assistance shall be furnished with reasonable promptness to all eligible individuals.[21]

SELECTED REFERENCES

Allen, Helen, "Application of the Fair Hearing Process," *Public Welfare*, April, 1949.

Annual Reports, Federal Security Agency, Social Security Administration.

Berman, Jules H., and Blaetus, George J., "State Public Assistance Legislation, 1951," *Social Security Bulletin*, December, 1951.

Bigge, George E., "Federal Grants-in-Aid: A Bulwark of State Government," *Social Security Bulletin*, November, 1950.

Bureau of Public Assistance, Circular No. 17, *Money Payments to Recipients of Old-Age Assistance, Aid to Dependent Children and Aid to the Blind*, Washington: Federal Security Agency, 1944.

Bureau of Public Assistance Report No. 18, *Characteristics of State Public Assistance Plans Under the Social Security Act*, Washington: Federal Security Agency, 1953.

Burns, Eveline M., *The American Social Security System*, Boston: Houghton Mifflin, 1949, chaps. 11 and 12.

[21] Added in the 1950 amendments.

Carlson, Victor J., and Perry, Ware L., "Prompt Payment of Assistance," *Social Security Bulletin*, October, 1951.

Cohen, Wilber J., "Social Security Act Amendments of 1952," *Social Security Bulletin*, September, 1952.

Cohen, Wilber J., and Myers, Robert J., "Social Security Act Amendments of 1950: A Summary and Legislative History," *Social Security Bulletin*, October, 1950.

Compilation of the Social Security Laws, Washington: Government Printing Office, 1951.

"Confidentiality of Assistance Records," *Social Work Journal*, April, 1952.

Falk, Myron, "Social Action on Settlement Laws," *Social Service Review*, September, 1944.

Goldman, Franz, *Public Medical Care*, New York: Columbia University, 1945.

Hill, Phyllis, "Aid to the Permanently and Totally Disabled," *Social Security Bulletin*, December, 1950.

Hoey, Jane, "Money Payments in Public Assistance," *Social Security Bulletin*, September, 1944.

Howard, Donald S., "Next Steps in Public Assistance," *Public Welfare*, June, 1949.

Howard, Donald S., and Gentile, Felix M., *General Assistance* (pamphlet), New York: American Association of Social Workers, 1949.

Lansdale, Robert T., "The Growing Complexity of Administering Public Assistance," *Public Welfare*, January, 1953.

Lansdale, Robert T., and Hipple, Byron, "Integration of Social Welfare Services—State Organization," *Social Service Review*, March, 1946.

Leet, Glenn, "Rhode Island Abolishes Settlement," *Social Service Review*, September, 1944.

Linford, Alton A., "Public Assistance Categories—Yes or No?" *Social Service Review*, June, 1948.

Perkins, Ellen J., "Old Age Assistance and Aid to Dependent Children," *Social Security Bulletin*, November, 1951.

Rickert, Marion, "Medical Care Under County Welfare Units," *Public Welfare*, May, 1948.

Scholz, Bernard W., "Hearings in Public Assistance," *Social Security Bulletin*, July, 1947.

Smith, A. Delafield, "Community Prerogative and the Rights and Freedom of the Individual," *Social Security Bulletin*, August, 1948.

"Tax Supported Medical Care for the Needy," *Public Welfare*, October, 1952.

U.S. Congress, *Issues in Social Security*, A Report to the Committee on Ways and Means of the House of Representatives, Washington: Government Printing Office, 1946, Part II.

U.S. Senate, *Public Assistance*, A Report to the Senate Committee on Finance, Washington: Government Printing Office, 1948.

CHAPTER 5

The Legislative Framework of Public Assistance

(CONTINUED)

The independence and unplanned, unregimented freedom of action of its rich and powerful members is not the test of a free society. The test of a free society will be found in the scope of right and privilege possessed by its weakest elements—those who are under the greatest pressure to surrender their independence.

> —A. DELAFIELD SMITH, Assistant General Counsel, Federal Security Agency

THE FINANCING OF PUBLIC ASSISTANCE

With respect to public assistance, the Social Security Act is a device whereby the federal government, through its wider taxing powers and financial resources, can redistribute income among the states for the purpose of relieving want. The public assistance titles of the act specify the conditions under which this aid can be received and establish the formulas by which the amount of such aid can be calculated. Since the passage of the act the formulas have been modified from time to time but the original principle has been retained—the principle of the uniform matching grant-in-aid; that is, with respect to each category, the federal government pays a specified proportion of the cost of assistance and administration. The accompanying schedule shows the changes that have taken place in the reimbursement formulas.

Changes in the Rate of Federal Reimbursement for Public Assistance

Date	OAA, AB (and AD after 1950)	ADC
1935	½ of individual grant up to maximum of $30 per month.	⅓ of individual grant up to maximum of $18 per month for first child; ⅓ individual grant up to $12 per month for each additional child.
1939	½ of individual grant up to maximum of $40 per month.	No change.
1946 [a]	⅔ first $15 of average monthly payment, ½ remainder up to average monthly grant of $45.	⅔ of first $9 of average monthly payment for first child, ½ remainder to maximum of $24 per month. For each additional child the same percent up to monthly maximum of $15.
1948	¾ first $20 of average monthly payment, ½ remainder to maximum of $50.	¾ first $15 of average monthly payment for first child, ½ balance to maximum of $24 per month. Same percent for each additional child to maximum of $15.
1950	⅘ first $25 of average monthly payment, ½ next $10 and ⅓ of remainder to maximum of $50.	⅘ first $15 of average monthly payment per recipient, ½ next $6, ⅓ next $6, to maximum of $27 for first child and for relative, and maximum of $18 for each additional child.
1952	⅘ first $25 and ½ of balance within federal ceiling of $55 per month.	⅘ of first $15 per person and ½ of balance within federal ceiling of $30 per month for first child and relative, and ceiling of $21 per month for additional children.

[a] Since 1946 federal reimbursement for administrative costs is equal to one half such costs. Prior thereto it was 5 percent of the individual grant in OAA and AB and one third of the cost of ADC administration but not to exceed specified maximum per child.

An examination of these formulas reveals several significant points. First, from the outset the formulas have been much more generous in the case of old-age assistance and aid to the blind than they have been in aid to dependent children. Even with the recent changes, which include reimbursement for aid to the needy relative caring for dependent children in addition to the children themselves, the formulas are still weighted in favor of the first two categories. The aged constitute the largest group of assistance recipients. The fact that the proportion of the total population sixty-five years of age and over is growing rapidly, that these people have votes and are becoming increasingly articulate in lobbying for their demands, should not be overlooked in casting about for reasons to explain this discrimination. The necessity for heading off such economically fantastic movements as those of Dr. Townsend and the "ham'n'eggers" has also influenced Congress.

Second, the increase in the rate of federal participation in public assistance has not kept pace with the rise in the cost of living. Between 1939 and 1946 the cost-of-living index rose by almost 40 percent whereas the maxima within which federal reimbursement applies increased only 12½ percent for OAA and AB and 33⅓ percent for ADC. As of September, 1950, the consumer price index of the Bureau of Labor Statistics reached an all-time high of 174.8 percent as contrasted to the base figure of 100 percent in 1939. The 1950 amendments to the Social Security Act, however, contained no increase in federal maxima within which there would be participation. Reimbursement of the cost of assistance to the "needy relative" in addition to that of the dependent child is equivalent to an increase in the rate of reimbursement in that category.

The method of determining the amount of the federal contribution, first adopted in 1946 and developed further in 1948, 1950, and 1952, provides for a higher rate of reimbursement in the lower ranges of a given grant of assistance within the maxima for the category. Thus the lower the average monthly grant, the greater will be the federal share of the payment.

During a given year, State "A" grants old-age assistance to 20,000 persons at a cost of $13,200,000. The average monthly grant is thus $55. On an average grant of this amount the Federal government will contribute $35. Thus, State "A" will receive $35x12x20,000 or a total of $8,400,000 from the Federal government. This represents 64% of the cost of assistance granted. Should the average monthly grant exceed $55 monthly, the excess would be borne exclusively by the state, hence the percentage of the total cost of assistance paid by the Federal government would be lower.

During the same year, State "B" grants old-age assistance to 20,000 at a cost of $6,000,000. The average monthly grant is thus $25. On an average grant of this amount, the Federal government will contribute $20. Thus, State "B" will receive $20x12x20,000 or a total of $4,800,000 from the Federal government. This represents 80% of the cost of assistance granted.

This reimbursement formula has naturally not been adopted to encourage low grants; rather, it has been based on the theory that states with low average grants cannot, as a rule, afford to pay higher ones. The formula thus provides additional assistance to the poorer states and enables them to maintain better assistance standards than would be possible were the federal contribution to match that of the states dollar for dollar.

One of the major problems in public assistance arises from the fact that there is usually an inverse relation between a state's financial resources and the degree of need which should be relieved. This is borne out by the fact that states with low per capita income tend to have substantially higher "recipient rates" than states with higher per capita income. Their average monthly grant, however, tends to be lower. The accompanying table contrasts the average monthly grant and total payments to recipients for OAA and ADC, for December, 1951, for the ten states ranking highest and the ten states ranking lowest in per capita income for that year. The table also includes the recipient rates for OAA as of June, 1950, ADC as of December, 1950.[1]

The disparity in recipient rates might have been even greater had it not been for the fact that the poorer states had such low

[1] See Walter M. Perkins, "Trends in Recipient Rates in OAA," *Social Security Bulletin*, October, 1948, and Elizabeth T. Alling, "Trends in Recipient Rates in ADC," *ibid.*, November, 1948.

State	OAA Grant	Total Payments	Rate [a]	ADC Grant [c]	Total Payments [c]	Rate [b]
1. D.C.	$52.87	$ 143,923	45	$26.16	$ 210,020	32
2. Conn.	65.29	1,034,452	84	34.68	478,310	18
3. Nev.	56.39	151,410	224	No federal participation		
4. N.J.	58.25	1,265,375	51	31.95	534,552	9
5. N.Y.	56.94	6,298,941	82	34.10	5,670,438	29
6 Ill.	41.66	4,461,297	134	31.54	2,572,098	24
7. Cal.	69.60	18,998,958	279	37.25	6,038,075	39
8. Wash.	66.09	4,361,348	289	33.72	960,000	28
9. Mich.	50.86	4,507,781	180	30.54	2,404,312	27
10. Ohio	51.49	5,794,906	150	21.74	1,033,229	15
40. La.	51.38	6,189,729	631	17.17	1,362,606	59
41. Okla.	66.13	6,322,759	464	29.84	1,780,166	59
42. Ga.	36.00	3,436,083	407	20.65	969,084	28
43. N.C.	29.40	1,495,034	210	15.30	929,385	30
44. Tenn.	36.74	2,213,310	241	13.63	984,321	46
45. Ky.	35.03	1,968,651	228	17.92	1,281,953	50
46. S.C.	31.45	1,327,924	342	11.88	287,016	22
47. Ala.	26.66	1,866,713	327	10.70	701,900	44
48. Ark.	32.52	1,871,926	361	14.80	705,123	51
49. Miss.	26.24	1,556,475	366	7.07	278,607	35
U.S.	48.82	128,632,515	199	23.47	46,720,062	30

a Rate per 1000 persons 65 years of age and over.
b Rate per 1000 persons under 18 years of age.
c Per recipient.
Data from *Social Security Bulletin*, March, 1953, Tables 12, 14, and 15.

standards of assistance that many needy persons were excluded
who could have been eligible for substantial supplementary assistance had they been living in wealthier states where the standards of assistance were higher. This is reflected in a comparison
of OAA and ADC grants in the ten richest and the ten poorest
states. In September, 1950, when the federal government was
paying up to $30 a month on OAA grants of $50, seven of the ten
wealthiest states were able to take full advantage of the maximum federal contribution, while two more had average monthly
grants close to that maximum. Of the ten poorest states, however,
only one had an average grant close to that maximum. In spite
of federal participation covering three-fourths of the first $20

and one-half of the remainder up to a maximum average grant of $50 a month, all but one of the poorest states had average grants under $30 a month. The disparity in ADC grants was similar.

The average monthly grant, however, is not too reliable an index of the standard of assistance. A low average monthly grant doesn't *necessarily* mean that the standard of assistance is low. The average monthly grant is a mean average based on all individual grants, which may range from full assistance to a small supplementary allowance. The mean average does not show how these grants are distributed. The higher the standard of assistance and the more liberal the policy with regard to evaluating resources (i.e., disregarding income from odd jobs, eliminating or reducing the requirement that relatives contribute to a needy person's support, etc.), the greater will be the number of persons who become eligible for supplementary assistance.[2] When many recipients are receiving small supplementary grants, the average grant will decline.

This fact is of particular significance in the light of the reimbursement formula first introduced in 1946. The reader will recall that, under this formula, the lower the average grant, the greater will be the proportion paid by the federal government. If a state, by judicious upward revisions in its standards of assistance, can raise its recipient rate substantially by granting small amounts of supplementary assistance to a larger number of persons, it may be able to bring about a reduction in the size of the average grant, increase total expenditures for public assistance, and at the same time secure an absolute reduction in the state's share of the cost. Whether or not states will take advantage of this windfall remains to be seen. In the absence of federal standards regarding the determination of need, however, it appears possible for them to do so.[3]

In spite of these factors, it is still reasonable to assume that

[2] In 1949, when Louisiana raised its standard of assistance and eliminated support provisions from the law, the OAA rolls increased by more than 100 percent. See *Social Security Administration Annual Report for 1949*.

[3] See Richard Hohous, "The Present Challenge to America in Social Security," *American Economic Security*, November–December, 1949.

low average grants generally indicate low assistance standards. As Eveline Burns points out:

The fact that by and large the lowest payments occur in the poorer states suggests that other resources are likely to be least where payments are smallest. The average recipient in Georgia or Kentucky receiving a payment of $17.04 and $17.38 respectively in June, 1947, was hardly likely to possess greater personal resources than the average recipient in Colorado or Washington with payments of $65.11 and $53.02. It is also known that the practices and policies of the states lead to the granting of widely different sums to applicants in similar circumstances.[4]

The poorer states are largely agricultural, but farm owners, tenants, and sharecroppers are excluded from old-age and survivors' insurance coverage. Although until the revision of the insurance benefit formula in 1950, the retirement and survivor benefits have been rather small, nevertheless, when added to whatever other resources the beneficiary possesses, they may make application for OAA or ADC unnecessary. Old-age and survivors' insurance benefits tend to reduce the recipient rates in the industrial states, where there is greater wealth.

Except in so far as the present reimbursement formulas result in greater federal participation in the lower ranges of the average grant, thus easing somewhat the burden on those states with lower average grants, the Social Security Act treats all states alike. States with a greater incidence of need must raise more money to meet their share of the cost. Percentage figures do not always tell the full story. Thus:

For example, in the calendar year 1947, when the rate of Federal participation was two-thirds of the first $15 in old-age assistance and aid to the blind and two-thirds of the first $9 in aid to dependent children, the Federal government paid only 52.7 percent of all costs of old-age assistance in the United States, 50.6 percent of the total cost of approved plans for aid to the blind, and 39.4 percent of the total costs for aid to dependent children. In the five states with the lowest per capita income, however, Federal participation in old-age

[4] Eveline M. Burns, *The American Social Security System* (Boston: Houghton Mifflin, 1949), p. 133.

assistance ranged from 62.5 to 64.7 percent of the total costs; in aid to the blind the Federal share ranged from 60.5 to 63.6 percent; and in aid to dependent children from 60.5 to 65.8 percent.[5]

Despite these favorable percentage figures, the poorer states, even with lower standards of assistance, are faced with a greater burden in financing their share of public assistance costs because of the greater incidence of need. Thus, even though state X may have to raise only 35 percent of the cost of OAA, as contrasted to 50 percent raised by state Y, when translated into dollars the amount that must be raised by state X may be greater in absolute terms or in relation to the number of inhabitants of the state.

These factors have led to proposals that the Social Security Act be amended to equalize the financial burden among the states through some form of variable grants-in-aid related to the capacity of each state to meet its obligations. The Social Security Administration has consistently recommended such a change, and it has also been advocated by the National Resources Planning Board, the American Public Welfare Association, the Social Security technical staff of the House Committee on Ways and Means (1946), and in a more guarded fashion by the Advisory Council on Social Security to the Senate Committee on Finance (1948). Proposals to this effect were incorporated in the bill introduced in the House (H.R. 2892) in the first session of the 81st Congress but were not included in the bill as passed in 1950.

As can be imagined, these proposals have not been welcomed by the wealthier states, whose taxpayers would have to supply the funds by which the federal government would provide additional aid to the poorer states, and, indeed, it is a problem which admits of no easy solution. What criteria, for example, should be used in determining whether one state should get more federal aid than another?

In the first place, ability as well as willingness to raise funds must be determined for each state. "Ability" is stressed because some states (not necessarily the poorest) have retained obsolete, inequitable tax systems which are inadequate for raising poten-

---

[5] U.S. Congress, Senate, Committee on Finance, *Public Assistance*, Report by the Advisory Council on Social Security (Washington: Government Printing Office, 1948), p. 10.

tially available revenue. The best test of ability is per capita income but this must be related to need. Thus state A may have a per capita income lower than state B, but its needs may be less because it has a low recipient rate. The recipient rate is directly related to the standard of assistance in use, but since each state has great latitude in establishing such standards, what measure can the Social Security Administration use in determining relative need among the states? Furthermore, the financing of public assistance should not be considered entirely apart from other public services. The volume of public assistance in a given state may be relatively low, but if the state has a high proportion of children of school age in its population, the cost of financing adequate public education may be high. Assistance and education may become competitors for state tax revenue. This situation would also have to be taken into consideration in varying the rate of federal aid for public assistance among the different states.

A number of measures have been developed to determine the financial resources of a state and the effort it is making to tap such resources. The evidence at hand, while it does not show a state-by-state correlation between per capita income and total operating expenses, as well as operating expenses for public assistance, nevertheless indicates that there is a clear tendency for the below average per capita income states to make a greater effort.[6]

Adequate safeguards for the sound administration of variable grants-in-aid have yet to be developed. In the bill introduced by Congressman Doughton in the 81st Congress, federal grants were to be based on the following factors: (1) the population of each state according to the most recent estimates, (2) the financial resources of each state, and (3) the degree of necessity, determined by the administrator, in order to effectuate the purpose of this title, the extent of a particular adult-welfare problem or problems or child-welfare problem or problems, as the case may be in the respective states.

[6] U.S. Congress, House of Representatives, Committee on Ways and Means, *Issues in Social Security,* Report by the Technical Staff on Social Security (Washington: Government Printing Office, 1946), pp. 285–294.

Quite aside from the fact that the basis upon which the "financial resources" of the states are to be determined is not specified, or even suggested, the latitude given the administrator seems questionable. The record of the FERA during the period 1933–1935, when similar powers were given an administrator with respect to allotments to the states for unemployment relief, is not an auspicious precedent.[7] The dilemma, which has yet to be resolved, is how to work out an equitable variable-grant program without conferring wide discretionary powers on an administrative official who may be subject to political pressure, or without writing detailed standards and controls into the federal act.

THE PROBLEM OF GENERAL ASSISTANCE

General assistance is the successor (often in name only) to poor relief. Theoretically, general assistance is available to needy people who cannot qualify for the special forms of assistance. In practice, unfortunately, this is not always the case. In many jurisdictions the standards of general assistance are so low, and eligibility requirements are so restrictive, that many genuinely needy people are deprived of aid.

We have seen that special assistance, limited in form and scope, existed prior to the Social Security Act. That act, because it made federal funds available, produced a vast expansion in categorical programs. Theoretically, federal participation in the cost of special assistance should have eased the burden on the states and enabled them to improve the quality of general assistance, but this, for the most part, has not been the case. The preceding section has perhaps illustrated the point that the federal reimbursement formulas have not been of sufficient help where the need is greatest. The nature of the matching formulas is such, however, that many states with limited financial capacity have tended to divert most of their limited funds into the special categories in order to attract the maximum amount of federal dollars, leaving little or nothing for general assistance.

[7] Edith Abbott, *Public Assistance* (Chicago: University of Chicago, 1940), Part V, sec. 2.

As of December, 1951, of the fifty-three states and territories listed in the statistical supplement of the *Social Security Bulletin* for September, 1952, eleven contributed no state funds for general assistance; in eight states the rate of participation ranged from 0.5 percent to 9.9 percent; and in twenty-seven states the rate of state participation ranged from 50 to 100 percent of the cost of general assistance. The extreme unevenness of administration among the several states makes generalization difficult.

The accompanying table contrasts the average monthly grant for OAA and ADC in December, 1951, for the ten high and ten low states in per capita income mentioned previously, with the average grant in general assistance. The contrast is the more impressive when we realize that in OAA and ADC the grant is per recipient whereas in general assistance it is per case.

State	OAA Grant Recipient	ADC Grant Recipient	G.A. Grant Case	% State Funds G.A.
1. D.C.	$52.87	$26.16	$62.23	100.0
2. Conn.	65.29	34.68	55.22	41.4
3. Nev.	56.39	–	34.29	–
4. N.J.	58.25	31.95	71.57	37.6
5. N.Y.	56.94	34.10	74.62	78.5
6. Ill.	41.66	31.54	62.95	63.8
7. Cal.	69.60	37.25	46.70	–
8. Wash.	66.09	33.72	60.33	69.9
9. Mich.	50.86	30.54	60.69	28.0
10. Ohio	51.49	21.74	43.79	91.8
40. La.	51.38	17.17	38.93	100.0
41. Okla.	66.13	29.84	N.A.	78.3
42. Ga.	36.00	20.65	16.97	0.5
43. N.C.	29.40	15.30	20.48	0.5
44. Tenn.	36.74	13.63	15.71	–
45. Ky.	35.03	17.92	26.37	–
46. S.C.	31.45	11.88	21.21	76.7
47. Ala.	26.66	10.70	23.70	76.9
48. Ark.	32.52	14.80	13.64	100.0
49. Miss.	26.24	7.07	12.54	–

Data on average grants from *Social Security Bulletin,* March, 1953, Tables 12, 14, and 17, pp. 34–36. Data on state participation from *Social Security Bulletin,* September, 1952, Table 40, p. 60.

It will be noted that, with one exception, the average general assistance grants in the ten poorest states were lower than the average grant per recipient of old-age assistance. Even in five of the ten richest states, general assistance grants were lower than the grants for OAA. Aptly has Joanna Colcord called the recipients of general assistance "the residual legatees of disesteem."

A recent survey of general assistance [8] reveals even more graphically the contrast between general assistance and the federally aided categories. Strict residence and settlement requirements serve to deny aid to many needy people; even the archaic practice of "warning out" is still resorted to in some areas. Three-fourths of the forty-seven local units studied in this survey denied aid to employable persons—although in cases of temporary illness or accident some help might be given. The term "employability" was subject to wide variations in interpretation, as were the methods by which such determination was made. In one community the policy was to consider a person employable if he was well enough to make his way to the assistance office. [9] In many localities the standard of assistance was so low that it virtually precluded the granting of supplementary assistance, since any outside income was generally more than would be allowed for full assistance. "Even the capacity to earn as little as $2.50 a month—whether or not this small amount was actually received—rendered applicants ineligible."

General assistance, where locally administered, and without state leadership or financial support, is often reminiscent of the worst days of the poor law. Unenlightened attitudes and practices add to the problems created by low standards and restrictions. None of the safeguards thrown around needy people by the Social Security Act—such as cash assistance, promptness in determining eligibility, fair hearings, and the like—are provided. Attitudes toward the needy are characterized by hostility and impatience, and the most shoddy devices are resorted to in order to deny assistance. In some localities administrators have been

[8] Donald Howard and Felix Gentile, *General Assistance*, pamphlet (New York: American Association of Social Workers, 1949), p. 11.

[9] Donald Howard, "Next Steps in Public Assistance," *Public Welfare*, June–July, 1949, p. 123.

known to invoke the archaic "vagabond laws"; thus, if an employable person who applied for, but did not actually receive, assistance refused to accept an available job to which he was referred, he would be charged with vagrancy, the penalty for which was incarceration for ninety days.[10]

The foregoing remarks illustrate the more extreme examples of inadequate service. Fortunately, some states, generally ranking high in per capita income, have general assistance programs that compare favorably with the other categories. In such cases the administration of general assistance has been integrated with the other programs. It is interesting to note that, of the ten states in which the average monthly grant for general assistance was $50 or more in December, 1949, four were among the ten highest ranked according to per capita income, while the remaining six were among the next eleven states so ranked. In five of these states, the state's share of the cost ranged from 71 to 100 percent; in four states the state's share ranged from 21.4 to 44 percent.

If, as seems to be the case, the problem of general assistance is due largely to difficulties in financing, the question arises: Why has not the federal government provided protection for this category? That it has failed to do so is not because of any lack of advocates; the National Resources Planning Board, the American Public Welfare Association, the American Association of Social Workers, and the Social Security Administration itself have supported such a move.

The objections that are offered against federal aid to the states for general assistance include the following:

1. General opposition, in principle, to the extension of federal responsibility in the area of social welfare.
2. Fear that federal participation in the assistance categories tends to overshadow the insurance programs; the belief that federal sharing of assistance costs was a stopgap remedy necessitated by the fact that the insurance programs, during their early years, could not pay adequate benefits or provide protection for enough people; the belief that, since federally aided assistance grants tend to be larger than insurance benefits, the

[10] Howard and Gentile, op. cit., pp. 7–8.

proper growth of the social insurances has been thwarted and the feeling that, as the social insurances are strengthened, the federal government should withdraw from public assistance— not become further involved.

3. The unpredictability of the general assistance case load. The other categories are relatively stable, but general assistance is subject to wide fluctuations depending upon conditions in the labor market. A prolonged recession would result in a great increase in general assistance, and need under such circumstances might better be met by special measures adapted to the characteristics of the emergency rather than by a relatively permanent program of assistance.

4. Lack of real conviction regarding the need of many people receiving general assistance. The other categories aid those who, as a matter of fact, or as a matter of social policy, are not considered employable. Does not the availability of general assistance weaken economic incentives? Are there not many people now dependent who could and would be self-supporting were it not for this assistance?

The last point needs further elaboration. The fact that experience has demonstrated that there is a close correlation between increases and decreases in the number of employable persons in receipt of assistance and the changes in the labor market has not dissipated the suspicion that there are many persons who prefer assistance to work. Another erroneous belief is that the general assistance rolls contain a large number of employable persons. Although general assistance is the last resort of persons who are in need for a variety of reasons, illness and disablement are a major cause for opening such cases. A study made by the Bureau of Public Assistance revealed that from April through June in 1946 and in 1947 the percentage of cases opened for these reasons was 35 and 40.2 percent, respectively.[11]

Employability, as we shall see in a later chapter, is not always easy to determine. In times of prosperity, high employment, and high prices the general assistance case load, in states where the

[11] "Reasons for Opening General Assistance Cases," *Social Security Bulletin,* October, 1947, p. 35.

program is reasonably adequate, will include a fairly large number of persons who, from a physical point of view, might be considered employable but who have so many other handicaps that their capacity to get steady work and earn enough to support their families is limited. It is this group that causes so many misgivings about general assistance, precisely because it is difficult to differentiate them from the "malingerers" and the "work shy." The nature of their limitations is not always understood or, even when understood, accepted as a valid reason for dependency.

Veteran Assistance

Veteran assistance, which is still found in a number of jurisdictions, is a sort of subcategory of general assistance. It came into being after the Civil War when many communities decided that poor relief was not good enough for veterans, their dependents, or survivors who were in need but who were ineligible for pensions or compensation from the national government. Legislation was passed in many states authorizing local government to appropriate funds for veterans' relief. Various administrative arrangements were worked out for the disbursement of these funds. A common practice was to have veterans' relief administered by a veterans' organization, or by a special committee composed of representatives of various veterans' organizations. Sometimes a special division was created in the public welfare agency, staffed by veterans or by members of their immediate family.

Poor relief being what it was, veterans' relief was a net gain in that it spared some people, at least, from its rigors. Its standard of assistance was higher, and, presumably, the attitude with which it was administered was less condemning, although why this should be, unless the dependency could be related to military service, would be difficult to explain. With the development of sound programs of public assistance, especially general assistance, the role of veteran assistance has become ambiguous. Many communities have retained their veteran assistance agencies, although they provide a service indistinguishable with respect to standards from general assistance. In some communities the separation of veterans from non-veterans has resulted in the creation of two assistance agencies, neither large enough for effective administration.[12] Since veteran assistance is not federally aided, it is not uncommonly restricted to persons who are not eligible for a federally aided category. A recipient of veteran assistance, upon reaching the age of sixty-five, will thus be transferred to old-age assistance, in which event his case will be handled by the same agency, perhaps by the same worker, that would have handled it had he previously been a recipient of general assistance rather than veteran assistance. Perhaps one argument for the retention of separate assistance agencies for veterans is that the staff of such agencies is presumably more familiar with the various monetary benefits and services that might be available for persons formerly in the armed services and for members of their families. Since at the present time the federal Veterans' Administration has many offices conveniently situated throughout the country, and since many states have established programs which enable local communities to appoint "veteran service officers" to advise veterans and the general public on resources available to veterans, this argument no longer carries as much weight. A final point is this: Should public funds for assistance be administered by private organizations? During the depression this question was answered in the negative, yet today there are communities in which public funds are turned over to veterans' organizations for relief purposes, often with little control or supervision by the public authorities.

SHOULD THE CATEGORICAL SYSTEM BE RETAINED?

Administration of public assistance by categories, though less than fifty years old, is well entrenched in American practice, especially because of the categorical provisions of the Social Security Act. From time to time, however, the question is raised as to whether this is a desirable method for aiding the needy.

The chief arguments against the categorical system are as follows: It is undemocratic; it sets up distinctions among the needy

---

[12] Some communities maintain separate public agencies to care for the children of veterans; thus, should a veteran be charged with neglect, the case would be handled by a special "veterans' children's worker."

on the basis of preferential treatment for certain groups; it is susceptible to political pressure, as is witnessed by the way in which the needy aged have captured the greater share of the relief dollar; it is cumbersome to administer, difficult to audit, and wasteful of staff time.

It would be difficult to defend in principle a system of public aid which provides different standards of assistance and service to human beings whose needs are presumably the same. It is doubtful, however, whether anyone could be found who would defend categorical assistance on these grounds. The arguments advanced in favor of it are pragmatic ones. As Gordon Hamilton said some years ago: "The chief value of the categories is to be a sort of temporary breastwork against regressive forces—not a permanent trench." [13]

That this "temporary breastwork" still serves a useful function has been demonstrated as a result of the spate of investigations of public assistance in the years following the close of World War II. Two trends in criticism could be detected in these investigations: one directed against agency policy and practice—which in many instances were thought to be too liberal and wasteful of public funds; the other directed against assistance recipients—especially of general assistance and aid to dependent children. Criticism took the form of questioning the validity of need; whether recipients were making use of available resources, particularly employment; and whether they were leading moral lives and managing their affairs in a proper manner. In many instances, these investigations revealed misapplication of policy, inadequate administrative structure and controls, and inept and misguided activity on the part of a poorly trained, poorly supervised, and confused staff. Unfortunately, there was a tendency to apportion blame equally between staff and recipients. The articles and letters appearing in the public press, and especially the revival of such derogatory terms as "reliefers" and "chiselers," the confusion manifested over good and bad practice, the failure to distinguish between recipients who were found to be ineligible and recipients

[13] "Categorical vs. Generalized Relief," Report on the Symposium on Categorical Assistance, *Social Work Today*, February, 1938, p. 7.

whose eligibility had not been established, suggested that public understanding and acceptance of the objectives of public assistance were more superficial than real. Amidst all this turmoil, however, there was relatively little criticism of old-age assistance, aid to the blind, or their recipients.

Whether or not it is justifiable, the fact is that when the public thinks about public assistance it thinks differently about the different categories. Moreover, the general assistance and ADC case loads present problems in eligibility determination and in socially acceptable behavior that are not found to the same extent in the other categories. Under the circumstances, is it not wiser to keep separate the needy groups whose claim to assistance is unchallenged? So long as Congress sees fit to extend financial support to certain groups and not to others, such discussion is largely academic; even if the distinctions among the federally aided categories were eliminated there would still be two categories—one federally aided, the other financed by state and local funds.

Concerning the arguments advanced against categorical assistance mentioned earlier, it must be admitted that such programs are frequently undemocratic, but it is doubtful if the general public can be induced to think democratically about need by lumping the various groups together. So long as it is easier for the public in general, and legislators in particular, to accept more readily the needs of special groups than the total problem of economic dependency, no favor is done anyone by blurring these distinctions. The substantial accomplishments in the areas of income maintenance in the past twenty years have been achieved through the categorical approach. One would have to be very optimistic to think that the time is now propitious for abandoning the instrument through which so much has been done. While one does not relish the idea that certain groups get preferred treatment because of their political strength, this is not an unmixed evil. After all, the old poor law was fragmented by just this approach. The record shows, moreover, that as one needy group has secured an improved level of aid through public support, other groups lacking such support have eventually benefited.

The time may come when our expanded programs of social insurance will materially reduce the need for assistance. At that time it will probably be advisable to do away with the categories.

MEDICAL CARE

Medical care for the sick poor has been a public responsibility as long as there has been a poor law. At the present time responsibility for providing medical care for persons who cannot afford to pay for it may be shared by many public agencies. State and local health departments provide diagnosis and treatment in cases of contagious and infectious disease; state departments or divisions of mental hygiene provide custodial care and treatment for the mentally ill and the mentally handicapped; large metropolitan districts may have separate departments of hospitals providing free care for the needy. Although public assistance agencies are no longer exclusively responsible for providing medical care, it continues to be an extremely important service, and an increasingly expensive one, especially since the cost of such care is often a local charge.

With respect to medical care, the assistance agency is concerned with the following groups:

1. Persons currently in receipt of assistance who require medical care.
2. Persons whose need for assistance arises from their health problems.
3. The "medically indigent"—persons who are otherwise self-supporting but who are unable to pay for medical care for themselves or their dependents.

According to the American Medical Association, a person is medically indigent when he "is unable, in the place in which he resides, through his own resources to provide himself and his dependents with proper medical, dental, nursing, hospital, pharmaceutical, therapeutic appliances care without depriving himself or his dependents of necessary food, clothing, shelter, and similar necessities of life as determined by the local authorities charged with the duty of dispensing relief for the medically indigent."

Traditionally, poor relief authorities provided medical care through the employment of a full-time or part-time town or city physician, or by authorizing a private physician to treat the needy person. If the sick person required hospitalization the poor relief authorities were usually responsible for the cost. In practice, medical care under the poor law was very inadequate, the quality of service being low, and limited to the direst emergency cases. Institutional care in the almshouse was the preferred method of care for persons suffering from physical handicap, chronic illness, or the degenerative ailments of the aged. The growth of public assistance and developments in medical science have improved the quality of care, but much remains to be done. In some areas care is little better than under the poor law.

In 1939 the Committee on Medical Care of the American Public Welfare Association set forth some of its ideas regarding the scope and character of medical service under public auspices. It recommended the following objectives:

1. Scope and amount of care sufficient to include all necessary preventive and curative service required by persons unable to procure it for themselves.
2. Good quality of service and personal attention.
3. Reasonable accessibility and promptness of service.
4. Continuous care of the patient including:
   a. Continuity of diagnosis and treatment by different types of service—home, ambulatory, and hospital.
   b. Continuity of preventive and curative service.
   c. Integration of medical and social treatment.
5. Reasonable payment to all participating medical practitioners and agencies.
6. Participation of medical professions and agencies in planning service; and as wide a participation in furnishing service as is compatible with quality, scope, and economy.
7. Economy of expenditure, consistent with adequate scope, amount, and quality of service.
8. Provision of service under conditions which will encourage its full use; avoidance of conditions that will deter the needy from securing the necessary medical care and discourage well qualified practitioners or agencies from participating in the service.
9. Adequate records of professional service and expenditure.[14]

[14] American Public Welfare Association, "Organization and Administration of Tax-Supported Medical Care," processed report (Chicago: 1939), p. 24.

The committee also made these additional suggestions:

Persons already accepted for maintenance at public expense should be accepted without further investigation for medical care at public expense.

The determination of medical need should be a medical responsibility and should precede the determination of financial eligibility.

Determination of eligibility should not delay necessary treatment.

Policies concerning the determination of eligibility should be made by the public authority after consultation with the agencies and professions concerned; and should include agreement between the agencies to avoid duplication of investigation.[15]

Franz Goldman elaborates on the components of an adequate program of medical care as follows:

1. Physicians' service including general practitioners and specialists.
2. Dental service including dentists and dental technicians.
3. Nursing service including institutional and public health nurses, nurse-midwives, nurses' aids, and visiting housekeepers.
4. Medical social service, including case workers and persons engaged in organization and administration of health services.
5. Diagnostic laboratory and roentgenological services.
6. Supply of drugs, diets, and appliances.
7. Special treatment services, such as physical therapy and roentgen and radium therapy.

[15] In the fall of 1952 a revision and expansion of the 1939 statement was published by the Joint Committee on Medical Care of the American Public Health Association and the American Public Welfare Association (*Public Welfare,* October, 1952). In this statement on "Tax-Supported Medical Care for the Needy," the persons to be served are defined as individuals who may require public aid in obtaining needed medical services when they have exhausted their personal resources and hence require public assistance to meet all their basic needs, including medical care. In addition, individuals who are normally self-supporting may find expensive medical care requirements too great a burden for a small budget. Persons seeking public aid under these latter conditions are often designated as "medically needy" or "medically indigent."

A concept of good medical care is developed which should meet both quantitative and qualitative standards. Common interests of health and welfare departments are indicated and patterns of coöperation between the two governmental agencies suggested. Problems and methods of administration are enumerated dealing with financing, arrangements with providers of the service, determination of eligibility, methods to promote quality of care, and organization.

8. Hospitalization in general and special hospitals, including convalescent homes and hospitals for the chronically ill.
9. Custodial care in institutions.
10. Ambulance service.[16]

Of all the items in the assistance budget, medical care involves the greatest difficulties. Should care be provided "in kind," or should a cash grant be issued so that the recipient can purchase his own care? Under what circumstances does a person need medical care? This is a question that even self-supporting persons under similar circumstances answer differently. If little Johnnie has a cold or an upset stomach, how severe must his symptoms be to warrant medical attention? Should the doctor come to the home; should Johnnie be taken to his office; or should he be taken to the clinic (assuming that there is a clinic in the community)? Under what conditions should little Mary have a tonsillectomy? If old Mrs. Jones, who is suffering from a chronic ailment, complains of feeling "poorly," should the doctor be called or should she be encouraged to attend the clinic? Are old Mr. Smith's infirmities so severe that he should be encouraged to give up his furnished room and move to a home for the aged or a nursing home (again assuming that there are such facilities in the community)? There is no problem in determining whether medical care ought to be authorized when a person has clearly defined symptoms, and the nature of the treatment is indicated, or even when further diagnostic work is indicated. The problem arises in connection with the "borderline" cases. But even allowing for the fact that some people tend to exaggerate their symptoms and become unduly alarmed every time they feel in the least unwell, it would be better to err on the side of providing medical care than of denying it.

The conflicting forces with which a local administrator must come to terms in establishing medical care policy are set forth by an experienced medical social worker as follows:

A county commissioner of public welfare must assume responsibility

---

[16] Franz Goldman, *Public Medical Care* (New York: Columbia University, 1945), p. 160.

for establishing and operating a medical program designed to satisfy a number of seemingly conflicting forces. Some of these are:

1. A system which will guarantee to the patient adequate medical treatment of the highest quality available and at a cost acceptable to the taxpayer.
2. Understanding of what the average citizen in his community expects to achieve in living standards for himself and his family, and maintaining the delicate balance between these criteria and the high standards which should be maintained in the medical care program. The county boards of supervisors, the officials elected to govern the county, cannot be expected to appropriate funds for a program which provides service far in excess of those which they provide for their own families.[17]

The adequacy of medical care for needy people is limited not only by appropriations for such care and the policies with respect to service but also by the quality of medical care in the community and the extent to which medical facilities are available. If specialized facilities are absent or inadequate, needy people, like others in the community, must do without, or delay treatment, or else arrangements must be made for care in another community at considerable expense and inconvenience. Regardless of these limitations, the assistance agency has the responsibility for developing as comprehensive a program as possible in coöperation with the medical professions and agencies. The basic policy areas are:

1. The conditions under which care will be authorized.
2. The method of service when alternatives are possible, e.g., home visit vs. clinic.
3. The amount of payment for service.
4. The method of payment.
5. Accounts, records, and supervision.

Most of these points involve medical considerations which need not concern us here. The method of payment, however, is closely related to other aspects of assistance administration and warrants

[17] Marion Rickert, "Medical Care Under County Welfare Units," *Public Welfare*, May, 1949, p. 99.

further discussion. At first glance it would seem that, in the light of the principle of the "unrestricted grant," payments for medical care should be made directly to the needy person so that he can purchase his own medical service or pay for care already received. Indeed, until 1951 the Social Security Act required that in so far as federal funds were used for such purpose they had to be paid directly to the recipient.[18] Although the amount of the regular monthly or semimonthly assistance grant is computed on the basis of budgetary needs, it is understood that the recipient is free to use his grant as he sees fit (subject to restrictions on the duplication of assistance); thus he can use part of his food money to purchase household supplies or other items which he considers sufficiently important to warrant depriving himself in other areas. But a check for medical expenses is issued for a specific purpose, and the assistance agency, if only from the standpoint of public health, has the duty of seeing that it is used for the purpose for which it was authorized. Granted that the great majority of recipients will not misapply such funds, nevertheless, medical care, especially if it involves hospitalization, an extended course of treatments, or a prosthetic appliance, can be very costly, and misuse of such funds, even if by only a few persons, can create a serious problem, particularly if the needy person still requires treatment. At any rate, the problem has been thought sufficiently acute for the unrestricted-grant provisions of the Social Security Act to be modified to permit payments for medical care to be made directly to the practitioner or supplier. Where hospital and clinic facilities are under public auspices, whether administered by the welfare department or some other public agency, payment for service need involve only bookkeeping transactions.

A program of medical care for needy people involves technical

[18] Federal participation in the cost of medical care is limited by the maximum average contribution per case. Thus, if the average OAA grant is $55 a month or more, no additional federal contribution can be secured. When the average OAA grant is less than that amount, funds up to the maximum can be secured—to be applied toward the cost of medical care. Federally reimbursed payments can now be made directly to vendors of medical service. This is a modification of the "unrestricted grant" policy. See Chapter 7 for further discussion of this topic.

and professional considerations outside the scope of the local director's competence. Even in the smallest local agency, therefore, it would be desirable to have at least a part-time medical consultant to assist the director in planning and administering the service. In larger agencies, a medical social worker and even a full-time medical director will be needed.

Institutional Care

Many persons in need of maintenance (especially the aged) have health problems which do not permit them to live alone. If they have no relatives or friends to care for them, or if their condition is such that the latter cannot provide the necessary care, then some sort of institutional care is indicated. The groups in need of such care may be roughly classified as follows:

1. Persons who are acutely and seriously ill. Such persons are in need of care in a general or special hospital and, therefore, do not differ in this respect from other persons in the community.
2. Persons who are in need of care in a mental hospital.
3. Persons who are in need of active and continuous treatment by a physician. They may not need to be in a hospital but they should be in an institution with an infirmary and adequate medical facilities.
4. Persons who need chiefly skilled care by a trained nurse, like the preceding group.
5. Persons who require care only by a practical nurse or attendant with medical and nursing supervision. Such people are chiefly in need of so-called "custodial care."
6. In addition to the above groups there are some aged or handicapped persons who, though able to live by themselves, might find it more satisfying to live in the protected environment of an institution, provided there were no stigma attached to it, their freedom of movement were not unduly restricted, and the facilities were reasonably adequate.

We are concerned primarily with the last four groups—those who are in need of custodial care or care in an institution for persons suffering from chronic ailments.

Under the terms of the Social Security Act, recipients of old-age assistance may live in private homes for the aged. These homes, however, are unevenly distributed throughout the country, and, even though they may admit persons from outside the community, elderly people may be reluctant to move away from friends and associations of many years. Many homes, moreover, are unwilling to admit or keep persons who are in need of continuous medical care and who are difficult to handle.

Private boarding and nursing homes (proprietary) are used extensively, but their standards are often low. Not only is the quality of service poor, but the physical facilities fail to conform to the most urgent safety precautions, so that many of them are "death traps." Most state agencies have neither sufficient legal authority nor adequate inspectional staff to insure that all institutions conform to minimum requirements.

In the absence of other facilities, the county or municipal home is used. This is far from satisfactory. Old-age assistance recipients lose their grants when they enter such institutions. While the character of the county home population has changed considerably with the development of public assistance, the facilities and quality of service have, for the most part, not been changed. Persons who reside in county homes are usually suffering from infirmities and diseases of the aged which are not acute enough to warrant hospitalization. In some instances, however, people who are in need of hospital care are kept in county homes either because their symptoms are not demonstrably severe enough or because the hospitals cannot accommodate them.

Where there are adequate programs of public assistance, no one need live in a county home because of economic need alone. Institutional care is necessary only where health conditions require it; hence, the county home as we have known it no longer has a reason for being. Much needed, however, are county infirmaries, and some states are endeavoring to convert their county homes for this purpose and are making them available not only to the needy but also to "paying guests." Not all of these attempts at conversion are well planned, as the Bureau of Public Assistance, in a study on sheltered care, reports: "It seems apparent that in some localities at any rate, former public homes are being converted without sufficient consideration of such factors as: unmet needs for medical care; the possibility of developing other types of care; the location and organization of the converted institution in relation to existing hospital facilities; the size and type of the building to be converted; the availability of competent professional staff and the cost of maintenance on a good standard of service." [19]

There has been a movement to modify the Social Security Act to permit old-age assistance recipients to retain their grants even though they enter public homes. The argument is that it is unfair to penalize people who need institutional care but who have no other recourse than public homes. Moreover, the added funds that would be represented by such persons' retention of their grants would enable the homes to improve the quality of their service. This argument is faulty since once the act was modified there would be no guarantee that the quality of care would be substantially improved. Most public homes are so poorly adapted for infirmary purposes that a large capital outlay would be required to make them satisfactory. Their very location is often one of their greatest handicaps—miles from the nearest center of population.

One approach to a solution is reflected in an amendment to the Social Security Act in 1951: Recipients of federally reimbursed assistance are permitted to retain their grants while residing in public medical institutions other than hospitals for the care of the mentally ill or for persons suffering from tuberculosis. Consequently, if a public home is converted into a bona-fide medical institution, as certified by the appropriate medical authorities, it may care for persons currently in receipt of public assistance. This provision is further strengthened by another 1951 amendment, which requires that the state plan must provide, if payments are made to individuals in private or public institutions,

[19] Social Security Administration, *Sheltered Care*, Public Assistance Report No. 5 (Washington: Government Printing Office, 1944).

for the establishment or designation of a state authority responsible for establishing and maintaining standards for such institutions.

SELECTED REFERENCES

See list at end of Chapter 4.

CHAPTER 6

The Measurement
of Economic Need

What is an acceptable "content of living"? Shall we include only what it takes to keep a man alive? Black bread and thin soup from a prison camp kitchen will do that. But we do not want just *any* content of living. We want a content of living in the United States of America that includes the goods and service that will at least assure a minimum of well being for every citizen.

—JANE HOEY, National Conference of Social Work, 1948

In this chapter we propose to give meaning to the phrase "adequate content of living" by translating it into practical terms, by examining various standards of living and the devices that have been worked out to measure them, and by considering some of the current issues related to the task of formulating suitable standards of assistance for those persons whose need obliges them to seek help from the state.

HISTORICAL BACKGROUND

The extent, form, and quality of public programs to relieve economic want depend not only upon actual conditions of want, and upon the financial resources of the state, but also upon society's recognition of this problem, and its attitude toward it. If the prevailing opinion is that poverty results from personal shortcomings, and that financial assistance tends to aggravate dependency rather than reduce it, the kind of help society will provide will differ markedly from that which would be provided were the prevailing opinion that poverty usually results from the faulty

139

economic arrangements of society. If society believes that the responsibility for relieving want is based upon the need to protect itself from civil disorders likely to arise if many people are in extreme want, the measures that will be adopted to deal with the problem will have slight resemblance to those that will be adopted if society believes that social justice and democratic principles require that no one unable to support himself be permitted to fall below a minimum but decent scale of living.

There are few persons who will not at least pay lip service to the idea that people in want should be helped by the community. Objections multiply, however, when specific proposals are advanced as to the manner in which want should be relieved. "The extent of the need has been exaggerated." "These people are not genuinely in need." "The proposals are too costly and will jeopardize the economy." "The proposals are too generous; they will demoralize the poor, reduce the incentives to save, make them content with relief rather than spur them on to return to self-support." These, and arguments in similar vein, have been used against almost every effort to increase the scope and content of programs designed to protect the economically insecure from the disaster of income loss.

American and British social history reveals striking similarities in the attacks made in the past on social welfare measures now commonly accepted and current objections to the extension of our social security system. This is not to imply that every liberalizing measure has been sound or that every objection has been unwise; many foolish proposals have been blocked, fortunately; many serious mistakes have been made. Unfortunately, in too many instances opposition to the extension of social legislation has been based on erroneous, outdated, or inadequate data. Attitudes tend to be inherited, but not the social conditions which once may have justified them.

Since feelings tend to exert as much influence on social change as facts, it will be revealing to consider the growth of contemporary social philosophy in this area, from the theories, prejudices, and occasional insights of the past.

Attitudes Toward Poverty and the Poor

Almsgiving and some form of organized charity can be traced far back in history, but, although many treatises have been written concerning the causes and conditions of poverty, it was not until relatively recently that objective investigations of living standards and economic needs were undertaken. In the first place, scientific knowledge of physiology, nutrition, and related fields was lacking, as were also the necessary techniques of social investigation and measurement. Secondly, developments in this area had to await a climate of opinion favorable for such study.

In the Middle Ages science was undergoing a rebirth. The bits and scraps of classical knowledge salvaged by the monks (often in distorted form) from the ruins of Roman civilization were being reëxamined and tested in the light of a new philosophy and theology. Emphasis was on the erection of a stable and orderly body of knowledge rather than on its mundane application.

The church, however, had developed a dynamic doctrine of charity based upon a distinction between "natural" and "supernatural" charity. According to this doctrine, the former virtue springs from natural motives—pity, identification, civic consciousness, etc.; while worthy of merit, it is not to be as highly regarded as supernatural charity. The latter is derived from the scriptural reminder that, when the poor are helped, Christ himself is helped; that Christ and the members of the church are one body. This doctrine gave a strong impetus to almsgiving and to the establishment of the various charitable foundations described earlier. Moreover, it colored the whole medieval attitude toward poverty. But in so far as total community needs were concerned, or, for that matter, the long-term needs of the individual, charity was to a great extent unplanned. The emphasis was on generous and unquestioned giving. Whoever asked for help was presumed to need it, and such help was granted as if Christ himself had requested it.

No doubt charity of this sort was sometimes misdirected; no doubt many persons were more concerned about the spiritual merit of their almsgiving than in how effectively such alms met the needs of those to whom it was given. But whether the attitudes that motivated medieval society resulted in less humane, less adequate help to the poor than the attitudes in the age that was to follow will be left to the reader to judge.

In many sections of Europe the Renaissance and the religious revolt of the sixteenth century led to a complete reversal of thinking regarding the poor. This was due partly to social and economic changes which rendered the old system unsuitable, partly to new theological conceptions, and partly to the need to discredit anything that was a reminder of the old social and religious order which had been forsaken. Helen Wright, Dean of the School of Social Service Administration of the University of Chicago, summarizes the changes:

It remained for the new religious ideas of the 17th and 18th Centuries, and the concomitant economic changes, to destroy almost entirely any concept of dependency not resulting solely from the fault of the dependent. As economic prosperity became the sign of the Lord's approval and poverty a sign that his anger had been incurred, it followed that the poor must be sinners in need of punishment. The economic changes which made possible the rise of many relatively poor to positions of affluence, served to emphasize personal responsibility and extraordinary worship of the virtues of industry, frugality, and self help.[1]

Another writer comments:

Religion still continued to exercise some faint influence over the administration of relief, but to say how much was lip service only would not be easy. Even this influence was inherently changed from that which had held sway throughout the Middle Ages. To give alms was no longer a mystic act of grace but a practical duty towards God. . . The poor, even to such persons as were still influenced by a religious motive, were no longer an opportunity, but merely a responsibility, and in time even this aspect of the religious duty of relieving the poor became entangled with other motives not even remotely religious. By the middle of the succeeding century Baily found nothing incongruous in writing in the same paragraph that it was both our duty to God and very good for our trade to provide for

[1] Helen Wright, "Dependency," *Encyclopedia of the Social Sciences,* Vol. V (New York: Macmillan, 1930), p. 94.

the poor. Thus he wrote, "to provide a comfortable subsistence for the Poor is most certainly a duty highly obligatory upon every person in whom the traces of moral virtue are not quite obliterated; the performance of which is equally required by Policy and Religion. This is a charity of the utmost extent; which, if conducted according to the following plan, by employing the Poor in Parish Workhouses, will very much promote the commerce, wealth and Peace of this kingdom. These Houses will also become proper schools to train up the children of the Poor to Religious sobriety and industry, who would otherwise be brought up in sloth, ignorance, and vice. They will likewise be nurseries for spinners, weavers and other Artificers, in the woolen, linen and cloth Manufacture, and give occasion to the Exercise of many other trades and useful Employments." Such an extract illustrates the great gulf which divided the religious motive for relief in the Middle Ages from that which influenced man in the early Eighteenth Century. The latter was not strong enough, and lacked the driving force to make a real and effective incitement to the relief of the poor.[2]

In any event, ideas regarding poverty and the poor became fixed, and any real incentive to investigate whether or not they had validity was precluded. The stratification of society was another obstacle to understanding. In seventeenth- and eighteenth-century England the great landowners, the merchants, the men of affairs who made the laws were far removed, spiritually and economically, from the great mass of working people; indeed, the latter, as we shall see, were thought to be almost a different breed —one whose needs were little above those of the brute. Although the history of British poor relief is brightened by the labors of many wise and noble men who strove to reintroduce concepts of justice and charity into the administration of the poor laws, prevailing opinion was against them.

Bernard Mandeville, a writer on economic and social matters, had this to say about the "lower classes" in 1723:

It is impossible that a Society can long subsist, and suffer many of its members to live in idleness and enjoy all the ease and pleasure they can invent, without having at the same time great multitudes of

[2] Dorothy Marshall, *The English Poor in the Eighteenth Century* (London: George Routledge, 1926), p. 19.

people that to make good this defect will condescend to be quite the
reverse, and by use and patience inure their bodies to work for others
and themselves besides.

The plenty and cheapness of provisions depends in a great measure
on the price and value that is set upon this labor, and consequently
the welfare of all societies, even before they are tainted with foreign
luxuries requires that it should be performed by such of its members
as in the first place are sturdy and robust and never used to ease or
idleness and in the second soon contented as to necessaries of life;
such as are glad to take up with the coarsest manufacture in everything they wear and in their diet have no other aim than to feed their
bodies when their stomachs prompt them to eat and with little regard to taste or refresh, to refuse no wholesome nourishment that can
be swallowed when they are hungry, or ask anything for their thirst
but to quench it. . . .

If such people there must be, as no great nation can be happy
without vast numbers of them, would not a wise legislature cultivate
the breed of them with all imaginable care, and provide against their
scarcity as he would prevent the scarcity of provision itself? No man
would be poor and fatigue himself for a livelihood if he would help
it: the absolute necessity all stand in for victuals and drink, and in
cold climates for clothes and lodging, makes them submit to anything
that can be borne with. If nobody did want nobody would work: but
the greatest hardships are looked upon as solid pleasures, when they
keep a man from starving.

Going to school in comparison to working is idleness, and the longer
boys continue in this easy sort of life, the more unfit they'll be when
grown up for down right labor, both as to strength and inclination.
Men who are to remain and end their days in a laborious tiresome
and painful station of life, the sooner they are put upon it at first, the
more patiently they'll submit to it for ever after.[3]

Lest this be thought an isolated and cynical example, consider
the views of the Rev. Joseph Townsend in his book, *A Disserta-
tion on the Poor Laws by a Well-wisher* (sic) *to Mankind:*

It seems to be a law of nature, that the poor should be to a certain
degree improvident, that there may always be some to fulfil the
most servile, the most sordid, and the most ignoble offices in the

---

[3] Quoted in Karl de Schweinitz, *England's Road to Social Security* (Philadelphia: University of Pennsylvania, 1943), p. 59.

community. The stock of human happiness is thereby much increased, whilst the more delicate are not only relieved from drudgery, and freed from those occasional employments which would make them miserable, but are left at liberty, without interruption, to pursue those callings which are suited to their various dispositions, and most useful to the state. As for the lowest of the poor, by custom they are reconciled to the meanest occupations, to the most laborious works, and to the most hazardous pursuits; whilst the hope of their reward makes them cheerful in the midst of all their dangers and toils.[4]

That this unfeeling attitude persisted is brought out in this quotation from a pamphlet called *The Curse of Beggars* published in the middle of the nineteenth century:

At every crossing an impudent urchin trails a dirty broom before us and would fair lay upon us a tax. . . . In short intervals we encounter the whining interruptions of the sturdy Irishman who is always starving, or that odious girl who is always taking God's name in vain. We enter a pastry shop for a modest luncheon of a biscuit or a bun; a family of ragged vagabonds watch every mouthful we eat.[5]

That the idea that the poor are a race apart has not been relegated to the pages of history is apparent when we read the following remarks made as late as 1936 by the president of the state medical association in one of our most populous states:

The idle, shiftless and subnormal, together with 3,000,000 aliens who are on the dole will be housed, nourished and medically cared for by the people whose property they begrudge and whose ideals they betray.

Matthew Carey, a Philadelphia merchant, writing in 1830, summarized what he called "Erroneous Opinions About the Poor":

1. That every man, woman, and grown child, able and willing to work, may find employment.
2. That the poor, by industry, prudence, and economy may at all

---

[4] *Ibid.,* p. 116.
[5] Helen Bosanquet, *Social Work in London 1869–1912,* quoted in Helen Witmer, *Social Work* (New York: Farrar & Rinehart, 1942), p. 140.

times support themselves comfortably without depending upon eleemosynary aid—and as a corollary from these positions:

3. That their sufferings and distress, chiefly, if not wholly, arise from their idleness, their dissipation, and their extravagance.

4. That taxes for the support of the poor, and aid afforded them by charitable individuals or benevolent societies, are pernicious as by encouraging the poor to depend on them they foster their idleness and improvidence and thus produce, or at least increase, the poverty and distress they are intended to relieve.[6]

Matthew Carey, it can be seen, was far in advance of his time. The reader may find it profitable to discover how many of his friends and acquaintances still hold these "erroneous opinions."

The Concept of Less Eligibility

Underlying the traditional repressive attitude toward the economically dependent was the concept of "less eligibility." This concept had its clearest expression in the British poor law reform of 1834, but it had influenced the administration of poor relief since the days of Queen Elizabeth and continues to be an issue for debate.

The term "less eligible" means "less desirable." In other words, the principle was laid down that no one should receive material assistance from the state if by that assistance his situation became more favorable than that of the poorest person who was maintaining himself through his own efforts. Poor relief recipients were thus to be kept in a condition less desirable than that of self-supporting persons. The British Poor Relief Commissioners of 1834 explained the practice thus: "However diligent an assistant overseer, or an officer for inquiry may be, there are numerous cases which will baffle his utmost diligence and sagacity; the only test of those cases is making their condition more severe than that of the lowest class of laborers who obtain their livelihood by honest industry."[7]

---

[6] Arthur Schlesinger, Jr., *The Age of Jackson* (New York: New American Library of World Literature, 1949), p. 65.

[7] De Schweinitz, *op. cit.*, p. 121.

An earlier explanation of this concept is found in a report of the poor relief program in Hamburg, Germany, in the latter part of the eighteenth century: "It was our determined principle to reduce this support lower than what any industrious man or woman in such circumstances could earn; for if the manner in which relief is given is not a spur to industry, it becomes undoubtedly a premium to sloth and profligacy." [8]

This concept, as can be seen, was logically derived from one of the major premises of poor relief administration, namely, that the poor naturally prefer to have even a meager sustenance for which they do not have to work than to support themselves. Actually, however, there is nothing unsound about the concept of "less eligibility"; the evil lay in its method of application. It is doubtful whether even the most altruistically inclined person would advocate a standard of assistance for dependent people higher than the living standard of persons who are self-supporting. The concept, however, was applied without any reference to what might constitute a reasonable standard of living. It was taken for granted that if a person did not seek poor relief he was self-supporting. The fact of the matter was, however, that poor relief was administered in such a manner that most people, if they had any resources, no matter how inadequate, would prefer to struggle along on starvation rations than to accept the niggardly, begrudging, and punitive terms of the overseer of the poor.

Since the standard of assistance was set at a point lower than the living standard of a self-supporting person (rather than being based on what a person needed), a vicious circle developed because the standard of what constituted a self-supporting person was artificially lowered by the repressive methods of poor relief, which discouraged many genuinely needy persons from seeking supplementary help. For example: Suppose that a parish overseer established a policy of granting six shillings a week in outdoor relief to a family unit of three, when there was no other resource in the family. A laborer earning five shillings a week, but with a wife and child to support, might prefer to struggle along on this inadequate income, rather than put himself under the poor law

[8] *Ibid.*, p. 92.

in order to get one shilling a week supplementation. If many workers did this, the overseer might conclude that his standard of assistance was too high in view of the "self-supporting" persons who were living on less. The standard of assistance for a family unit of three might then be decreased to four shillings, sixpence.

The Workhouse Test

Although the policy of making poor relief so irksome that none but those in direst straits would seek it was not new, it remained for the poor law reform of 1834 to carry this policy to its logical conclusion by prohibiting outdoor relief and requiring all needy people to enter the workhouse. Here husbands were separated from wives, parents from children, and in terms of meager fare, lack of privacy, loss of personal liberty, and moral obloquy there was little that could distinguish it from a common gaol.

We have noted that "workhouses" and "houses of correction" were part of the paraphernalia of poor relief from earliest times. Institutionalization, however, was but one method of caring for needy persons, used as circumstances seemed to require. Later, institutionalization became more or less a general policy—a policy based on the belief that willingness to enter the workhouse constituted the only reliable test of genuine need. The extent to which the "workhouse test" was used, rather than outdoor relief, varied. When economic conditions were bad, and the number of needy persons increased, the test was relaxed, largely because the workhouses could not accommodate all who requested help. At such times it was not uncommon to require that only the able-bodied head of the family enter the institution, his family being assisted in their home.

The very existence of this test served, however, as a barrier to an understanding of the needs of the poor. When the test was rigorously applied, it was not uncommon to find a sharp decline in the number of persons requesting help. This was interpreted as proof that many people who would have accepted outdoor relief were not really in need since they avoided the "offer of the house." That even among the poor there was sufficient self-respect, love of family, and desire for freedom for them to prefer a starvation existence to surrendering all they held dear probably never occurred to poor relief officials.

The cost of maintaining the poor in the workhouse served as a rough guide to what might be allowed in cases of outdoor relief. The cynicism with which such policies were administered is reflected in the reasons for granting outdoor relief. Enterprising officials, in reckoning the charges per inmate, hit upon the idea that money could be saved by offering destitute persons less than the cost of their maintenance in the institution if they stayed outside. The following statements reveal the factors that motivated them:

I may aver that the parish has saved, by having a workhouse, between 1,000 and 1,100 pounds. For the people of the parish having been sorely afflicted with the smallpox and fevers and agues and because they would not come into the house, they have made shift with a shilling when four before would not content them.[9]

A chairman of a Board of Governors, addressing a widow with two children applying for a renewal of relief, "If you can't earn enough to keep you with what we give you, you must come into the workhouse, *we don't profess to give you* enough to keep you out of the workhouse!" [10]

Another writer called attention to the fallacy of this policy, not out of concern for its failure to meet need, but with regard to the savings that could be secured:

A family applies for relief; if they are given out-relief to the amount of four shillings a week they will be satisfied; if they come into the workhouse, their maintenance will cost ten shillings a week. The economists, therefore, argue that by giving out-relief they will save six shillings per week. Now the very same Guardians who have used this argument have frequently acknowledged to me, that when the workhouse test is offered it is not accepted in more than one case out of ten. By offering the workhouse then in ten such cases the Guardians would indeed lose six shillings a week in the one case in which it was accepted, but in each of the remaining nine cases they would

[9] *Ibid.*, p. 63.
[10] *Ibid.*, p. 157.

save four shillings so that their total gain upon the ten cases would amount to thirty shillings a week.[11]

There is no need to elaborate further. Where such unfeeling attitudes prevail, there can be no incentive to ascertain the facts with regard to need. As things actually worked themselves out in English poor relief, there was no pretense at meeting need; assistance in amounts just sufficient to pacify the poor was granted so that there would be no danger of their resorting to violence. As inhumane as the workhouse may strike us today, there were times when it represented an actual improvement over some methods of providing care. The reader need only recall the practice of "auctioning off" the poor described in an earlier chapter.

The Allowance in Support of Wages

An early but abortive attempt to establish some reasonable standard of living for the poor occurred in the latter part of the eighteenth century. It took the form of grants to supplement inadequate wages, the grants being adjusted to fluctuations in the price of bread. Although the measure was crude, and the economic results were disastrous, it is of significance because it represents the first attempt to relate an individual's resources to the cost of living, and because it illustrates the problems that arise when government tries to subsidize employers who pay substandard wages.

From the middle of the eighteenth century until well after the close of the Napoleonic Wars the condition of the British working class was depressed. Beginning in the early years of the century there had been a revival of the process of enclosure, and this now began to affect the "common land." Most agricultural villages included land that was used communally—a vestige of the medieval system. For the poor man it was a source of fuel and served as pasture for his cow, his donkey, and his flock of geese. The "common," moreover, was used by persons who had no legal title to it. Bills of enclosure, sponsored usually by the more wealthy and influential members of the community, permitted the pasture and

[11] *Ibid.*, p. 158.

meadow land to be divided up among those who could establish legal claim to it. Consequently, not only were those who had no title to the land deprived of an important resource, but others, whose claim was small, were compensated in money which was soon spent. The growth of the factory system, moreover, resulted in the decay of the cottage industries—an important source of supplementary income to the small farmer. Circumstances thus conspired to deprive the poorest elements of British society of the means of a decent livelihood. Prices were high and wages were low, and finally the plight of the poverty-stricken laborer could no longer be disregarded. Perhaps for the first time, the dominant elements in British society were confronted with the inescapable fact that poverty was not necessarily the result of incompetence, intemperance, and laziness, for it was obvious that fully employed workers were living in poverty.

Various measures were considered for solving this problem, but the most obvious one, that of setting minimum wages, was rejected, although there was ample legal precedent for such action. In 1795 the magistrates of Berkshire, meeting at Speenhamland, evolved a plan that soon spread throughout England—the "allowance in support of wages." De Schweinitz summarized the plan as follows: "The scale which they drew up provided that when the gallon loaf sold for one shilling, enough relief would be added to the laborer's wages to bring his income to 3 shillings; if he had a wife, to 4 shillings 6 pence; if a wife and one child, to six shillings, and so on according to the size of the household."

Other devices to cope with the problem of the unemployed farm laborer included: (1) sending the unemployed man from house to house to seek work—householders willing to employ such men were required to pay sixpence a day and provide food, while the parish would add fourpence a day for the support of the family; (2) auctioning off farm labor by the parish, the latter supplementing whatever wages the successful bidder had agreed to pay; (3) threatening householders that if they did not employ such laborers their tax rate would be increased.

The net result of this system was quite different from that which had been anticipated. All these devices combined to depress wages still lower and thus increased the number of persons who became entitled to the "allowance." It needed only a few shrewd employers of agricultural labor to recognize that here was a way in which a substantial part of their labor costs could be subsidized by the government; all other employers of such labor had to follow suit, willy-nilly. Vast numbers of the British working class became dependent upon some form of poor relief, and the tax rate rose sharply. As De Schweinitz points out: "The burden of this failure was placed upon the relief system, and in particular upon relief to the able bodied." It was the reaction to this failure that resulted in the poor law reform of 1834 with its emphasis upon "less eligibility" and the "workhouse test." De Schweinitz' opinion is that this delayed for three-quarters of a century the development of a constructive program of assistance. Thus we see that programs of social welfare, even though designed to relieve distress, can do more harm than good if they are poorly conceived. We also learn from this experience the futility of trying to improve the economic position of an underprivileged class by relief measures alone, and the necessity of coördinating such measures with plans to strengthen the overall economic structure.

Present-Day Attitudes

The lag in the establishment of adequate programs of assistance is a reflection of the very gradual change in attitudes toward poverty and the poor. Until relatively recently there was no concerted effort to deal with the problem in its entirety. We have seen that a largely sentimental concern for the problems of certain dependent groups resulted in the establishment of certain programs of preferential assistance. It took an unprecedented, nation-wide economic catastrophe, however, to awaken the American people to the necessity of a comprehensive attack on economic need.

Changes in the method of dealing with economic dependency, resulting from the experience of the great depression, have, indeed, been far reaching, and they could have been achieved only through widespread acceptance by the American people.

It would be unduly optimistic, however, to assume that this acceptance is a reflection of widespread and fundamental changes in attitudes toward poverty, its nature and cause. To be sure, there has had to be some intellectual acceptance of the fact that poverty is not due entirely to personal causes; the record of the depression years, when the number of persons dependent upon some form of public aid reached almost twenty-eight million, is too dramatic a refutation of this theory to be disregarded. Nevertheless, whenever evidence of mismanagement or inefficiency on the part of an assistance agency is brought to the attention of the public, or whenever a particularly dramatic case of misbehavior or the fraudulent receipt of assistance by recipients becomes known, the hue and cry that is raised in the press, in popular magazines, and in "letters to the editor" suggests that there are still many people who are willing, perhaps even anxious, to find justification for the old contention that the poor are poor through their own fault, that the receipt of assistance corrupts. No doubt some people find this conception more comforting than the thought that our economic structure is so delicately balanced that thrift, industry, and business acumen are no longer guarantees of economic security. We would not suggest that the public should not protest when evidences of deceit and mismanagement are revealed. Unfortunately, protests too often take the form of confused and emotional attacks on the principle of adequate assistance to the needy rather than of intelligent inquiries as to why the system has broken down in a particular instance.

THE NATURE OF POVERTY

What, then, is poverty? It is not an absolute term but denotes, rather, a state of insufficiency. But insufficiency in relation to what—to the standard of living of the wealthier members of the community or nation; to the standard of living of the majority; or to the standard of living that everyone could enjoy were all economic resources utilized effectively? Can poverty be determined objectively, or is it subjective and based upon what individuals desire? Once we move beyond the point of thinking of poverty only as that state in which an individual lacks the necessities of life, this question allows no simple answer. Optimum and minimum living standards vary greatly, not only with regard to geographic and historical differences, but also in terms of individual judgments regarding personal needs and the needs of others. Thus, in estimating *my* essential needs, I am likely to be much more generous than in estimating the essential needs of someone else, especially if that "someone" is dependent.

I. M. Rubinow points out that the determination of the state of poverty must be based upon some distinction between legitimate and excessive desires—a distinction resting not only upon physiology but also upon some underlying theory as to the purpose of human existence.[12]

Francis J. Haas discusses human needs under the following headings:

Primary Physical Needs: (a) Life, (b) Health, (c) Home Life, (d) Property.
Primary Non-Physical Needs: (a) Truth, (b) Good name and social approval, (c) Liberty, (d) Government, (e) Mental development, (f) The arts, (g) Religion.[13]

Professor Helen Harris Perlman comments thus on the changing concept of human needs:

We are living, and so are persons on relief, here and now, in the second half of the 20th Century, United States of America. It is a time and place when materialistic values are high. One may decry this, but it is a fact. The things one must eat to be well, wear to be accepted, own to "belong" are infinitely multiplied over what they were fifty years ago. Moreover, it is a time and place when knowledge of what people have a right to want is spread by unending communication from radios, newspapers, billboards, movies. Only recently the chairman of one of America's greatest corporations said, "There is a definite correlation between education and the consumption of commodities." Had he been speaking of persons on relief he might have added ". . . or in the sense of need for those commodities."

[12] I. M. Rubinow, "Poverty," *Encyclopedia of the Social Sciences,* Vol. XII (New York: Macmillan, 1930), pp. 284–292.
[13] Francis J. Haas, *Man and Society* (New York: Appleton-Century, 1930), p. 201.

Every person's sense of his needs is greater, far greater, than was the sense of need of fifty years ago. I remember my grandfather said that he never saw an orange until he was twelve years old, and when he ate it, rind and all, he wondered why people considered it such a delicacy. Nowadays every mother considers oranges a basic need for her baby's health. People's felt needs rise and multiply as standards of living rise and they become more complex. It is fallacious to speak of the days when one's grandfather raised seven fine sons in a one-room log cabin, because this took place in a different setting, a different time, a different culture from ours today. In a culture of one-room log cabins the seven sons grew up feeling equal to their peers. In a culture where people are supposed to have bedrooms the sense of inequality is keen when these cannot be had. In a community where bread and cheese are the normal diet people will live on bread and cheese with equanimity, even though the sickness rate among them may be appalling. In a community where people know that balanced diets secure health, and where, moreover, lavish varieties of foods spill over from grocery counters and colored advertisements, the persons who must confine themselves to bread and cheese feel both cheated and defeated.

The fact is that in our present stage of technological and psychological development, nobody—but nobody—considers subsistence living to be enough to meet his needs. Sometimes we consider it to be enough for somebody else, but never for ourselves. Nor does the client on relief consider it to be enough for himself. He may feel it is all he deserves, or know it is all he can hope for. But underneath this seethes the feeling that there is a very great disparity between what he wants, and thinks he needs, and what society gives him. He is left again with the sense of being a second class member of the community; again feelings of frustration and helplessness may undermine the sense of adequacy and security which is basic to his self-dependence.[14]

The psychological component in human needs is discussed by Professor Charlotte Towle:

Obviously, the conditions which make for maximum physical health are important from the standpoint of creating a citizenry physically powerful and efficient in contributing to the Nation's wealth in time

[14] Helen Harris Perlman, "Are We Creating Dependency?" *Illinois Public Aid*, July, 1951, p. 4.

of peace and to its safety in time of war. We are interested also in physical health from the standpoint of personality development. . . .

Another essential element in enabling the individual to grow toward greater freedom from irrational emotional forces is the opportunity for the maximum development of his intellectual capacities. . . . This requires provisions . . . to make possible the kinds of training and education appropriate to the individual and the kinds of educational method most suited to the development of citizens for a democracy. It also implies provisions in the community which make it possible for every individual to obtain, under conditions conducive to productive learning, the education essential for the full realization of his powers. This objective involves such measures as adequate enforcement of child-labor laws and removal of restrictions against minority groups. It involves also at least a minimum economic security. . . .

This leads to recognition of a third important element in a life experience conducive to personality growth—the kind of relationships which an individual experiences in the early years within the family and throughout his life in other groups. The early family relationships are generally conceded to be of primary importance, since they determine the basic personality patterns and influence in considerable measure the nature of subsequent relationships. In the human personality there is a natural and inevitable impulse toward growth from the original state of dependence to a state of greater self-sufficiency and independence. It is generally agreed that the human personality grows, develops, matures through relationships with others, and that there is an innate tendency to gravitate into relationship with others in the interest of survival. Man's social needs, that is, what he seeks in relationships throughout life, will vary with the age, changing circumstances, and prior relationship experiences. . . .

But, literally, man does not live by bread alone. Demoralization and disintegration of the individual are prevented, in part, through opportunity to work and to take one's place in the community. But spiritual needs of the individual must also be recognized, understood, and respected. They must be seen as distinct needs and they must also be seen in relation to other human needs. This entails provisions which safeguard church attendance, the use of church resources, and in human-conduct problems, respect for the individual's religious convictions. Through the influence of religion the purpose of human life is better understood and a sense of ethical values achieved. With that understanding comes keener appreciation of the individual's relationship to his fellow man, his community, and his nation. The need for religious influences is particularly acute in childhood and throughout adolescence, when the individual is likely to require definite guidance and supportive judgments to help him toward becoming an emotionally mature adult.[15]

Thus we see that, once we get beyond the core of physiological necessities, human needs are largely psychological—which, however, renders them no less real. To underestimate the significance of psychological needs aggravates the misery of the poor, handicaps them in their efforts to improve their situation, and retards national well-being. Whether or not an individual is in a condition of poverty will be determined by the extent to which he can, through his own efforts, or the help of others, satisfy these basic needs.

Before proceeding farther it will be helpful to explain what is meant by "standard of living." The late Edward T. Devine formulated the following excellent definition:

In simplest terms the standard of living means all those things which one insists upon having. It is not merely a collective name for the commodities enjoyed at a given time, but those which are so related to one another, and so important to the consumer, that if any one of them is lacking, forces to restore it are immediately put into action. . . . Elusive and kaleidoscopic though it may be, nevertheless the conception represented by this phrase is a definite and powerful reality. The expression means something to everyone; the thing itself is the controlling force which shapes every life. . . . Each individual has his own standard, determining every choice he makes. Each family has its own, the result of combinations, consolidations, and compromises. Each locality and each nation has its standard, produced by the interplay of an infinite number of economic, social and psychic forces.[16]

When individuals and families suffer a substantial decrease in income they must reduce their standard of living, but the *way* in which they make this adjustment is a reflection of that stand-

[15] Charlotte Towle, *Common Human Needs*, Public Assistance Report No. 8 (Washington: Federal Security Agency, 1945), pp. 3–9.
[16] Edward T. Devine, *The Normal Life*, quoted in Hazel Kyrk, *Economic Problems of the Family* (New York: Harper, 1933), p. 373.

ard. For example, one family may place a high value on diet; the quantity and variety of food it consumes may remain the same even though it must deprive itself of other necessities, and even though it might possibly economize on food with no deterioration in nutrition. Another family may give priority to the quality of its living quarters: it may refuse to move to a cold-water flat, or to a part of town it considers undesirable, even though failure to reduce rent may result in its going on short rations. From the point of view of meeting basic physiological needs, some of the adjustments that are made are obviously unsound. In many instances, however, although the adjustments do not appear "sensible" to the outsider (who is not in a position to appreciate the motives that prompt them), they may have a compelling logic to the persons who are making the adjustments. It may not be "sensible" for a man, frantically looking for work, to go without lunch in order to buy a trinket to celebrate his little son's birthday, but if this action reassures him of his significance as a father and as the head of the household, who will assert that it has no value in maintaining his sense of responsibility and self-respect? When, by force of outside pressure, people are obliged to disregard psychological needs, such violence may be done to their morale that feelings of dependency and hopelessness may be stimulated.

There is no necessary identity between poverty and low living standards. According to our standards, a primitive tribe may have a low standard of living, but this does not mean that the tribe is in a condition of poverty. Tribal life may be hard and material possessions meager, but if felt wants are few and easily satisfied, there is no poverty, despite a marginal existence. On the other hand, the conditions under which most assistance recipients are obliged to live may strike us as appalling poverty, yet they may exceed the most optimistic expectations of teeming millions in Asia.

Poverty, then, is to a great extent based on the discrepancy between recognized wants and desires and the opportunities for their satisfaction—especially in the light of the prevailing standard in a given society. As a nation grows in material wealth, what formerly were thought of as luxuries become comforts, and what formerly were considered comforts become necessities. This process is particularly noticeable in the United States because of our high productivity and our susceptibility to novelties and the blandishments of advertising.

From the point of view of public assistance, our interest lies in considering how much purchasing power people need in order to live in health and decency.

Serious attempts to investigate the nature of poverty can be traced back to the latter half of the eighteenth century. Interestingly enough, these investigations were not undertaken by officials responsible for the relief of the poor, but by persons of a philosophic and scientific turn of mind who were concerned about the conditions of the working classes in agriculture and industry.

In 1767 Arthur Young, a writer on agricultural matters, published a series of *Farmer's Letters* in which he discussed the living conditions of farm labor. David Davies, rector of Barkham, published the *Case of Laborers in Husbandry* in 1795, in which he included actual budgets of the families of farm laborers in his own and other parishes. Frédéric Le Play, the French engineer and economist, made detailed studies of European workers and their families, particularly with respect to their living conditions, income, and expenditures. His classic study, *The European Worker*, published in 1855, contained a selection of thirty-six monographs drawn from three hundred case studies of actual families. Carrol D. Wright (1840–1909), a former United States Commissioner of Labor, made elaborate studies of the economic condition of the laboring man and the means whereby his welfare could be secured. Charles Booth (1840–1916), an English shipowner and amateur sociologist, conducted prolonged investigations of the life of the poor, which were reported in his monumental work *Life and Labor of the People of London.* He essayed to show "the numerical relation which poverty and misery bear to regular earnings and comparative comfort, and to describe the general conditions under which each class lives." Benjamin Seebohm Rowntree, another English investigator, made detailed studies of poverty and living standards of the working class in York. His findings were reported in a series of volumes, the most recent being *Poverty and Progress,* published in 1941. Rowntree revealed how low-income families actually earned and spent their income.

These studies, rudimentary at first, but later refined through the development of improved techniques of social investigation, have challenged the highly moralistic, unsubstantiated generalizations regarding the nature and cause of poverty which are still all too prevalent. In addition, they served to focus attention upon the necessity for more accurate measurement of the amount of purchasing power needed by families in order to achieve a given scale of living.

Various systems have been worked out whereby families may be classified according to their income and the scale of living they are thereby able to maintain. Such arrangements are admittedly arbitrary, but for the purpose of analysis they are useful because they enable us to reduce a large number of households with various incomes to a few broad groupings.

One of the first to adopt such a scheme was Booth, who, in order to study living conditions, divided the population of London into eight groups, four being above the "poverty line" and four below. "My poor," he said, "may be described as living under a struggle to obtain the necessaries of life and to make both ends meet, while the 'very poor' live in a state of chronic want."

Rubinow proposed a schedule containing five levels based on income: insufficiency, minimum subsistence, health and decency, comfort, and luxury.

Insufficiency

As Jane Hoey has suggested, "black bread and thin soup are enough to preserve life," and, indeed, World War II and its aftermath have taught us grim lessons in how little is necessary in order to keep body and soul together. Existence at this low level makes the individual prey to disease and distorts his outlook on life, while his offspring, should they survive, become stunted in mind and body—an expensive social problem for future generations. Existence at this low level, moreover, deprives the individual of energy and the ambition to seek or to undertake productive work. The shiftlessness, improvidence, and squalor often found among the chronically poor, which so often arouse the scorn and ire of those more fortunately situated, are probably an effect rather than the cause of their poverty. Economic deprivation begets social maladjustment, and vice versa. Our Elizabethan and Victorian forebears, in their omniscience, were certain that the poor were poor because of their bad habits, so they took pains not to demoralize them further by relieving any more than their most exigent wants. The poor law standard of assistance was designed to keep the needy in a state of insufficiency—to spur them on to help themselves. When the needy failed to respond to this treatment, they were looked upon as confirming society's distrust of the poor. Less relief, rather than more, seemed to be a more appropriate method of dealing with the problem. Even today, when assistance recipients do not behave the way society thinks they ought to behave, advocates of this method are still to be found.

Minimum Subsistence

The full significance of what it means to live at a level of minimum subsistence is vividly conveyed by Rowntree:

A family living upon the scale allowed for in this estimate must never spend a penny on railway fare or omnibus. They must never go to the country unless they walk. They must never purchase a half-penny newspaper or spend a penny to buy a ticket for a popular concert. They must write no letters to absent children for they cannot afford to pay the postage. They must never contribute anything to their church or chapel or give any help to a neighbor which costs them money. They cannot save nor can they join sick club or trade union because they cannot pay the necessary subscriptions. Their children must have no pocket money for dolls, marbles or sweets. The father must smoke no tobacco and must drink no beer. The mother must never buy any pretty clothes for herself or for her children, the character of the family wardrobe, as for the family diet, being governed by the regulation, "Nothing must be bought but that which is absolutely necessary for the maintenance of physical health and that which is bought must be of the plainest and most economical description." Should a child fall ill it must be attended by the parish doctor; should it die it must be buried by the parish. Finally, the wage earner must never be absent from his work for a single day.

If any of these conditions are broken the extra expenditure involved is met *and can only be met* by limiting the diet or, in other words, by sacrificing physical efficiency.[17]

Rowntree wrote this graphic passage to illustrate the conditions under which one must live at the "poverty line." By this he meant the income level which is just sufficient to maintain a family of normal size in a state of physical efficiency, provided that all resources are economically administered. It can be seen, however, that families living at the margin of poverty are in a very restricted and precarious position since any increase in expenditures, as in illness, or any decrease in income, such as loss of a few days' pay, will bring the family below the poverty line.

Rowntree was primarily interested in calculating the earnings needed to keep a family above the poverty line, but his comments are relevant to families in receipt of public assistance. Poverty is related to income rather than the source of that income. Thus it is quite possible for families in receipt of assistance in a community with high assistance standards not to be in a condition of poverty, whereas certain low-income families not in receipt of assistance, but living in a community with low assistance standards, are in a condition of poverty.

Health and Decency

A modest but considerably more adequate budget, more in keeping with what we would like to consider the "American standard of living," has been developed recently by the U.S. Bureau of Labor Statistics. This standard, first worked out in 1947, is based on certain minimum standards of nutrition, housing, clothing, health, etc., recommended by various national agencies, such as the Food and Nutrition Board of the National Research Council, the American Public Health Association, and

[17] Benjamin Seebohm Rowntree, *Poverty and Progress* (London: Longmans, 1941), p. 103.

the Federal Housing Administration. These recommendations were tested in the light of expenditures of a number of actual families who were studied over a period of years, particularly 1934–1936, 1941, and 1942. In the words of Ewan Clague, director of the Bureau of Labor Statistics, "It does not represent the 'ideal' budget or one based on a few people's notion of what workers should have; rather it is based on the kinds of goods and services workers' families in the United States actually select." [18]

The New York *Times,* on December 12, 1947, summarized the budget for a typical urban American family of four, consisting of father, mother, and two school-age children, as follows:

It furnishes a family caloric intake of about 3000 calories per person on quantities of food rather substantially below the average per capita consumption for the United States as a whole. . . . It provides six loaves of bread, twelve quarts of milk, twenty eggs, and one half pound of butter a week. Cheaper cuts of meat on week days make possible a chicken or roast on Sundays and a turkey on Thanksgiving. School lunch was not important enough volume-wise to be computed.

The rented dwelling has five rooms, including kitchen and bathroom, hot and cold running water, daylight and electric light in each room, and heat to 70 degrees. It is within walking distance of food stores and elementary schools. The wife does all the cooking, cleaning and laundry, uses an electric or gas stove, mechanical refrigerator, and washing machine. Those making the study did not consider a telephone essential but allowed an average of three local calls from a pay station a week.

The husband gets an overcoat once in seven years; the wife a coat once in four years. He gets a wool suit every two years, a light suit every three years; she four dresses a year. However the total clothes budget for the husband is more than for the wife. The wife, however, gets slightly more for medical care.

A ratio of seven autos for ten families was used in all cities except the three largest, New York, Chicago and Philadelphia—where a four-car-to-ten-families ratio was used.

[18] "The City Worker's Family Budget," quoted in William Haber and Wilber J. Cohen, *Readings in Social Security* (New York: Prentice-Hall, 1948), p. 25.

In medical care, the family was allowed four doctor's calls apiece a year, and a serious illness or accident about once in four years.

In miscellaneous items, families were allowed school books, one newspaper, one monthly magazine, tobacco, an occasional movie, some treats, gifts, church and club money . . . one bottle of beer a week for the parents and soft drinks for the children.

For the obvious reason of rapidly fluctuating price levels, monetary figures have been omitted. It is interesting to note that in December, 1947, an annual income of $3447 would have been needed by a "typical family" in order to achieve this standard of living.

Since the comfort and luxury budgets provide a standard of living higher than that enjoyed by most self-supporting families in the United States, not to mention those that are in receipt of public assistance, they need not concern us here.

SELECTED REFERENCES

Bureau of Public Assistance, Circular No. 17, *Money Payments to Recipients of Old-Age Assistance, Aid to Dependent Children and Aid to the Blind*, Washington: Federal Security Agency, 1944.

Bureau of Public Assistance Report No. 18, *Characteristics of State Public Assistance Plans Under the Social Security Act*, Washington: Federal Security Agency, 1953.

De Schweinitz, Karl, *England's Road to Social Security*, Philadelphia: University of Pennsylvania, 1943.

Dimond, Blanche, "The Basis for Adequate Standards of Assistance," *Public Welfare*, June, July, August, 1943.

Encyclopedia of the Social Sciences, New York: Macmillan, 1930, articles on "Dependency," "Poverty," "Family Budgets."

Haber, William, and Cohen, Wilber J., *Readings in Social Security*, New York: Prentice-Hall, 1948, No. 4, "City Worker's Family Budget," by Ewan Cleague, and No. 54, "Looking Ahead in Public Assistance," by G. E. Bigge.

Meriam, Lewis, *Relief and Social Security*, Washington: Brookings, 1946, chaps. 18, 19.

Proceedings of the National Conference of Social Work, Chicago, 1952, New York: Columbia University, "Economic Factors Affecting Family Living," by Clague, Ewan.

Ibid., Atlantic City, 1948, "Economic Programs for the American Standard of Living," by Rev. George C. Higgins, "The Content of Living as a Basis for a Standard of Living and Service," by Jane Hoey, and "How Adequate Should Assistance Standards Be?" by Val M. Keating.

Ibid., San Francisco, 1947, "The Social Services and the Maintenance of Optimum Standards of Living," by Donald S. Howard, and "The Philosophy and Use of Budget Standards," by Vocille M. Pratt.

Reed, Ellery F., "Family Income and Living Standards," *Public Welfare*, February, 1947.

Riley, Sarah, "How Adequate Should Assistance Be?" *Public Welfare*, July, 1948.

Perlman, Helen Harris, "Are We Creating Dependency?" *Illinois Public Aid*, July, 1951.

CHAPTER 7

Standards of Assistance

In terms of goods and services are we willing to underwrite less than food, clothing, shelter (including fuel, water, light, and cleaning supplies), personal care and medical care? Would we dare go so far as to consider as an essential a modest sum for recreation, reading and even a little bit for church contribution? Which of these basic items would anyone, even the guardians of the exchequer, classify as non-essential if he believes, as we profess to believe, that the assurance of the individual's welfare and dignity is the purpose and form of government? If we grant that these are the essentials for all, how do we translate their cost into dollars?

> —VAL M. KEATING, "How Adequate Should Public Assistance Be?" *Proceedings of the National Conference of Social Work,* 1948

THE ELEMENTS OF THE ASSISTANCE BUDGET

We now come to what is undoubtedly the central issue in public assistance administration—the development of standards to determine the amount of assistance needy individuals and families are to receive. How desperate must a person's economic plight be for him to get aid from his government? To what economic level should assistance raise him? Should the assistance grant be calculated to keep him below the "poverty line," on the theory that hunger is the best spur to self-support? Should the grant bring him just above the poverty line? Or should assistance enable economically unproductive persons to achieve a standard of living approaching health and decency? What relation should assistance standards bear to the general economic level of the community? Can they be used to raise the standard of living?

Even the National Resources Planning Board finds this a knotty problem:

Determination of the plane of living which should be assured is perhaps the most difficult practical question in the entire realm of public aid policy. We believe that the long run objective should be to provide a standard of living that is not too widely at variance from what we like to think of as the "American standard." Apart from the important humanitarian considerations, we believe, further, that the present international situation only increases the desirability of making it possible for all Americans to enjoy a way of life which they will value sufficiently to be prepared to defend.[1]

Although this statement points up the issue sharply, it is perhaps unfortunate that the phrase "enjoy a way of life" was used in connection with a discussion of assistance standards. Assistance is a grim necessity for those who receive it; no matter how adequate the standard, it can hardly make possible a "way of life" that anyone can "enjoy."

In 1949, the American Public Welfare Association issued a report on assistance standards. While stated in general terms, this report reveals the thinking of officials responsible for developing and operating assistance programs. It is reproduced here in its entirety: [2]

PUBLIC ASSISTANCE STANDARDS—A REPORT BY A COMMITTEE
OF THE AMERICAN PUBLIC WELFARE ASSOCIATION [3]

I. PHILOSOPHY AND PRINCIPLES OF PUBLIC ASSISTANCE

General Background

The declaration of human rights as approved by the United Na-

[1] *Security Work and Relief Policies* (Washington: National Resources Planning Board, 1933), p. 514.
[2] Mimeographed report, American Public Welfare Association (Chicago: 1949).
[3] This report of the Committee on Assistance Standards is the result of intensive work over a period of almost two years including eight meetings of the committee, and presentation of draft statements and discussion at regional and annual meetings of APWA. The committee acknowledges the constructive criticisms given by many persons who analyzed the report and helped to discuss and refine it.

tions General Assembly, December 10, 1948, for all people of the world declares in part:

> Everyone has the right to a standard of living adequate for the health and well-being of himself and of his family, including food, clothing, housing, and medical care and necessary social services, and the right to security in the event of unemployment, sickness, disability, widowhood, old age, or other lack of livelihood in circumstances beyond his control. . . . Article 25:1

In the United States certain rights of the individual have been established by Federal and State legislation as a recognition that it is in the public interest to provide income to those in the population who are temporarily or permanently unable to be self-supporting. The will to be financially independent, to be a producing member of the community, and to improve one's standard of living is a predominant characteristic of American society. This will can be weakened by inability to purchase the essentials of life, by prolonged inability to find work, or inability to contribute otherwise to community enterprise.

Citizens in our democratic society have a responsibility to develop the opportunities available to them and make their maximum contribution to themselves, their families and their communities. Primary emphasis, therefore, should be placed upon the development and maintenance of conditions under which workers and potential workers may secure for themselves and their dependents a standard of living essential to their own well-being and that of the community. To the extent that private and governmental efforts fail to assure opportunities for self-support, and to the extent that persons are unable to work, or for other reasons lack the essentials of life, government has a further responsibility to supply them or to see that they are supplied. This may include social insurances, so-called "social utilities," such as medical care, housing, school lunches, and public works; and public assistance programs. All of these programs are essential to the protection and the development of our human resources.

Role of Public Assistance

The social insurances and "social utilities" need to be extended so that their benefits will become available to large groups of persons not now included; and the level of insurance benefits should be increased to meet current living costs more adequately. Even when this is done the responsibility of government to meet the need for public assistance will continue because of special exigencies in the lives of individuals which are not adequately met by measures intended for large numbers of people on a mass basis. Public assistance is designed to complement the programs of other welfare agencies, and to supplement resources available to the individual. The term, "public assistance," as used in this report, includes not only the special categories for the aged, children, and the blind, but also assistance from public funds for all other needy persons.

Assistance should be readily available to all who meet the requirements of economic need without exclusion because of race, religion, political belief, citizenship, personal habits, residence or artificial classification of people into categories. Essential to the protection of the health and welfare of the individual and of the community is a comprehensive program of public assistance which makes it possible for everyone to secure a minimum standard of human decency and security.

The conditions of eligibility for public assistance should be a matter of public information. The right of eligible persons to assistance should be upheld by legislation and by administration. It should be clearly indicated to those applying for or receiving assistance, and to the public generally, that the right to assistance carries with it the responsibility for maximum self-support, maximum self-direction, and active participation in plans for rehabilitation.

Adequacy of Assistance Grants

Public assistance should be adequate to meet the cost of a minimum standard of living. Inadequate food, clothing, housing, medical care, and the like may impair the health of the individual and weaken his capacity for self-direction and self-support. Assistance grants should not be arbitrarily limited because the standard of living made possible by the grant exceeds that which families can achieve for themselves when all employable members are gainfully employed. Eligibility for public assistance and the amount of the assistance grant should be determined on the basis of objective standards which include all requirements necessary for health and decent living.

The failure of employment opportunities and certain wage levels to make possible an acceptable standard of living presents a serious social problem. Minimum wage laws, uninterrupted employment, and family allowances are better methods of achieving adequate family income than assistance. In the absence of full development of these measures and conditions, an inadequate family income should be supplemented by a public assistance grant. In families with children this has special importance so they may have the opportunity for normal growth and education leading to later self-support and useful citizenship.

Method of Payment

The assistance grant should be in the form of cash. In our present industrialized society persons are dependent on a money economy and wages. Unrestricted money payments permit recipients the greatest possible freedom in managing their own affairs, thus facilitating their maximum degree of rehabilitation and self-support. However, in the case of needs that are unpredictable and variable, such as medical care and nursing and housekeeping services, requirements may be met through cash payments or may be provided through direct services on either a salary or fee basis.

Related Services

Public assistance agencies have the responsibility for seeing that children and others incapable of caring for themselves have appropriate services made available to them, either through provision of such services or through referral to other agencies. Public funds can be conserved by early and adequate medical and social services. Necessary rehabilitative services should be provided by public assistance agencies or utilized as resources available from other community agencies in order that individuals may become wholly or partially self-supporting. A general referral and information service on available local, state and national welfare resources should be maintained by the assistance agency.

Equitable Application of Standards

Standards of assistance should be uniformly applied within states without personal discrimination, and should assure comparable levels of adequacy in the different political subdivisions.

Recipients of public assistance should be under no duress as a condition to the receipt of aid. Courts, health and other authorities exist in communities to prohibit action inimical to a community's well-being and to compel action required in the interests of the public good. Such instruments of social policy applicable to all persons regardless of economic status, rather than the withholding of public assistance, should be relied upon when required to assure standards of conduct demanded by the best interests of the community.

Appeal procedures should be established to assure equitable treatment of all public assistance applicants and recipients regardless of the type of aid needed.

Responsibility for Adequate Financing

Since the provision of funds to finance a public assistance program is a responsibility of legislative bodies, it is necessary that assistance agencies present to the public and to the legislature the facts on the reasons for economic dependency, the content and cost of a minimum standard of living, the number of persons in need, and the total appropriation required to finance the program adequately.

Methods of financing by levels of government should aim to prevent variations that would otherwise exist because of differences in fiscal capacity or revenue measures.

In spite of the best efforts of public officials to match anticipated obligations for a fiscal period with expected revenues, it sometimes happens that the funds appropriated fall short of the total cost of providing a minimum standard of living for all needy persons. There can be no satisfactory answer to such a situation other than additional appropriations.

II. LIVING REQUIREMENTS

Public welfare agencies should establish standards in terms of quantity and quality for estimating the living requirements for individuals, and standards for evaluating resources in order to determine the amount of assistance needed. The standards for living requirements should be translated into dollar values on the basis of current prices and expressed as cost schedules. These schedules should be reviewed at least once a year and adjusted to current prices. Standards should be uniform throughout the agency, and provision should be made for modifications under specified circumstances such as illness, infirmities of old age, and physical and mental handicaps.

In a standard of living there are certain items which are essential to all people all the time, and others which are essential under specified circumstances. The items of basic living requirements which should be considered in all family budgets and for which allowances at current prices should be made are: food, shelter, fuel, utilities, clothing, personal incidentals, and household supplies.

Food

Food should be adequate in the quantity and quality necessary to promote growth in children and maintain health in adults. The food cost schedule should be varied for age, sex, activity status, and geographic food patterns.

The United States Department of Agriculture provides food standards for three cost levels based on nutritive requirements determined by the National Research Council. The low-cost diet in the series meets all the nutritive requirements for the various age, sex, and activity groups. This standard, or a comparable adaptation, should be priced currently and the resulting cost schedule used as the basis for assistance food allowances.

Since specifications for pricing food items are based on "family size" packages the food allowances for one or two persons should be increased to allow for smaller size units and the purchase of more ready to eat items. Any decreases in the total food allowance for a family consisting of four or more persons should be based on a study, in the local community, of (1) the availability of larger units, and (2) the lower unit prices of large quantities of food if available. The extent of variations to be made for the size of household unit needs further scientific study.

Restaurant allowances should be established for one, two, or three meals a day for use in case of individuals lacking cooking facilities or persons physically unable to prepare their own meals. The meal allowance should be based upon the current local cost of purchasing such meals of a type to meet the nutrition standard.

Shelter [4]

Housing should be free from hazards to health and safety and in

[4] It is recognized that there is an acute and widespread shortage of good housing available at economical cost, and this fact has an important bearing on work with families applying for public assistance. The establishment of standards for shelter may appear theoretical since it is not possible in a large percentage of cases to relate the cost of shelter to a reasonable standard for this requirement.

In spite of the importance of factors affecting costs which are beyond the control of either the agency or the family, it has been considered worth while to define standards of shelter requirements which may be regarded as a minimum from the point of view of the assistance agency. The American Public Health Association through its Committee on the Hygiene of Housing has recently taken the lead in formulating specifications for healthful housing.

reasonably good repair, weather tight and dry. The number, size and arrangement of rooms should provide adequate space for performing all of the necessary activities of family life, with privacy of sleeping quarters for parents, adolescent children of each sex and aged individuals. There should be adequate heating and cooking facilities, and storage space for food, household equipment and clothing.

The need for shelter may be met by an allowance for rent or for carrying charges on a client-owned house or through a board and room allowance. The shelter cost should be based on prevailing rents and family size.

Fuel and Utilities

The cost schedule for fuel and utilities should be based upon the size of the house, the kind of heating equipment, and the climate. It should be adjusted to the current prices of each type of item used in heating, cooking, lighting, refrigeration, electricity for household equipment, water and refuse disposal. Any or all of these items may be included in the rent or the board and room allowance.

Clothing

The clothing cost schedule should be based on the current price of clothing sufficient in kind and amount to protect health, permit a desirable standard of cleanliness and warmth, and conform in general to the standards of the community of which the recipient is a part. The kind of clothing being worn by a majority of children in the local school must be taken into consideration in order that the child in a family receiving public assistance will not be conspicuous because of his clothing.

The allowances for clothing should vary according to age, sex, activity, and climate, and should be based on durable low cost quality. There should be included in the clothing allowance an amount for up-keep, cleaning and repairs.

Personal Incidentals

There are a number of incidental items needed by individuals which should be recognized and included regularly in the budget. The particular items vary with individuals. The amount of money that represents the allowance of the agency should be set on the basis of the cost of typical rather that comprehensive needs. Such items as haircuts, sewing materials, stamps, newspapers, stationery, carfares, toilet articles, first aid supplies, church contributions, and recreation should be given consideration.

Household Supplies

There are certain basic recurring needs for housekeeping supplies. These will vary according to the composition of the household. A household supplies cost schedule should be based on the current price of laundry, cleaning and toilet materials; replacement of such items as sheets, pillow cases, towels, light bulbs, dishes; and other household items regularly needed.

Items of Special Need

In many family situations there is need for special items of assistance. Items of special need may be regularly recurring or non-recurring depending upon the nature of the items and the circumstances and resources of the recipient.

The more common items of special need which should be considered in the budget under established specified circumstances and for which allowances at current prices should be made are:

therapeutic diets	housekeeping service
expenses incident to handicap	expenses incident to employ-
expenses incident to education	ment
telephone	household furnishings
medical and dental care	home repairs
laundry	nursery care
transportation	nursing care
	burial

III. RESOURCES

Since public assistance supplements resources available to the individual, standards for evaluating resources are just as essential as those for estimating living requirements. The public assistance agency should develop policies and procedures for the exploration, evaluation and application of all resources of the client. The grant should equal the difference between the estimated living requirements and the resources available to meet them, this difference being usually known as a budget deficit.

All income and other resources should be taken into account. However, only resources immediately available, significant in amount, and predictable should be applied against current living requirements.

Some resources, such as current income from any source, bank accounts, and savings bonds, are immediately available; others are potentially available and the applicant should be expected to develop them. Public assistance agencies should give applicants whatever help is essential to them in developing these potential resources.

Potentially available resources include real estate, stocks, insurance, contributions from relatives, benefits, and earnings from possible employment. Where cost of production is involved, net rather than gross income should represent the available resource. As a general rule, real and personal property, other than that neded to help meet current living requirements, should be converted into cash and used to reduce or eliminate—temporarily at least—the need for assistance.

In order that persons not be completely destitute in order to be eligible for public assistance, provision should be made for needy persons to retain a reasonable reserve as a safeguard against minor unpredictable needs and specific non-recurring items. It should not be required that real property used as a home be liquidated. Resources available on a voluntary basis from such sources as friends, relatives, churches, and private welfare agencies, may by mutual agreement be set aside for needs for which an assistance grant is not made.

Another potential resource is support from relatives. The extent of support to be sought by or on behalf of the applicant should depend on the degree of relationship, living expenses, income level, and unusual financial obligations.

Earnings from employment are a normal means of support for those able to work and available for employment and should be developed as any other potential resource.

Resources, like living requirements, should be reviewed as a whole. When total resources fall short of total living requirements when both are measured against the standards of the agency, then financial need has been established and the agency has a firm basis on which to make an assistance grant to meet the budget deficit of the individual or family.

Let us examine in greater detail the major items in the preceding report:

Method of Payment

Assistance in the form of cash is a rather recent innovation. There was some experimentation with cash payments in pre-Social Security Act programs of preferential assistance and unemployment relief, but it did not become widespread until the Social Security Act made it mandatory in order to receive federal reimbursement. Even today, many states with poorly developed programs of general assistance do not provide cash assistance.

The historic objection to cash relief arose from the belief that poverty and need were caused by incompetence, by sloth, intemperance, and thriftlessness. Cash relief, it was believed, would only aggravate the plight of the poor by making relief more palatable and by increasing their opportunities for misuse. "Misuse" applied not only to the more obvious forms of squandering money in strong drink, gambling, and the like but also to expenditures for such items as tobacco, beer, quality foods, and entertainment. In short, the poor could not be relied upon to use money intelligently, and it was thought inappropriate for tax funds to be used for frivolous and "unnecessary" purposes. Since relief was granted only in amounts sufficient to prevent the most dire want, any expenditures for items such as those mentioned above were looked upon as an indication that the needy family was depriving itself of essentials, or that it had an undisclosed source of income. In consequence, relief was provided "in kind," that is, in the form of supplies or by vouchers which could be redeemed at designated stores for certain specified items.

Despite some initial resistance to providing assistance in cash, experience has dissipated the fear that it would result in wholesale squandering of public funds. It was found that, by and large, needy people are as capable of handling money as the general run of self-supporting people. To be sure, most public assistance case loads include a few people who run into difficulties in handling cash. In some instances, they are so deteriorated and disorganized as to require institutionalization; in other instances, skilled guidance and supervision may help them overcome their difficulties. Sometimes, it may be necessary to withdraw cash assistance temporarily or permanently and substitute voucher relief or make the cash payments to some responsible relative in behalf of the recipient.

Withdrawal of cash assistance means the loss of federal reimbursement. Some assistance agencies may be more concerned about what this means in terms of state and local costs than with what the best interests of the needy person require, and may therefore be reluctant to authorize voucher relief. Sometimes, moreover, individual workers are overly hopeful that through their guidance irresponsible recipients may be enabled to grow in maturity and stability; hence they postpone recommending transfer to voucher relief—with disastrous results.

A somewhat similar problem arises when old-age assistance recipients require institutional care. If they can enter a private home for the aged, or a public or private medical institution, they may retain their OAA grant. Most of the grant is applied toward the cost of their maintenance. But if they enter a public home, the grant must be withdrawn and they become a full local charge. In some communities the needs of the aged person are outweighed by the financial considerations—reluctance to lose state and federal reimbursement—and the aged person may be retained on OAA rather than transferred to a public home, even though he is in need of congregate care.

The chief advantages of cash assistance may be summarized as follows: It removes the stigma of untrustworthiness from the recipient; it permits him greater freedom in shopping and does not reveal his status as a dependent person; it eliminates the danger (and temptation) of the occasional dishonest store-keeper's marking up goods sold to recipients on voucher relief, or discounting vouchers to enable recipients to secure "forbidden" items. Finally, it simplifies the whole clerical and accounting procedure of the assistance agency.

The Bureau of Public Assistance has interpreted the term "money payment" to mean that "payments must be in cash, checks, or warrants immediately redeemable at par, and that the payments must be made to the grantee or his legal guardian at regular intervals *with no restriction on the use of the funds by the individual.*" [5]

The "unrestricted grant" requirement means that, while the

[5] Social Security Administration, *Guide to Public Assistance Administration,* Bureau of Public Assistance Circular No. 9 (Washington: Government Printing Office, 1940), p. 1.

assistance agency computes the amount of the individual grant by referring to a budget schedule based upon the amount and cost of various items of consumption, the recipient is not obliged to spend his grant in accordance with this schedule. Thus, if a grant includes a certain amount for clothing, but the recipient prefers to use it for some other purpose, such as additional food or household supplies, the agency cannot exact conformance by threatening to withhold from his next check an amount equivalent to that which he failed to spend for the purpose designated by the agency. The presumption is that the recipient is in a better position than anyone else to decide the most useful way his grant should be spent. Naturally, if recipients, either through mismanagement or because of some emergency, run short of funds before their next grant is due and request supplementary assistance, the assistance agency is obligated to look into the situation carefully and institute controls to see that such difficulties are not repeated.

In 1950 the "unrestricted grant" provision of the Social Security Act was modified to permit direct payments by assistance agencies to medical practitioners and other suppliers of medical service. Thus, it is no longer necessary (in order to obtain federal reimbursement) for assistance agencies to pay for hospital charges, physicians' home visits, medicines, etc., by making additional payments to recipients. These charges may now be paid directly. Medical expenses are not regularly recurring items and often run into large sums. Since even among self-supporting people there seems to be a strong temptation to delay paying such bills, welfare officials and the medical profession favor this direct method of payment. It is interesting to note that the medical profession, although strongly disapproving of any form of governmentally administered prepaid medical care, nevertheless prefers reimbursement directly by the assistance agency rather than by the recipient-patient.

Food

Of all consumption items that make up a budget, food requirements are probably the least difficult to determine. The science of nutrition has reached the point where it is now possible to calculate individual requirements, in accordance with age, sex, type of work, and condition of health, for the basic food elements such as fats, proteins, carbohydrates, minerals, and vitamins. Various kinds of food have been analyzed to determine their value in terms of these elements. Thus, it is now possible for nutritionists to work out fairly accurate and satisfactory low-cost diets for individuals in varying circumstances. Since these food elements can be found in varying quantities and combinations in different kinds of food, considerable leeway is possible in determining what is needed for a well-balanced diet. On the basis of price studies made in different parts of the country and in different seasons, dietary requirements can be translated into monetary terms so that the cost of satisfactory nutrition can be calculated with a high degree of accuracy.

Even though the cost of such diets can be worked out in terms of current prices, the provision of an adequate food allowance is not without its problems. Lewis Meriam of the Brookings Institution raises the following points:

From the standpoint of the individual, a satisfactory low-cost diet may be unsatisfactory for three principal reasons: (1) it does not appeal to the individual's food tastes and habits; (2) it may be lacking in variety; and (3) it may require more time and trouble in preparation than the individual may care to expend. The individual left to follow his own tastes and practices would spend far more for food, although as a result of the additional expenditure he might get no greater nutritional value. In fact, in some instances he might get lower nutritional value, in spite of the additional expenditure.

Thus an issue arises as to whether an individual or a family is in need for food if resources are available to purchase a scientifically adequate low-cost diet. Is the desire for a more expensive diet a need that calls for payment of benefits from public funds? [6]

The question with which the above quotation concludes seems gratuitous. The answer is obviously "no" even though the food schedule of the assistance agency might allow some slight margin.

[6] Lewis Meriam, *Relief and Social Security* (Washington: Brookings, 1946), p. 573.

Of course, it is probably true that an extremely low-cost "scientifically adequate" diet can be developed, but it would also probably have to be administered under laboratory conditions.

The problem lies not so much in the willingness or unwillingness of people to subsist on a "scientifically adequate" low-cost diet as in their ability to do so. The ability to prepare reasonably palatable and varied meals over an extended period demands not only considerable intelligence and marketing and culinary skill but also great strength of will. These qualities are probably to be found among the needy in the same proportion as in the general run of the populace. It is the needy, however, with no margin of income, who are put to the test. The trained home economist can manage on a limited budget with, perhaps, something left over, whereas the average housewife, even one who prides herself on her domestic arts, will fail.

These remarks must not be construed as a plea for indulgence, but rather for some leeway to be allowed in computing low-cost diets, in recognition of the difficulties that most persons would have in managing on them. Lifetime food preferences cannot be changed overnight, nor can long-established patterns of shopping for and preparing food be adapted easily to the exigencies of a reduced income. Where there are young children, the problem is accentuated since they cannot be expected to understand the fact of their dependency and adapt their behavior accordingly. Limited budgets, moreover, do not permit quantity purchases, on which there is likely to be some saving, nor do low-cost budgets make provision for carfare so that the housewife can search for bargains. If the needy person is aged or suffering from physical handicaps which restrict movement and adaptability, his management problem is also aggravated. Help should be available to recipients who are having difficulties in managing their grants, but even if the assistance agency has a staff of home economists, it is questionable whether they will have the time to do the kind of reëducation job that is needed. It is also doubtful whether the average public assistance worker can be of much help because of lack of specialized training or even familiarity with the problems of managing a home.

Shelter

The computation of a shelter allowance is much more difficult than that for food. Should the shelter allowance be based on the size of the family or on the number of rooms? Should it be based on the type of facilities provided (i.e., plumbing, heating, lighting, etc.) or on the actual rental? In the case of homeownership, should the actual amount for taxes and other carrying charges be allowed—even though the dwelling has a high assessed valuation? Such questions arise because of lack of flexibility in housing. To quote Meriam again:

Since housing is relatively permanent, it does not respond quickly to changes in demand. Changes in the economic activity of the community may take place that create either a surplus or a shortage of houses. Rents are quickly responsive to such changes. There may be wide differences in rents for comparable accommodations between two different communities or at different periods in the same community. The newcomer to a crowded community may find it necessary to pay higher rent than fellow workers who have the advantage of arrangements made in an earlier period. Circumstances may force him to pay more rent and occupy better quarters than he would have taken if he had a wider choice or if he could have selected a house as he would food or clothing. Thus one cannot say what a family should pay for rent except on the basis of averages which may be entirely inapplicable in the face of existing housing in the community where the family lives.[7]

Departing a moment from the problem presented by the type of housing that might actually be available, let us consider the kind of shelter that an assistance agency, through its shelter allowance, ought to provide. Meriam agrees that such a dwelling should provide protection from the elements, suitable sanitary facilities, adequate light and ventilation, and sufficient space and privacy for decent living. He makes no mention of such specific items as private toilet and bathing facilities, hot and cold running water, electricity, central heating, or mechanical refrigeration; nor does the APWA report on assistance standards mention them.

The fact is that the extent to which such conveniences are used,

[7] *Ibid.*, p. 181.

or even thought necessary, varies with different regions. What a particular rural district considers an adequate minimum standard for self-supporting people might be well below the minimum standard for a metropolitan area. Perhaps, in such instances, the community has not been conditioned to the desirability of modern conveniences; perhaps the expense of providing them, in areas where cheap municipal services are not available, is more than many rural dwellers care to undertake; perhaps they prefer to save their money, or to spend it for what are to them more important purposes—such as new farm equipment. Assistance standards must be related to general community standards. It follows that, in a particular state, city dwellers may receive a shelter allowance which will permit them to enjoy conveniences that may not be available to some rural recipients.

Clothing

The determination of the clothing schedule presents problems of a somewhat different nature. Food and shelter represent regularly recurring charges, whereas there are wide variations in the need for different items of apparel. Thus, an overcoat will last much longer than an undershirt; children's garments will wear out much sooner than those of adults. As in the case of shelter, climatic differences affect the size of the clothing allowance. The monthly or bimonthly clothing allowance does not represent the clothing needs for that period; rather it is prorated allowance for clothing for a year, or possibly several years. It is not uncommon to provide a regular clothing allowance which does not cover total clothing needs—the more expensive items such as overcoats, wool suits, and the like being provided on an "as needed" basis, through special supplementary grants—because of the temptation to spend the small regular clothing allowance for other purposes, instead of letting it accumulate so as to have enough money to purchase some more expensive garment.

Both Dr. Meriam and the APWA are in agreement that clothing not only provides protection against the elements but also has a psychological function. Clothing, therefore, should conform to the general pattern of the community, so that the recipient not only will not be conspicuous but will be able to take some pride in his personal appearance.

Personal Incidentals

One of the most controversial items in the assistance budget is "personal incidentals." As can be seen from the APWA report, this term includes a large number of subitems. Personal needs of the recipient (apart from the basic items of food, shelter, etc.) cover a wider range of possible expenditures than we can conveniently discuss here. We will consider, therefore, only those items about which there has been some question.

Dr. Meriam does not consider the whole range of personal incidentals but confines himself to a discussion of expenditures for recreation. Although he concedes that a modest provision for recreation should probably be allowed, especially in the case of children, in characteristic fashion he begins his discussion by calling attention to abuses—especially to expenditures for alcoholic beverages, gambling, and the ownership, maintenance, and operation of automobiles. "Although they may not constitute a heavy item in the average budget of low-income families," he points out, "exceptional families may give a high priority to expenditures of this nature, so high a priority that funds are not available for more essential purposes." [8] Since abuses are admittedly exceptional, it would seem sensible to deal with them on an individual basis rather than to adopt restrictive practices that penalize all recipients. Let us consider the question from a more positive viewpoint.

The aphorism that "man does not live by bread alone" applies even to recipients of public assistance. When a person is obliged to seek assistance from the state, he does not thereby withdraw from normal contacts with relatives and friends, or from community activities—nor should he be expected to do so. His affairs, of necessity, will be circumscribed, but if he is to retain his self-respect, his initiative, and his physical and mental health, he must be enabled to keep some semblance of his former way of life. Outdoor relief under the poor law pauperized those it was supposed to help, since, even with the most determined and skillful

[8] *Ibid.*, p. 577.

management, they never received enough help so that they could rise above the margin of bare existence. Of necessity, they formed a class apart, for, unless they supplemented their grant surreptitiously, they were unable to take part in the life of the community. They tended to develop a subculture based upon deprivation, deceit, and despair. Developments in geriatrics, child psychology, and juvenile delinquency underscore the necessity for individuals to have opportunities to participate in the life of the community if they are to respect, and make effective use of, the society of which they are a part.

Whether or not the assistance budget includes an allowance for personal incidentals, ways will be found to purchase items such as newspapers, haircuts, tobacco, etc., even though it means going on short rations. It will be a rare parent who will not deny himself so that his children may have a little pocket money for candy, comic books, or an occasional movie. If not carried to excess, this diversion of funds is probably a wholesome sign, even though it aggravates an already difficult situation.

A recent controversy reflects the difficulty of formulating acceptable standards for personal incidentals: In the latter part of 1949, the New York City Department of Welfare reduced its food schedules to conform with the decline in food prices. This reduction touched off a heated discussion in which the City Council, the local chapter of the American Association of Social Workers, and various private social agencies became involved. The legitimacy of the percentage drop in the food schedule was not challenged, although it was pointed out that the downward revision of the allowance followed much more promptly the decline in prices than had the last upward revision followed increases in prices. The major objection to the reduction was that, while the food allowance was reasonably adequate, the overall budget was inadequate because it failed to make provision for certain needs—especially in the area of personal incidentals. It was argued, therefore, that there should be no reduction in individual grants.

The chairman of the New York State Board of Social Welfare took exception to these arguments and at the midwinter meeting of the State Public Welfare Association in Albany in February, 1950, delivered an address in which he analyzed the significance of an allowance for cigarettes, insurance, medicine chest supplies, and church contributions in the assistance budget.[9] He pointed out that, in the case of cigarettes, it would be impossible to differentiate between smokers and non-smokers and hence every adult would be entitled to an allowance for cigarettes. To supply each potential smoker with funds to buy a half a pack a day would cost $10,000,000 a year! With respect to church contributions, he said that he had been assured by leaders of the three great religious faiths that no one would be unwelcome in church or synagogue simply because he could not make a donation. He further questioned the spiritual significance of church contributions made, not at the expense of the ostensible donor, but at the expense of the taxpayer. Finally, such allowances would have to be made to all recipients, since there would be no way to distinguish the churchgoer from the non-churchgoer.

There is no doubt that if personal expenditures are broken down into a large number of subitems with a specific amount assigned to each one the total allowance for personal incidentals could reach staggering proportions. It must be noted, however, that the APWA committee on assistance standards does not recommend such a detailed breakdown. It says, with respect to personal incidentals, "The amount of money that represents the allowance of the agency should be set on the basis of typical rather than comprehensive needs." Thus, the item for personal incidentals should be large enough to permit some choice on the part of the recipient. A recipient who has strong church ties may then satisfy his desire to make an offering by cutting down on cigarettes or some other expenditure; the recipient who sets great store by his personal appearance may forgo his newspaper so that he can have some extra money to apply toward his grooming. Even though provision cannot be made for every possible expenditure, there will be some margin, however slight, within which the needy person can maintain his individuality.

[9] Henry Root Stern, in an address to the New York State Public Welfare Association, Albany, 1950.

It is ironic that this controversy arose in New York State, where overall assistance standards are superior to those in any other state.

The Dilemma of Public Assistance

In the attempt to develop a scientifically accurate and socially desirable standard of assistance, legislators, public welfare officials, and social economists are confronted with the question: Should public assistance be used to underwrite a minimum standard of living for the total population? At first glance we may wish to answer this question in the affirmative, but further analysis is likely to create some doubts. Government, through its agencies of public assistance, has definite responsibility for helping those persons who, for one reason or another, cannot work and support themselves and their natural dependents. But does it follow that public assistance should be used to supplement the earnings of fully employed workers when economic factors create a wide disparity between wage scales and the price level? Public assistance supplementary grants are not satisfactory substitutes for a living wage. Assuming, therefore, that enough essential goods and services are being produced, more fundamental economic readjustments are called for. The dilemma arises from the fact that, although need should be relieved where found, regardless of the cause, in so doing public assistance agencies may be perpetuating substandard wages.[10] The reader need only be reminded of the "allowance in support of wages" scheme in England which depressed wages so that laborers and their families in increasing numbers were maintained on a minimum standard at a rapidly increasing cost to the public treasury.

Assistance standards cannot be too far out of line with the prevailing standard of living in the community or region. In these days of rising prices, an acute problem for welfare administrators is the fact that, as they increase the dollar amounts of the grants to meet increased costs of living, not only is the cost of maintain-

[10] See Val M. Keating, "How Adequate Should Assistance Standards Be?" *Proceedings of the National Conference of Social Work* (New York: Columbia University, 1948), pp. 302–309.

ing current recipients greatly increased, but thousands of additional persons become eligible for supplementation. Moreover, in view of the wide disparity between standards of general assistance and the federally reimbursed categories in many localities, recipients in the latter categories may be better off than, or at least as well off as, "self-supporting members" of the community.

DETERMINING THE SIZE OF THE GRANT

The legal mandate to provide public assistance to needy persons will be found in the statutes of the several states and territories. In the great majority of cases, however, the *standard* of assistance is implied rather than fixed by law. A review of the assistance plans of the various states [11] reveals that they may be classified into three groups: those which refer to need in general terms, those which set maximum amounts, and those which set minimum amounts. The states which set legal maximum or minimum limits generally confine these restrictions to OAA and AB. The standards for ADC are stated generally as in the first group of states.[12]

Group I. Forty-two states and territories fall into this group. While there is some variation in the legal terminology of the statutory provisions, they tend to conform to the following pattern:

Has insufficient income and resources to provide a minimum subsistence level of living compatible with decency and health as defined by the Department. (Arkansas)

Has insufficient means to support self. (Connecticut)

Has been deprived of the essentials of life. (Delaware)

Has insufficient income to provide a reasonable subsistence compatible with decency and health. (Illinois)

Has insufficient income and available resources to provide the budgetary requirements established by the State Department. (New Jersey)

[11] Social Security Board, *Characteristics of State Public Assistance Plans Under the Social Security Act,* Bureau of Public Assistance, Report No. 18 (Washington: Federal Security Agency, 1953).

[12] Standards for Aid to the Permanently and Totally Disabled are usually similar to OAA.

Unable to support self, in whole or in part, and without other
means or sources of income by which he can be maintained.
(New York)

Under these provisions, the actual standards of assistance are
developed by the state agency or, in states where there is local
administration, by the local agency. There are, naturally, wide
differences in the interpretation of such terms as "health and
decency," "unable to support self," and even "essentials of life."
Regardless of the standards, moreover, the actual grants depend
upon the funds authorized by appropriating bodies. Many states
in this group have implied maxima in that they will not provide
grants in amounts greater than that necessary to secure the full
federal contribution.[13]

Group II.   There are only two states in this group. Their OAA
provisions are as follows:

$100 maximum amount for assistance plus other income if in the
household with self-supporting relatives; $110 if not in house-
hold with self-supporting relatives; need below maxima determined by budgetary method. (Arizona)

$75 statutory amount for "basic maintenance" with special needs
as related to circumstances included above statutory amount.
Statewide standard supports statutory amount for basic maintenance. (California)

Group III.   Seven states are in this group—all setting minimum
standards for OAA, only two setting such standards for AB, and
none for ADC. Typical OAA provisions are as follows:

Has insufficient income to meet need as determined by State Department; $45 statutory minimum for assistance plus income.
(Colorado)

Has insufficient income or other resources to maintain a content
of living compatible with health and decency. Amount of payment determined by budgetary method but monthly income,

[13] For example, in OAA the present maximum federal contribution is $35
on a monthly grant of $55. Any amount over this figure must be financed
out of state or state and local funds.

including assistance payment, cannot be less, for persons living within a family group (defined as three or more), than $30 for each recipient, $50 for brother and sister, plus $15 for each additional brother and sister; and for persons living apart from family group, $40 for one recipient, $65 for married couples or brother and sister. (Massachusetts)

Income plus assistance must not be less than the statutory amount of $60 for "basic maintenance," with special needs as related to circumstances included in the above statutory amount. (Washington)

Regardless of the statutory provisions, the usual method of determining the extent of an individual's need is through the "budget deficit" method. Under this method, need is measured with reference to a list of consumption items, to which the agency allocates specific amounts of money in accordance with its budgetary standard. The total amount of these items represents the need of the individual or family group. The amount of assistance will equal the deficit between this amount and whatever resources are available.

This method of calculating the grant has many advantages. Its very detail serves to keep the adequacy of the budget in sharp focus. How many items are allowed? What do these items include? How realistic are the amounts allocated to each item in relation to price levels? The effect upon the total budget schedule of changes in the general level of prices, or of fluctuations as between the cost of various items, can be easily determined.

Another advantage is that it permits a considerable degree of individualization. Thus, the amount allowed for food or clothing may be varied according to age, sex, and degree of activity. The allowance may also be adjusted according to the size of the family unit, thereby taking into consideration the fact that the needs of smaller family units are proportionately more expensive.

A final advantage of this method is its high degree of flexibility. Since the standard of assistance is derived from policy rather than law, it is relatively easy to make adjustments in the budget schedule to take into consideration changing conditions.

The budget deficit method, however, has certain disadvantages.

Its very complexity makes it practically impossible for a potential applicant to anticipate just how much assistance he would be entitled to receive. It is, moreover, cumbersome to work with. The initial calculations, as well as the innumerable minor adjustments that must subsequently be made (which often do not alter the total budget), are wasteful of time and productive of error.

States which have introduced minimum dollar limits into their statutes are attempting to set a floor below which no one will be permitted to fall. The important question with respect to statutory minimum or maximum limits is the manner in which they have been determined. Have these figures been "picked out of a hat" by the legislature or by an administrator, or are they based on sound budgetary studies which reflect typical needs? In the latter case, if provision is made for additional grants in instances of special need, and if the legislature is disposed to adjust the statutory limits to changing living costs, this method retains the principal advantages of the budget deficit system while eliminating most of its disadvantages.

We have already referred to the variations in average grants of assistance between states within the same category of assistance, and the variations within a given state between different categories of assistance. In the first instance, variations may be due, to a limited extent, to differences in the cost of living and in willingness to provide adequate assistance. In the main, however, these variations are the result of differences in financial capacity. The wealthier states can provide larger grants not only because their financial resources are greater but also because relative need tends to be less. The wealthier states are industrial states in which more people are protected from income loss by social insurance; consequently, they have to provide public assistance for proportionately fewer people. In the second instance, variations between categories is, to a great extent, a reflection of the national legislature's unwillingness to establish equitable reimbursement formulas for all categories. The more insistent demands of the aged, moreover, find expression in higher grants for OAA in many states —even above the federal reimbursement formula.

A graphic illustration of the inequities of present assistance standards is found in a study made a few years ago by the Indiana State Department of Public Welfare.[14] This department developed a hypothetical application of old-age assistance, which it submitted to four OAA districts in each of the forty-eight states and the District of Columbia with a request that a determination be made as to whether or not a person in these circumstances would be eligible for assistance according to the agency's standard of assistance. The facts in this test case were as follows:

An aged man lives with his son and daughter-in-law. The son has earnings of $200 a month, including an admitted surplus of $5 a month for himself and wife, in addition to $5 a month savings. The applicant can earn $5 a month from odd jobs in addition to the produce from his garden, valued at $1 a month.

Of the 125 agencies in 44 states and the District of Columbia that replied, 57 would have denied assistance. In nine states the application would have been accepted in some districts and denied in others. In the agencies that would have accepted this application there were wide variations in the amount of assistance that would be granted.

Some states, because of either inability or unwillingness, have very low standards of assistance; other states have a fairly reasonable standard but because of limited appropriations grant only a percentage of the budget. There is this to be said for the latter method: it emphasizes the discrepancy between what the state considers a minimum standard and what it actually provides for needy persons.

It is, perhaps, too strong to say that assistance depends not so much upon what a person needs as upon where he lives, yet geography plays a very important part in determining the kind of help he receives. It is doubtful whether uniform standards of assistance can be achieved by anything short of a federally administered program. Nevertheless, it should be possible to achieve greater equity, while avoiding the dangers of a monolithic, centralized federal program, if means can be developed to deal with the following points:

[14] Virgil Sheppard, "Standards for Old Age Assistance," *Public Welfare in Indiana,* February, 1943.

Uniform reimbursement formulas for all categories of assistance under the Social Security Act.

More adequate financing of general assistance. Although federal participation in the financing of this program is one solution, it is not so much the lack of federal financial participation that has created the problem as lack of state financial participation. In theory, substantial federal reimbursement of assistance costs of the other categories should enable the states to develop stronger general assistance programs.

Additional financial assistance to states in which a wide gap between needs and resources can be demonstrated. The difficulties inherent in working out such a plan were touched upon in an earlier chapter.

A conviction about the necessity for conserving human resources. Financial considerations will naturally limit what some states can do about helping the needy, but if the people of a state look upon the needy with ill-disguised contempt, if they fail to recognize that the well-being of dependent groups is related to the economic and social well-being of the total community, they will be unwilling to provide even that minimal assistance which they could afford.

SELECTED REFERENCES

See list at end of Chapter 6.

CHAPTER 8

Client Resources

Public assistance is intended to supplement rather than replace continuing income and resources. The lack of income or resources to meet requirements, therefore, becomes the determining factor in establishing need. Income and resources, whether in cash or in kind, should be considered in establishing that need exists and in determining the amount of assistance granted.

—*Manual of Public Assistance,* State of Iowa

THE MEANS TEST

Regardless of budgetary standards, assistance grants will bear some relation to the resources of the applicant and the way in which such resources are evaluated. By resources is meant anything possessed by the needy person that represents income or its equivalent, actually at hand or immediately available. Thus, it may mean earnings, property, savings of various kinds, help from relatives or friends—almost anything which might contribute to his maintenance and which might be given monetary value.

The primary function of the public assistance worker is to determine the extent of the applicant's or recipient's need by a process of investigating, verifying, and evaluating his resources. Historically, this process has been known as the "means test" and, apart from the condition of economic want itself, is probably the most distasteful aspect of the needy person's dealing with the assistance agency.

Lewis Meriam, in his trenchant criticism of the entire American social security system, develops the thesis that elaborate and costly programs of social insurance have been established "to relieve the recipients of the embarrassment and humiliation of the means test." He suggests that needy persons dislike the means test because they are reluctant to face the fact of their dependence upon the taxpayer for their support. They find social insurance more acceptable, because the fact that a substantial portion of the average insurance benefit must be paid by the general taxpayer is less obvious, and because the conditions under which the benefit is received are less restrictive than in the case of assistance. Dr. Meriam contends that social insurance is both uneconomic and unnecessary—uneconomic because it is much more costly than public assistance (". . . It costs more to provide each person with a minimum of subsistence regardless of his need than to give a person in need only such sums as may be necessary in addition to what he already has to bring his total resources to a minimum of subsistence.") [1] and unnecessary because the means test needn't be painful to undergo if it is only administered properly. Thus: "The means test is to many persons anathema. Almost anything, except the total neglect of need, is better than a means test. The explanation of this antipathy lies at least in part in the fact that the means test was an essential element in a system cursed with many other defects. To it were attributed faults that on analysis appear to have resulted from other features of law or practice." [2]

This observation seems overly optimistic. To be sure, there is a vast difference between a means test administered in the begrudging, suspicious, contemptuous manner characteristic of traditional poor relief and a means test administered with the sensitivity, tact, and warmth characteristic of the best professional practice. Nevertheless, no matter how humane the method, it cannot be made palatable. The means test is an enforced inquiry into personal affairs which the individual would normally prefer to keep to himself were he free to do so. Even at best, it implies a measure of control over the scope of choice and activity of the person who must submit to it in order to receive help.

[1] Lewis Meriam, *Relief and Social Security* (Washington: Brookings, 1946), p. 564.
[2] *Ibid.*, p. 593. See chaps. 18, 20, 33, and 34 in this book for a more detailed treatment of Professor Meriam's views.

Sometimes an attempt is made to draw a parallel between the means test and the kind of financial investigation a businessman must undergo in negotiating a bank loan. There is this distinction, however; whereas a bank loan is an indication that the lender has confidence in the probity, competence, and hopeful prospects of the borrower, the assistance grant is an indication that the recipient is without any immediate economic prospects—is, in fact, helpless and on the verge of desperation. It is difficult enough for a person to accept the fact of his dependency, no matter how understandable the cause, and it is made more painful by the necessity of proving one's helplessness in order that public aid can be justified.

The means test, however, is an essential element in public assistance. Regardless of the way in which the state extends financial help, if the means test is absent it is not public assistance. In a democratic society, a fundamental assumption is that the state must have regard for the feelings of those whom it has been created to serve, and this includes even those who are dependent upon the state for their basic needs. It follows, then, that the means test must be conducted with thoroughness and yet with an understanding of its painful nature so that those who must submit to it are not needlessly hurt.

Resource policy is as essential to the means test as the latter is to public assistance. Without some sort of resource policy there would be no way of determining how much help a needy person should get. Nevertheless, the development of principles and methods with respect to the treatment of resources is relatively recent. Although treatises on the investigation of need may be traced to the Middle Ages, the traditional methods of administering relief reflected a distrust of such investigations. In the Middle Ages they were thought to be inconsistent with the practice of charity, while, in later periods, there was doubt whether such investigations could actually reveal the true circumstances of those who asked for help. We have noted the great reliance that was placed on the workhouse test as the most effective means of determining need. Outdoor relief was not favored and, when granted, was generally for emergency periods and was predicated upon the taking of the "pauper's oath," which was supplemented by whatever general knowledge of the applicant the poormaster could glean from his familiarity with the community. Though there were exceptions, the prevailing policy, often required by statute, was that only paupers were eligible for help—that is, one had to be destitute of resources. If a needy person had resources, no matter how meager, he was required to exhaust them before receiving help.[3] Two developments were necessary before public assistance could replace poor relief: one was the development of a budgetary standard of assistance which took into consideration the kind and quantity of basic human needs translated into monetary terms, and the other was the development of standards for evaluating resources.

The variations in resource policy and practice are too numerous for us to present a clear picture of what is done in the United States as a whole. With a few minor exceptions, the five assistance categories are found in all fifty-three states and territories. Each program in each state has its own plan, which may differ with respect to resource policy from the other programs. Many states, moreover, allow considerable discretionary power to local administrative units. In spite of these variations, the underlying issues are similar, and policies, while differing in detail, are related to a common objective. If we analyze some of these issues, illustrating the problems that arise in actual practice, the reader should be able to formulate a point of view which will be useful in the subsequent evaluation of resource policy in given agencies.

For the purpose of analysis, resources may be grouped under five headings: (1) income from work, (2) income, or its equivalent, from real property, (3) support from relatives, (4) savings, and (5) other resources. We will consider each in turn.

INCOME FROM WORK

The major premise upon which eligibility for public assistance rests may be stated thus: The applicant or recipient is not working, or is not earning enough from work to support himself and

[3] See Edith Abbott, *Public Assistance* (Chicago: University of Chicago, 1940), Part I, sec. 3, pp. 107–112, case of Coffeen v. Town of Preble.

his natural dependents at a minimum level established by the assistance agency. If he is not working but is physically able to do so, he must demonstrate his willingness to accept suitable employment. A corollary is that, if he is not employable by reason of health or lack of appropriate skill, he must be willing to correct this condition. We shall see that the terms "employable" and "suitable work" have undergone considerable modification in recent years.

It follows from this that the recipient of public assistance has the obligation of keeping the agency informed as to income from any source; conversely, the agency has the responsibility of keeping a continuous check on the earnings of recipients and on their efforts to become self-maintaining. All income from work must be deducted from the budget, but not until the latter has been adjusted to cover expenses incidental to employment. Agency practice differs with regard to the number of items that may be allowed for this purpose; they may include increased food and clothing allowance for the employed person, carfare and lunch money, and an allowance for tools and union dues.

Employability

It is far easier to develop policies concerning the obligations of employable recipients than it is to determine who is employable. Employability is based upon a number of interrelated factors such as physical condition, emotional and temperamental qualities, mental capacity, training, and the personnel policies of employers. It is unrealistic to think of employability solely in terms of physical capacity. A person is never just "employable"; rather, he is employable in relation to specific jobs.

A and B are both suffering from the same ailment, which, while it requires treatment and impairs physical efficiency, does not prevent them from working. A's experience and training have been in work of a sedentary nature. If there were openings in his line of work or a related one his illness would not prevent him from taking employment. B, on the other hand, has always worked as a manual laborer. His physical condition prevents him from continuing in his customary occupation, and he lacks the skill (and, perhaps, the learning ability) to secure employment of a kind that his health would permit him to undertake. Whether or not either of these two men is employable depends upon his skill in relation to the kind of work that is available.

C is in good health and is highly skilled, but technological changes have eliminated the need for his special abilities. If C is young, and has the ability (and opportunity) to learn a new skill, he may eventually earn even more than before. But if he is older and finds it difficult to adapt himself to new demands, he may find it impossible to get work. At best he may secure a much lower-paid job. D is elderly but in excellent health and has retained his skill. Even though there are openings for workers with his skill, he may be unable to get work because of arbitrary age restrictions.

F is in good health and is a highly skilled worker. His work history reveals, however, a long record of accidents, illnesses, and disputes with fellow workers or supervisors so that there have been numerous resignations or dismissals after relatively short periods of employment. What of this man's employability? Can he be said to be employable except in times of labor shortage?

G is in good health but lacks training. His mental capacity is so limited that he can undertake work of only the simplest kind and has difficulty doing that. If there is any excess in the labor supply, G will be the last to be hired and the first to be fired.

There are many others in this lexicon: H, who has never done anything but housework, but now, being widowed, must try to find a job; I, whose work history is punctuated by a succession of illnesses, real or fancied; J, who is physically handicapped; K, who, in addition to being unskilled, belongs to a minority group against which there is much discrimination. These thumbnail sketches, while oversimplified, suggest, perhaps, that when we hear about the number of employable persons receiving public assistance we must subject such statements to several qualifications.[4]

[4] See Elizabeth Hoffman, "How Employable Are Employables?" *The Family* (now *Social Case Work*), October, 1942, pp. 203–209; also Myra Shimberg and Alfred G. Lockitt, "Some Are Unable to Work," *Public Welfare,* July, 1947, pp. 154–156.

Recipients of assistance in the federally aided categories are, as a matter of course, considered not to be in the labor market— that is, eligibility for such assistance is not conditioned on willingness to accept available work.

Old-age assistance, for example, was not adopted on a nationwide basis until the depression years, when it was accepted as a way of increasing employment opportunities for younger people by making it possible for the elderly to retire from the labor market without fear of destitution. It also enabled employers to lay off older workers. Today circumstances have changed. Economists warn us that ways must be found to keep the rapidly growing numbers of older people productive, lest the economic burden on the rest of the population become too great. From geriatrics, moreover, we are learning the importance of keeping older people active and useful, if they are to retain their physical and mental health. In spite of these changes, it has not been thought necessary to introduce a work requirement in old-age assistance. Although the fact is that the percentage of persons sixty-five years of age and over who are gainfully employed has shown a marked drop in recent decades, this is not necessarily an indication that there has been a proportionate decrease in work opportunities. Nevertheless, available evidence suggests that it is increasingly difficult for older people to get work. Ironically, the private retirement systems designed by industry to protect the older worker are often a barrier to the employment of older workers.[5] The record of the war years, moreover, has demonstrated that there is little need to *require* older people to work; with few exceptions, they will do so if the opportunity presents

[5] In 1870, 80.6 percent of the nation's elderly men were employed or in the labor force; by 1947, this figure had decreased to 48.4. In spite of the vast increase in women employed or in the labor force, the number of elderly women in this category increased from 5.8 percent to only 8.0 percent during that period. In spite of the increased rate of aging of our population, there was a steady decrease in the old-age assistance rolls from 1942 until 1945—from 2,227,000 to 2,055,000. Not until 1947 did the OAA case load surpass that of 1942—2,332,000. Annual Statistical Supplement, *Social Security Bulletin*, September, 1950, Table 58. Part of the decline in the OAA case load could be attributed to increased contributions from relatives.

itself. The great task that lies ahead is opening up work opportunities for older people which will make most effective use of their skill and dependability, with allowance for the limitations imposed by the aging process.

In ADC the situation is similar. The "mothers' pension" was introduced so that widowed mothers could remain at home with their children instead of going to work. It was believed to be more economical for society to pay this "pension" than to pay the ultimate social cost of having young people grow up deprived of a stable and supervised home life and of the care and protection of a parent. Today ADC grants may be given in behalf of children to relatives other than the mother, and in circumstances other than widowhood. The original purpose, however, remains the same—to provide an economically and socially secure home for children, the nation's greatest resource. Generally speaking, the relative who receives the grant in behalf of the dependent child or children will not be expected to work outside the home, unless adequate provision can be made for the care and supervision of the children during working hours. As in OAA, situations may arise in which it is to the best interest of the total family group that the mother or other relative do some work outside the home. In such instances the agency will help the mother or other relative work out a plan that will best meet her needs and those of the children. Willingness to take a job will rarely be a condition of eligibility for this type of assistance.[6]

In AB and AD particular attention is paid to the diagnosis and treatment of the handicap and to vocational guidance, so that the recipient may become at least partially self-supporting.

Willingness to work, at least in so far as it affects eligibility for assistance, is an issue confined largely to general assistance. Today, when employment conditions are favorable, the number of individuals in receipt of general assistance at any one time is probably less than half that being helped through the other categories—and it includes children as well as adults, the sick and the well. The issue of employability is particularly acute in juris-

[6] See Riley Mapes, "Whose Decision in ADC?" *Public Welfare*, April, 1950, pp. 74–77.

dictions where general assistance is denied to employable persons and members of their families.[7]

As we have seen, the difficulty in determining employability lies in the necessity of relating it to many variable factors. Even mere physical efficiency is not easy to determine. Competent medical examiners are often unable to recommend that a person is fit to do "light work" or "sedentary work" because they are seldom sufficiently familiar with occupational requirements to be more precise.[8] Physicians are concerned primarily with the health of their patients rather than with other aspects of their lives and hence will be inclined to give them the benefit of the doubt when they maintain that they do not feel well enough to work. Even so, differences arise between doctor and patient—the doctor reporting that the patient is employable while the latter claims that he is not equal to the demands of a particular job.

Work Refusals

One of the most vexatious problems in public assistance administration is that of refusal of available work (and its correlative failure to make adequate effort to find work). This problem is not large in volume, but it consumes a disproportionate amount of time, often exposing the agency to community criticism, and it requires a great deal of effort and skill to distinguish legitimate work refusals from those that are not valid. There are many reasons for job refusals but the most common is on the grounds of health. Sometimes, when examining physician and recipient disagree, the situation may be sufficiently unclear to warrant a reexamination, perhaps by another doctor, to make certain that the original diagnosis and recommendation are free from error.

Even where the original recommendation is confirmed, it would be unjust to assume that the recipient has thus been proved a malingerer. There can be many reasons why someone sincerely desirous of returning to work will resist taking a particular job. It is not uncommon, moreover, for a person who is uncertain and

[7] See Donald Howard and Felix Gentile, *General Assistance,* pamphlet (New York: American Association of Social Workers, 1949).

[8] Competent medical advice must, of course, be secured.

under conflict to take refuge in illness, real or fancied, in the unconscious belief that illness may be a more acceptable excuse than
his real reason. Even though the real reason may not be acceptable in the light of agency policy, it will be helpful if it can be
brought into the open. If the public assistance worker is skillful
enough to do this, she may be able to help the recipient face the
reality of his situation. At any rate it is more likely to produce a
satisfactory resolution of the problem than if the worker becomes
enmeshed in a futile dispute that does not reach the heart of the
matter.

Although it would be equally unwise to assume that every
able-bodied person who refuses a job is "emotionally ill," on the
theory that it is "normal" to want to work and to support oneself,
it is nonetheless true that there are people who are too disturbed
emotionally to be employable. We do not intend to enter into a
discussion of the psychological implications of such conditions or
to advocate that assistance agencies temporize, evade the issue,
or engage in prolonged and futile efforts at treatment for which
the staff has neither time nor training. Since, in such situations,
decisions that are fair to both the recipient and the taxpaying
public can be made only through careful psychiatric examinations, it follows that psychiatric consultation is as necessary to
assistance agencies as is medical consultation. Some of the most
serious criticism of public assistance administration arises from
misunderstanding on the part of the community and confusion on
the part of the agency when the latter, because of its mandate to
help all persons in need, has to deal with emotionally disturbed
persons without the protection of psychiatric guidance.

Unfortunately, because of the dearth of psychiatric facilities
in most communities, and because the public assistance staff is
usually insufficiently trained to arrange appropriate referrals for
diagnosis and treatment, many, if not most, assistance agencies
will probably have to struggle with this problem and bear the
brunt of much unmerited criticism for years to come.

Suitable Work

Public assistance is granted on condition that the employable
recipient accept work that is available. Conflicts may arise be-

cause of this requirement when the recipient considers a particular job unsuitable for him. Usually policy does not permit much flexibility in this regard; nevertheless, it is important to consider some of the issues that may be involved.

During the depression the problem of suitable work often arose in connection with referrals to work relief jobs. The early work projects were mostly of the type requiring unskilled manual labor and usually involved outdoor work. There were bitter protests from unemployed white-collar workers, skilled workers, artists, entertainers, and professional people assigned to such projects from the relief rolls. In addition to their feelings regarding loss of dignity and status that such assignments involved, they complained that the work was too arduous for them; that they were unaccustomed to hard physical labor, exposed to the elements; that work of this kind would deprive them of their skill (e.g., as in the case of musicians); and that it would deprive them of opportunities to make contacts for work in their own fields.

Many people (generally those who are in comfortable circumstances) have little sympathy or patience with such attitudes. As Karl de Schweinitz points out, "Such a person almost invariably says, 'If I were out of work, I'd take any kind of a job, even digging ditches.' Actually most people would do nothing of the sort. One of the reasons they try to save money is to avoid having to take 'just anything.' Who does not want to maintain his skill, his level of salary, and the position he has reached in his occupation?" [9]

Obviously no assistance agency could accept every reason for refusing work, but there should be some flexibility, and even when the refusal is not acceptable, the agency staff should be able to handle the situation with tact, understanding of motivations, and imagination so that the agency decision will not provoke resentment and discouragement.

A man employed as a window washer in office buildings is taken sick, his symptoms being dizziness and loss of conscious-

[9] Karl de Schweinitz, *People and Process in Social Security* (Washington: American Council on Education, 1948), p. 49.

ness. He is obliged to stop work and is ineligible for unemployment compensation. Having exhausted his savings, he applies for public assistance. After receiving assistance for several months, his condition responds to treatment and he is pronounced fit to return to work. The only work available is his former job, to which he refuses to return. What should be the decision of the assistance agency?

Suppose this man had been able to state his real reason for refusing this job—his fear that should his symptoms recur while he was at work it would be extremely dangerous. Should the agency deny further assistance because of his refusal of available work? Suppose he could not admit this fear—even to himself? Suppose that instead he tried to think of other reasons that might justify his refusal. What is the agency's responsibility in this situation?

In arriving at a decision as to whether assistance should be continued after a recipient has turned down a job, the agency should be able to answer the following questions: In the light of the recipient's general physical condition, is the job such that he could have undertaken it without impairing his health? Is the job one that presents special hazards to the recipient in the light of his health, skills, and aptitudes? What are the long- and short-term prospects of this job; has he reasonable prospects for securing a better-paying job, one with greater promise of permanence and of chances for advancement? The assistance agency cannot afford to continue helping people who are waiting for a job that suits them exactly; on the other hand, it cannot afford to disregard the personal element in each job referral. A hard and fast "take this job, because if you don't your relief will be discontinued anyway" approach to the problem may force potentially capable workers into blind alleys and so discourage them that their dependency is increased.

The Problem of the Part-Time and the Marginal Worker

Many people who go on and off the assistance rolls at frequent intervals have very low earning power. Their best earnings are insufficient to meet their needs or merely approximate what they would receive in full assistance. It is not surprising that persons so circumstanced should weigh the relative advantages and disadvantages of work as against assistance. It is not surprising, moreover, that some decide that they are better off receiving full assistance than working and receiving supplementary assistance, or working and earning only the equivalent of a full assistance grant. Naturally, the assistance agency cannot allow them to choose assistance instead of work; they are expected to work, if they are able to do so, even though working may result in only a slight reduction in their grant. It is often difficult, however, to determine the motivations of applicants and recipients. Assistance agencies are still confronted with the old problem of needy people who appear to prefer relief to work. The reader will recall that poor law history is replete with references to the fear that relief was demoralizing and that the poor would come to prefer it to maintaining themselves through their own efforts. The reader will also recall that this fear has been strenuously denied. Yet there is a kernel of truth in the contention—a truth, however, which wears a somewhat different aspect from that originally suggested.

In theory, it is preferable to be partially dependent than fully dependent, to be independent rather than dependent, even though "independence" allows a content of living no higher than that of recipients of full assistance. The standards of even the most liberal assistance agencies are not so high that they constitute the dividing line between sufficiency and want. Self-supporting persons with incomes substantially greater than the assistance level can, with good reason, consider themselves economically deprived. It is doubtful if many persons at the margin, or just below the margin, of "independence" are influenced very much by such considerations as civic responsibility, the moral obligation to be self-supporting, and the satisfactions to be derived from work. More probably they will be absorbed by such immediate and practical questions as to whether there will be enough milk for the children, where the rent money is to come from, and a hundred other items of worry and expense.

Nevertheless, there are probably few people who would not

prefer to work if they could earn enough to get off the relief rolls and free themselves from the necessary but distasteful supervision of the agency, *provided* that there would be no loss in net income. Moreover, few people would refuse a full-time or part-time job, even though supplementary assistance would be required, *provided* that there would be no loss in net income. Unfortunately, many assistance agencies do not take into consideration all of the expenses incidental to employment, and hence, when they budget the income from employment, the recipient may actually be penalized. The penalty may be only a few dollars a month, but when one is living at the subsistence level this loss can loom very large—enough to outweigh the advantage of working. If, moreover, the job does not produce sufficient income so that the case can be closed, the recipient has nothing to show for his labors—not even the satisfaction of being rid of public assistance.

Another factor which must be faced frankly is that some recipients supplement their grants by income from various sources not reported and hence not budgeted. Such income may be highly unpredictable—such as an occasional odd job—or it may be a regular part-time job which the recipient is able to conceal from the agency. The temptation not to report income is very strong, especially in jurisdictions where assistance standards are low. Additional income, even though it is only five or six dollars a month, may make life a little easier for a large family. Some assistance agencies recognize the fact that recipients may have opportunities to earn money and do not require that small sporadic earnings be budgeted. A recipient who has been supplementing his grant by unreported income will take this into consideration in deciding whether it is to his advantage to take a job where the earnings are known to the agency, because not only will his earnings be budgeted but the job may prevent him from continuing with his other (unreported) work and thus he may actually suffer a loss in total income.

Of course, it is wrong for recipients to practice such deception, and it is the job of the assistance worker to see that it does not occur, but it would be naïve to think that outside income is seldom successfully concealed. We cannot condone such viola-tions of the law, and yet it is not entirely fair to label those who engage in such practices "chiselers." The great majority of recipients who conceal earnings do not earn enough to affect their grant materially were they to report these earnings. Before heaping opprobrium upon them, critics should first consider whether they would have the moral fortitude to resist this temp-tation if they were under similar pressure. They might also review their past federal income tax returns to see if they have always exercised as nice a sense of discrimination with respect to their obligations.

In most communities there are a few families that are socially as well as economically maladjusted. Since they are usually in need, they are frequently to be found on the assistance rolls. Whether because of genuine delinquency or because of physical and psychological difficulties, their behavior is a source of con-cern to the community. The assistance agency is often blamed for not "doing something" about them. Unfortunately, neither advice, persuasion, nor threats seem to have much effect. Special pro-cedures are needed to help them, or at least to protect them from their own disorganized impulses. Too often the total assistance case load has been judged, and restrictive and punitive policies have been instituted, on the basis of the behavior of these few families.

Earnings of Family Members

How shall the earnings of persons other than the head of the family (especially children) be handled? During the depression (and today in many general assistance agencies) it was a regular practice to treat the earnings of a son or daughter living at home in the same manner as those of the head of the household. The entire income would be budgeted after allowing for minimum expenses incidental to employment. This policy led to very un-satisfactory results. Young people resented the fact that all their earnings were taken from them and found it hard to solace them-selves with the thought that because of their earnings their families were only partially dependent. So far as they could see, their economic situation remained the same except that, whereas before they had had leisure, they now had to labor. Many young people gave up their jobs or, if their earnings permitted, left home. A policy which led to discouraging young people from working, or inducing them to leave their families, could hardly be condoned even though in some instances it resulted in slight reductions in the cost of assistance. Accordingly, various modifications were introduced. One plan permitted the employed non-head of the family to retain 40 percent of his earning (up to a certain maximum—about $25 a week) to cover all personal needs. Sometimes, if earnings were sufficient, the working member was removed from the family budget. Another plan required the budgeting of the entire income but included work expenses and an additional amount, roughly 10 percent of weekly earnings, for the personal expenses of the employed person. The following policy from a recent manual of a local agency reflects still another approach:

Income from an employed non-head of the household is applied first to his individual needs including his share of the household maintenance, expenses of employment and personal needs. The allowance for personal needs may cover the expenses of clothing, life insurance, medical and dental care, and recreation to permit the wage earner to take part in the normal activities of his group. Such an allowance for personal use ordinarily should be considered only where the income of the wage earner is more than sufficient to cover his own maintenance and employment expenses. In exceptional cases where income is derived from employment in the form of vocational training, etc., and is not sufficient to meet the maintenance needs and employment expenses, application of income is considered on an individual basis. Income over and above budgeted needs of the employed person is applied to the family budget.[10]

Self-Employment

Some persons who conduct their own businesses need assistance because they lack sufficient income to maintain themselves.

[10] *Manual of the Department of Public Welfare,* City of Jamestown, N.Y., November, 1946, p. 20.

Usually the enterprises are small and employ only the owner and members of his family. Except for farming, they are usually general service enterprises—shoe repair shops, lunch stands, carpentry and plumbing businesses, and the like. The advisability of assisting needy persons so that they can continue in business depends upon several factors.

The major factor is whether or not the business produces a net income. It would obviously be inappropriate for government to subsidize an enterprise the gross earnings of which were insufficient to meet operating expenses. The enterprise must, therefore, earn enough income so that there will be some profit to apply to the living expenses of the proprietor. Another factor concerns the probability that the enterprise will become sufficiently profitable for the proprietor and his family to return to self-support. If this factor is doubtful, it may be wiser to require the needy person to abandon the enterprise and look for more remunerative work. This requirement would not apply to aged or handicapped recipients since, so long as the little business could meet expenses, the major consideration would be whether the business contributed to the physical and psychological well-being of the proprietor.

Farming presents a special case in that it is not only a business but also a way of life. There are various types of farms, some producing crops such as tobacco and cotton exclusively for the market, others being more in the nature of subsistence homesteads, where the bulk of the produce is raised for home consumption. Unlike the small business discussed in the preceding paragraph, agricultural enterprises may appropriately be subsidized by government—but not by means of public assistance. The governmental programs for the improvement of agricultural conditions have been instituted presumably because of need, but their benefits are available because of other factors.[11]

Public assistance, nevertheless, is available to people who farm, but the major consideration is still whether or not the farm has a net income. In calculating such income, the value of farm

[11] See Chapter 13 for further discussion of farm programs.

products consumed in the home is naturally taken into consideration. Operating expenses such as feed, seed, fertilizer, agricultural equipment, etc., may entail considerable outlay. Taxes and mortgage payments may also represent a substantial expense, which may be difficult to differentiate from the carrying charges of the farm home. Whether or not the farm can yield a net income may depend upon many complicated factors such as whether it would be better for the needy farm owner to work only part of his land and to rent the rest or let it lie idle.

In determining the value of the agricultural commodities consumed at home, allowance must be made for the cost of preserving. Consideration must also be given to the kind of commodities raised and the extent to which their market value should be deducted from the food budget. A farm family may be able to raise considerable quantities of a limited number of food items, for example, potatoes, onions, beans, and cabbage. The value of these commodities, when prorated over a six months' period, might be equivalent to the greater part of the family's food budget. It would be unfair, however, to budget the full amount for these products since the family would be condemned to live on a poorly balanced diet and deprived of funds with which to purchase meat and dairy products. If families were to be penalized thus, they might well be discouraged from being as productive as they might be.

Treatment and Retraining

Unemployment may result from illness or physical handicap or the lack of training in a currently marketable skill. In either case, agency policy alone cannot provide a solution to the problem. Medical and vocational guidance and retraining facilities are needed. The assistance staff, moreover, needs to be sufficiently well trained to recognize when referral to such facilities is indicated and to be able to help recipients who are uncertain or in conflict about the best course of action to meet their needs. Although the assistance agency may have policies regarding corrective treatment and training, an arbitrary application of such policies on a "do it or else" basis is likely to be costly and harmful in the long run.

INCOME OR ITS EQUIVALENT FROM REAL PROPERTY

Except for emergencies of short duration, assistance under the old poor laws was conditioned upon destitution. There was thus no need for detailed policy with respect to real property. If a needy person possessed property, he was expected to sell it and live on the proceeds. The advent of categorical programs (especially old-age assistance) and the unemployment relief programs of the 1930's brought about a change. Assistance agencies were called upon to help many needy families who owned property, often free and clear. The social and financial disadvantages of requiring that such property be liquidated were soon recognized. Carrying charges, taxes, and interest were often found to be less than the cost of providing rented quarters. The result has been that all states have formulated policies concerning conditions under which assistance recipients may retain property.

The first major distinction is that between property used as a home and other real property. The latter is usually considered a capital asset which must be liquidated. Property used as a dwelling may be retained subject to certain limitations. About half the states set some dollar maximum to the value of real property that may be retained—a maximum related to the equity in the property, or its assessed or real value. All states will take into consideration the cost of maintaining the property and the income derived from it—roomers, rental of store space, and especially net savings over the cost of providing equivalent rented space.

Even states which set no maximum to the value of property take into consideration the advantages and disadvantages of allowing property to be retained. Sometimes a needy person, generally one whose descent in the economic scale has been rapid, owns a home far in excess of his needs. The carrying charges, moreover, may exceed a normal rent allowance, and the sale price may be sufficient to purchase an adequate but more modest dwelling and leave some surplus. A refusal to include carrying charges in the assistance budget is usually sufficient inducement for the needy person to dispose of his property.

If property produces substantial income, as in the case of a two-family dwelling or rental of store space, it may be treated as a small business.

It is socially undesirable to force needy people to give up their homes, especially when the timing of the sale, as in a period of depressed values, may result in a capital loss to the owner. If retaining of the property does not add to the burden of the general taxpayer, who must finance the cost of assistance, it will be advantageous to have the recipient retain this capital asset—particularly if he is likely to return to self-support.

A somewhat different situation prevails in the case of old-age assistance recipients, who usually continue receiving assistance until death. In most instances, elderly recipients are permitted to retain their homes. Sometimes aged recipients are required to deed their property to the agency so that at the time of death of the surviving spouse the agency can dispose of the property and reimburse itself from the proceeds. Any surplus from the sale goes to the estate of the deceased. A deed, however, transfers title to the assistance agency so that in effect the recipient surrenders his property, although allowed life use of it. A more satisfactory arrangement, one which is preferred by the Social Security Administration, is for the agency to take a lien on the property. Title is thus retained by the recipient though he cannot transfer the property until the claim secured by the lien is satisfied.

There are two reasons why it is desirable for assistance agencies to recover from the estates of deceased recipients. The first is the actual savings to the taxpayer that will result. The second relates to the attitude of children toward the support of elderly parents who own property. There is some reason to believe that children are willing to support aged parents rather than have property which they hope to inherit encumbered by a lien. If parents have no property, or if the assistance agency does not require a deed or a lien, some children may have no qualms about allowing their parents to be supported by the state.[12]

Many states have legal provisions which disqualify persons from receiving assistance if they have transferred property for the purpose of making themselves eligible for assistance. We ought not to conclude, however, that many people willfully try to defraud the government. Transfer of property prior to applying for assistance may be quite understandable. Aged persons finding it necessary to seek assistance may wish to give a final and tangible reminder of their love for their children. What would be more natural than to turn over to them the only thing of value they have? They may actually be trying to repay their children for the very real sacrifices the latter may have made in supporting them over a period of years. On the other hand, it might be that the children have persuaded their parents to do this against their will. Perhaps it has never occurred to the aged couple that by transferring property prior to seeking old-age assistance they are jeopardizing their application. At any rate, provisions against the transfer of property are designed to preserve that property so that it may be applied toward the maintenance of aged people in time of need.[13]

SELECTED REFERENCES

Griffing, Ethel, "—And Must Not Have Transferred Property," *Public Welfare*, October, 1948.

Hoffman, Elizabeth, "How Employable Are Employables?" *The Family*, October, 1942.

Mapes, Riley, "The Mother's Employment—Whose Decision in ADC?" *Public Welfare*, April, 1950.

Meriam, Lewis, *Relief and Social Security*, Washington: Brookings, 1946, chap. 20, also pp. 839–844.

Mertz, Alice, "Working Mothers and the Aid to Dependent Children Program," *Public Welfare*, July, 1952.

Sheppard, Virgil, "Standards for Old Age Assistance," *Public Welfare in Indiana*, February, 1943.

[12] See David H. Stevens and Vance G. Springer, "Maine Revives Responsibility of Relatives," *Public Welfare*, July, 1948, pp. 122–125.

[13] See Ethel Griffing, "—And Must Not Have Transferred Property," *Public Welfare*, October, 1948, pp. 200–203.

Shimberg, Myra, "The Employment Program of the New York City Dept. of Welfare," *Public Welfare,* October, 1951.

Shimberg, Myra, and Lockitt, Alfred G., "Some Are Unable to Work," *Public Welfare,* July, 1947.

Steininger, Fred H., "Desertion and the ADC Program," *Public Welfare,* October, 1947.

CHAPTER 9

Client Resources

(CONTINUED)

There is something about the idea of families on relief having bank accounts, however vestigial, that the public cannot apparently endure. The rare case of some slick rascal who gets his family on relief while he still keeps his own sizable hoard intact is always good news for some newspaper headlines if not for a public scandal. It is this occasional grafter who is responsible for the rigidity of rules which "just don't make sense" and which, in the opinion of those close-in to their administration, work unnecessary humiliation on numbers of sincere self-respecting people helpless in the cogs of the great relief machine.

—GERTRUDE SPRINGER, "Miss Bailey Says—" *The Survey*, December, 1933

THE RESPONSIBILITY OF RELATIVES TO PROVIDE SUPPORT

The idea of mutual obligation among closely related members of a family group to help one another in time of trouble is deeply imbedded in our culture—indeed, in most cultures. At common law this sense of moral responsibility has been reinforced—at least with respect to the obligation of husband to wife and parents to minor children. Prior to the enactment of the Elizabethan poor law, however, there was no other legal provision of a civil nature which required related people to contribute to each other's support in time of need. The "relative responsibility" provisions of the poor law were enacted, not to enforce a moral obligation, but rather as a fiscal measure to reduce the burden of maintaining the poor, on the theory that the primary responsi-

215

bility in this regard rested with relatives rather than with the taxpayer. This thinking was incorporated into colonial poor relief legislation together with many other features of the Elizabethan act. It flourishes today in a majority of the states although with wide variations in policy and procedure.

The stronghold of the so-called "support laws" is in the Northeastern and North Central states which have been deeply influenced by the stern traditions of New England. Many states in the South and West (often poorer states) have no such requirements. Whether or not legal provisions exist regarding support, the help which relatives provide, or which they may be induced to provide, constitutes an important factor in public assistance administration. It is significant to note, however, that the Social Security Act, although it requires that all income and resources be taken into consideration in determining need, makes no reference to relatives as a resource, nor has the absence of support laws in many states jeopardized federal grants-in-aid. One can deduce, therefore, that the Bureau of Public Assistance, which interprets the provisions of the federal act, is not an advocate of the principle of relative responsibility.

Considerable controversy has arisen in recent years regarding the social desirability and fiscal necessity for support laws, and some of the contrasting views are summarized here:

At one extreme we find those who advocate repeal of all support laws except domestic relations legislation, which applies to the responsibility of husband to wife and parents toward minor children. This school of thought maintains that other support legislation is unnecessary because the sense of family solidarity is still so strong that people will help their close needy relations if they are able to do so. They point out that few needy people have relatives who are in substantially better economic circumstance than they. As a consequence, unless these laws are enforced in a ruthless and arbitrary manner, reducing the relatives to a lower standard of living so that they will have a surplus to contribute to the needy person, the savings in tax funds will be slight. The process by which support is obtained, moreover, is socially undesirable. It is degrading to all the family and may create, or at least aggravate, family tensions. Hard feelings are likely to arise among relatives when some are required to contribute more than others, or resentment may be directed toward the unfortunate needy person. The process, moreover, is costly to the taxpayer in time and money, and even though court support orders are obtained, they are difficult to enforce. Often the needy person will do without support rather than call its lapse to the attention of the assistance agency or court. Instances in which a single relative is able to provide full support but is unwilling to do so are rare and are generally the result of long-standing family quarrels, which the courts are likely to take into consideration in denying support orders.[1]

At the other extreme are those who believe that the support laws should be extended and strengthened. They fear that the rapid rate of social change and the many distracting influences of the modern age have tended to weaken family ties and have tempted people to shirk their responsibilities—rather than make sacrifices that might deprive them of the many gadgets and creature comforts of contemporary life, they prefer to shift the burden of the care of relatives to the state. A relaxation of the support laws, therefore, will not only increase the cost to government but further demoralize family life.

A wide range of opinion separates these two points of view. The middle ground is, perhaps, best represented by those who would continue the support laws but would interpret them liberally. They believe that family feeling is still strong; that most people are willing to assume the burden of supporting close relatives if they are able; that opinion still prevails that failure to do so constitutes a grave reflection upon the character of those who would shirk this duty. But they also believe that the way people think about these matters is strongly influenced by prevailing social attitudes. Support laws are a reflection of social attitudes. Were these laws to be repealed, people might begin to think differently about the extent of their moral obligations. Those who at present are making sacrifices to help needy rela-

[1] Edith Abbott, *Public Assistance* (Chicago: University of Chicago, 1940), pp. 155–176 and 258–283.

tives and who would be shocked at the thought of doing otherwise might begin to consider it acceptable to withdraw this
help and let the state provide full assistance. It is not so much
that the support laws are being used to dragoon unwilling relatives into providing help as it is that support laws reinforce
moral sanctions and strengthen the convictions of those who
believe it is necessary and right for them to help their relatives.
This point of view takes issue with the first position on the
grounds that the extent to which people are "willing" and the
extent to which they are "able" will be influenced by social
sanctions. As a consequence, the advocates of this middle course
would retain the support laws but would invoke them rarely,
since their function would be not so much to give authority to
the state to compel that which people are unwilling to do as
to encourage people to continue doing that which they now
think fitting.

Because of the absence of adequate statistical data it is difficult
to determine the problem of relative responsibility—that is, the
extent to which relatives are contributing to the support of needy
persons, and the extent to which it is a burden to them. We
obviously have no way of knowing the number of needy persons
who are receiving sufficient help from relatives to make public
assistance unnecessary. Even to determine the extent of the
problem within the case load of a given agency would require a
research project involving intensive, individual case reviews. In
spite of these limitations, it might help us to see the problem in
sharper perspective if we consider that public assistance case
loads may be broken down into the following categories:

1. Recipients who have no legally responsible relatives.
2. Recipients with legally responsible relatives, none of whom
   is in a position to help.
3. Recipients with legally responsible relatives who are helping
   to the best of their ability.
4. Recipients with legally responsible relatives whom the
   agency deems to have ability to help but who refuse to do
   so, or who refuse to make an adequate contribution.

It is only with this last category that real problems arise. In this connection, we must point out that disputes between the assistance agency and relatives seldom involve amounts that would be sufficient to provide the needy person with full maintenance. The point at issue is more likely to be whether the relative can provide any help so as to reduce the amount of assistance granted, or whether the contribution can be increased so as to render supplementary assistance unnecessary. Disputes often involve several relatives and the way in which the cost of support should be apportioned among them. Sometimes needy people deny that they have legally responsible relatives or that they know where they are, either because they do not want to be a burden to them or because they feel less humiliated in accepting help from the state. Sometimes the relatives, fearful of what the agency may demand, try to conceal their assets. It is important for the student of public assistance to remember that serious disputes regarding support, while time-consuming and difficult to adjust, are not frequent.

The following are the major elements in support legislation:

1. Applicability.
2. Degree of relationship.
3. Location of relatives.
4. Method of approach.
5. Criteria of "sufficient ability."
6. Method of enforcing support.

Applicability

Support legislation may be based in the original poor law of the state; it may be included in a comprehensive state public welfare law; or it may be a specially enacted support law. Most states have some form of support legislation but its applicability varies. It may apply to all forms of public assistance; certain categories, such as old-age assistance, may be excluded; or it may apply only to general assistance.

Degree of Relationship

Parents and children are the relatives usually held responsible under support legislation. Grandparents and grandchildren may also be held responsible. A few states hold brothers and sisters responsible. There is a tendency to exclude minor children with property from the terms of the law.

Location of Relatives

Although the provisions of state support laws can apply only to relatives living within the state, there is considerable variation in the extent to which states will try to secure support from non-residents. Generally, some effort will be made to get in touch with such relatives by letter, or by having a local welfare agency visit them, in order to ascertain their economic condition and, perhaps, induce them to provide some help. Jules Berman, writing on public assistance legislation in 1949, has this to say:

Another outstanding development in 1949 was the enactment by seven states of desertion and non-support laws that provide for mutual cooperation among the States in obtaining support from out-of-state relatives. State laws with comparable provisions were enacted this year in Connecticut, Indiana, Iowa, Oklahoma, New Hampshire, New Jersey and New York. Though the exact provisions vary, the laws in general enumerate the relatives—wives, children, mothers, fathers, grandparents, and grandchildren—the States expect to be responsible for the support of dependent persons. A procedure is set up whereby the dependents of such persons may, through the State courts, obtain an order requiring the relatives, even though they may live in another State, to support in such amounts as the court may order. The laws then provide on a reciprocal basis for one State to honor similar support orders issued by courts of other states.[2]

Concern has been mounting over the desertion and nonsupport of minor children. Such an act is generally considered a felony and falls within domestic relations law as well as support legislation. Felonies are extraditable offenses; hence, quite apart from the reciprocal arrangements mentioned above, there is a way of enforcing parental financial obligations. The high proportion of ADC cases in which a parent (usually the father) has deserted,

[2] Jules Berman, "Public Assistance Legislation in 1949," *Social Security Bulletin,* December, 1949, p. 9.

as well as the large number of cases involving children born out of wedlock in which no help is provided by the natural father have been major reasons for this concern. Congressional concern has been reflected in a 1950 amendment to the Social Security Act which requires that state plans include a provision for reporting to appropriate law enforcement officials all Aid to Dependent Children cases in which a parent has deserted. The shift in thinking that has taken place is highlighted by the contrast between the aforementioned requirement and the following quotation from a bulletin on the interpretation of the term "Deprived of Parental Support and Care" issued by the Bureau of Public Assistance in November, 1944:

C. *Recommendation for Eliminating Requirements that Legal Action be Taken to Establish Absence or Secure Support.*
   It is recommended, therefore, that the decision of one of the parents to assume parental responsibility *without support* from the absent spouse, not be a barrier to receipt of aid to dependent children, if the children are otherwise eligible. (Italics mine. H. M. L.)

Where the needy applicants are living in the homes of legally responsible relatives, there are wide variations as between different programs. At one extreme is the practice of treating all related persons living in the same household as a family unit, budgeting their total income accordingly; at the other extreme is the practice of taking into consideration only the income of the needy applicant.[3]

Method of Approach

The method by which the assistance agency deals with the problem of securing support from relatives falls more properly within the realm of practice and procedure rather than law, but they are so closely related that it is appropriate to consider it here.

The need for legal provisions to safeguard the rights and in-

[3] See Virgil Sheppard, "Standards for Old Age Assistance," *Public Welfare in Indiana,* February, 1943.

terests of both needy persons and their relatives is brought out by
two cases cited by Edith Abbott.[4] The first case indicates what
can happen when almost unlimited discretion is given to officials
who are apparently unmoved by the most piteous of circumstances:

> An important Wisconsin case dealt with the tragedy of an aged
> woman who had been removed from the county poorhouse "the only
> home she had in the world" by order of one of the superintendents
> of the "county poor," apparently on the theory that her sons could
> and should support her. The poor woman was carried "with some
> goods" to the place where her children lived. "The goods were put
> in a barn and she was left in the public street, 'sitting on the wood-
> pile.' Her children turned her from their doors and suffered her to
> wander about the country and to find shelter and food where she
> could." When a third person finally took her in, boarded her, and
> cared for her, the court held that the county was liable to this kindly
> citizen for her maintenance.

It must be noted that this instance of appalling neglect reached
the courts not because of the heartlessness of public officials but
because the third party was attempting to secure reimbursement
for the care he had rendered.

The second case, while not quite so shocking, demonstrates the
ultimate cost of failure to institute sound procedures:

> The wasteful litigation arising from controversies regarding support
> by relatives is illustrated in a recent Iowa case, Cherokee County v.
> Smith. . . . Here the parents of an adult son were sued by the
> county for the support of the son and his family by the overseer of
> the poor of Cherokee County. The county had paid the rent of the
> house from which the landlord proposed to evict the adult son and
> his family because of inability to pay the rent. The case finally went
> to the district court and was tried by jury. The parents claimed, first,
> that the son had never applied for relief and, therefore, they, his
> parents, were not liable. But the court held that since the owner of
> the house had told the overseer that the son and his family were to
> be evicted if the rent was not paid, and since the overseer acted to

[4] Abbott, *op. cit.*, p. 26, Mappes v. Iowa County, and p. 171, Cherokee
County v. Smith.

prevent the eviction of the family, this was equivalent to an application for aid.

The parents also claimed, as a defense, that the son was "not a poor person" under the statutory definitions. But the Supreme Court pointed out that the statutory definition of a poor person as one who "had no property" and was "unable because of physical or mental disabilities to earn a living by labor" was modified by a further statutory provision which said that "this section shall not be construed to forbid aid to needy persons who have some means, when the board shall be of the opinion that the same will be conducive to their welfare and the best interests of the public."

Finally, after the district court had decided that the parents must pay the $55, appeal was taken to the Supreme Court and this court considered the claim that there had been evidence that the parents were really able to support the son and his family. The court carefully reviewed the family responsibility sections of the poor law and reached the not very helpful conclusion that the father's ability "to render the support for which the county now seeks to recover," and, since "there was no evidence as to such ability" on the part of the father, the judgment of the district court was reversed and the county was not able to collect the $55 after the time of the courts, county attorney and other attorneys, jury, judges, attendance of poor law officer as witness, had all carefully considered the prepared elaborate legal opinions, not about whether Bob Smith and his family were being properly cared for but whether $55 could be collected from his parents—all of which cost the taxpayers of Cherokee County much more than their officials tried to collect.

The moral of this case is not that there should be no support laws, or even that there should never be resort to court action, but rather that case decisions in matters of support should be based on a thorough and tactful ascertaining of the facts and weighing of all the evidence.

A major requisite of sound support laws is that they safeguard needy persons from being deprived of assistance simply because they may have legally responsible relatives who are able but unwilling to help. Some support laws have such safeguards although they do not always apply to all categories. Thus the New York State Social Welfare Law (section 210) stipulates that old-age assistance shall be granted to an otherwise eligible person who has "no legally responsible relatives able and willing to support him. . . ." The state's attorney-general has rendered an informal opinion that the relatives are still responsible under this section of the law but that appropriate action against them should be taken after assistance is granted. Assistance should be provided on the basis of need, and no resources not actually available and regularly predictable should be taken into consideration in determining that need. The 1950 amendments, however, exempt the first $50 per month of earned income for recipients of Aid to the Blind.

An essential of sound practice should be that the applicant (unless he is so disturbed as to be incapable of making rational decisions) decide whether his relatives should be interviewed regarding support. He must, of course, understand the nature of the legal requirement and the conditions under which support might be expected. If he chooses, he should be allowed to prepare his relatives for the agency contact. Dealings with the applicant and his relatives should be direct, businesslike, and tactful. Policy should be sufficiently flexible so that the agency can take into consideration the painful feelings that are often aroused and the fact that it might take a little time for the applicant and his relatives to come to an acceptable decision. Sometimes policy with regard to support can be arbitrary. Thus, the state of Maine, reacting from rather liberal policies regarding support, revised its old-age assistance laws in 1947 to provide that "an application shall not be considered unless accompanied by an individual sworn statement of inability to support the applicant made on the part of each adult child or spouse of such applicant residing in this State, and such statements shall include full information regarding individual incomes, assets and liabilities." [5] One wonders how anyone could say whether or not he was able to support a relative unless he first had an opportunity of knowing what the law expects of him in the light of his resources and his own family responsibilities.

The skill of the assistance worker is, perhaps, the most im-

[5] David H. Stevens and Vance G. Springer, "Maine Revives Responsibility of Relatives," *Public Welfare,* July, 1948, p. 124.

portant element in dealing with problems of support. The sound-
est policies are to no avail if the worker is inept. Even with the
best of intentions, a confused and clumsy worker may make a
botch of the job of determining whether or not a relative is in a
position to help. If she is not a skilled interviewer, doesn't know
what information is essential, or lacks sensitivity and tact, she is
likely to antagonize the applicant and his relatives or overlook
significant data. In either case she may unwittingly jeopardize
the application of one who is genuinely in need or grant assistance without adequate verification of need.

Criteria of "Sufficient Ability"

Whether or not support laws contain specific references to
"sufficient ability," the assumption is that only those relatives who
are able to do so are expected to provide support. Unfortunately,
the practice has often been to leave the establishment of criteria
to the discretion of the worker, supervisor, or local administrator,
whose personal feelings on this delicate subject set the pattern
for cases coming to their attention. Wide variations and inequities
have been the result. The two cases just cited suggest the dangers
that can arise from arbitrary decisions made without reference to
guiding principles or standards, or even a complete understanding of all the facts.

As public assistance began to emerge from poor relief, efforts
were made to develop some criteria for measuring the ability of
relatives to provide support. These efforts have ranged from
"rules of thumb" to specific provisions in the law. The difficulty
of developing realistic criteria is that no two situations are exactly alike. If it is hard enough to ascertain how much income a
needy person has, how much more difficult it is to determine the
resources of relatives who are not themselves applicants. And
how shall decisions be arrived at regarding that portion of the
relative's resources which he can retain for his personal and
family needs? Relatives should obviously not be expected to live
at the relief level in order to help the applicant, but to what extent should they be expected to reduce their standard of living?
Should consideration be given to the fact that the relative is

saving money so that his son of high-school age can go to college? Suppose he is making payments on an automobile or television set, or is saving money to go into business, or is paying for orthodontia for his daughter?

While the very existence of support laws is an indication that people are expected to make some sacrifices to help their needy kin, a major premise should be that relatives ought not to be obliged to impoverish themselves or substantially reduce their scale of living. Sound policy supports the idea that a person's first responsibility is to his spouse and children living at home, and that they should not be deprived in order to provide a surplus to help a needy relative living elsewhere. But how can this be worked out?

In recent years, the trend has been to develop written formulas (either in the law or as policy derived from the law) which set forth in fairly precise fashion the amounts that responsible relatives might be expected to contribute under varying conditions. Two illustrations are cited. The first is from Maine:

1. In the case of a relative with no dependents, the applicant (recipient) becomes ineligible if the relative's gross income exceeds $2,000 plus the amount needed for verified medical care, not to exceed $200. In the case of two applicants (recipients) with the same responsible relative, both become ineligible if the relative's gross income exceeds $2,500. If the relative with no dependents is living with an applicant or recipient and has income between $1,000 and $2,000, he or she is to be assessed $12 a week for board and room of which $6 is to be considered net income.

If the responsible relative has dependents, $500 is allowed for each dependent up to a maximum of $4,000 plus the amount needed for verified medical care not to exceed a total averaging $200 a person.

2. If the responsible relative has net assets in excess of $5,000, the applicant or recipient becomes ineligible. In the case of two applicants (recipients) with the same responsible relative, both become ineligible if the net assets exceed $7,000.

Any responsible relative having a gross income or net assets in amounts in excess of the income and assets formula results in the automatic denial of the applicant or discontinuance of the recipient.

Procedures have been established whereby specified relatives, having gross incomes less than the amount deemed by the Department as constituting ability to furnish complete support will be referred to the legal unit. This unit will attempt to make collections for the partial support of responsible relatives where the contributions either in cash or in kind are not up to the Department's standard of partial support.

The following scale has been set up by the Department regarding partial support. Where the relatives live apart from the applicant this schedule is effective:

No. of Dependents	Gross Income	Contributions 50% of Earnings Over
None	$2,000 or less	$1,500
One	2,500 " "	2,000
Two	3,000 " "	2,500
Three	3,500 " "	3,000
Four	4,000 " "	3,500

Where the relative maintains a household and lives with the applicant, the relative shall contribute shelter, heat and light, if his gross income is over $2,000.[6]

The following schedule has been worked out by a local agency in Indiana:

Family Status of Relatives	Voluntary Contribution Range (gross, minus withholding tax). Ascertain amount of contribution and budget accordingly.	Negotiation Range (gross, minus withholding tax). Ascertain amount of contribution after personal interview, self-support budget, and negotiation, and budget accordingly.	Support minimum (gross, minus withholding tax). Ascertain amount of income over support minimum and budget accordingly.
Single son or daughter	0–$199 per mo.	$200–224 per mo.	$225 and up
Married son or daughter	0–$274 per mo.	$275–299 per mo.	$300 and up

[6] *Ibid.*, p. 125.

Married son or daughter and one dependent	0–$289 per mo.	$290–349 per mo.	$350 and up
Two dependents	0–$314 per mo.	$315–374 per mo.	$375 and up
Three dependents	0–$339 per mo.	$340–399 per mo.	$400 and up
Four dependents	0–$364 per mo.	$365–424 per mo.	$425 and up

The following comments give a general explanation of the table:

Voluntary Contribution Range. When a legally responsible relative falls into this income level, the case worker discusses with him the needs of his aged parents and requests a contribution. If the relative maintains that he cannot financially contribute, the visitor accepts his statement and attempts to get the relative to visit the aged parent, offer him a little recreation, offer personal service in time of illness, and offer other services.

Negotiation Range. When the legally responsible relative falls into this income level, the case worker requests that the relative make out an itemized personal or family budget. Whatever surplus remains after the budget has been made out is the contribution expected from the relative. If the relative refuses to "negotiate" on this basis the case is referred to the Prosecutor's office for action under Chapter 82, 1947 Acts.

Support Minimum. When a relative falls into this income level, the case worker requests that all sums over the support minimum be contributed to the aged parent. If the relative refuses to contribute the sum over the support minimum the case is referred to the Prosecutor's office for action under Chapter 82, 1947 Acts.

There is a separate standard of application of income in situations where there is more than one income in the household of the responsible relative and where the relatives are living apart from the applicant or recipient.[7]

The two policies reveal certain important differences. The Maine policy applies only to old-age assistance, whereas the Indiana policy applies to all categories. The Indiana agency is in a heavily industrialized area on the periphery of one of the nation's largest metropolitan areas. Maine is predominantly rural. Not only is the Indiana policy substantially more liberal but its application seems to be more flexible. The Maine provisions would appear to disqualify a needy person if he is unable to submit, along with his application, sworn statements from his legally responsible relatives, or if, in the opinion of the agency, the data submitted indicate that the relatives should be able to provide full support. Presumably, if such help is not forthcoming, the needy person must take his relatives to court. How he maintains himself while awaiting a decision from the court is apparently not a matter for concern to the agency. The Indiana agency, on the other hand, seems to play a more active role in trying to per-

[7] Dorothy Nierengarten, "We Don't Believe in Relative Responsibility," *Public Welfare,* May, 1950, p. 103.

suade relatives to help. Assistance may be granted even though there are relatives who are able to help. Thus, Miss Nierengarten, the case supervisor, says: "The amount of assistance should not be determined on the basis of a promise to support on the part of a responsible relative or the fact that a responsible relative is financially able to contribute. The support should actually be given before it influences the amount of the grant."

The dilemma faced by assistance agencies in developing criteria of "sufficient ability" stems from the fact that, although specific policies are needed to insure equitable treatment, the more specific the policies, the more difficult it is to take into consideration the atypical situation.[8] Perhaps such policies should be used primarily as a guiding principle rather than hard and fast rule, so that, when conditions warrant, exceptions can be made after careful study and proper authorization.

Method of Enforcing Support

Though there are many differences among the states with respect to the legal structure and procedures through which support laws are enforced—the type of court, the persons responsible for bringing action, etc.—these details need not concern us here. It is sufficient to point out that most states fall into one or the other of two categories: those which vest in the state or local welfare commissioner the power to initiate action on behalf of the needy person, and those which place this responsibility on the needy person himself. In either case the latter is confronted with a painful choice, since the assistance he needs is contingent upon bringing his relatives into court or upon acquiescing to such action by the assistance agency.

What is of paramount importance is the social policy developed by the agency to determine whether or not court action should be taken. The criteria of sufficient ability, especially the

[8] Consider Smith and Jones, both of whom are called upon to support their parents. Neither has enough current income to do so; Smith has invested his savings in a house, while Jones has put his savings in the bank. In many jurisdictions Jones would be required to contribute his savings to the support of his parents but Smith would be exempt—because he had no liquid assets.

income schedules already mentioned, are one way of determining the help that relatives should provide, but even they become arbitrary if used to decide automatically the cases that must be referred for legal action.

In considering whether or not legal action should be taken, several factors should be carefully weighed—the likelihood of the court's sustaining the action, the likelihood of the relative's complying with the court order, and the total cost of the action in relation to the amount of support sought. With respect to the first point, there can be no guarantee that the court will see eye to eye with the agency. Even though the plan of enforcing support and the criteria of sufficient ability have been worked out in advance in coöperation with the judges, individual circumstances may prompt the court to make no order of support, or to enter an order for an amount smaller than that which the agency might have secured through negotiation. Some welfare officials are beginning to think that the courts are adopting a more liberal attitude toward support than that of assistance agencies. Some judges seem to think that if the assistance agency has not been able to persuade relatives to extend help, there is little that can be accomplished even with the authority of the court, if they persist in their refusal. Although the courts may be severe with parents who fail to support young children, they are likely to be more lenient with adult sons and daughters, with families of their own, who claim they cannot help their aged parents.

With respect to the second point, the court can issue an order of support, can require that the respondent post a bond, and, as a last resort, can send him to jail for failure to carry out the court's order. This, however, is often a game of bluff. To be sure, most people will be sufficiently intimidated by the prospect of thirty or sixty days in jail to comply; in reality, however, the court will be reluctant to send to jail a person with natural dependents of his own simply because he refuses to support a relative for whom he is legally responsible. Often, a relative will make a show of complying with the court order but will fall behind in his payments, delay making them, or fail to pay the full amount. He is often aware that it takes time to bring him back to court, and when he has another hearing he can offer numerous excuses which might induce the court to cancel the arrears.

The difficulty and costliness of securing support, even when there has been a court order, is illustrated as follows:

An adult married son has been ordered by the court to contribute $20 a month toward the support of an aged parent with whom he is on unfriendly terms. After several months his payments fall into arrears. The aged parent may be unwilling to call this to the attention of the authorities either because he realizes the economic sacrifices his son must make or because he finds it too painful to participate in further court action. As a result, he tries to manage on the supplementary assistance grant alone. But suppose necessity drives him to reporting his son's default? An effort will be made to bring the son back to court, first by writing to him to report for an interview; if that fails, several other letters may be sent. If he still refuses to report, a summons may be sent, and, if he does not answer that, a warrant for his arrest may be issued. All of this may take from six weeks to two months or more. When he finally appears before the judge he may present a picture of changed circumstances that the judge will take into consideration. The assistance agency may doubt his story and more time will elapse while an effort is made to determine the facts. But assuming that his excuses are unconvincing, the judge will continue the order and require that he make up the arrears. What then? The whole process may be repeated a few months later. Meanwhile, either the aged parent is doing without or the agency is making up the deficit. For reasons which we have mentioned above, the court will hesitate to take drastic action against the recalcitrant son, and the situation may drag on for years with the contributions amounting to far less than the cost of court and agency action.

The above illustration is admittedly a more extreme case; nevertheless it highlights the issues that must be considered. When an assistance agency meets with a refusal on the part of a relative who is deemed to have "sufficient ability," it should look first to whether the worker handling the case has made an accurate analysis of the facts and a skillful interpretation to the relative of the role of the agency and of his responsibility. If coöperation is to be secured, if relatives are not to be antagonized, the subject of support must be broached with the greatest delicacy, with the worker being sensitive to their feelings and adapting her approach accordingly. Although it would hardly be correct to say that every court case is an indication of failure on the part of the agency, the number of court cases can be reduced materially if policies are flexible and the staff is well trained.

Do contributions from relatives reduce materially the cost of public assistance? Unfortunately no precise answer to this question can be given. Naturally, the more that relatives contribute, the less the assistance agency will have to expend. It is important to know, however, whether the cost of public assistance would be greatly increased were there no support laws—taking into consideration the administrative cost of determining "sufficient ability" and the enforcement of court orders. Would most relatives who are now contributing continue to do so?

From time to time states have relaxed or strengthened their support laws. These changes, however, have been accompanied by so many changes in legislation, in policy, and in social and economic conditions that it has not been possible to isolate the fluctuations in costs and case loads that may have been due to modifications in law and policy with regard to support. Nothing short of detailed case and application studies would provide the data we need. What evidence we have on hand is inconclusive.

Commissioner Stevens of Maine comments as follows:

As a result of the new laws regarding responsibility of relatives to support and the policies formulated by the Department to carry out the provisions of the law, some 2,150 old-age assistance cases have been closed. About three-fifths of the cases were closed because sworn statements revealed income or assets in excess of the standards set by the Department, while the remaining two-fifths were closed because of the failure of responsible relatives to file sworn statements. Approximately eight percent of these cases have been reinstated for assistance payments because of errors in the sworn statements or for other reasons.[9]

Otto Walls, former Administrator of the Indiana State Department of Public Welfare, seems to be of the opinion that there are many people who will support their relatives only under some form of compulsion. Writing in *Public Welfare*,[10] he points out that when Indiana repealed the lien provisions of its law, thus making it impossible for the state to recover the cost of assistance from the estates of old-age assistance recipients, there was a significant increase in the volume of such assistance.

Official records show that in March, 1941, during which month the provision was repealed, there was an increase of 791 applications over the previous month. This was an increase of sixty-three percent. In April there was an increase of 2,347 applications, or one hundred eighty-eight percent over February. During the twelve months' period following repeal of the recovery clause, there was an increase of more than forty-five percent in the number of applications over the previous year. Though upon investigation more than half of the new applications were rejected, by May, 1941, there had been a sharp increase in the case load and expenditures. This was a reversal of the decline from the peak load which had previously been in effect, and was in the face of marked improvement in economic conditions.[11]

When the lien and recovery provisions were reënacted in 1947, some six thousand old-age assistance recipients, approximately 10 percent of the case load, failed to execute lien agreements, thus giving tacit consent to the withdrawal of assistance. "As had been anticipated, a fractional part of this number later found that they could not maintain themselves without public assistance and so signed the lien agreement." Mr. Walls points out that a few of these aged persons probably failed to sign the lien agreement not because they wished to avoid having a claim upon their property but in anticipation of the effects of companion legislation which required able-bodied children to support needy parents.

[9] Stevens and Springer, *op. cit.*, p. 125.
[10] Otto Walls, "Indiana Re-enacts Its Lien Law," *Public Welfare*, May, 1948, pp. 108–111.
[11] *Ibid.*, p. 108.

Mr. Walls suggests that the decline in the case load following reënactment of the lien and recovery provisions was brought about by children's deciding that it was preferable to support their parents rather than to have their property, which they hoped to inherit, encumbered. Mr. Walls further suggests that old-age assistance has often been confused in the public mind with various types of pensions—a much more acceptable kind of help. The absence of lien provisions as well as support laws contributed to this confusion in Indiana. Now that such laws have been enacted, it is easier for relatives to recognize public assistance for what it is, and to recognize their responsibilities.

Professor Alton Linford reports the results of investigations in Massachusetts of the question of relative responsibility and its effect upon the cost of public assistance.[12] In May, 1944, the total number of OAA cases was 76,633, of which 14,747, or 14 percent, were getting some help from relatives. This help was valued at $228,780 for the month, and it was estimated that, on an annual basis, help from relatives would amount to $2,745,371. In addition, the amount of help given on those cases that were closed and on the applications that were rejected because of the ability of relatives to help was estimated at $2,425,000. The total amount of financial assistance contributed by relatives was estimated to be $5,170,371 for the year. In May, 1944, Massachusetts spent $3,044,968 on OAA and, on an annual basis, $36,539,616. The amount contributed by relatives was equal to 14 percent of the public funds provided for the care of the needy aged. It must be assumed, moreover, that help provided by relatives was even greater, the unknown quantity being the amount contributed to needy people who therefore found it unnecessary to seek OAA.

The crucial question, still unanswered, is: How much of this help would be forthcoming if there were no legal requirements regarding support? Obviously, those who are unwilling contributors would discontinue or reduce their help. But how many persons whose voluntary contributions are now sufficient to keep their aged parents off the assistance rolls would have a change of

[12] Alton Linford, "Responsibility of Relatives in the Massachusetts Old Age Assistance Program," *Social Service Review*, March, June, September, 1945.

attitude and begin to think that their parents' receipt of OAA would no longer be a reproach to them?

SAVINGS

Cash, whether kept at home or in a bank, stocks, bonds, and other negotiable instruments are resources which normally must be used before a person is eligible for assistance. In the case of OAA applicants, an exception may be made if they have no life insurance—a small sum may be retained for burial purposes.

Life insurance is a form of savings that requires more detailed treatment. With respect to this resource, Dr. Meriam comments as follows:

Two different points of view may be taken with respect to insurance. The first is that the family is not in need if it can even for a short period get along on the cash which can be obtained by surrendering the policy. The other is that it is in the interest of both the family and the public treasury to appraise the situation and take action with consideration of the probable future. What are the chances that the insured will again earn and be able to continue the policy in force? What are the facts with respect to his expectation of life? To take a possible case, let it be assumed that the need arises from the disability of the insured and that the prognosis of the physician is unfavorable. Under such circumstances it is clearly in the interest of the public treasury that the policy be maintained in full force if there are dependents for whom provision will have to be made. The insurance, in other words, is from the standpoint of the public treasury worth far more than is its cash surrender value.

Many life insurance contracts contain provisions under which adjustments can be made to meet the new situation. It is always possible, moreover, for the law to authorize the public agency, unless the policy is unassignable, to continue payments of the premiums and to take a lien on the policy itself or on the policy and other property, either for the amount advanced as premiums or for all the money expenses in assisting the family. Use of the lien procedure may justify continuing even a fairly substantial policy in full force during a considerable period, if satisfactory arrangements cannot be worked out with the insurance company or with local banks.[13]

[13] Lewis Meriam, *Relief and Social Security* (Washington: Brookings, 1946), p. 258.

Generally speaking, life insurance is considered as a resource for burial only. Where policies are in effect for a substantial amount, and premiums are correspondingly high, the applicant will be required to take an adjustment on his policy—that is, have it reduced to a smaller amount. He may be expected to apply the proceeds to living expenses, or else they may be applied, in whole or in part, to paying advance premiums. If the case appears to be a "short term" one, such adjustment may be waived. Agencies with more liberal policies follow the plan suggested by Dr. Meriam with respect to insured persons whose prognosis is unfavorable; that is, arrangements are made to pay the premiums, and a lien is taken on the policy.

Often it is found that the life of an applicant is insured but that the person who is paying the premiums and who is the beneficiary is a friend or relative. In such cases the policy is a resource of that person rather than of the applicant. As in the case of real property, it is important to ascertain whether or not the policy was transferred by the applicant to avoid an insurance adjustment.

The agency must examine all policies held by the applicant, those that have lapsed as well as those currently in effect. Frequently applicants are unaware that policies that have lapsed because of inability to keep up the premiums have some cash value. Each year considerable sums of money are realized for needy people because the assistance agency has been able to collect on such lapsed policies.

Many agencies do not require that stocks, bonds, and other securities be liquidated if a reasonable price cannot be obtained for them. In such instances they may be assigned to the agency, or at least held by it for possible liquidation at a more favorable time.

OTHER RESOURCES

Personal Property

Many states set limits to the amount of personal property that may be retained by a recipient. There may also be limits to specified types of property. The limits may range from as low as

$150 to a high of $1500. Except in periods of economic crisis, when the decline from affluence to poverty can occur almost overnight, it is unlikely that many applicants will be overburdened with a surplus of material possessions. Nevertheless, questions do arise concerning the possession of such items as jewelry, silverware, antique furniture, art objects, expensive fur coats, television sets, and motorcars.

It is not unreasonable to expect needy persons to utilize their resources for maintenance, but there are limits to the extent to which this should be required. Jewelry, for example, is a luxury, the disposal of which would not materially reduce one's standard of living. Yet it would be needlessly harsh to expect that a wedding ring or some other treasured keepsake be sold, when its personal value may far outweigh the price it would bring. The same may be said of many other personal items the sale of which would produce very little compared to the total requirements of the family unit. To some people an automobile may be a necessity, especially if they live in remote rural areas, or if it is a means whereby employment might be secured; to others it is a luxury.

In general, policy with respect to personal property should be sufficiently flexible so that distinctions can be made between cases of long-term and short-term dependency. It is uneconomic in the long run to require needy persons to sacrifice personal goods if their return to self-maintenance is fairly probable.

Other Sources of Income

Other possible sources of actual or potential income are too numerous to mention. We can merely call attention to some of the more common ones. The agency has the responsibility of verifying not only whether applicants or recipients are in receipt of such income but also whether or not they are, or can become, eligible for it. These possible sources are:

1. Social insurance.
   Old-age and survivors' insurance benefits.
   Unemployment compensation.
   State disability and sickness insurance.

Railroad retirement and survivors' insurance.

Railroad unemployment compensation.

Workmen's compensation.

2. Federal and state benefits and pensions to veterans, their dependents and survivors.

3. Disability and retirement pensions from public or private employers.

4. Money payments from fraternal and labor organizations.

5. Private insurance annuities, disability and retirement policies.

6. Income from trust funds and lawsuits.

7. Inheritances.

8. Assistance from private agencies.

As part of their treatment plan, private social agencies often provide financial help to recipients of public assistance. This financial assistance is usually for items that cannot be provided by the assistance agencies. Since it is the policy of most private agencies not to supplement the regular maintenance budget, which is the responsibility of the public agency, such help will be discontinued if the public agency budgets it. Most public agencies, therefore, do not deduct such income from the budget.

SELECTED REFERENCES

Abbott, Edith, *Public Assistance,* Chicago: University of Chicago, 1940, Review Introduction to Part Two, pp. 155–176.

"Developments in Reciprocal Non-Support Legislation," *Public Welfare,* December, 1951.

Griffin, John J., "The Standard Budget and Children's Responsibility in Mass.," *Social Service Review,* September, 1944.

Hart, Ethel J., "The Legal Responsibility of Relatives in the Care of the Aged," *Social Service Review,* March, June, 1941.

Hitrovo, Michael K., "Responsibility of Relatives in the Pennsylvania Old Age Assistance Program," *Social Service Review,* March, 1944.

Laitinen, John A., "Our Program of Relative Responsibility," *Public Welfare,* October, 1948.

Linford, Alton A., "Responsibility of Relatives in the Massachusetts Old Age Assistance Program," *Social Service Review,* March, June, September, 1945.

Nierengarten, Dorothy, "We Don't Believe in Relative Responsibility," *Public Welfare*, May, 1950.

Stevens, David H., and Springer, Vance G., "Maine Revives Responsibility of Relatives," *Public Welfare*, July, 1948.

Walls, Otto, "Indiana Re-enacts Its Lien Law," *Public Welfare*, May, 1948.

CHAPTER 10

Social Investigation

"Social investigation" as applied to public assistance means the collection, verification, recording and appraisal of factual information on the basis of which a determination is made of eligibility and degree of need or ineligibility for any form of public assistance. In such determination the applicant, recipient and agency share responsibility.

—New York State Department of Social Welfare, Bulletin No. 91b, "Determination of Initial and Continuing Eligibility for Public Assistance or Care"

Increasingly, the authority which formerly one individual, the director of the poor, exercised over another, the person receiving relief, has been transferred to a code of law and organizational policy. The public assistance worker serves in fact as well as in title as the representative of the agency of government and acts through the medium of principles, requirements, specifications and considerations that form the elements of the process of social administration.

—KARL DE SCHWEINITZ, *People and Process in Social Security*

THE CONTENT OF THE PUBLIC ASSISTANCE JOB

Having examined the major objections, standards, and requirements of public assistance as reflected in law and policy, we now turn to a consideration of the way in which the purpose of the public assistance agency is translated into service through the activity of the public assistance personnel. From what has already been considered, we may deduce the following summary of public assistance functions:

1. To provide financial assistance in appropriate amounts to all

needy persons whose eligibility for that assistance has been verified and to withhold assistance where need is not sufficiently acute by agency standards.

2. Through understanding of the individual causes of economic dependency, and of the limitations and capacities of the needy person, to help him, in so far as that is possible, to return to a condition of self-maintenance.

3. To determine eligibility and to administer assistance and related services so that the experience can be a constructive one for the needy person—one wherein his capacity for self-direction is maintained or strengthened; one in which he can face the disagreeable reality of his dependency without accepting it as a desirable or inevitable condition or feeling personally degraded by his misfortune.

Karl de Schweinitz has attempted to find the core of skill and knowledge common to both forms of income maintenance—insurance and assistance. Although there are some fundamental differences which we will consider shortly, his analysis of the common process of eligibility determination has considerable pertinence.

1. *Ascertaining facts.* These are the special facts about the life and work of the individual that form the basis of the decision whether or not he shall receive the benefit or money payment for which he has applied. Sometimes they are in his possession and at his command; sometimes they must be obtained elsewhere from people or from documents. They need to be accurately established. This is not easy when memory is fallible and definite evidence is not at hand. These facts, moreover, often touch closely upon things intimate to the person involved. How often and how intimately depends upon the nature of the insurance or of the assistance, but this element of intimacy is always potentially or actually present.

2. *Determining with the individual the extent of his responsibility for establishing eligibility.* What is the area of the responsibility of the individual and that of the organization in this respect? How much of the proof necessary to determine eligibility should the individual obtain for himself? To what extent should he be expected to report changes in work and wages and pertinent circumstances? How much can the process be made something the individual does for

himself, rather than something that is done to him or about him? While the organization as a whole can establish general policies—and the trend of development is in the direction of the retention of a maximum of responsibility by the individual—there are always variants in the individual and his circumstances, his condition, and his capacity, that call for special and immediate decision.

3. *Evaluating facts in relation to law and regulation and deciding whether and in what amounts an individual is entitled to benefits.* This process requires not only knowledge of the Social Security Act but, in the case of unemployment compensation and public assistance, of State law and, in all services, of the interpretation of the act as provided by the decisions of the Social Security Board, amplified or particularized in the State and local administrative units. Regulation, policy, and procedure are inherent in a service that undertakes to deal equitably and predictably with all persons in the same status or condition, and the insurance or assistance worker must be able to determine fairly and appropriately in relation to such regulation and policy whether the individual, in the light of his special facts, is entitled to the benefit or payment for which he has applied.

4. *Explanation.* No other skill is so universally important to the success of the program as this. The quality of the working relationship between the organization and the applicant largely depends upon his understanding what the requirements of eligibility are; what, as indicated above, is expected of him; and whether he is or is not eligible, and why. The extent to which the individual appreciates what social security involves as it relates to him not only affects, often decisively, the whole process of determining eligibility, but also influences the development of a popular understanding of the program. Explanation calls for a high degree of individual activity; it is not something done by rote. It varies as people vary, and it calls both for insight into human nature and for facility—frequently ingenuity—in statement.

These four processes in the establishment of eligibility—ascertaining facts, evaluating facts, determining responsibility, and explanation—demand a disciplined skill which is variously required throughout the program. The chief medium through which they are carried on is the interview. That interview takes place usually under circumstances which have a high emotional content. Sorrow, anxiety, fear, even anger may all or any of them be present when death, unemployment, and needed income are the occasion of the discussion. Complicating the situation still further is the fact that the issue is personal. There is a world of difference, for example, between having to make an explanation of eligibility for insurance or assistance to an individual whose interest is academic and not immediate, and having to make the explanation involved in telling an individual he is or is not eligible for something he wants.[1]

In spite of these common elements, the contrast between qualifying for insurance and qualifying for assistance is marked. Insurance benefits, unlike assistance grants, are based on coverage rather than need; hence, those aspects of the applicant's life that must be investigated are much more restricted. Resources need not be evaluated, nor need relatives be interviewed, nor are there limitations on real or personal property. Though continuance of insurance benefits may be subject to conditional factors (e.g., the acceptance of suitable work provision in unemployment compensation), the area within which such factors apply is much narrower than in public assistance. Thus, insurance beneficiaries may inherit fortunes, dispose of property, alter their living arrangements, and even have regular incomes without affecting eligibility for, or the amount of, the benefit. They are free to manage their own affairs subject only to those norms to which everyone in the community must conform. Unlike assistance recipients, their behavior is not judged more rigorously simply because of their status as insurance beneficiaries.

Since the growth of social insurance in this country, the point is sometimes made that assistance recipients are, in a sense, discriminated against; that need for assistance arises primarily because of the absence of insurance coverage; and that this lack of coverage is due solely to the failure of Congress to provide the necessary protection. Some people, when they are in need, can get insurance; others, although in similar circumstances, must seek public assistance. The proposition is advanced, therefore, that assistance should be administered in a manner approximating that of social insurance. The rights and duties of the recipient and the agency should be clearly defined in written policies and regulations; the area within which those who administer assist-

[1] Karl de Schweinitz, "The Basic Skill in Social Security," *Social Security Bulletin,* January, 1944, p. 24.

ance exercise discretionary judgment should be held to a minimum; the behavior of the applicant or recipient, except in so far as it affects economic need, should not be a matter of concern; the agency should confine itself to problems related to economic need and should not try to deal with any of the other environmental or psychological problems the needy persons may appear to have. Should the latter request help with such problems, they should be referred to other community agencies.

This approach to assistance administration is an extension of the point made by De Schweinitz in the quotation heading this chapter. It is a reaction from poor law methods, in which one's moral character, racial or national origin, religious or political affiliation, personal habits, degree of gratitude, and conformity to the predilections of the administering official were as likely to influence the kind of help received as economic need. It is also a reaction from a later approach when, under the first flush of psychiatric theory, there was the tendency to suspect that emotional dependency or other maladjustment underlay most requests for financial aid.[2]

In spite of its good points, this approach to assistance administration is impractical precisely because assistance is the last line of defense against want. Eligibility for insurance benefits is based on prior events which, though of great importance to the claimant, do not touch closely upon the more intimate aspects of his life. The factors determining eligibility are so closely related to specific occurrences in the area of employment and earnings that there is a marked similarity among thousands of claims. Claims interviewers need not concern themselves about how claimants or

[2] "Probably nothing more important has happened in the history of casework than this discovery that under the mask of poverty are the unsolved problems of all of us, not merely the special problems of economic failure." Grace Marcus, *Some Aspects of Relief in Family Casework* (New York: Russell Sage, 1929), p. 3.

"The expert caseworker recognizes emotional dependency as a potential in every case she must investigate and evaluate before she can formulate plans for treatment which are based on accurate appraisals of assets and liabilities." *Ibid.*, p. 67. Contrast this viewpoint with that of contemporary social work as reflected in the article by Helen Harris Perlman, "Are We Creating Dependency?" *Public Aid in Illinois,* July, 1951.

beneficiaries are managing on their income, or about their other problems, because the assistance agency can help them if they run into difficulties.

The contrast between administration of insurance and administration of assistance is illustrated by problems arising in connection with the "suitable work" provisions in unemployment compensation and in general assistance. Eligibility for unemployment compensation is dependent upon willingness to accept suitable work. The conditions which make for "suitable" work are clearly defined. Any beneficiary refusing such job referral, regardless of the strength of his personal reasons, loses his benefits. The reason there can be such clarity and firmness on this point is precisely because public assistance is available if the person whose claim is disallowed is in need.

In general assistance, the staff cannot take the relatively detached and objective point of view of insurance personnel because decisions regarding the granting or withholding of assistance are fraught with much more serious consequences. The public assistance worker, if he has any feelings of responsibility, must be aware of the consequences of denying aid to someone who is, in fact, in need. The factors on which the decision to deny assistance are based may seem clear enough on the surface, but there is always the nagging thought that the decision may have been based on incomplete or erroneous data. The fact is that, while need is the primary requirement in public assistance, it is not the only requirement. Intent is frequently an issue. Thus, when a recipient declines a job, the worker must determine what his intentions are. Is he trying to avoid work? Once the worker enters the realm of intentions and motivations, written rules and policies are an uncertain guide. They can never be sufficiently specific to anticipate the infinite variety of human circumstances. Ultimately, the worker must rely upon his ability to interpret the meaning of the behavior he observes.

The difficulty of applying policy and the necessity of basing it on an accurate diagnosis of the social situation are reflected in the following case brought to light during a recent investigation of public assistance administration:

A recipient of general assistance was repeatedly referred for work but without success because he would always report to his prospective employer clad in a red fez and a long yellow robe. Thus, although he never actually turned down a job, his attire, outlandish in our culture, guaranteed that no one would hire him. The question naturally arose as to whether this was a ruse to avoid work. The recipient maintained that this garb was required by his religion. Although this was doubtful, there was the possibility that he might be a sincere adherent of some obscure sect in which this garb was required. Apparently it was difficult to prove that this was *not* the case. On the other hand, it was more likely that he was an eccentric or a disturbed person. Finally, there was the possibility that he was a shrewd, calculating individual who, for one reason or another, preferred not to work and had adopted this costume to confound the agency. Whether or not this was the case, the agency *was* confounded, and continued to grant assistance without arriving at an understanding of the situation. Had this man been unattached, a decision to discontinue assistance might not have been so difficult to make, but he had a wife and several children for whom discontinuance of assistance would have worked hardship. Would the withdrawal of assistance have forced this man to change his behavior? Would he then have made serious efforts to support his family?

The case just cited is an extreme one, yet complicated situations arise with sufficient regularity to make it imperative for the public assistance staff to know how to deal intelligently and responsibly with the intangible factors that bear on eligibility and for which there can be no written provisions. Thus, when Mrs. Jones claims that she doesn't know where her husband is, is this a fact, or is she trying to protect him from being brought to court on a charge of nonsupport? When Mr. Smith says that he has no living relatives, is this true, or is he trying to avoid the humiliation of having his relatives visited? When Mr. Brown disputes the medical report that he is fit to work, does he really consider that he is too ill to work, or has he some ulterior motive? Or conversely, when Mr. Black withdraws his application, is it because he is not in need or because he considers living on starvation rations preferable to the humiliation of having his relatives know his plight? Or when Mrs. White maintains that her son is contributing to her support, is this a fact, or is she trying to conceal the shame of her son's indifference to her needs?

The content of the public assistance job includes a high degree of technical knowledge, skill in social investigation and in human relations so that that knowledge can be applied, and a rigorous professional self-discipline. The Committee on Social Work Education and Personnel of the American Public Welfare Association has outlined the content of the job as follows:

BASIC KNOWLEDGE REQUIRED FOR PUBLIC ASSISTANCE WORKER

A. Legal and philosophic basis for public assistance programs.
   1. Knowledge of the law under which the agency operates and of basic structure of the agency set-up.
   2. Knowledge of the eligibility requirements for services through the worker's own agency and of its policies and procedures.
   3. Knowledge of the rights, privileges, duties and responsibilities of applicants and their relatives, of recipients and their relatives, and of the workers as defined in the law.
   4. Knowledge of the sources of funds for public welfare programs.
   5. Knowledge of the objectives of the program, and of the underlying philosophy which governs the manner in which public welfare programs are administered.
   6. General knowledge of governmental structure.
B. Knowledge of social and economic factors and how to use this knowledge for the benefit of the individual served.
   1. The public assistance worker needs to understand the problems and processes of social change that affect people such as the aged, family without a wage earner, the physically and mentally handicapped.
   2. The public assistance worker needs to understand the relationship between the public assistance programs and other income maintenance programs, such as social insurance, minimum wage laws, employment services, public housing.
   3. The public assistance worker needs to know and understand preventive treatment and rehabilitative programs in physical and mental health.

4. The public assistance worker needs to have a recognition and understanding of the other community programs, public and private, and sufficient knowledge of these programs to use their services effectively.
5. The public assistance worker needs to have an understanding of the impact of economic change and a knowledge of the economy of the particular community in which the worker is employed.
6. The public assistance worker needs to have an understanding of cultural and ethnic groupings in the community where the worker is employed.

C. Elementary understanding of need for and use of research and statistics for social purposes and appreciation of scientific methods.

D. Understanding of human behavior.
1. The understanding of human behavior is a lifetime task. A minimum essential for the public assistance worker is a knowledge of normal growth and development and of individual differences.
2. The worker should have an awareness of the need to be nonjudgmental toward the behavior of others and to be aware of their role in diverse situations.
3. He also has a need to be aware of his own feelings and attitudes so that assistance and other services may be provided with equity and helpfulness.
4. In addition, he should be able to recognize marked deviations from the normal in order to use his energies suitably with and for the client, and to use appropriately the agency and community resources.

BASIC SKILLS AND ABILITIES REQUIRED OF A PUBLIC
ASSISTANCE WORKER

A. Skill in communications.
1. Skill in interviewing in order to bring out pertinent feelings and facts and in securing participation in the intervew.
2. Skill in observation of factors in specific situations, of attitudes, feeling tones, and relationships.
3. Ability to write and speak clearly, concisely, and effectively.
4. Ability to establish and make use of constructive relationships with clients, co-workers, workers in other agencies, and other interested individuals.

5. Skill in recording briefly and clearly that which is pertinent.
6. Ability to report accurately and to select what is relevant.

B. Ability to use and work within agency policies and procedures, and to interpret these in the community.

C. Skill in the exploration of the applicant's and recipient's eligibility for assistance and for his desire for other services.

D. Skill in extending the appropriate social services of the agency, and in referring the applicant and recipient to suitable community resources.

E. Ability in planning, organizing, and in administering own work load.

F. Ability to participate constructively in the development and revision of inter- and intra-agency policies, procedures, and agreements.[3]

It is obvious from the above statement that the public assistance job involves highly specialized, professional activity. The Committee on Social Work Education has gone on record that graduate training in social work, with a specialization in public welfare, is the best means of acquiring this background of knowledge and skill. Since immediate personnel needs rule out graduate training as the main source of training for some years to come, the committee recommends that there be an extension of undergraduate sequences in public welfare, and that there be further development of in-service training programs and educational leave for persons already employed.[4]

The skill inherent in public assistance administration cannot be learned from books alone. It requires arduous, criticized practice under intensive supervision, based upon knowledge drawn from many other disciplines—notably psychology, psychiatry, and cultural anthropology. Since its nature and function are frequently misunderstood, its place in the process of public assistance must be examined. It can be considered from two related aspects: social investigation and human relations. The former is focused on *what* the worker must know about the needy person

[3] "The Public Assistance Worker," *Public Welfare,* June, 1951.
[4] The extent to which welfare administrators share this conviction about the desirability of professional training is, to say the least, uncertain.

in order to help him, while the latter is focused on *how* he secures these data and *how* he provides the needed assistance.

SOCIAL INVESTIGATION

Social investigation is both delicate and distasteful—delicate because of the necessity of maintaining a balance between the desire to help and the withholding of help unless need can be established (particularly difficult since the needy are often not *sufficiently* needy to qualify under agency policy); distasteful because of its association with the means test, and because of the requirement that proof be secured for all significant assertions made by applicants and recipients.

Investigation is not unique with public assistance. It is a condition for many things that man requires. It is a particularly sensitive issue in public assistance, however, because, apart from criminal investigation, there are few more searching inquiries into the intimate details of one's life and because, until relatively recently, it was assumed that the *poor as a class* could not be trusted but preferred relief to work and would exaggerate their need and lie about their affairs if they thought the truth would jeopardize the benefits sought. Although this assumption has been largely rejected, the need for proof has not lessened, though the way in which it is obtained has been modified.

It is undoubtedly distasteful to reserve judgment on the credibility of what one is told until verification is secured. Experience has demonstrated that most people who seek help tell the truth, as they understand it, even though, because of unfamiliarity with agency requirements, they may not be able to present a clear picture of their situation. Since some, either wittingly or unwittingly, distort the picture of their needs, the public assistance worker must have proof, since he is the guardian as well as the purveyor of public funds.

One of the greatest disservices to both the needy and the taxpayers has been the slipshod methods of eligibility determination revealed by legislative inquiries into the administration of assistance. These inquiries have often brought to light a disturbingly large number of recipients found to be ineligible, and an even larger number of genuinely needy persons whose eligibility had not been adequately established. The public has not always been able to distinguish lack of need from lack of *proof* of need, and, as a result, recipients generally have been exposed to suspicion, contempt, and hostility. There are some persons who shrink from a frank discussion of social investigation because emphasis on proof of need suggests that the needy are to be distrusted. Nevertheless, failure to give status to this art and to teach it systematically as an essential professional tool of the public assistance worker has in the long run worked hardship on persons who must seek assistance.

Evidence

A few years ago a number of public assistance workers first employed within the preceding year were interviewed by the training consultant of a state welfare agency. The purpose of the interviews was to find out how these young workers had been trained for the job and what they thought about it. One of the questions that baffled them dealt with what they had learned about social evidence and its relation to the determination of eligibility. When the question was rephrased, that is, when they were asked what they did about determining whether assistance should be granted, they were able to mention a number of specific points they had to "check." But as to any understanding of the nature of evidence *per se*, or of the probative value of different kinds of evidence, or of the inferences that might be drawn from evidence they were completely ignorant. Yet social evidence is the raw material with which they were dealing daily. Without evidence there could be no diagnosis, no effectual treatment.

Evidence, according to the *Encyclopaedia Britannica,* is "a term which may be defined briefly as denoting the facts presented to the mind of a person for the purpose of enabling him to decide a disputed question." In public assistance, eligibility is a "disputed question" until it has been proved.

It should not be too surprising to find that the young workers mentioned above had had no training in the use of evidence. In recent years the literature of social work has contained little on this subject. Mary Richmond, a pioneer in the development of social casework, was one of the few social workers who attempted to formulate ideas about its nature and application to social work. She comments as follows:

The words evidence and proof are often confused. *Evidence* is the ultimate fact or facts offered as a basis for inference; *inference,* a part of the process of reasoning from this fact or facts to another—unknown—fact; while *proof* is the result of reasoning. In social diagnosis, the kinds of evidence available, being largely testimonial in character, can of course never show a probative value equal to that of facts in the exact sciences. All that is possible for us is to obtain proof that amounts to a reasonable certainty.[5]

The question whether a thing be a fact or not is the question whether it can be affirmed with certainty.[6]

There are four main classes of evidence: real evidence, testimonial evidence (direct and hearsay), circumstantial evidence, and documentary evidence.

REAL EVIDENCE

"In real evidence the very fact at issue is represented to our senses." [7] Thus, if Mrs. Smith applies for ADC for her three children, and a visit to the home reveals three children for whom she has birth certificates, this is real evidence of the children for whom Mrs. Smith is seeking help. If the Jones family reports that their home has been destroyed by fire, and a visit confirms the fact, it is also real evidence. Unfortunately, much that is of greatest importance in determining eligibility for assistance cannot be established through real evidence. The facts that are most needed are usually of a negative nature: i.e., the applicant is *not* working; he has *no* income; he is *unable* to work; he has *no* savings; or he has *no* legally responsible relatives.

[5] Mary Richmond, *Social Diagnosis* (New York: Russell Sage, 1917), p. 55. Although this book was published in 1917, it represents the only attempt to deal systematically with the technique of social investigation. It contains a great deal which still has pertinence.
[6] *Ibid.,* p. 53.
[7] *Ibid.,* p. 56.

TESTIMONIAL EVIDENCE—ASSERTIONS

They may be direct ("I am in need of public assistance") or indirect ("Mrs. Jones said that she was in need of public assistance"). This testimony may be verbal or written. Since most public assistance work is carried on by means of interviews, it follows that testimonial evidence is plentiful. While of great significance, assertions made by applicants, recipients, or members of their families are not in themselves adequate proof of need.

In the past, great reliance was placed on the assertions of other, presumably disinterested, persons regarding the need of the applicant. Thus, neighbors, storekeepers, clergymen, etc., were asked for their opinions. We have come to realize that these are doubtful sources of evidence. Such testimony is largely hearsay; it is likely to be based on incomplete or erroneous information. Moreover, it is likely to be colored by conscious or unconscious bias either for or against the presumptively needy person. Nevertheless, under certain circumstances, the testimony of outsiders may be useful in establishing facts tending to verify need. A present employer may confirm the applicant's statements as to part-time employment, his earnings, and the length of employment. A former employer may confirm the fact that the applicant is no longer employed and his statements concerning the reason for termination of employment, past earnings, prospects for future employment, etc. Landlords and merchants may verify the applicant's debts; clinics may verify the applicant's state of health.

Modern practice favors securing this evidence indirectly, that is, by having the applicant or recipient obtain written testimony wherever possible. This may spare the applicant the embarrassment of having his plight become widely known, as he can often secure the necessary written data without having to reveal the reason he is requesting them. Furthermore, it makes the applicant an active participant in the joint process of establishing eligibility. Although evidence of this kind usually carries considerable weight, it too must be analyzed. Thus, a typewritten, signed statement from a former employer on his official letterhead will usually be acceptable, whereas a scrawled note on plain stationery may require further corroboration.

CIRCUMSTANTIAL EVIDENCE

Mary Richmond calls this the "catch all." It includes everything that is not a direct assertion of a human being. An object, event, or situation may be real evidence for one thing but only circumstantial evidence for something else. Thus, a home that is in an extreme state of disrepair, cold, draughty, unsanitary, and sparsely furnished is real evidence of the condition under which a family is living. As evidence of poverty and of need, it is circumstantial. Each year, newspapers in great cities report cases of people who, while living under every appearance of misery and squalor, are actually possessed of considerable wealth. Such cases are, of course, rare, and circumstantial evidence of this kind will normally carry weight.

A neighbor may complain that a woman who is receiving assistance is actually working, as it is observed that she leaves her home every morning at seven-thirty and does not return until six in the evening. If this complaint is confirmed, it is still only circumstantial evidence of employment. Actually the woman might be caring for her aged and ailing mother while her father is at work.

Circumstantial evidence is of importance because it may suggest the direction in which further investigation should be made. Circumstantial evidence that tends to confirm a person's claim that he is in need will more probably be accepted as valid than circumstantial evidence that suggests that he is not in need. In the latter case, more evidence will be sought for before the application is rejected. Miss Richmond comments on the cumulative effect of adding item to item in indirect evidence, each a comparatively weak basis for inference in itself, but gaining in cogency with each circumstance added:

Circumstantial evidence is always indirect, is characteristically cumulative. Moreover, any fact in the material universe or in the mind of man may become the basis from which some other fact is inferred. The trustworthiness of this indirect evidence, apart from the bias and competence of the witness through whom it may have come, depends upon a set of considerations which may vary with the nature of the subject matter . . . whereas the trustworthiness of direct evidence depends upon certain human traits possessed in varying degrees by all witnesses, such as honesty, bias, attention, memory, suggestibility, etc. . . .

Despite the difficulty of drawing correct inferences from circumstantial evidence, it has the advantage over direct testimonial evidence that the inference does not depend upon the elusive personal trustworthiness of a witness; for example, if a child's back is wounded in a certain way, the shape of the wound may be such as to indicate infallibly that it was beaten with an instrument and that the father's assertion about the child's falling downstairs must be false. The case worker will have to use both kinds of testimonial evidence—direct and indirect. In using indirect evidence, moreover, he will have to adapt his tests to an infinitely varied subject matter.[8]

DOCUMENTARY EVIDENCE

This is any kind of written evidence, from formal legal instruments to informal written statements of individuals. As such, it may be real, testimonial, or circumstantial evidence, depending on its nature. Direct testimony from a former employer that the applicant is no longer employed is testimonial evidence; a written statement to the same effect on the employer's letterhead is also testimonial evidence as well as documentary evidence. An official record of a deed of property ownership is real and documentary evidence of ownership. In both instances, documentary evidence is merely circumstantial with respect to need.

The written word carries great weight, and hence care must be taken not to overvalue evidence simply because it is in writing. In establishing a person's exact age, an official certificate of birth, or a transcript thereof, is probably the most reliable evidence. A baptismal record may also be acceptable, provided the record appears to be authentic. A birth record in a family Bible may be an acceptable proof of age, since it is assumed that at the time the entry was made the possibility of its being used to perpetrate a deception would not have been anticipated. But of what value is

[8] *Ibid.*, p. 60.

such an entry in proving that someone is over sixty-five if the Bible was published years after the passage of the Social Security Act?

We have already suggested that increasing reliance is being placed on documentary evidence in proving need. For this reason it is essential that such evidence be subjected to strict tests of credibility. Is it authentic? What facts does it establish? What inferences may be drawn from it? What additional evidence is needed?

Sources of Social Data

The determination of initial or continued eligibility for public assistance is now thought of as a joint undertaking between the applicant or recipient and the assistance agency. Although the burden of proving need may rest with the presumptively needy person, and he may be expected to participate actively in the process of eligibility determination, the major responsibility still rests with the public assistance worker. As the representative of the agency, he knows the services that the agency can provide and the conditions under which they are available; furthermore, he is the only one who can suggest ways in which these conditions can be verified or fulfilled. He, primarily, is responsible for the direction that the investigation takes. Unless he is well prepared for the job, he is likely to march off in all directions at once and become involved in prolonged, unnecessary, and unproductive explorations.

The following statement, drawn from the manual of a large welfare agency, sets forth clearly the purpose of the social investigation:

1. To permit the applicant to state his need in his own terms; why he is applying for assistance; and to explore with him in a preliminary way what use he has made or might make of his own resources in lieu of application for assistance.
2. If he decides to make application for assistance, to acquaint him with the provisions of the laws, regulations and other requirements relevant to his application.
3. To inform him of the nature of the proofs required to establish

eligibility and to help him in securing those proofs insofar as he needs or wishes such help.

4. To examine the proofs as to their validity for the purpose of establishing eligibility.
5. To arrive at a decision with respect to eligibility.
6. To discuss with the applicant the manner of calculating the amount of the grant and to arrive at a decision regarding the amount of the grant.
7. To inform the applicant of the decision.
8. To discuss with him the conditions applicable to his acceptance of a grant; the nature of his responsibility to report relevant changes; the periodic reconsideration of the grant; and any other conditions or arrangements which in the opinion of the local department require consideration.[9]

We thus see that the first step in a social investigation is to secure from the applicant a preliminary statement as to his situation. On the basis of this material, the worker is then able to advise him of his presumptive eligibility, and of the things that must be done in order to prove such eligibility.

A determination of eligibility is a decision by the agency on the basis of factual information that eligibility to receive assistance exists. The kinds of factual information that are acceptable as a basis for a decision concerning eligibility are oral statements, written material, and the observations of the worker. Acceptable sources of factual information relating to eligibility include the applicant, members of his family, the agency worker, and other qualified persons. Information presented by the applicant concerning a condition of eligibility, if it is pertinent, consistent, and complete is a satisfactory basis for the agency decision insofar as that condition is concerned.[10]

The reader will note that the term "factual information" is used three times in the above paragraph. Facts, however, must be distinguished from mere assertions. It will be recalled that

[9] Quoted in Anita J. Faatz, *The Nature of Policy in the Administration of Public Assistance* (Philadelphia: Pennsylvania School of Social Work, 1943), p. 33.
[10] Social Security Administration, *The Application Process in Public Assistance,* Bureau of Public Assistance Report No. 14 (Washington: Federal Security Agency, 1948), p. 12.

a fact is something that can be affirmed with certainty. If an applicant states that he has no savings, the only fact of which the worker can be certain is that he has made this assertion. It remains for further investigation to reveal whether or not this assertion is "in fact" true.

The importance of the applicant in the process of eligibility determination is brought out by Karl de Schweinitz:

> The chief source of information is the individual. There was a time when this was not the case. In the years before the coming of social security, particularly during the nineteenth century, the person who sought aid because of the economic distress of himself and his family was regarded as a lay figure not capable of participating in the development of the facts required in determining his need, or if capable, not to be trusted with this kind of responsibility. The method used was that of detection. The effort was to obtain information about the individual without his realizing what, during the course of an interview, he was revealing. No notes were taken lest he discover the importance placed upon what he might say. Clues to other sources of fact were sought in his unwitting remarks, and these sources were then consulted without his being told.
>
> Today the tendency is to look upon the individual as a principal source of evidence required to determine his eligibility for benefits. The assumption is that he is honest and able to take part in developing the information required, that he is entitled to know what the process of getting these facts involves, and what responsibilities the receipt of benefits or assistance payments places upon him. The purpose of the interview is stated and an application blank is used to indicate the specific facts that are required. The individual knows that he is being interviewed.[11]

The Bureau of Public Assistance supports this view, thus:

> The use of the applicant as the primary source of information in determining eligibility means that the applicant and the worker are jointly responsible for the facts and that, in many instances, the agency can determine eligibility or ineligibility on the basis of the facts supplied by the applicant. Moreover, the agency criteria for determining when the facts are pertinent, consistent, and complete may prop-

[11] Karl de Schweinitz, *People and Process in Social Security* (Washington: American Council on Education, 1948), p. 36.

erly include acceptance of facts presented orally by the applicant concerning his current circumstances or his personal and family history that, when related to other known facts and combined with the observations of the worker, substantiate the applicant's assertions concerning specific conditions of eligibility. In other words, the worker tells the applicant what conditions of eligibility he must meet and the factual information necessary to establish each condition. The applicant and the worker review and discuss such information as the applicant has at hand, and determine for what conditions of eligibility, information does not meet the agency's criteria of adequacy or is not in the applicant's possession. They must agree then as to what additional information must be obtained from readily available sources and who will obtain it—the applicant or the worker at the applicant's request. . . .

The worker takes no step in the exploration of eligibility to which the applicant does not agree. If, however, as is true in some cases, the information that an applicant is prepared to present is incomplete, inconsistent, or indeterminate, the agency should tell him that additional information is required. Usually, in such instance, the applicant and the worker can reach an agreement as to the sources to be used. Occasionally, however, the issue may be such that the applicant must decide whether to permit the agency to seek essential information, to drop his application, or to face having his application denied.[12]

The key point in this quotation is that the applicant is the primary *source of evidence* and that he and the worker are *jointly responsible for the facts*. It does not mean that the unsupported statements of the applicant are acceptable proof of need. It is necessary to stress this point because there is danger that in reacting from the old-fashioned "detective" type of investigation there will be a tendency to swing to the opposite extreme. A prime example of this reaction can be seen in the following letter used by a large public assistance agency in lieu of periodic investigation of active OAA cases.[13]

[12] *The Application Process in Public Assistance*, pp. 12–13.
[13] Commission on Governmental Efficiency and Economy, Inc., *The Department of Welfare in the City of Baltimore* (Baltimore: December, 1947), p. 40.

Feb. 28, 1947

My dear Mrs. Client:

We are in the process of reviewing continuing eligibility for Old Age Assistance.

We are writing to find out if there has been any change in your situation since you were last seen on July 5, 1946.

Unless we hear from you by March 10, 1947, we shall assume that there have been no changes in your living arrangements or needs.

Very truly yours,
(signed)
Social Worker

It is questionable whether this letter would be a fruitful source of evidence for determining continued eligibility. In the first place, the recipient might not understand what the worker wanted when she inquired about "any changes in your situation" and "changes in your living arrangements." But even if the recipient understood, it is not at all certain that he could compose a reply which would convey a clear picture of whatever changes had taken place. Secondly, if in the previous eight months there *had* been changes in the recipient's circumstances which would result in closing the case or in reduction of the grant, it is questionable whether the recipient would now report them, particularly since the wording of this letter appears to invite the recipient not to answer. Finally, this inquiry seems to be based on the assumption that the reply, if there is any, will contain the kind of evidence that would warrant continuance of assistance.

The Content of a Social Investigation

In discussing the subject of "attention," Mary Richmond makes the following point:

The closeness of attention on the part of any witness to an incident in his own or another's situation depends upon the importance which at the time he attaches to it, or, it may be upon the existence of a similarity between some part of that incident and something which he has experienced before—upon his "funded thought." This "funded thought" is his material for thinking, the sum total of ideas which his tradition, education, and experience have made an integral part of his mind. New experience which is entirely strange, which he can relate to nothing in his past thinking, he will not heed.[14]

Miss Richmond illustrates this point:

A post-graduate student in sociology had been sent, after careful directions, to visit a family, but apparently there were no hooks in his mind on which to hang instructions. He could not tell, when he returned to the office, whether the wife and mother seemed in good health or bad, he had no idea of the woman's approximate age, or the number of her children (there were a lot, he thought) or of the number and size of the rooms and their condition. But he did learn that the husband and father was working and that he was a member of a union. As the young man was writing a thesis upon Trade Unionism, the inference was obvious. He saw what he knew enough to notice.[15]

Section 172 of the *Public Assistance Manual* of the New York City Department of Welfare summarizes the kind of information required in order to determine need:

Any or all of the following items (the list is not inclusive) as well as any other items which have a bearing upon eligibility should be investigated in relation to the determination of eligibility. All available or potential resources should be completely explored and frankly discussed.

a. Past Maintenance

In an initial investigation, information shall be obtained regarding maintenance prior to application for assistance, and verification thereof shall be of such a nature as to establish clearly the exact way in which the present situation differs from the past, why public assistance is now necessary, and what resources are still available. In a reinvestigation, information regarding past maintenance and verification thereof, if pertinent to the determination of continuing eligibility, and information regarding management while in receipt of assistance shall be obtained. This information shall be of such a nature as to establish present and continuing need

[14] Richmond, *op. cit.*, p. 66.
[15] *Ibid.*, p. 68.

and to insure that the public assistance grant meets the purpose for which it was issued.

b. Employment

The investigator shall be responsible for determining if the applicant or client or any member of his family is employed.

1. The following information shall be secured and verified for each member of the family of employable age:

(a) Name and address of employers.

(b) Earnings—length of employment.

(c) Reason for termination of jobs.

(d) What type of work is he qualified to do?

(e) What are the job prospects in his field?

(f) The efforts he has made and he is making to secure employment—with what results?

(g) What efforts he has made to secure employment outside his field?

(h) Registration with the New York State Employment Service and eligibility for unemployment insurance benefits.

(i) Union affiliations.

(j) Odd jobs.

For those workers who have had what are called "odd jobs" or workers who have not had training and who have gone from job to job as the opportunity presented itself, a careful analysis of why such contacts are no longer available is important. Determination should be made regarding:

(1) Present availability of odd jobs.

(2) What source has the applicant or client used to secure these jobs?

(3) Have these jobs been in his trade or outside his trade?

(4) What have been the earnings?

It is important that addresses, periods of such employment, and earnings for each job be secured, since this is an aid in understanding the applicant's or client's past and present management as well as resources for future management.

(k) Seasonal employment.

Those workers who have been engaged in industries which have seasonal slack periods would normally be expected to plan through their own resources for those recurring slack periods. Therefore, the following must be explored in each such situation:

(1) What resources has the applicant or client used to manage previously during slack periods?

(2) Why are those resources not now available?

(3) Is the present slack period longer than usual?

(4) When does the season begin?

(5) Has he any borrowing capacity?

(6) Is he eligible for any unemployment insurance benefits?

(l) Educational or trade training as it relates to employment re-employment possibility.

2. The following information, as well as the pertinent information listed above, should be obtained and verified from each employed applicant or client or any member of his family whose earnings are not sufficient to enable him to maintain himself and his family without public assistance supplementation:

(a) Specific information regarding the wages paid, the work schedule, and the nature of the duties performed by the employed person.

(b) Is he employed at his maximum capacity?

(c) Does his work schedule permit him to get additional employment?

(d) Could he increase his wage-earning capacity by a program of retraining?

(e) Does his field of employment have slack periods? If so, what has been his plan for self-maintenance during such periods?

(f) What opportunities does the family have for supplementing his income through its own resources?

3. If the applicant or client is unable to continue working because of his own ill-health, the investigator should ascertain:

(a) The nature of the health problem.

(b) What medical care he is receiving.

(c) Specific data as to the probable duration of his illness and incapacity.

(d) Whether he is receiving any wages or disability allowance from any sources during his illness.

(e) Whether his old job is being held for him.

    (f) His ability to work part-time during his illness.

    (g) Whether he is fully or partially employable at an occupation other than his regular trade.

Verification of all statements is important and careful control of such cases in terms of time is essential. When a collateral visit is made to an employer, its purpose is not only to verify the employment status and to determine the possibility of re-employment, but to obtain information regarding possible openings in the industry, its seasons of greatest activity, its wage scale, and its methods of employing. This enables the investigator to discuss employment possibilities intelligently with the applicant or client and to stimulate his interest in seeking employment in his trade at a time when work is available. If any of the applicants or clients are employed or employable, current procedure with respect to payroll clearances with the Division of Placement and Unemployment Insurance shall be followed.

c. Relatives

Relatives of applicants or clients constitute an invaluable resource to the applicant or client and to the Department. The relative can often supply necessary and pertinent information regarding the eligibility of the client, his past maintenance and present need. Relatives are frequently an important employment resource as they can often suggest employment opportunities which would be available.

A careful and individualized consideration of the ability of relatives to support is essential to determine eligibility and degree of need. For this purpose, all legally responsible relatives must be contacted, as well as socially responsible relatives from whom there is a possibility of assistance. Every effort should be made to obtain full support from the relatives. If it is established that resources are insufficient for them to provide full or partial maintenance for the applicant or client, effort should then be directed toward obtaining their assistance in supplying such special needs as clothing, medical care, surgical appliances, care of children during employment of the applicant or client, or help with housekeeping during illness. Such assistance from relatives is important for its monetary value and in maintaining and strengthening family ties.

In situations where there is a deserting husband, putative or adjudicated father, who is not contributing to the support of the family, child or children, it is the primary responsibility of the applicant or client to make every effort to find or assist in finding the missing husband or father, and obtain support. When it appears that relatives who are legally responsible for the support of the applicant or client are able but unwilling to provide such support in full or in part in accordance with the relatives' circumstances, it is the responsibility of the applicant or client to seek support through appropriate court action. When court action is indicated or necessary, failure on the part of the applicant or client to institute or cooperate with the Department in the necessary legal proceedings will result in ineligibility for assistance.

d. Friends

When friends have assisted in the past it is important to know the names, addresses, the extent of their assistance and under what circumstances the assistance was given. Their present willingness and ability to assist should be explored. Are any other friends possible resources at the present time? Information obtained from friends should be carefully evaluated as to its objectivity.

e. Landlords

Present landlords should be contacted with reference to the following: What is the rent? Is the rent paid to date? Does the applicant or client pay his rent regularly? What amount has he paid? By whom has the rent been paid? Is the applicant or client a janitor; if so, what is his compensation for this service? Can the landlord give any information regarding boarders or lodgers?

Has the rent been established in accordance with legal controls, or is the rent not subject to control? The legal rent must be verified with appropriate agencies exercising control.

In some instances it may be advisable for the Investigator also to contact the previous landlord for pertinent information concerning the applicant's or client's eligibility for assistance.

f. Resources

The Investigator is responsible for determining the total available resources of each applicant and client and each member of the family.

1. Insurance

What insurance policies are carried by each member of the family? Have they been reviewed by the Resource Consultant? Has any cash or benefits been realized from insurance policies, the selling of policies or from death benefits, loans, disability or accident insurance? Is sickness or disability insurance carried now? How is the family paying the insurance premiums?

2. Banks

In the initial investigation there shall be an inquiry and a determination regarding present or past bank accounts and safe deposit boxes. Whenever there has been or is an indication of a bank account, this should be cleared in accordance with current procedure. The Investigator should see the bank book or bank statement to correlate withdrawals and deposits with the story of past management and assets. A review of the amount of withdrawals is important since cancellation of an account in one bank does not necessarily mean there is no account in another bank. In a reinvestigation, it is essential to determine whether adequate information has been obtained concerning present or past bank accounts or safe deposit boxes. When necessary, clearances or reclearances shall be initiated.

3. Postal Savings

The above points regarding bank accounts apply to postal savings. A statement of the applicant's or client's consent is necessary to obtain verification from the postal authorities and must be secured by the Intake Interviewer or Investigator wherever there is indication of postal savings.

4. Property

There must be a discussion with each applicant by the Intake Interviewer or Investigator regarding what real or personal property he has had in the past or now has, and such property must be evaluated with the Resource Consultant in order that complete information may be obtained to determine how it can be utilized for the applicant's present maintenance.

In a reinvestigation, it is essential to determine whether adequate information has been obtained concerning real or personal property the client has had or now has. When necessary, clearances or reclearances shall be initiated.

5. Compensation

(a) Has the applicant or client or any member of the family had an industrial accident? Is Workmen's Compensation possible? Is claim pending? Has applicant or client ever received an award?

    (b) Is applicant or client or any member of the family receiving disability insurance or allowance?

6. Pending Civil Suits

    (a) Are there any pending civil suits?

    (b) Can damages for personal injuries (accidents) be collected?

    (c) Can outstanding loans be collected?

7. Pensions and Benefits

    Is any member of the family eligible for:

    (a) Pensions for service in a public department such as Police, Fire, Education, or other.

    (b) Pensions or benefits from private industry; for example, from railroads or for personal service over an extended period.

    (c) Unemployment Insurance Benefits.

    (d) Old-Age and Survivors' Insurance Benefits.

    (e) Veterans' bonus, pensions, benefits and other allowances.

8. Allowances

    (a) Is applicant or client or any member of the family receiving an allowance through Family Court, Supreme Court, Court of Special Sessions or other legal process?

    (b) How often are these payments made? What is the amount?

    (c) Should applicant or client be referred to one of these sources?

9. Trust Funds and Estates

    Can monies be obtained from these resources at this time?

10. Other resources which the family may have such as

    (a) Janitorship: Is the compensation free rent, utilities, etc.?

    (b) Lodgers or boarders: Is there any present income from this source? Was it ever a source of income to the family? Is it a feasible plan at this time?

    (c) Lodges and unions: Does the family belong to any organization granting benefits? Under what circumstances are they paid? Does any member of the family have union affiliations? Are current dues paid? Date of last payment, amount, and how met? What are the possibilities for reemployment through this source? How often does each employable member contact this union?

g. Debts

> Amounts and dates should be secured in relation to past management. To whom owed, and under what circumstances borrowed? Has any part of the debt been repaid? What arrangements have been made for repayment? Does the applicant have further borrowing facilities? If money has been borrowed, were there co-makers to the loan? If so, who were they? Have they been contacted?

The public assistance worker cannot, however, rely upon a list of "points to be covered" alone because, no matter how detailed, such a list can never be exhaustive enough to cover all the combinations and permutations of circumstance that go to make up life. He needs a well-organized frame of reference concerning the problems and opportunities that people encounter in making a living and in managing their affairs. He must analyze each new bit of material brought out by his investigation with respect to its relevance, its consistency, and the inferences that can be drawn from it.

SELECTED REFERENCES

De Schweinitz, Karl, "The Basic Skill in Social Security," *Social Security Bulletin,* January, 1944.

De Schweinitz, Karl, *People and Process in Social Security,* Washington: American Council on Education, 1948.

A Guide to Content of the Public Assistance Case Record, Albany: New York State Department of Social Welfare, 1951.

"The Public Assistance Worker," *Public Welfare,* June, 1951.

Richmond, Mary, *Social Diagnosis,* New York: Russell Sage, 1917.

Social Security Administration, *The Nature of Service in Public Assistance Administration,* by Grace Marcus, Bureau of Public Assistance Report No. 10, Washington: Federal Security Agency, 1947.

Social Security Administration, *The Application Process in Public Assistance Administration,* Bureau of Public Assistance Report No. 14, Washington: Federal Security Agency, 1948.

Weber, Alice, "Interviewing," *Social Security Bulletin,* April, 1940.

CHAPTER 11

Human Relations
in the Administration
of Public Assistance

American culture has been greatly influenced by what has come to be called rugged individualism. This has resulted in the glorification of such characteristics as self-reliance, self-maintenance, and the smug virtues of the "self-made man," to the point where recognizing that a problem cannot be met unaided and seeking assistance from an outside source have become indictments of one's personal worth and integrity.

    —REV. SWITHUN BOWERS, O.M.I., *The Nature and Definition of Social Casework*

THE MEANING OF HUMAN RELATIONS

The term "social investigation" refers to that part of the public assistance worker's job which deals with the collection and analysis of social evidence bearing upon eligibility, but the worker is concerned with more than this. He must understand individual causes of need, discover ways in which to help recipients return to self-maintenance, and so deal with them that the experience of qualifying for and receiving assistance is not destructive. The term "human relations" may be applied to that aspect of the job which considers the applicant or recipient as a human being with hopes and fears, with conscious and unconscious biases, with blocks to understanding such things as cultural differences, language difficulties, and feelings that may interfere with his capacity for effective participation in the

269

establishment of eligibility and in the constructive use of assistance.

The primary responsibility of the assistance agency is to
provide help for eligible persons requesting it. In theory, it
might be said that the process of assistance administration consists in securing evidence concerning need and in applying
appropriate policy. In practice, however, it is not so simple.
Establishing eligibility is a complicated process. Often the cases
in which eligibility is hardest to prove are those in which need
is greatest. To the extent that the agency denies assistance to
genuinely needy persons because they are unable to prove need,
it fails in its obligation to the community. Though the burden of
proof rests with the applicant, this holds only if the latter is
equal to the task. Experience has shown that there is wide variation in ability to cope with it. The agency representative cannot,
therefore, fulfill his trust by sitting back and saying, "There are
the requirements; take them or leave them." His role must be
much more active. He must be able to distinguish between those
whose problem in establishing eligibility arises from the fact
that they actually are ineligible and those whose problem stems
from other causes.

The reader will recall that evidence of need is largely negative:
the applicant is *not* employed; he has *no* savings; he has *no*
legally responsible relatives; he *cannot* find work. Furthermore,
this evidence is, to a great extent, circumstantial; eligibility is
determined by piecing together an accumulation of data—none
of which by itself is clear proof of need, but which indicates a
presumption in favor of eligibility. Finally, much of the most
significant evidence comes not from direct observation or from
documentary sources but from the testimony of applicants, recipients, relatives, friends, and other interested persons. The
willingness and *ability* to give reliable testimony depend not so
much upon the shrewdness and thoroughness with which questions are put as on the *relationship* which the worker establishes
with the applicant.

A social investigation is not a cross-examination. The worker
who relies on a barrage of questions may get correct answers

to those he asks, but he doesn't get answers to those important questions he is unable to ask, because he doesn't know enough to ask them. To be sure, social investigation involves a certain amount of questioning—perhaps a great deal of questioning—but if too great reliance is placed on interrogation, the person interrogated may well feel that his only responsibility is to answer rather than to volunteer anything unasked.

An interview involves give-and-take. The person interviewed is encouraged to speak freely about matters of mutual concern. The interviewer may guide the interview, but he does not seek to force it into a set pattern because of the danger of shutting off important information that otherwise might be revealed spontaneously. If the interview is to be productive, the person interviewed must accept the purpose of the interview, understand the reasons why information is needed, and have confidence that what he reveals will not be used to trap him, to exploit him, or to condemn him—or persons close to him.

The worker is frequently faced with the necessity of confronting applicants and recipients with two unpleasant alternatives: conforming to certain requirements of the agency (such as consenting to have relatives visited, bringing a husband into court for nonsupport, agreeing to a lien on property, surrendering insurance, etc.) or having assistance denied or withdrawn. To apply agency policy firmly and appropriately and yet not add to the burden of bitterness, discouragement, or resentment of the needy person requires considerable sensitivity and insight into human nature. Thus, as De Schweinitz reminds us:

That skill must always be focused on the purpose of the agency. To see this purpose and the relationship with the client as incompatible is a denial of skill. There are workers who have failed to deal with a job refusal thinking that to do so would jeopardize the relationship. The same thing has happened with refusals to take court action in desertion or in non-support where a resource may reasonably be involved and the policy of the agency requires such action. In not meeting this kind of situation the worker is revealing his lack of skill.

On the other hand, an unwarranted assumption of authority can likewise stem from an absence of professional discipline. The intrusion of the worker's unwanted concern about a client's behavior or the implication that manners, morals or the ways of bringing up children must change simply because the client is receiving assistance, can violate the individual's sense of independence and confuse him about what is and what is not required, and also defeat what the worker would like to achieve.[1]

Obviously, the relation between worker and client cannot be like an impersonal business transaction; it involves hard choices and is charged with feeling—and the worker must be prepared to cope with the feelings. He must try to understand what they mean to the client—not how the client "ought" to feel, or how he, the worker, thinks he would feel were he in similar circumstances. It does not necessarily follow that public assistance workers should be trained to diagnose and treat personality disorders, but they should at least be sufficiently familiar with psychology to recognize the causes and symptoms of emotional stress and how feelings may interfere with logical behavior.

Feelings, Behavior, and Policy

Professor Alexander Leighton summarizes types of stress and the way people react to them as follows:

A. TYPES OF STRESS

The following specific types of stress are disturbing to the emotions and thoughts of the individual:

a. Threats to life and health;
b. Discomfort from pain, heat, cold, dampness, fatigue and poor food;
c. Loss of means of subsistence, whether in the form of money, jobs, business or property;
d. Deprivation of sexual satisfaction;
e. Enforced idleness;
f. Restriction of movement;
g. Isolation;
h. Threats to children, family members and friends;
i. Rejection, dislike and ridicule from other people;

[1] Karl and Elizabeth McCord de Schweinitz, "The Contribution of Social Work to the Administration of Public Assistance," *Social Work Journal*, October, 1948, p. 162.

j. Capricious and unpredictable behavior on the part of those in authority upon whom one's welfare depends.

The following general types of stress are derived from the more specific types, but are in themselves particularly disturbing to the emotions and thoughts of the individual:

a. Persistent frustration of goals, desires, needs, intentions and plans;
b. Circumstances that promote the dilemma of conflicting and mutually incompatible desires and intentions;
c. Circumstances creating confusion and uncertainty as to what is happening in the present and what can be expected in the future.

B. THE WAY PEOPLE REACT TO STRESS

Cooperation, withdrawal, and aggressiveness are three universal kinds of behavior with which individuals react to authority when subject to forces of stress that are disturbing to the emotions and thoughts of the individual.

Cooperation and compliance with authority resulting from disturbed emotions and thoughts may:

Operate to free the individual from the forces causing the disturbed emotions and thoughts;

Operate to permit the continuance of the forces causing the disturbed emotions and thoughts;

Lead the individual to extremes of blind submission that rob him of the ability to take care of himself.

Withdrawal, apathy, and indifference arising from disturbed emotions and thoughts may:

Serve to protect the individual from some of the forces causing the disturbed emotions and thoughts and enable him to survive until conditions improve;

Operate to permit the continuance or increase of the forces causing disturbed emotions and thoughts;

Lead to extremes of selfishness, isolation, personal deterioration and unreliability.

Aggression arising from disturbed emotions and thoughts may:

Stimulate the individual to take decisive actions that will free him from the forces causing the disturbed emotions and thoughts;

Lead to confused and violent action wholly inappropriate to the circumstances of the individual.[2]

Economic need, if it is unmet, produces stress—in fact, the needy person may be subject to several kinds of stress. Need is a threat to his life and health; it causes discomfort; it implies a loss of subsistence; it may involve idleness, and so on. Moreover, if the needy person is at all aware of the traditional attitudes of society toward the dependent, he may well suspect that he will be subject to dislike and ridicule, and to capricious and unpredictable behavior on the part of those from whom he must seek help.

The circumstances which have caused economic need are usually a source of stress that would be painful even if economic need were not present. Need is usually caused by the death, desertion, sickness, incapacitation, or unemployment of the principal family wage earner. Thus, a young woman recently widowed or deserted might well be overwhelmed by her loss even though she has resources sufficient for herself and her children. A man forced to retire at sixty-five though still in excellent health may become discouraged and depressed even though his savings and pension are ample for his needs. A person forced to give up work because of a serious accident or illness may well be overcome with anxiety regardless of his resources. When need is added to these problems, the stress may become unbearable.

In this competitive society, moreover, success or failure is measured in terms of economic status. The public's attitude toward the dependent still tends to range between condescension and contempt. The needy person, therefore, finds his situation humiliating, not only because of community attitudes, but also (since he is likely to share the views of the society of which he is a part) because of his own feelings of failure.

Finally, as we have seen, the conditions on which assistance is granted are hard to accept.

Whether an individual will react to stress by coöperation, withdrawal, or aggressiveness will depend on his personality

[2] Alexander Leighton, *The Governing of Men* (Princeton: Princeton University, 1945), chap. 16.

structure. Whether his reaction will be positive or negative depends upon how great the pressure is upon him; and concerning this there can be no generalizations—it is an individual matter. Of two individuals faced with serious illness, one is able to mobilize the strength to compensate for it while the other breaks down; yet if these same individuals were faced with a different kind of problem, unemployment, for example, the roles might be reversed. A man who behaves with courage and resourcefulness on the battlefield may become confused and unreasonable when obliged to ask for help.

Most people who ask for public assistance have emotional resources adequate to cope with their problems. Though troubled, if their basic needs are met, if their needs are studied with tact and understanding, they can adapt themselves to changing circumstances. If the public assistance worker is crude and inept in his approach, his failure to appreciate the feelings of applicants or recipients may so add to the latter's burden that they will be incapable of reacting positively.[3]

There are some people who, though functioning fairly well when things are running smoothly, are unable to bear up under stress. They are easily overwhelmed by external pressures and adopt behavior "wholly inappropriate to the circumstances." Thus, some people may become so resentful of the fact of need that they must challenge even the simplest requirement of the assistance agency. Others may be so distrustful that they go to extremes of deceit and concealment about matters which, if they were known, would in no way affect eligibility. Still others may fall easily into a pattern of blind submission and dependency.

In every community, moreover, there are some persons who are feeble-minded or mentally ill. Their condition may be un-

[3] The following incident, recently called to the attention of the writer, illustrates the need for tact and sensitivity in dealing with needy persons. An ailing man was denied assistance because he refused to secure medical confirmation of his inability to work. When this man subsequently asked for help from a private welfare agency, the reason he had refused to get medical verification came to light: The public assistance worker had told him he had to get a statement from the clinic certifying that he was "unemployable."

diagnosed or, if diagnosed, not considered sufficiently acute to warrant institutionalization. Often such persons are in need. Their behavior, however, makes determination of eligibility extremely difficult.

Finally, most communities have at least a few individuals and family groups who are "marginal"; that is, they are socially, psychologically, and economically on the fringes of society. They are ineffectual in making a living, in rearing a family, in managing a home. Delinquency, immorality, alcoholism, marital discord, illegitimacy, disinclination to work, and filth and disorder are commonly present. Chronic poverty, running, perhaps, through generations, is merely one symptom of their disorganized lives. It should not be a matter for surprise that persons so inadequate are known to the assistance agency. They constitute one of its most difficult administrative and public relations problems because their behavior is often unrecognized as symptomatic of serious emotional instability, but instead is judged to be willfully obstructive, irresponsible, and delinquent. In some cases this may be true, but how are they to be distinguished and on what basis is treatment differentiated?

"The role the profession may have in the future administration of public assistance," comments Donald Howard, "may well depend upon social work's skill in either demonstrating how the 'hard core' cases—the 'ne'er-do-wells,' the 'chronic loafers,' the 'chronically unmarried mothers,' the 'deserting spouses and putative fathers'—can really be helped, or in defining the limits beyond which this skill cannot yet be expected to be of much help." [4]

We have already pointed out that need is the primary requirement for eligibility (apart from the requirements for specific assistance categories) but that the behavior of the needy person may affect eligibility. Thus, the worker must decide whether need is caused by the failure of the applicant or recipient to take certain actions which would make assistance unnecessary. The worker, moreover, must insist that the needy person accept

[4] Donald Howard, "Public Assistance Returns to Page One," *Social Work Journal,* July, 1948, p. 116.

certain conditions even though they do not affect need. Thus, the refusal of an aged man to have his children interviewed will result in denial of assistance even though, in fact, the children cannot contribute to his support.

In the above situations, the responsibility of the worker is clear: He must be able to help the needy persons accept these requirements. If they do not, agency policy requires that he deny or withdraw assistance. But if the failure of the needy person to accept these requirements results from the worker's lack of skill, then the agency has failed to discharge its obligations.

Behavior may be an issue in assistance administration in still another way, one in which the role of the agency is by no means as clear—because society is not clear as to what its role should be. We refer to those needy persons whose need has been caused by past mistakes, indiscretions, delinquencies; and to those needy persons whose present behavior, although it has no bearing on need, runs counter to behavior the community deems acceptable. Consider, for example, the young woman who could be supporting herself were it not for the fact that she has two children born out of wedlock; or the family that has squandered an inheritance; or the man who is in need during his "off" season because he failed to save when he was employed. These people are in need, and nothing they can do *now* can alter that fact.

"What can we do," complained a young public assistance worker, "when we find that an ADC mother has a paramour living in her home? If we tell her this relationship must terminate, she is likely to try to deceive us, or else the man will take a room around the corner and the relationship will continue. Meanwhile, we have aroused her resentment and distrust. On the other hand, if we say that the man should contribute to the support of the home, we are in effect condoning an illicit relationship. If we withdraw ADC because the home is 'unsuitable,' the family becomes eligible for home relief which in this state has standards identical with ADC. If we deny home relief, we can do so only on the basis that there is no need— presumably because the paramour is in a position to provide full support. Here again we are in the position of condoning the relationship. But suppose the paramour is on assistance himself? What then? Of course, we could bring the case into children's court on a petition of neglect, but if the mother provides adequate physical care and seems to love her children there is little likelihood that the court would commit the children to foster care unless there was evidence of gross and flagrant immorality. Even if the finding of neglect were made, the court would only order the man out of the home and place the woman under the supervision of a probation officer. This would mean that assistance would have to be continued and we would be right back where we started."

This young worker was understandably troubled. She realized that whatever decision she made would affect this woman and her children for good or for ill—and she didn't know which. She realized that it is unjust and ineffectual to try to use the power to grant or withhold assistance as a means of enforcing society's moral code—unjust, because it subjects certain people in the community to controls to which others are not subject, although their behavior is equally reprehensible; ineffectual, because threats and penalties rarely have lasting effect and are often, indeed, detrimental. She was particularly concerned, moreover, because she realized that she didn't know enough about the art and science of human relations to know what course of action would be to the best interests of the children.

Granted that Sam Brown rather than the taxpayer has the primary responsibility for supporting his family; but Sam is barely literate; not only is he completely unskilled but he is clumsy and unreliable. Should he get a job, his employer will soon find him a liability and discharge him at the first opportunity. Suppose that Sam makes no real effort to find work; suppose that he "likes to lie a-bed of mornings"—can we be sure that this is due to plain "cussedness"? Could it not be that his "not feeling like working" might be the result of a lifetime of poor nutrition, of rotting teeth, of bad eyesight, of a profound but unrecognized discouragement?

Sarah Smith, ADC recipient, is the mother of four children, all born out of wedlock to different fathers—two, since she began to receive public assistance. If Sarah is in need, and if the men who fathered her children cannot be located or are unable to provide support, should she be denied assistance simply because of her behavior? Is the denial likely to impress upon her the advantages of a virtuous life? Is it likely to benefit the children?

Bill Jones has deserted his wife and three children and is living with another woman by whom he has had three more children. For years Mr. Jones supported both families; now he can support only one. Should Mrs. Jones be denied assistance because it is her husband's responsibility to support her and the children? Is this likely to prompt Mr. Jones to return to the bosom of his legitimate family? If so, what will happen to his other children?

Such cases constitute a relatively small proportion of the average public assistance case load, but the trouble they cause is far out of proportion to their number. From time to time, when the public becomes conscious that people like this are being supported by the taxpayer, the assistance agency is deluged with criticism. The complaint is heard that "easy and generous relief" encourages behavior of this sort. There is just enough truth in this generalization to make it exceedingly dangerous.[5] Probably

---

[5] An astounding lack of appreciation of the limitations under which public assistance agencies operate is reflected in two articles in the *Saturday Evening Post*. The first, by Judge Jacob Panken of the New York City Domestic Relations Court, appeared in the September 30, 1950, issue and was entitled "I Say Relief Is Ruining Families." The second, by reporter Paul Mallow, appeared in the September 8, 1951, issue and was entitled "The Relief Chiselers Are Stealing Us Blind." The authors of both articles are understandably irritated at evidences of gross mishandling of individual cases, but they also make sweeping generalizations regarding the effect of relief on its recipients and about the "failure" of assistance agencies to prevent misuse of relief funds and the misbehavior of recipients.

Judge Panken summarizes his views thus: "Every day, sitting in court, I amass new evidence that the relief set-up is sapping their will to work; that it is encouraging cynicism, petty chiseling and barefaced immorality; that it is inefficient, profligate and unwilling to distinguish between those in need and those who are taking a paid vacation at the public expense." It is

there *are* a few persons who would behave with greater circumspection if assistance were more difficult to get. For the most part, however, they are enmeshed in social, emotional, and economic difficulties of such long duration that they are often unable to disentangle themselves even with the most skilled help.

The responsibility which the community sometimes seems to expect the public assistance worker to assume is greater than that of a judge. Sarah Smith gets no relief because she "should have known better" while Sam Brown gets relief because "he couldn't help himself." For the person who does not have to take responsibility for these decisions it is easy enough to play at being God.

The public assistance job is further complicated by the fact that problems of behavior that jeopardize eligibility are usually found in only one or two members of a family group; the others—particularly the children—are innocent victims. Of course, it is often suggested that in such cases the children should be removed from the home. This, however, is no solution. In the first place, substitute parental care in either foster homes or institutions is much more expensive than public assistance. Secondly, existing facilities are limited and it would be impossible to expand them sufficiently to accommodate all those children removed from their natural homes because of the community's desire to punish the parents. Finally, child care specialists have learned that substitute parental care, no matter how efficient, is a poor substitute for care by the children's own parents—even though they be inadequate in many respects. Parents, moreover, cannot be deprived of their children except for grave reasons and only by order of the court. The latter is reluctant to take such action if there is any possibility of improving the home situation.[6]

surprising that the Judge's experience in court has not made him aware that untrained staff can do little about changing a person's behavior; that even professional staff are often defeated in this effort; that threats and penalties frequently fail to have lasting effect; that the causes of a person's circumstances are often extremely difficult to discover. Mr. Mallow apparently supports the view that people whose behavior is objectionable should get no relief; that children born out of wedlock should be taken from their mothers and placed in "orphanages."

[6] Because of conflicting public opinion, assistance agencies often find

Society will have to reconcile itself to the existence of that "hard core" of irresponsible people of whom Donald Howard writes—whether or not they get assistance, they will continue to be irresponsible. Consequently, if they are not to starve or more probably be driven to a life of outright crime, and if society is unable or unwilling to institutionalize them, they will have to get assistance if they are in need.[7]

THE ROLE OF SOCIAL CASEWORK IN THE ADMINISTRATION OF PUBLIC ASSISTANCE

A recent definition of casework runs as follows: "Social casework is an art in which knowledge of the science of human relations and skill in relationship are used to mobilize capacities in the individual and resources in the community appropriate for the better adjustment between the client and all or part of his total environment." [8]

The three functions of a public assistance agency outlined in the opening paragraphs of the preceding chapter conform closely to the above definition. The provision of financial assistance based on need is certainly "mobilization of appropriate resources in the community"; helping people to return to a condition of self-support is clearly "mobilizing capacities in the individual"; and administering assistance in a constructive manner requires "skill in relationship." The points we have stressed thus far concerning the relation of total behavior to eligibility for assistance have been made for the express purpose of demonstrating that

themselves in the wrong regardless of what they do. Thus, when the New York City Department of Welfare withdrew ADC in certain cases in order to get relatives with whom the children were living to consent to foster placement (their homes were considered unsuitable) the department was severely criticized by Judge Hubert T. Delany, a colleague of Judge Panken, for "usurping" the function of the Children's Court.

[7] Granted that assistance payments should not be used to exact a standard of behavior for recipients higher than that for others in the community, what should be done when assistance *enables* someone to indulge in undesirable behavior? For example, a mother is granted ADC so that she can quit work and remain at home caring for her children; instead, she spends most of her time out of the home carousing with unsavory companions.

[8] Rev. Swithun Bowers, O.M.I., *The Nature and Definition of Social Casework* (New York: Family Service Association of America, 1949), p. 19.

"knowledge of the science of human relations" is an essential element in public assistance administration.

Recently there has been controversy regarding the place of casework in public assistance. The controversy seems to have arisen at least in part because the term "casework" is used in two different contexts: to describe a general method that may be used in administering a variety of social services, and to describe a specific social service, namely, psychological counseling, directed toward the diagnosis and treatment of personality difficulties interfering with a person's ability to maintain constructive and satisfying social relationships. Often the term is used without indicating the sense in which it is applied.

Even when this distinction is made clear, opinion differs as to whether casework in its latter sense should be a part of public assistance. Some authorities, as has been already noted, maintain that assistance should be administered as nearly like social insurance as possible; others argue that it is impossible to determine need and to help people to return to self-support if the psychological factors related to need are disregarded; still others advocate that assistance agencies provide "casework treatment" as an additional service for all persons in the community who seek it, regardless of economic need—in other words, that assistance agencies take on the function provided usually by voluntary family service agencies.

Whether or not this should be done need not be debated here. For the present it is administratively and financially impracticable. Should this service be assumed by the assistance agency, however, there are sound arguments in favor of administering it separately from the public assistance function.

The diagnosis and treatment of personality difficulties are expensive. It can be done only by highly specialized staff under intensive supervision and with close psychiatric consultation. Social workers qualified to do this sort of work are few in number. Their training is costly, and they can command relatively high salaries as far as social work compensation goes. Although, theoretically, it might be desirable if every public assistance worker were thus trained, it would not be practicable. Public assistance is essentially a mass program; relatively few needy people would either want or need this type of service. Hence it would be a misapplication of professional and tax resources to employ such staff when there would be little demand for their specialized skill.

Although "psychological counseling" is not essential to public assistance, the casework method is a sine qua non. Without it public assistance becomes a mere dole. The distinction between casework as a method of administering a social service (such as public assistance) and case work as a distinct social service concerned with the treatment of personality disorders is, however, easier to make in theory than in practice. How can the two be differentiated, especially in situations in which economic need is inextricably entwined with emotional problems? Can the worker determine eligibility and administer assistance constructively without taking into consideration the relation between the applicant's or recipient's behavior and his need?

The following case illustrations may point up the distinction:

The worker, who was inexperienced, could not understand why John Standish was always late for his job in the factory and, as a consequence, was fired. She superficially saw Mr. Standish as a big, strapping fellow who was too lazy to get up in the morning. When he applied for relief, the worker argued with him, taking the attitude that his present situation was entirely his fault.

Mr. Standish was used to having people take this fact for granted. His wife did, his boss did, his wife's mother did. He unconsciously looked upon all these people with hostility. Now this person from whom he must get a relief order or else go home to a hungry and resentful family empty handed, was making the same assumption. He had long ago given up trying to explain his situation to anyone. No one would believe what he said, anyway. Besides, how could he explain that his wife either wept or argued far into the night and then objected when he wanted her to get up and get breakfast for him. She even complained that he disturbed her when he got up to get it for himself. The last person to whom he would explain his situation was this young woman before whom he was now sitting and who was telephoning his last place of employment about his work record. When his boss told her that "the only time John was on time was when he wasn't there" she had turned on him and said, "You lost your job for being late, what right have you to come here and ask for relief?" Instead of explaining, he got sullen and demanded the order, saying that he would stay there until he got it. After all, as bad as this situation was, it was better than facing an angry wife and hungry family.

The worker, finally, reluctantly gave him an order. Mr. Standish went out vowing that he would never come to that place again. He had formed his opinion of relief, or relief workers, and of his government, and in no sense was it complimentary. He classed them all as his enemies. He never did come back; instead, when the order was gone, he left home. The worker never knew what became of him but it is probable that he joined the ever increasing group of men wandering from city to city. As a result, the relief organization had a fatherless family to care for.[9]

The trouble with Bill Rogers was not so much that he couldn't *get* a job as that he couldn't *keep* it. In the past five years he had had twelve jobs—none lasting more than eight months. Sooner or later something would happen: the situation would become intolerable and he would quit, or else he would be discharged—ostensibly because of trouble-making, Mr. Rogers admitted, but actually because of the hostility of his fellow workers. When he applied for assistance, he discussed his situation frankly, adding that he needed vocational guidance because he had begun to realize that his employment difficulties were due to the fact that he was temperamentally unsuited to this particular line of work. Perhaps, as he said, he could be directed to work he would find more interesting and where he could associate with more congenial people.

The worker, who was trained, realized that there was more to the problem than met the eye and she was not misled by Mr. Rogers' honest and superficially plausible explanation of his difficulties. As she explored his needs, she got him to talk about his work, his relations with his fellow workers and superiors; bit by bit she began to piece together a picture which revealed Mr. Rogers as a profoundly discouraged and frightened man who, in spite of his rationalizations, was beginning to suspect that his difficulties in relation to work were due to causes deep within himself. Although she did not attempt to diagnose the problem, she was aware that the evidence pointed to a serious maladjustment and that at this point Mr. Rogers would not be able to function effectively no matter what line he was in. The prob-

[9] Ella Lee Cowgill, *A Guidebook for Beginners in Public Assistance* (New York: Family Service Association of America, 1940), p. 22.

lem was not that of finding him another job—for he was anxious to work—but in *not* referring him until the case could be studied further. She suspected that Mr. Rogers was near the breaking point and that another job failure—which was a foregone conclusion— would be more than he could tolerate and would precipitate a complete breakdown.

The worker did not deny Mr. Rogers' request for vocational guidance, but as part of the plan she arranged for a psychiatric interview which corroborated her findings. Although Mr. Rogers was feeling too threatened by his problems to accept an outright psychiatric examination, he could accept it as part of a counseling plan. The worker, the psychiatrist, and the psychologist carefully refrained from adding to his great need to get a job and prove to himself that he was capable. Instead, he was helped to accept treatment at a mental hygiene clinic; meanwhile assistance was given.

In this case, six months of assistance plus skilled care enabled Mr. Rogers to improve to the point where he could take a job—and keep it. Had he been encouraged to take the first job available and thus get off relief, it might well have resulted in his being hospitalized for years—perhaps life.

In the first case, although we do not have the entire story, we see a man whose economic problems arose because of his inability to cope with a family problem. His wife appears to be a disturbed person, and his weakness is also not without significance. To establish himself economically, he needed not only immediate financial assistance but help with the situation that was causing this need. One of his needs, therefore, was to have someone try to understand his situation *as he saw it*. The fact that he did not express this need in so many words made it none the less real. He couldn't, in fact, discuss it until he had some assurance that the worker was capable of understanding him. She wasn't. In spite of the fact that she was employed to deal with problems such as this, she had no more competence than any lay person. Had she been trained in human relations, she could have averted a broken home and long-time dependency and saved the taxpayers thousands of dollars.

In the second case, we see a worker who used her casework knowledge not to treat a problem that was beyond her powers and the function of the agency, but to administer assistance in as helpful a fashion as possible within the limitations imposed by that problem. This is casework of the highest order.

Relatively few public assistance workers are able to deal skillfully with problems such as these. Casework training is not a requirement for employment nor is any serious attempt made to teach it on the job. Although public assistance workers deal with hundreds of needy persons (and presumptively needy persons) and are responsible for the authorization of from $75,000 to $100,000 in relief funds annually, there is little organized effort to help them learn the job. To be sure, a great deal is said about "in-service training" but, like the weather, "everybody talks about it but nobody does anything about it." What passes for in-service training in most jurisdictions is barely distinguishable from orientation and staff development, which are necessary for all workers —whether or not they have had previous training.

Training, such as it is, usually consists of a few weeks of orientation, after which the neophyte is given a case load and turned over to a supervisor who is herself untrained and beset with a hundred other responsibilities. The worker learns—but only after a fashion. As many young workers put it, it is "trial and error," or "hit and miss." When human welfare and public funds are at stake this can be expensive.

Ironically enough, when legislative investigations of public assistance administration have revealed inefficiency, confusion as to purpose, misapplication of policy, inadequate social investigation, and misguided attempts at "treatment," the blame for this state of affairs is often placed on the fact that the staff is composed of "social workers" rather than trained financial investigators. Thus, Lewis Meriam, although accepting the necessity for trained case workers to handle certain types of problem cases, doubts whether they are equipped by temperament or training to conduct the kind of investigations needed in public assistance.[10] "The necessity of finding good," he points out, "tends to

---

[10] Meriam, *Relief and Social Security* (Washington: Brookings, 1946), p. 808. Dr. Meriam does not explain how "financial investigators" would be able to recognize emotional and social problems that should be called to the attention of a case worker. The overly sympathetic worker may see eligibility where none exists; the "hard-boiled" worker may deny help to

make caseworkers attorneys for the defense. The client's short-comings must be so explained that there can be no verdict of total depravity."[11] Be this as it may, the fact that case workers are trained to help rather than to condemn does not prevent them from carrying out policy—even when they disagree with the policy.

The distrust of specialized education, at least in so far as it applies to public assistance, is reflected in the report on the Department of Welfare of the City of Baltimore, in which the statement is made that "No amount of school training can ordinarily take the place of ability that is based on common sense and practical experience."[12] "Practical experience," as any golfer will admit, will never get one out of the ranks of "duffers" unless it is accompanied by training. As for "common sense," if this book accomplishes anything, it should make clear that what is needed is not "common sense" but "uncommon sense"—that "common sense" which is so useful when applied to everyday affairs can lead one astray when applied to problems of great complexity, subtlety, and delicacy.

Actually, of course, few public assistance workers (or supervisors) have had any formal training. Public assistance agencies do not pay salaries that attract professionally trained social workers. The errors in case handling that are brought to light reflect not the philosophy and method of social case work but rather well-intentioned though misguided efforts of untrained (or partially trained) people to do what they think trained case workers would do.

Since, in many jurisdictions, public assistance workers have the civil service classification of "caseworker," it is only natural that they take trained case workers as their model. Unfortunately, the few professionally trained persons in public assistance are usually

---

genuinely needy persons. It is the ineptitude of the former, however, that comes to the attention of the public because his mistakes are easier to discover.

[11] *Ibid.*

[12] Commission on Governmental Efficiency and Economy, Inc., *The Department of Welfare of the City of Baltimore* (Baltimore: December, 1947), p. 50.

in administrative positions or else in the higher echelons of supervision, where they have little direct contact with the case-load carrying staff. The latter, from reading professional litera-ture (which tends to ignore public assistance), from attendance at conferences and institutes, and from occasional part-time courses in schools of social work, have acquired bits and snatches of casework knowledge which have not always been too well assimilated. They have tended, moreover, to take the casework practice of social workers in other agencies for their criterion. But since the function of family service agencies, medical social work bureaus, and child guidance clinics is quite different from that of public assistance, confusion is inevitable. Thus, it was not a trained case worker who was involved in either of these two cases:

A man applying for assistance was asked by the worker about his feelings toward his wife, his wife's feelings toward him, his feelings toward their children and the children's feelings about him, the wife's feelings toward the children and their feelings toward her, and, finally, about his feelings about the children's feelings toward the wife. Whereupon the applicant said, "Lady, I only came here to ask for assistance." To this the worker replied, "But before we can help you we must understand you."

A recipient of public assistance seen by a psychiatrist, was told that there was nothing he needed so much as a job. After receiving assistance for eighteen months the man was again referred to a psychiatrist who reaffirmed his earlier recommendation, expressing some surprise that nothing had been done in the meantime to help the man find employment. When the assistance worker was asked why the record showed no evidence that employment possibilities had been discussed, the worker replied, "Several times during the year and a half he was given the opportunity to discuss the problem of employment. When he nevertheless avoided the subject I knew it must be painful to him but thought it not up to me to intrude into our relationship anything so painful." [13]

Many of the most promising young workers, those who are in-experienced and untrained but eager to help people, have con-ceived the idea that only to the extent that they are counseling

[13] Donald Howard, *op. cit.*, p. 115.

people on complex social and emotional problems are they functioning as social workers. The determination of eligibility and related duties are accepted as necessary but unpleasant chores
which interfere with their efforts in this direction. Thus, as De
Schweinitz points out: "Another public assistance agency may
have escaped being caught in this net because as one perplexed
young worker put it, 'The extent to which we delve into the
causative factors of emotional problems is limited by our time.'
Considering how much clients have been spared because of high
case loads and the immediacy of demands of the job, one sometimes feels that the weight and volume of the work in public
assistance is not without its compensations." [14]

Training is one of the most urgent problems in public assistance. As the social insurances take over an increasing number of
cases in which income maintenance is the only major problem,
the public assistance load will become a residual one—one in
which the proportion of "problem" cases will increase. If assistance agencies do not take steps to secure staff skilled in docu-
menting the reasons for granting or withholding assistance and
skilled in dealing with (not necessarily "treating") behavior
problems, the criticism of public assistance will increase rather
than diminish.

SELECTED REFERENCES

De Schweinitz, Karl and Elizabeth McCord, "The Contribution of
Social Work to the Administration of Public Assistance," *Social
Work Journal,* July, October, 1948.

Hamilton, Gordon, "The Role of Social Casework in Social Policy,"
Proceedings of the National Conference of Social Work (Chicago),
New York: Columbia University, 1952.

Howard, Donald, "Public Assistance Returns to Page One," *Social
Work Journal,* April, July, 1948.

Leibling, A. J., "Horsefeathers Swathed in Mink," *Social Work Journal,*
January, 1948.

Linford, Alton A., "Which Way Public Assistance Administration?"
Social Work Journal, July, 1952.

[14] De Schweinitz, *op. cit.,* p. 162.

Meriam, Lewis, *Relief and Social Security,* Washington: Brookings, 1946, chap. 34.

Method and Skill in Public Assistance (Journal of Social Work Process), Philadelphia: University of Pennsylvania, 1938.

Perlman, Helen Harris, "Casework Service in Public Welfare," *Proceedings of the National Conference of Social Work* (San Francisco), New York: Columbia University, 1947.

"The Real Crisis in Public Assistance," *Social Work Journal,* April, 1950.

Social Security Administration, *The Implication of the Federal Social Security Act for Social Work Agency Practice* and *Money Giving in Social Work Agencies—in Retrospect and in Prospect,* by Elma H. Ashton, Bureau of Public Assistance Report No. 11, Washington: Federal Security Agency, 1947.

Towle, Charlotte, *Common Human Needs,* Bureau of Public Assistance Report No. 8, Washington: Federal Security Agency, 1945. (Now published by the American Association of Social Workers.)

Witmer, Helen, *Social Work,* New York: Farrar & Rinehart, 1942, chap. 10.

CHAPTER 12

The Structure of the
Public Assistance Agency

The size of a unit organization being usually restricted very narrowly by the necessities of communication, it follows that growth of organization beyond the limits so imposed can only be accomplished by the creation of new unit organizations, or by grouping together two or more unit organizations already existing. When an organization grows by the addition of the services of more persons it is compelled, if it reaches the limit of size, to establish a second unit; henceforward it is a complex of two unit organizations. All organizations except unit organizations are a group of two or more unit organizations. Hence, a large organization of complex character consists not of the services of individuals directly but of those subsidiary unit organizations. Nowhere in the world, I think, can there be found a large organization that is not composed of small units. We think of them as having descended from the mass, whereas the mass can only be created from the units.

— CHESTER BERNARD, *The Functions of the Executive*

THE PATTERN OF ORGANIZATION IN
LOCAL OPERATING AGENCIES

The Influence of Legislation on Structure

Although we have had a glimpse of the magnitude and complexity of public assistance operations, thus far we have concentrated on the formulation and application of policy. Policy, however, is meaningless without instruments through which it can be effectuated. These instruments are the public assistance agencies established by law to administer the programs. Although the structure of the agencies is, of course, determined by policy, it is also true that the nature of policy, or at least the way in which policy works out in practice, is influenced by the structure and functioning of the agency.

Public assistance administration, that is, all the processes necessary to translate the intent of the legislature into specific services to people, is too complex a subject to receive adequate treatment here; therefore, we shall confine ourselves to a consideration of only those aspects of administration and organization which are of immediate concern to the social service staff of assistance agencies.

The statutes which provide the legislative mandate for public assistance stipulate either directly or indirectly the structural framework within which service is to be rendered. We have seen that public assistance is a state responsibility, but one that can be delegated to local government. Whether assistance is administered by a branch of local government (e.g., a county department of public welfare) or by a local branch of the state assistance agency, the Social Security Act requires that there be some state supervision and financial participation for those assistance categories covered by the act. It is perhaps more convenient than accurate to make a distinction between states on the basis of whether they have a state-administered or a state-supervised, locally administered system.

What are the characteristics of a state-supervised program of public welfare? Of a state-administered program? Can we differentiate clearly between the two? An examination of state public assistance legislation reveals not only variations from state to state, but variations among programs within the states. In those programs which are clearly state-supervised, the controlling state legislation contains the following characteristics: The state act creates or designates a local agency which is authorized, subject to the policy standards and procedures adopted by the state agency (1) to accept applications; (2) to determine eligibility; (3) to select personnel; and (4) otherwise manage the operation of the program within the county. The act also requires that the local unit participate financially in the program. Old-age assistance legislation in fifteen states contains all these characteristics. In so far as old-age assistance is concerned, this group of states would be classified by this standard as having state-supervised programs. Eighteen states, the District of Columbia, Alaska and Hawaii have none or less than two of these characteristics and, therefore, occupy the opposite position of state administered programs. In these states, the local units operate as branch offices of the state department, whether or not the local units have the advice of citizen boards. Between these two groups are fourteen states representing considerable variation in the method of state control and local administration. Five of these fourteen states require local financial participation but otherwise they place responsibility for decision in the state agency. Nine of the fourteen states have relieved the local units of financial participation but six of these nine require the local unit of government to administer the program. There are still further variations among and within the states when aid-to-dependent children, aid-to-the-blind and other state welfare legislation is considered.[1]

States differ, moreover, in the extent to which the administration of the various assistance categories is integrated, that is, the extent to which the five programs are administered by the same agency, and perhaps the same worker. New York, for example, has a completely integrated, locally administered program, whereas Pennsylvania has a completely integrated program for only those categories for which there is federal reimbursement, general assistance being left entirely to the localities. In some states there may be variation even among the federally reimbursed categories; thus, in New Jersey, aid to dependent children is state-administered, while aid to the blind and old-age assistance are locally administered. In Delaware until 1951–1952 each of the federal categories was administered by a separate state agency; since then OAA, ADC, and AD have been consolidated in a Board of Welfare which administers the programs while AB is administered by a Commission for the Blind.

These variations can be understood only in the light of the social and political history of the respective states. Whether a state-administered system is better than a state-supervised, locally

[1] Reba Choate, "Two Types of Public Welfare Administration," *Proceedings of the National Conference of Social Work*, 1948 (New York: Columbia University, 1949), p. 146.

administered system is not an issue of vital importance. What *is* important is the extent to which all the assistance programs are integrated, so that standards are substantially the same for all needy people, and so that people are not shunted from one agency to another because of different categorical eligibility requirements.

DISTRIBUTION OF LOCAL OFFICES AND EMPLOYEES
BY SIZE OF STAFF

Number of Full-Time Employees	Offices		Full-Time Employees	
	Number	Percentage Distribution	Number	Percentage Distribution
Total	2,956	100.0	31,970 *a*	100.00
None *b*	93	3.1	0	0.0
1	276	9.3	276	.9
2	520	17.6	1,040	3.3
3	489	16.5	1,467	4.6
4	282	9.5	1,128	3.5
5	236	8.0	1,180	3.7
6–9	474	16.0	3,394	10.6
10–49	527	17.8	10,066	31.5
50 or more	59	2.0	13,419	42.0

a Excludes 152 child welfare workers for whom information on size of office was not comparable.

b Part-time employees only, or all positions vacant as of date of report.

The above figures are for employees actually on pay roll; they do not include unfilled positions.

As used above, the term "local office" refers to a local operating unit even though it may have several district offices.

SOURCE: Social Security Administration, *Personnel in Local Offices of State Assistance Agencies,* Public Assistance Report No. 12, p. 5.

The size of the local operating unit, whether a branch of a state agency or an agency of local government, depends upon the geographic area served, the population of the area, the number of programs administered, and the incidence of need. In locally administered systems the area of operation is usually the county; less often, the city or township. In state-administered systems the area of operation is usually the county or, in sparsely populated territory, a group of counties. The differences in area and population in these subdivisions make for a wide range in size. Contrast, for example, New York City and Hamilton County in the Adirondack Mountains, and Philadelphia and Tioga counties in Pennsylvania. A few local units have staff running into the thousands, but the great majority have a total staff of less than ten. In 1946 the Bureau of Public Assistance reported that three-fourths of all local office personnel were employed in offices with ten or more staff members, but these large offices comprised only one-fifth of all the local offices in the country.

The Local Administrative Authority

Even the smallest local agencies are usually headed by a staff member charged with administrative responsibility. In the study of public assistance personnel to which we have just made reference it was found that in 64.1 percent of the one-person offices that person was classified as a director, while in 78.1 percent of the two-person offices the staff consisted of a director and a clerk. In such offices, of course, the director combines administrative duties with carrying a case load. In the majority of local offices, that is, offices with a total staff of less than thirteen, there is rarely any staff member specifically designated as a supervisor. In such instances the director may combine administrative and supervisory functions.

The following statement on executive functions was developed by a state supervising agency; but the functions are not dissimilar to those of an administrator in a state-administered system:

Executive functions should normally include: providing leadership to staff and community; developing agency budget; selecting qualified personnel; defining responsibilities of individuals and groups of staff; establishing lines of relationship and appropriate delegation of authority; developing and integrating programs; coordinating the work of the supervisory and consultant staff; and developing working relationships with other public officials and bodies. Each of the above functions should be carried out in such a manner as to assure individualized consideration to the needs of persons whom the agency serves.[2]

[2] New York State Department of Social Welfare, "Standards Governing the Administration of Public Assistance Care and Service in Public Welfare Districts," processed report, 1946.

The functions of the local administrator vary, depending on the size of the agency, its structural and staff pattern, the service it provides, and whether it is a branch of local government or a state assistance agency. The local administrator is distinguished from the supervisor in that the latter is responsible for carrying out the social service functions of the program, whereas the former is responsible for the execution of the total program— planning, personnel, securing and disbursing of funds, fiscal and statistical controls, etc. In locally administered systems the director may be responsible for programs other than public assistance, such as child welfare and the county home and infirmary. In large multiple-function agencies the executive usually has a number of subadministrators in charge of the various programs or staff services, i.e., director of public assistance, director of child welfare, superintendent of the county home, director of personnel, office manager, chief accountant, etc.

To whom is the local director responsible, and whence comes his authority? In state-administered programs he is a state employee, although in about one-third of these states he is appointed by a local citizens' advisory board. This, however, is often a formality, since he must be appointed from a civil service list. In state-supervised systems the local director is appointed by a local policy-making board, except in California, where he is appointed by the county board of supervisors, and in New York, where the majority of local welfare commissioners are elected. (In most of the larger districts in New York, however, he is appointed by the county or city executive, or by a local welfare board.)

The authority of the local director is defined and circumscribed by the terms of the statutes, and by policy derived from such legislation by the state agency. Local policy-making boards (which are also limited by such legislation) are technically the head of the local agency, while the director is responsible for executing the program. Local directors and policy-making boards may retain considerable discretion, especially in these areas:

1. Standards of assistance. Development of a specific definition of need; standards for the assistance budget—items to be included and the amount per item in relation to living standards

and costs in the community; standards relating to the evaluation of resources. *The Federal Bureau of Public Assistance,
however, is putting increasing pressure on the states to establish state standards of assistance.*

2. Personnel. Size of staff, job assignments, qualifications, compensation, other personnel policies, hiring and releasing.

3. Responsibility for decision. Authority to accept or reject applications for assistance, subject only to the rulings made by the
state agency on cases in which there have been "fair hearings."

Generally speaking, local discretion in matters relating to
assistance standards and to personnel is limited by minimum requirements imposed by the state. As the latter defines more precisely the minimum standards which local agencies must maintain, there is a corresponding decrease in the ability of the local
agency to function freely as a branch of local government and to
reflect prevailing local opinion. It is argued, therefore, that this
trend, in effect, changes state-supervised, locally administered
systems into state-administered systems without legislative authorization. While there may be truth in this contention, it is hard
to see what the alternative could be, if needy people are to receive equitable treatment regardless of where they live in the
state. In a state in which three-fourths or four-fifths of local expenditures for public assistance are reimbursed by the state or
federal government, it is difficult to justify a situation in which a
needy person is denied assistance in one county whereas, were he
living in a neighboring county, under precisely the same circumstances, he would be eligible for at least supplementary assistance. The establishment of minimum standards does not mean
uniform standards, since the localities are still free to adopt varying standards above the minimum; nor do minimum standards
mean uniformity in amounts of assistance. The minimum in
monetary terms may vary from locality to locality in accordance
with living costs and community standards.

The Case Unit and the Role of the Supervisor

In the study of public assistance personnel to which we referred earlier in this chapter it was found that in thirty-eight

states in which supervisors were employed in local offices only 440 out of a total of 2603 offices were large enough to employ persons in this category. This position was generally not included in the staffing pattern of local agencies unless the total office force (clerical and social service) numbered at least thirteen. In small agencies supervision is provided by the director or is delegated to a "senior worker," who combines limited supervision with carrying a case load. In the smallest agencies some supervision is provided by state field staff. The majority of public assistance workers, however, work in the large agencies where full-time supervisors are employed.

Supervision, although it has administrative aspects, must be distinguished from administration *per se*. The administrator is responsible for the execution of all phases of the program. While he retains ultimate responsibility, he must work through others to whom he delegates authority. The unique function of the supervisor (at least the *social service* or case supervisor) is to direct the activity of the social service staff in the discharge of their professional duties. In public assistance the supervisor is responsible for seeing that her staff carries out the mandate of the law and of policy relating to the provision of opportunity for everyone who considers himself to be in need to state his case; investigates applications promptly, in accordance with eligibility requirements and with due regard for the feelings of the persons investigated; authorizes assistance in the appropriate amounts; and provides related services. Furthermore, she must see that her staff maintains clear, accurate, and up-to-date records, reports, and statistics.

Her responsibility to the administrator is stated succinctly by an experienced supervisor:

. . . The case supervisor has the following responsibilities to the county superintendent: to accept his leadership as executive director of the Department; to report to him at frequent intervals on all aspects of the work; to bring to his attention all acute problems and situations in which the supervisor and case workers need his supervision and direction (or which he should be aware of); to bring to his attention staff problems, agency-client problems, client-community problems, problems of organization, procedure, policies, which arise within the total job responsibility; and, as requested, to help in formulating agency policy.[3]

In addition to the above functions, which are largely administrative, the supervisor has important teaching functions which fall under two headings: (1) teaching that is inherent in the job of case supervision and (2) teaching necessitated by the fact that most newly employed public assistance workers are completely untrained.

With respect to the first teaching function, it is perhaps unnecessary to elaborate on the fact that the public assistance job is professional in nature. This means that the staff member responsible for providing direct service should be allowed considerable leeway in the exercise of judgment and in the selection of methods of approach in each case. The supervisor must guide rather than give detailed instructions to her staff. Each case situation is unique, and the supervisor can understand it only as the facts are reported to her by the worker. It is her task to help the worker analyze each case, to recognize its unique character behind superficial similarities to other cases. Because of her wider experience and precisely because she is not immediately involved in dealings with the needy person, she can examine each situation with a fresh and objective eye and thereby help the worker gain new perspective.

The supervisory conference—in which the worker and supervisor jointly examine the evidence, consider alternative methods, interpret the facts, and evolve a plan of action—is one of the most important tools of public assistance administration. It is, however, essentially a teaching device in which the worker, by means of the case study, is helped to develop understanding and skill. The supervisor, of course, is ultimately responsible for the decisions made with respect to each case. The process of arriving at a decision, however, is a joint one.

In addition to the individual supervisory conferences, the supervisor is responsible for group teaching, through staff meet-

[3] Anna A. Cassett, "Relating the Case Supervisor's Job to That of the County Director," *Public Welfare*, February, 1944, p. 56.

ings in which new policy and procedure are interpreted, common problems are analyzed, and new techniques are discussed.

With respect to the second teaching function, the supervisor must help her workers acquire the basic knowledge and skill without which they cannot function. It is as if the chief accountant had to teach the elements of bookkeeping to his staff at the same time they were auditing the books. The extent to which the supervisor must devote time to this basic training and the extent to which she is equipped to train will affect the overall quality of work in her unit.

To make this concrete, let us look at the job of the supervisor in the public assistance organization. Roughly, we may say that a supervisor carries 10 visitors (the number may range from eight to fourteen) each with a case load of 150 (this may range from 100 to 400). He is responsible for a client case load which may range from 1500 anywhere up to several thousand. For what does a supervisor assume responsibility and what skill is required of him? If he comes straight from the visiting job, his tendency is to go at supervising as if he were a visitor, i.e., to work on each case presented by a worker, to straighten out the tangle in it for the sake of getting relief to the case. In addition, he tries to find some way of checking on the facts of eligibility and budget allowance in every case. In other words he tries to take responsibility for a case load of 1500 to several thousand cases. This is obviously impossible, as the intelligent supervisor must see, and his next problem is how to devise ways in which his enormous case load of clients is getting just and considerate treatment and the agency's policies are being correctly and fairly expressed to them. I have watched many beginning supervisors go through this struggle and have tried to help them in class and conference. What is involved for them first of all is not the learning of new techniques but a complete reorientation of their place in the job. Formerly as worker, he learned policies in his own way and interpreted them to his clients, now he has to help ten different visitors assimilate those policies so that they can use them with clients. I have in mind such a policy as that which enforces the legally responsible relatives to contribute to the support of the applicant for assistance. This policy is not difficult to learn in words but to assimilate its intent and explain it and stand by it with clients and relatives who are almost without exception embarrassed and antagonized by it, takes a great deal of work with oneself. Many workers, armed with the words of this policy alone, either go down before the assaults of the indignant relatives or they lose themselves completely in sympathetic identification with the problem of those people faced with so punishing a requirement. I believe every visitor has to protest and fight this policy before he can use it at all. The role of the supervisor then is to help workers straighten out their reactions to this policy to the point where they can present it to clients and stand by it. If the supervisor has really helped the worker take in the full force of the policy and work through a stable attitude toward it, the visitor will be able to let the client and the relative work out their attitudes on him in the same way and come to the same terms with the policy and the help the agency can give, if the client and relative contribute their share. Another type is the worker—perhaps more common among those without training—who will seize a policy and go out and inflict it, do or die, over the dead body of the client. The supervisor must again and again present the client in his humanity to these workers.

Abstracting from this description, I would say that the supervisor's job requires: first that the supervisor find a new orientation to clients. This involves that he give up his direct relation to clients and take a responsibility for workers. He now represents more completely than any individual worker is able to do, agency function, purpose and policy. . . . If he is soundly oriented to agency administration and visitors he is ready to develop the essential skills of supervision, the skill which enables him to help visitors carry out their jobs, become clearer and more responsible in their relation to policies and eligibility, see that relief moves to clients as fast as eligibility can be established. His skill must include the responsiblty for constant evaluaton of his staff and for knowing how to inject the stimulus that will keep them moving ahead in speed and quality of performance without putting a pressure that is too great to be tolerated. There is always pressure on the supervisor. I doubt that any kind of administration, no matter how good, will take the pressure out of it for the supervisor. If he accepts the job professionally it is a requirement that he absorb that pressure so that he does not deposit it on the workers but frees them to do the best possible job which a good worker with a good use of his time and self can do.[4]

[4] Virginia P. Robinson, "The Cultivation of Skill as the Preliminary Factor in a Social Work Curriculum," *Proceedings of the American Association of Schools of Social Work* (Washington: 1940), p. 8.

Local agency structure is distinguished chiefly by the organizational pattern into which units composed of workers and supervisor are grouped. All other functions—administrative consultant, fiscal, etc.—facilitate the work of these units. As the number of these units increases, so will levels of supervision.

In single-unit agencies the supervisor usually serves as assistant to the directors; that is, in addition to supervising the social service staff, she participates in the formulation of local policy and procedure, in developing methods for implementing state policy, in preparing the budget, and in matters of personnel. She may also share with the executive the task of public interpretation of the program and in other aspects of community relations. In two-unit agencies one supervisor is usually designated a "senior supervisor," or else the director coördinates the work of both units. In agencies with three or more units there will usually be a chief supervisor in charge of the social service program, to whom the unit supervisors are responsible. In the largest agencies, groups of units are districted under a district supervisor who, in turn, is responsible to a chief case supervisor.[5]

Supervisory functions tend to change with the size of the agency and with the number of supervisory levels interposed between worker and administrator. In small agencies the supervisor is a direct link between worker and administration; in large agencies supervisors at the unit level are concerned almost exclusively with supervision of workers and with carrying out policy developed by others. High-ranking supervisors are responsible for supervising the unit or district supervisors and for assisting the director and his administrative staff in policy development. Although this pyramiding of supervisory personnel is necessary in large agencies, it introduces problems of control and communication. Staff responsible for development of policy and procedure are far removed from personnel responsible for its execution. Important decisions regarding program and even individual case handling are reserved for top-level staff, whose decisions are based on data transmitted through several lower supervisory

[5] There is no uniform method of classifying supervisory staff; each state (sometimes the individual agency) has its own titles.

levels. There may thus be delays and distortion of data in transit, and opportunities for face-to-face discussion on issues are limited. The larger the agency, therefore, the more important it is to keep open channels of communication and to guard against unnecessary proliferation of top-level supervisory controls. If supervisors at the unit level are so inept that they cannot be relied upon, the solution lies not in instituting administrative controls but in getting new supervisors.

Among the major structural problems in public assistance are the following: What is the optimum size for a case unit? For how many units can a chief supervisor be directly responsible? At what point should districts be organized? To what extent can the execution of the social service program be decentralized?

No specific answer can be given to these questions. Among the variables that must be taken into consideration are the size of individual case loads, the geographical distribution of the cases, the quality of the supervisory and worker personnel. Other factors are the extent to which supervisors have duties other than staff supervision and the rate of staff and case turnover.

We may assume that a well-trained supervisor can supervise from eight to ten workers at the maximum, provided they are reasonably experienced and their case loads are of manageable size —say from eighty to one hundred cases. If case loads rise to more than one hundred, and if staff turnover is such that the supervisor must train three or four new and inexperienced workers in the course of a year, then a unit of ten workers is too large. When such conditions prevail—and they are all too frequent—we should not be surprised if the quality of work is poor. Few public assistance agencies require that supervisors have training for the job, nor do they make provisions for systematic in-service training for persons appointed to such positions. Supervisors usually have to learn the job on their own—and while doing it. This also makes for a poor quality of work. Budget limitations and restrictions on recruitment may interfere with the employment of a sufficient number of competent supervisors, and yet, the quality of the agency's work is probably more dependent upon the adequacy of unit supervision than on any other single factor.

The number of units for which a chief supervisor can be directly responsible is dependent to a great extent on the quality of the unit supervisors. If they are well trained, a chief supervisor may be able to supervise as many as eight or ten. If they are poorly trained, she may not be able to deal with more than four or five because of the extent to which they depend upon her help and because of the need for extensive controls to compensate for their lack of training.

Some Observations on Policy, Judgment, and Decentralization

As we have already noted, the modern trend in public assistance administration has been to define, by means of written policy, the intent of the law and the rights and duties of applicants and recipients, so that everyone in similar circumstances receives similar service, and so that the general public and potential applicants can understand the services the agency is authorized to provide. In theory, the more specifically policy defines the conditions and standards of service, the less extensive is the scope of decision and discretion of worker and supervisor and the greater is the likelihood of equality of treatment. In practice, however, this is not necessarily the case; at any rate, it has not lessened the need for skillful handling of technical materials or the need for professional judgment.

Detailed policies and administrative controls, though often necessary, are not an adequate substitute for professional judgment, and the rapid proliferation of such policies and controls should be a matter of concern to public assistance administrators. The attempt to anticipate alternative courses of action on the part of worker or supervisor, the issuing of detailed instructions covering various contingencies, and the requirement that higher-level supervisory approval be secured before certain services can be granted are self-defeating. Many agencies have developed a body of policy, procedure, and controls that has reached enormous proportions. No doubt they have been formulated because those agencies do not believe that their poorly equipped staff can do its job in an efficient and equitable manner without them. Variations in human circumstances, however, are too great for policy to serve other than as general guiding principles. In attempting to relieve staff of the burden of exercising discretion, these agencies impose upon them a different but even heavier burden—that of mastering a complex and often confusing set of rules and regulations. It is unrealistic to expect the average worker (who remains with the agency only a few years) to become familiar with, much less to know how to apply, so vast a body of rules. Large agencies that resort to highly centralized operations create as many problems as they attempt to solve, since the top-level staff which formulates detailed policy and controls for workers and unit supervisors is too far removed from actual operations to formulate them realistically.

The Relation of Facilitative Services to the Case Unit

Since the social service staff deals directly with needy people and is responsible for investigating applications for help and for recommending appropriate action, it is only natural that it consider its activities of major importance. While this position is substantially correct, nevertheless, without certain supportive activities the social service staff would be of small help to persons in need. The major activities facilitating the work of the case unit are these:

AGENCY BUDGETING

It is the responsibility of the agency executive to secure an appropriation adequate for the discharge of the agency's program. The budget is an estimate of the cost of assistance and administration for the next year and is based on an analysis of past experience and of trends likely to affect the volume of anticipated work. The data on which the estimate is based are derived from financial, administrative, and social statistics, as well as studies of economic and social conditions in the community.

CLEARANCE, REGISTRATION, AND THE MAINTENANCE OF RECORDS

The agency needs an elaborate set of records to justify its expenditure of public funds, and to assure the state, the federal government, and the community that its activities are in accordance with the intent of the law. These records include: (1) the individual or family case history, in which agency contact with people who seek its help is recorded, the applicant's or recipient's eligibility is documented, his social situation and changes therein are described, and the nature of the service rendered is reported: (2) the financial record, in which the amount of each grant paid to or in behalf of recipient is posted; (3) statistical records, which for given periods reveal fluctuations in the volume of work, the composition of the total case load, reasons for initiating or discontinuing service, etc.

Since there must be a case history for every individual or family group currently receiving help or who in the past received help or at least applied for it, the number of histories, even in a small agency, may run into the thousands. For convenience in filing, it will usually be desirable to give each history a case number and to file them in numerical order. Each record will have to be cross-referenced with an index card filed alphabetically. The index card must contain sufficient identifying data, in addition to the case number. To avoid duplication of assistance, and to make sure that all relevant social data are available to the worker, the name of every person who applies for help must be cleared with the files. The application is also cleared with the social service exchange, or central index (if the community has one), to see if the applicant has been known to other health and welfare agencies in the community. An accurate and readily accessible set of files is an essential adjunct to agency operations. A detailed procedure must be worked out so that the workers will report, in a uniform fashion, the information necessary to keep the files up to date.

FISCAL CONTROL AND THE ISSUANCE OF ASSISTANCE

The mechanics of getting an assistance grant to a recipient are handled by the clerical staff, but the worker must initiate action by preparing an authorization form. This form contains such identifying data as name, address, and case number; the amount of the monthly or semimonthly grant; and the period during which the grant is to be received (e.g., three months, six months, a single grant, etc.). When the assistance issuance section receives this authorization, the data are transcribed to a card which constitutes the permanent record of all assistance authorized for this case. To make sure that each case receives the assistance that has been authorized, another form is prepared and filed in such a way that on a particular day each month (in cases receiving grants monthly) the forms for all persons who are to receive grants are removed from the file and a pay roll is made up. When the pay roll has been certified, it is transmitted to the appropriate financial office (in a locally administered system, probably the county treasurer's office; in a state-administered system, the state finance office). Here checks are written and either sent directly to the recipient or returned to the agency for mailing. In the meantime, the amount of the check that has been issued has been posted to the recipient's "record of assistance granted" card. Should it be necessary to close the case, extend the period for which assistance should be granted, change the amount of the grant, or issue a supplementary grant, the worker must make out a new authorization form, which cancels or replaces the preceding one. Here again, it will be noted that the worker is responsible for initiating action and for supplying the necessary data.

STATISTICS

Statistics are essential for effective administration because they summarize agency activities for a given period. Like all summaries, statistical reports are shorn of many details so that certain developments may be brought into sharper focus. Statistical reports are concerned with data which can be extracted from each case, separated from their individualizing context, and combined with similar data from all cases for the purposes of comparison, generalization, and the prediction of trends. The mathematical treatment of data, the calculation of percentage fluctuations, the preparation of charts, tables, and graphs are a function of the statistical staff, but, once more, it is the worker who is responsible for furnishing the raw data. Case histories contain much material that may be subject to statistical analysis even though it was not reported for that purpose. From time to time the agency may wish to study certain aspects of its operations, and this may entail a careful review of case histories, or at least of a sample block of such records in order to extract significant data. Studies of this nature need not concern us here. What we are concerned with is the worker's responsibility for reporting regularly and in a uniform manner certain raw data from which the periodic statistical reports are prepared. Data will usually be required on the following points:

Case load activity. Number of active cases carried over from the preceding month; number of applications made during month; number of applications accepted for service; number of active cases transferred to other districts, or out of agency; number of transferred cases received; number of cases closed.

Changes in case load composition. Number of persons receiving assistance in each category; number of persons transferred from one category to another; age, marital status, and perhaps other social data on recipients.

Assistance received. Number of persons receiving full assistance, supplementary assistance; amount received during month—by category.

Major reasons for opening or closing cases.

Number of office interviews, home visits, collateral visits, conducted by worker during month.

Statistics are meaningless unless they are based on carefully defined categories of raw data and reported in a uniform manner, and unless the person supplying the data understands the purpose for which they are required. The necessity for clarity in definition is reflected in the problem of getting an accurate "case count," that is, the number of persons receiving assistance and the category in which they are found. For example, a family unit consists of a husband, wife, and two minor children, all receiving general assistance; the wife's aged parents, each receiving old-age assistance; the wife's brother, receiving blind assistance; and a widowed daughter, receiving Aid to Dependent Children in behalf of an infant son. This family unit actually consists of five cases—two OAA, one AB, one ADC, and one general assistance case. Should the husband become permanently disabled, he would be eligible for Aid to the Disabled, while his wife and minor children could be transferred to ADC. Then there would be two OAA cases, one AB case, two ADC cases, and one Aid to the Disabled case. Should one of the minor children become eighteen, he would no longer be eligible for ADC but would be transferred back to general assistance. In view of the different rates of reimbursement and differences in sources of funds, it is obviously necessary to account statistically for these changes. Cases like this are probably rare; nevertheless, they illustrate the care that must be taken in reporting. They also illustrate how the number of cases may fluctuate without any actual change in the number of persons receiving help.

OFFICE MANAGEMENT

Under this heading come all those activities connected with the provision of working facilities—the securing of office space and equipment, telephone service, janitorial and messenger service, the stenographic pool, etc.

PERSONNEL

We have noted elsewhere that the Social Security Act requires that state and local agencies in receipt of federal funds under the titles of this act operate under a merit system for personnel. Prior to this requirement relatively few states, only a few cities, and even fewer counties had civil service systems. The Social Security Act does not require a complete civil service system for public employment, but in the absence of such a system some form of merit program must be in effect in agencies disbursing federal social security funds. The federal requirements are stated in general terms. The following are the major merit system standards:

Classification Plan. A classification plan based upon observation and analysis of the duties and responsibilities of positions should be established and maintained. The classification plan should include a job description and a statement of minimum requirements of education, experience and other qualifications for each class of position.

Compensation Plan. A compensation plan should be established and maintained. Such a plan should provide a salary range for each class of position, adjusted to the responsibility and difficulty of the type of work to be performed, and in line with the prevailing rates for comparable positions in other departments of the state. It should include regulations for salary advancement on the basis of periodically evaluated service.

Merit Examination. Provision should be made for open competitive examinations administered by a civil service commission or a qualified supervisor of a merit system under a non-partisan committee appointed by the state agency from persons of known sympathetic interest in and knowledge of the problems of public personnel management.

Appointment. Employees of the agency should be appointed by its administrative head from among a limited number of persons certified by the merit system supervisor in the order of their standing in the merit examination. A definite probationary period should be established for all new appointees.

Separations. Job security should be assured satisfactory employees within the limits of need for staff. Provision should be made for the lay-off of surplus employees under an equitable system and for dismissal of employees for cause with impartial review of such dismissals.

Service Ratings. A system of periodic service ratings for the evaluation of performance should be established and maintained. The use of such ratings in the promotion, salary increases, and separations should be covered by regulation.

Prohibition of Discrimination. Political and religious discrimination in merit system administration should be prohibited. Participation of any employee of the agency in political activity direct or indirect should be prohibited except that an employee should have the right freely to express his views as a citizen and to cast his vote.[6]

Civil service and merit systems have been most successful in achieving the negative goals of eliminating discrimination and political favoritism and equalizing opportunities for public employment. They have been less successful in achieving the positive goal of securing the best-qualified persons for public service, partly because of the great difficulty of devising suitable tests of

---

[6] Albert H. Aronson, "Merit System Standards in Social Security Administration," *Social Security Bulletin*, February, 1939.

competence, and partly because of legislative restrictions on the setting of qualifications, compensation, and other matters of personnel policy. The existence of a merit system, of course, is no guarantee that even the above-mentioned negative goals will be achieved. The system is no better than the people who operate it. While merit systems can be perverted, those responsible for such perversion run a grave risk, unless the legislature and public opinion are indifferent, or are actually hostile to the merit idea.

Our discussion of personnel will be confined to social service and administrative staff and will relate to the following topics: job qualifications, method of selection, and promotions.

Job Qualifications

Before a person is eligible to take a merit system examination for public assistance, he must fulfill certain requirements, which may include some combination of special training, general education, and experience. Usually, however, there is no requirement of special training or experience for the beginning job; neither is there any requirement for special training for promotional examinations. The experience requirement is generally confined to experience in the job immediately below that for which the examination is being given.

In view of the professional content of the public assistance job, as brought out in the preceding chapters, this failure to demand that candidates for employment have at least some preparation for the job they are seeking is surprising; yet there are practical reasons for it. In the first place, legislatures seem averse to the establishment of educational requirements that will exclude most of the electorate from competing for public employment, except for positions that are generally recognized as requiring professional training such as in law, medicine, and engineering. Public assistance is essentially social work, a field not yet universally acknowledged to have professional status. Graduates of schools of social work, moreover, are so few and their services are in such demand, especially by private social agencies, that they can demand a salary which public assistance agencies are not prepared to grant. Furthermore, the time-consuming process of securing a merit system appointment, the restrictions on mobility imposed by residence requirements, and the limitations on rapid advance also contribute to the lack of interest among professionally trained persons. Relatively few assistance agencies can offer working conditions sufficiently attractive to induce trained persons to enter into competition with college and even high-school graduates.

Some public welfare administrators criticize schools of social work for not giving sufficient emphasis to public welfare; they even complain that graduates of these schools are "worse off" for their training.[7] All schools of social work require at least one course in public welfare; most of the larger schools have an extensive sequence of courses in this subject and in related fields such as social insurance; and there are opportunities for field work in public agencies. It must be admitted, however, that public welfare is usually not emphasized as much as other areas of social work. This is no basis for criticism. The fact of the matter is that most students are not interested in public employment *per se,* and, for the reasons we have given above, very few consider a career in public assistance. If there were an effective demand for trained personnel on the part of assistance agencies, not only would more students be interested but the schools would increase their offerings in this field.

Another point to consider is this: While some specialized training is clearly needed prior to employment, the two-year curriculum in schools of social work is, perhaps, more than would be necessary for the beginning public assistance job. An alternative program, however, such as one year of graduate training, would be effective only to the extent that assistance agencies would pay for persons so prepared and the merit system would allow additional credit on examinations for this advanced work.

In the absence of requirements for specialized training, the level of general education required is of particular importance. A bachelor's degree is a usual requirement, although equivalents

[7] See Joseph E. Baldwin, "A Local Public Welfare Administrator's Reaction," *Proceedings of the American Association of Schools of Social Work* (Minneapolis: 1948), p. 31.

may be offered, such as a specified number of years of employment in a related field. Unfortunately, equivalents are not often defined with any great precision, so that a high-school graduate who has sold life insurance for five or six years or who has been a bill collector might well be eligible to take the merit system test.

A college degree is no guarantee that its possessor is better prepared, or even better educated, than some high-school graduates. But usually it is safe to assume that a college graduate has a better foundation, that his college training will enable him to grasp the requirements of the job more quickly and skillfully. Unfortunately, college programs vary greatly as to content, a fact that is not always taken into consideration in evaluating educational qualifications. Thus, a graduate in engineering, in pharmacy, or in fine arts competes on the same terms with a person who has had a solid liberal arts education including work in economics, sociology, political science, psychology, and anthropology. If written tests were so constructed as to bring out the need for a solid foundation in the social sciences, the social science major would be at an advantage. This is not always the case at the present time.

Method of Selection

The steps in the selection of staff include announcement of the examination, recruitment, application for the examination, the examination (which may include a written test, an oral test, an evaluation of education and experience), the promulgation of the list, and finally, appointment.

The task of recruiting potentially well-qualified people for public jobs is considerably more difficult than for other employment. Yet precisely because the qualifications for taking the examinations are so often lower than is desirable, it is a matter of great importance. For example, even if the salary range is comparable to what recent college graduates can get in other lines of work, public employment may be hedged about with so many restrictions that the most promising college graduates, those whose primary concern is not mere job security, may prefer to look elsewhere for employment. Local residence requirements are one of the most discouraging barriers to public employment. For example, a capable young college graduate may be interested in public assistance, but the county in which she has residence has no vacancies. A neighboring county, however, has vacancies, but this young woman is not eligible because she lacks residence. A year later, when she has obtained other work, her county may have openings in public assistance but only a few candidates who fulfill even the minimum qualifications for the job. Because of the same residence restrictions, this county cannot recruit capable young people from neighboring counties. The existence of local residence requirements tends to discourage many of the most promising college graduates from considering public employment. Alice Campbell Klein comments on this problem as follows:

> The narrower are residence restrictions territorially, the more hampering are they to a system of appointing and promoting on merit. They not only limit recruitment of qualified personnel but prevent advancement from state to state or county to county. . . .
>
> Despite the attitude of taxpayers, it scarcely seems that local benefits to be derived from rigid restrictions of this sort are sufficient to offset their cost. Each community presumably wants the best personnel it can get for public service; but ability to do a special job does not necessarily come with residence. Even a large city or a whole state may not produce a person qualified for a single specialized job. No one would object to preferment of local personnel when and if it ranks equally with outsiders in respect to qualifications. Those interested in good government do object to the substitution of residence for merit.[8]

The closed promotional system is, perhaps, as pernicious as local residence requirements. Under this system, eligibility to take an examination for a position higher than the entry job is restricted to persons who have served in the job immediately below that job for which the examination is being given. No "outsiders" can compete, even though they may have had sub-

[8] Alice Campbell Klein, *Civil Service in Public Welfare* (New York: Russell Sage, 1940), p. 71.

stantially similar experience in other agencies or, of course, in other localities. The closed promotional system restricts mobility and is attractive only to those who fear competition. Capable and ambitious personnel are encouraged to leave the service because of lack of promotional opportunities. For example, an able young public assistance worker is employed in a small operating agency in which there are only one or two supervisory positions. Although there may be vacancies in supervisory jobs elsewhere in the state, she cannot compete because of the closed promotional system (or at least to the extent that it is in effect elsewhere). She must wait until death, retirement, or resignation creates an opening in her own agency. Usually she has left before that happens.

This system is particularly detrimental to agencies in their effort to secure well-qualified persons for top supervisory and administrative jobs. For example, a large agency needs to fill a vacancy for chief case supervisor. A sound procedure would be for this agency to encourage people holding similar positions in smaller operating units in the state to compete for the job. Usually they would welcome this opportunity because of the added prestige, responsibility, and compensation that would be involved. But a closed promotional system obliges the agency to promote from within. Looking at it from another angle, it would be to the advantage of supervisors in this agency if they could compete for more responsible positions in smaller agencies, rather than be restricted to competing only for that job in their own agency—a job that entails greater responsibility than their experience has fitted them to assume. A combination of local residence requirements and a closed promotional system results in inbreeding that is as unwholesome administratively as it is biologically.

A final difficulty is that a closed promotional system denies to an agency the full advantages to be derived from improved personnel standards. An agency may have had a very low salary schedule for many years and, as a result, a staff of mediocre ability. But it is from the ranks of those poorly qualified people

that supervisory positions must be filled. If, under a new administration, the agency attempts to improve the quality of its staff,
it can only do so from the bottom up. Poor supervision destroys
the effectiveness of the most promising workers; it causes the
best of them to leave the agency, or else renders them unfit for
supervisory responsibility when their turn comes. But the change
which is most needed—a strengthening of the supervisory staff—
cannot be made because of the requirement that promotions be
from within.

Veterans' preference, while necessary and desirable, can create
difficulties if the method of preference is not well thought out.
No reasonable person can object to a plan which enables veterans, whose years of military service have prevented them from
moving ahead in their civilian careers, to compete on favorable
terms with those who not only did not have to risk their lives but
could prepare themselves for advancement. The usual method of
preference is to allow the veteran a certain point bonus on entry
examinations and, perhaps, on promotional examinations. The
point bonus may vary, depending on whether or not the veteran
has a service-connected disability. If the point bonus is very high,
or if veterans are given an absolute preference (i.e., they go to
the head of the list so long as their grade on examination was
passing), non-veterans may well be discouraged from seeking
public employment.

THE EXAMINATION

The examination may involve three parts: a written test, an
oral interview, and an evaluation and rating of education and
experience. The successful candidate's position on the civil service list is usually based on a composite score. The written test
usually receives the greatest weight. Sometimes the oral interview and the evaluation of education and experience are for
qualifying purposes only; that is, the candidate must pass the
oral test, and he must have the minimum requirements of education and experience, but they do not affect his position on the
list. If the examination is one in which the candidate's scores on

the oral interview and on the evaluation of education and experience are averaged in with the score on the written test, the latter must first be passed.[9]

Historically, the written test was usually an essay-type examination designed to test the candidate's knowledge of the job for which he was competing. The emphasis was upon knowledge of law, policy, regulation, and procedure. It is now recognized that this type of examination is unsatisfactory. Essay questions are difficult to score objectively, and they test abstract knowledge rather than ability to apply such knowledge. The candidate with a good memory had an advantage over other candidates whose qualifications for the job, in all other respects, might have been superior.

Modern tests are usually of the objective, short-answer type. Not only are they easier to score but, precisely because they are of the short-answer type, they make it possible to include a wider range of questions, and thus reduce the element of chance that always was present when only a relatively few essay questions could be asked. The questions, moreover, are designed to test the candidate's potential ability to do the job. The emphasis is on general knowledge, current events, exercise of judgment, verbal comprehension, and the like. In some jurisdictions a single examination is used to test candidates for a variety of jobs, ranging from public assistance worker to statistician, junior administrative assistant, and even for engineering positions. The different parts of such an examination are weighted differently according to the job for which the candidate is applying. Thus the section of the examination designed to test the candidate's ability to deal with numbers and concrete relationships receives greater weight when the applicant is competing for a position in the field of statistics, accounting, or science, whereas the section that tests ability to handle human relationships and knowledge of social issues receives the greater weight when candidates for public assistance jobs are being rated.

[9] For some positions, especially technical and professional openings in the federal service, unassembled examinations are used; that is, candidates are rated solely on education and experience.

We have already noted that the qualifications for most jobs in public welfare do not include professional or technical training, and that even the general education requirements are quite low. Public policy may demand that these requirements be kept low so that persons are not denied the opportunity to compete for public employment simply because they have not had the advantage of advanced education. If this is so, then persons with advanced education or relevant experience should be given additional credit; otherwise, persons who are potentially best qualified for the job may be discouraged from competing, since the written test, no matter how skillfully prepared, does not give them a clear-cut opportunity to demonstrate how their additional qualifications better fit them for the job.

THE APPOINTMENT PROCESS

Successful candidates are ranked numerically in accordance with their score, which may be a composite of the scores on the written and oral tests and on experience and education. Appointments are made from persons on the list in accordance with their standing. Thus, Jones, whose score is 87.6, will be appointed before Smith, whose score is 87.4. Unfortunately, the method of scoring is not so precise as to guarantee that Jones is actually better than Smith (even 0.2 percent better). In a popular examination there may be forty or fifty persons whose scores fall within a range of only 1 percent. Some may be appointed, while the others may have to wait years before their turn comes. Strict numerical ratings based on these measurements suggest a high degree of accuracy which in fact is not present. Appointing officers have little leeway in selecting staff. They are restricted to making appointments from among the first three candidates on the list. It has been suggested that the quality of public personnel might be improved if candidates were grouped, according to their scores, into a few broad categories such as "outstanding," "qualified," "unqualified." On the basis of personal interviews, the administrator should then be free to appoint anyone from the "outstanding" category whom he thought fit. After all persons in this group had had an opportunity to accept employment, the administrator could then drop down to the "qualified" category.[10]

Promotions

Policy with respect to promotions affects all phases of public assistance administration. We have already considered some of the issues, especially in connection with recruitment and job qualifications.

The usual line of promotion is from public assistance worker to supervisor to the administrative ranks. In each category there may be several grades. At the administrative level, positions may also be filled by persons coming up the promotional ladder from the fiscal and business management sections of the agency. Top administrators may also be drawn from other governmental agencies, or from business or other professions. Though there is an increasing tendency for top administrators to be career people, their appointment by the chief executive of the governmental unit, or the legislative body, may be influenced by political considerations.

Opportunities for advancement and the qualifications for promotion will affect the caliber of the personnel that have chosen public assistance as a career. Obviously, advancement is limited by the number of higher positions in the agency (or in neighboring agencies that have abandoned local residence requirements) and their ratio to the number of persons employed in the beginning job. It will also be affected by the rate of turnover—especially among staff at the entry level. If beginning workers see promotion only as a remote possibility, or if it appears that the promotional process does not enable the best-qualified persons to demonstrate clearly their superiority, many of the most promising workers will find their jobs stultifying and will seek employment in other fields. This, in effect, gives the advantage in promotional examinations to workers who, because of either lack of initiative or inability to get employment else-

[10] The Commission on Organization of the Executive Branch of Government (the Hoover Commission), *Task Force Report on Federal Personnel* (Washington: Government Printing Office, 1949).

where, "outsit" everyone else. In time, they will become the supervisors.

It is customary, except in the case of some of the higher positions, to permit staff to qualify for promotion if they have served satisfactorily in the grade immediately below that for which they wish to compete. From the point of view of building a career service, this system has advantages. But if the qualifications for the entry job are low, and if the promotional system is closed and fails to give adequate credit for advanced education, the agency may be prevented from securing supervisory staff of a high quality. We have already considered some of the reasons why most agencies find it impossible to demand even partial preëntry social work training for their beginning staff. We have also touched upon the problems involved in trying to make up for this deficiency through in-service training. Supervisors who are themselves untrained cannot be expected to train others with any degree of efficiency.

From the point of view of sound staff development it would seem reasonable to require all supervisory personnel to have at least one year of professional education. This requirement could not be enforced, however, unless assistance agencies could pay salaries that would induce persons with such training to remain with them, and unless they could provide opportunities for such training, through educational leave or work-study plans, for public assistance workers who seemed to be good supervisory material.

SELECTED REFERENCES

Archer, Olive M., "The Nature of Authority in State Supervision," *Public Welfare*, April, 1950.

Aronson, Albert H., "Merit System Objectives and Realities," *Social Security Bulletin*, April, 1950.

Baldwin, Joseph E., "Welfare Administration Looks Ahead," *Social Work Journal*, January, 1952.

Cassett, Anna A., "Relating the Case Supervisor's Job to That of the County Director," *Public Welfare*, February, 1944.

Chickering, Martha A., "Some Suggested Principles in the Organization and Direction of a Field Staff," *Public Welfare*, June, 1944.

Chickering, Martha A., "Administrative Supervision," *Public Welfare,* October, 1944.

Choate, Reba, "Two Types of Public Welfare Administration," *Proceedings of the National Conference of Social Work,* New York: Columbia University, 1948.

Drake, Russell, and Leirfallom, Jarle, "Organization and Administration of the Local Public Welfare Program," *Public Welfare,* June, July, August, October, November, 1943.

Fietz, Louise, "Caseload Standards," *Public Welfare,* July, 1947.

Fink, Roland W., "Caseload Management in Public Welfare," *Public Welfare,* April, 1948.

Klein, Alice Campbell, *Civil Service in Public Welfare,* New York: Russell Sage, 1940.

Laird, Angus, "The Merit System and Public Welfare," *Public Welfare,* February, 1951.

Lansdale, Robert T., Long, Elizabeth, Leisy, Agnes, and Hipple, Byron T., *The Administration of Old Age Assistance,* Chicago: Public Administration Service, 1939.

Miles, Arthur, *An Introduction to Public Welfare,* Boston: D. C. Heath, 1949, esp. chaps. 14, 15, 17, and 18.

Mitchell, William, "The Administrative Review in Federal-State Social Security," *Social Service Review,* July, 1946.

Schmidt, Carl L., "Highlights of Administration," *Public Welfare,* November, 1949.

Social Security Administration, *Characteristics of State Public Assistance Plans Under the Social Security Act,* Bureau of Public Assistance Report No. 18, Washington: Federal Security Agency, 1950.

Stevenson, Marietta, *Public Welfare Administration,* New York: Macmillan, 1938.

CHAPTER 13

Some Related Income-Maintenance Programs

The accomplishments of the works program are the more creditable because won in the face of grievous handicaps. By design the program was asked to employ some persons who, though capable of rendering service to society, were deficient in respects that made their private employment unlikely save in the tightest of labor markets. To utilize the labor of such persons was in itself a sheer social gain, quite apart from their salvage as self-respecting individuals. In a narrow economic sense the process was inefficient, since among others, it employed marginal labor. It was inherently inefficient, moreover, so far as financial and other limitations required skimping in the use of mechanical equipment and in the outlay for materials. These difficulties, far from being faults of the works program, were rather the measure of the necessity for its distinctive methods. With such handicaps went another that was deeper. Projects, said the law, must be useful but not competitive. This stipulation meant that with exceptions important in themselves but relatively minor the works program was barred from participation in the production of prime necessities. It does not detract from the value of what it wrought to say that there was sometimes tragic irony in the preoccupation of the works program with embellishment while elementary human needs for useful goods were insufficiently satisfied. Those involved in the program, whether as administrators or as workers, were the last to deserve blame for this condition. Yet they labored under the cloud of vague public restlessness because, despite continuous governmental outlays, the energies of the country were not being utilized fully in the production of necessities, any final judgment on the effectiveness and value of the works program must make due allowance for the extent to which it was deliberately barred from an organic relationship to the economy in which it operated.

   —McMahon, Millett, and Ogden, *The Administration of Federal Work Relief*

WORK PROGRAMS

Historical Background

From the very inception of public poor relief it was a generally accepted principle that, with respect to the able-bodied poor, work was preferable to direct relief. The motives underlying this principle, however, were mixed. Perhaps paramount was belief in the efficacy of work as a test of good faith. The poor, it will be recalled, were thought to prefer easy living on relief to honest labor. It was also believed that those supported at public expense could reduce the cost of their keep if they were set to useful tasks. Still another belief was that children and young people should be trained in habits of industry and taught useful trades, so that they would have the inclination and ability to maintain themselves in later life. Since it was thought that the poor considered work distasteful, it followed that the imposition of so unpleasant a requirement as work would do much to strengthen their character. Early commentators generally overlooked the possibility that the poor might have sufficient dignity and character to prefer self-support to dependence on alms or direct relief.

With the exception of the workhouse, which was primarily a punitive instrument and only incidentally a work project, early efforts to provide work for the poor were failures. Thus, it was discovered that work relief was more expensive than direct relief or almshouse care, not only because of the cost of materials and the spoilage which arose because the poor were set to tasks with which they were unfamiliar, but also because the high rate of turnover prevented such enterprises from achieving any real efficiency. Undoubtedly, some of those who returned to self-support and who had been so employed profited from their training—but the number was small. An undesirable economic consequence of ill-conceived work programs was pointed out by Daniel Defoe:

> Suppose now a work-house for employment of poor children, sets them to spinning worsted. For every skein of worsted those poor children spin, there must be a skein less spun by some poor family or person that spun it before. Suppose the manufacture of making bays to be erected in Bishopsgate-Street—unless the makers of these bays can at the same time find out a trade or consumption for more bays than were made before, for every piece of bays so made in London there must be a piece the less made at Colchester. . . .
>
> 'Tis only the transposing the manufacture from Colchester to London, and taking the bread out of the mouths of the poor of Essex to put it into the mouths of the poor in Middlesex.
>
> If these worthy gentlemen who show themselves so commendably forward to relieve and employ the poor, will find out some new trade, some new market, where the goods they shall make shall be sold where none of the same goods were sold before; if they will send them to any place where they shall not interfere with the rest of that manufacture, or with some other made in England, then indeed they will do something worthy of themselves, and may employ the poor to the same glorious advantage as Queen Elizabeth did, to whom this nation as a trading country, owes its peculiar greatness.
>
> If these gentlemen could establish a trade to Muscovy for English serges, obtain an order from the Czar, that all his subjects should wear stockings who wore none before, every poor child's labor in spinning and knitting those stockings, and all the wool in them would be clear gain to the nation, and the general stock would be improved by it, because all the growth of our country, and all the labor of a person who was idle before, is so much clear gain to the general stock.
>
> If they will employ the poor in some manufacture which was not made in England before, or not bought with some manufacture made here before, then they offer something extraordinary.
>
> But to set poor people at work, on the same thing which other poor people were employed on before, and at the same time not increase the consumption, is giving to one what you take away from another; enriching one poor man to starve another, putting a vagabond into an honest man's employment, and putting his diligence on the tenters to find out some other work to employ his family.[1]

[1] Karl de Schweinitz, *England's Road to Social Security* (Philadelphia: University of Pennsylvania, 1943), p. 55.

Work relief is sound only if it increases total production and purchasing power through the creation of new markets, domestic or foreign. Even the production of goods consumed by work-house inmates is a detriment if it displaces persons who formerly made goods purchased by the workhouse.

Work programs have taken many forms. At one extreme is so-called "work-for-relief." A historical example is the workhouse in which the inmates were required to work in return for their keep. A more modern illustration is the work project to which are assigned able-bodied assistance recipients who are required to work a certain number of hours a week to offset their assistance grant.

At the other extreme are the "public works programs." Public works, of course, are a regular function of government, but in time of economic distress governments frequently expand such activity not only to stimulate employment through the employ-ment of workers directly engaged in such projects but also to stimulate "off-site" employment through the purchase of raw materials, machinery, and other equipment. As has already been noted in an earlier chapter, public works are not relief; they are carried on through the normal channels of public business. Plans are made, estimates are drawn up, bids are submitted, and the work is carried on by contractors and subcontractors, who employ workers on the basis of their competence and at prevailing wages. The volume of public works projects will have an important in-fluence upon direct relief and work relief programs.

Between these extremes are a variety of intermediate forms, carried on directly by some agency of government rather than through contractors. In times of heavy unemployment there is generally a special agency established for this purpose. When the number of needy unemployed is low, there is less likelihood of work programs, and if there are any, they are likely to be espe-cially set up by various units and bureaus of government in coöperation with the assistance agency.

Usually, work relief programs are restricted to able-bodied assistance recipients, or at least to persons who can satisfy the needs requirement. During the depression several attempts were made to depart from this requirment. The federally administered and financed Civil Works Administration was designed to put four million unemployed to work promptly—half from the relief rolls, half from the unemployed not on relief. Lewis Meriam comments on this program as follows:

This program was, however, short-lived. The cost was high; the number of dissatisfied persons not on relief who felt they had a right to a job but could not get one was large; and in the haste to get people at work, numerous projects were undertaken which aroused hostile criticism and ridicule. A wage scale was initially established identical with that used for P.W.A. Under it, hourly rates varied with skill and geographic area, influenced, however, by minimum and prevailing wage principles. Schedules of maximum hours were set up, so a definite weekly wage could be earned by all workers on the programs, irrespective of individual differences in personal or family needs. Average earnings approximated $15 a week when the program was in full swing, but because of costs maximum hours were sharply cut, reducing average earnings to $11.52 for the week of January 27, 1934. By the end of April C.W.A. was discontinued for all practical purposes. In a period of about five months it had cost some 931 million dollars of which the national government had contributed about 90 per cent.[2]

When WPA was created the following year, it endeavored to establish safeguards against one of the greatest problems faced by CWA. Eligibility for assignment to a work project was restricted to employable, unemployed persons in need. The latter status was generally certified by the state or local relief agency. Mr. Hopkins, the Administrator, tried to point out the difference between WPA work and work relief (or, more properly, work-for-relief):

I should like to clarify here the difference between work relief and a job on a work program such as CWA and WPA. To a man on relief the difference is very real. On work relief, although he gets the disciplinary rewards of keeping fit, and of making a return for what he gets, his need is still determined by a social worker, and he feels himself to be something of a public ward, with small freedom of

[2] Lewis Meriam, *Relief and Social Security* (Washington: Brookings, 1946), pp. 351–352.

choice. When he gets a job on a work program it is very different. He is paid wages and the social worker drops out of the picture. His wages may not cover much more ground than his former relief budget but they are his to spend as he likes. I am told that all over the country the response was the same when the people went off work relief (and we had over 2,000,000 on work relief) and on to Works Progress. The wife of the WPA worker tossed her head and said, "We aren't on relief any more, my husband is working for the government." [3]

This suggests that once a person had been assigned to WPA he was no longer on relief. This was technically correct, but as the years passed, pressure from Congress obliged the WPA to adopt stricter measures. Thus, efforts were made to see that WPA workers were not refusing jobs in private employment; they were required to submit quarterly statements on their total earnings, including any from outside employment; from time to time local assistance agencies were asked to certify their need; finally WPA employment was restricted to only one member from any household and, except for veterans, was limited to a term of eighteen months and there could be no reassignment until thirty days had elapsed and need had been recertified.

It was undoubtedly an unrealistic policy to seek to divorce work programs from relief. Public works programs are differentiated from all other work relief programs in that the former are designed to stimulate employment while the latter are designed to put needy unemployed persons to work, not as a substitute for relief but as a substitute for direct relief.

Some Major Characteristics of Work Relief

We have noted that work programs fall into three main types: public works, work relief, and work-for-relief. Work programs are of significance only during periods of heavy unemployment. When the nation is prosperous and the employment rate is high, the needy unemployed are few in number. They are for the most part, moreover, marginally employable; that is, because of physical, mental, educational, or social handicaps, they are at a com-

[3] Harry Hopkins, *Spending to Save* (New York: Norton, 1936), p. 114.

petitive disadvantage in the labor market. Work programs during good times, therefore, will be limited in scope and directed primarily toward helping such "marginally employable" persons maintain their work habits and acquire marketable skills. Certain elements of the work test may be present, however, because the community often fails to understand how any employable person should be out of work and in need when employment opportunities are presumably good. Work programs, during good times, precisely because they are limited in scope, are likely to be locally administered and financed and to be of the work-for-relief variety. The real test of their value and their intent depends upon the extent to which there is emphasis on retraining and preparation for return to the labor market.

Public works and work relief are of importance only during depression periods. Since it would be naïve to think that such times will never return, and since the extent of such work programs will affect the scope and nature of public assistance, the student of public assistance cannot afford to overlook them.

Public works, as we have seen, are often used to stimulate employment. They are more than a mere substitute for work relief or direct assistance. The theory of public works is closely related to economic theory, especially to such matters as full employment policy, public finance and fiscal policy, the national income, and theories regarding public and private investment. At the risk of gross oversimplification we can point out that the theory, in brief, is this: When the volume of private business declines, there is a drop in both production and purchasing power. A decline in purchasing power brings about further decreases in production, and so on. It is believed that government can prevent, or at least retard, this downward spiral by extensive investment in public works. The effectiveness of such public works depends to a great extent upon the ease and swiftness with which they can be undertaken; a delay of sixty or ninety days in taking up the slack caused by the decline in private business may result in a full-blown recession.

Unfortunately, public works cannot be dreamed up overnight; they require careful planning. Projects such as highways, bridges, hospitals, schools, flood control, moreover, are generally under-taken when they are needed for their own sake, rather than timed to coincide with the requirements of a full-employment policy. Whether or not government can carry out a large-scale and swift program of public works in an area affected by adverse business conditions depends upon whether there is a nation-wide calendar of projected public works that have been planned in anticipation of future requirements, and which can be executed in advance, if economic conditions warrant it. Another difficulty inherent in public works is that they are confined almost entirely to con-struction and to durable goods industries. It takes time for the benefits of increased public spending to filter down to those who are most directly affected by the decline in business. This in-ability of public works programs to relieve immediately the distress caused by unemployment prompted the national govern-ment to embark on its CWA and WPA programs.

Inasmuch as work relief is a substitute for direct assistance, it is more germane to our subject than public works; hence we will consider its characteristics in more detail.

The Nature of Work Relief Projects

Since work relief programs are undertaken in times of heavy unemployment, and since work relief is a substitute for direct unemployment relief, the program has to be extensive; the projects, moreover, have to be of a public nature. Employment that is created has to be additional—that is, the projects cannot involve activity that normally would be carried on by private business or by the regular agencies of government, since it would defeat the purpose of the program to take away jobs from people who would otherwise be employed. The projects have to be of such nature that the labor costs are high relative to the cost of materials. That is, the major expenditure has to be a substitute for relief. Finally, the projects have to be such that they can be undertaken by workers who are not trained. Even during the depression, when people from all walks of life were unemployed, and when the work program was extensive, it was impossible to assign people only to jobs for which their training equipped them. The limitations on the projects that could be set up resulted in an emphasis upon construction, physical improvements, and maintenance work. Many experienced salespeople and clerical workers, even technicians and professional people, had to take assignments as unskilled laborers.

Work relief agencies are faced with the difficult task of developing projects that are sufficiently useful not to be criticized as "boondoggling" or "leaf raking" and yet not so useful that they can be criticized for competing with business.

Assignment of Personnel

Work relief personnel falls into two categories: the supervisory staff responsible for the planning, overseeing, and general administration of the program; and the workers. The former have a non-relief status and are roughly analogous to the public assistance personnel; they are employed, presumably, on the basis of competence. The latter are employed because they are employable and in need. The two major aspects of a work relief program, namely, the necessity of giving work to employable needy people and the necessity of doing as efficient a piece of work as possible, inevitably conflict. "Employability," as we have noted in an earlier chapter, is a vague term; it takes on meaning only as it can be related to the demands of a particular job. But in the case of work relief the major requirement is need, while the term "employable" is applied very loosely to almost anyone who is physically able to function. Most people who are assigned to work relief jobs are anxious to work, but many of them are assigned to jobs for which they have neither training nor interest. In too many instances the jobs lead nowhere; they are not in line with the workers' past experience and they are not of a nature that will materially increase a worker's stock of marketable skills. Sometimes the assignment may actually be resented as signifying loss of status, as, for example, when an artist is assigned to a humdrum clerical job which brings him no more money but which reduces the time available for the practice of his art.

Under these circumstances there is likely to be a difficult problem in maintaining discipline and *esprit de corps*. Under private enterprise, and even in governmental service, certain criteria automatically determine an employee's worth; these are largely inoperative in work relief. The project supervisor may be eager to do a good job, but he is confronted with the fact that need rather than ability is the primary requisite for employment. He is under pressure to keep persons on the job unless they are grossly incompetent or recalcitrant.

The problem is accentuated where the work relief and public assistance programs are administered and financed by different levels of government. The assistance agency will naturally be desirous of unloading as many recipients as possible onto the work relief program, since every assignment reduces its costs while most work relief dismissals will raise its costs. It will probably, therefore, take a very broad view of what constitutes employability. Where both programs are operated by the same unit of government this issue is less likely to come up.

Compensation

Work relief is distinguished from work-for-relief by the fact that it is compensated on the basis, not of need, but of work performed. On what basis, then, should monthly earnings be computed? Regardless of the maximum or minimum monthly earnings allowable, it has to be recognized that some workers will be unable to earn enough to meet their total family needs; others, because they are unattached or have outside income, may earn substantially more than they would receive through direct assistance. This discrepancy cannot be avoided. The earnings of the first group will be supplemented by public assistance; the latter group will simply fare better than before.

Under WPA, monthly earning schedules were worked out on the basis of four work classifications: unskilled, intermediate, skilled, and professional and technical. The earning schedule also allowed for regional variations.

Another problem that must be dealt with is the matter of relating earnings to prevailing rates of compensation in the community. On the basis of past experience, organized labor will be most likely to favor an hourly rate of pay comparable to that prevailing in the community, for fear that anything less might serve to depress wages generally. Business interests, on the other hand, will probably be opposed to monthly earnings that can be compared favorably to earnings in private employment. Work relief, while it lacks the status of private employment, has certain characteristics that may appeal to some workers—particularly those who are "marginal"—such as security, guaranteed monthly income, a more relaxed tempo, and less emphasis on efficiency and productivity. Private employers may fear that, if enough workers consider these characteristics advantageous, they will be used as a lever to force up wages generally. This action might well be possible, since work projects do not provide for a social service staff to investigate workers' efforts to secure private employment, and to check on need.

The solution seems to be to set an hourly rate in line with prevailing community wage scales but require only enough hours of work a month to earn the "security wage." An advantage of this arrangement is that it permits workers to have some free time in which to look for private employment. A disadvantage is that skilled workers, since their hourly rate is higher, will put in fewer hours than unskilled workers, so that several shifts of skilled workers may be working on the same project during a given month, with resultant inefficiency.

Some Social Service Problems

Whether or not the administration of assistance and work are completely separate, there is need for a close working relationship. The labor force for the work projects is drawn from the assistance rolls. The assistance agency in making work referrals will have to take into consideration the characteristics and requirements for such work. The bulk of the project workers, moreover, will have a monthly "security wage" approximating the income to which they would be entitled if on assistance, but, if the monthly wage is based on the number of hours of employment during a given period, there is the possibility of loss of income due to illness, interruptions in the project due to weather conditions or other factors, or the termination of the project. If such conditions result in a budget deficit, there will be need for prompt supplementation. Hardship may ensue if even one or two days' work is lost. WPA attempted to solve this problem by paying workers for time lost owing to weather conditions or temporary interruptions beyond their control, provided the workers reported for duty and were officially dismissed for the day. While it seems sound in principle to allow for supplementation of work relief wages if, because of absences due to illness or other pressing personal reasons, the monthly "security wage" results in a deficit, difficulties arise in determining whether or not such absences are justified. The assistance agency must try to evaluate a situation that has passed and that is difficult to verify. The administration of one-payment supplementary grants to cover reductions in work relief pay is, moreover, expensive and complicated.

Sickness and injuries present additional problems. Long-term illness naturally results in dismissal from work relief; short-term illness necessitates not only supplementation but also medical care. Illness in the worker's family also requires medical care by the assistance agency. Injuries arising out of work relief can have just as serious effect as any other work injuries, and therefore project workers should be protected by some form of workmen's compensation.

Policies with regard to initial and continued eligibility for work relief need to be clearly thought out. We have already suggested that it is artificial to distinguish between direct assistance and work programs (except public works) on the basis that one is and the other is not relief. Work programs are established for the specific purpose of putting the unemployed to work, presumably because they are in need. Projects must be such that they would ordinarily not be undertaken because of either private or public demand; while they are, it is hoped, useful, they are nonetheless "made work."

In the first instance, it will be relatively simple to restrict work assignments to persons who are already on the assistance rolls or who have been certified by the assistance agency as being in need. But how shall continued eligibility be determined? How can we be sure that persons on work relief are making real efforts to return to private employment? Is it a matter of indifference whether the total family income of a person on work relief, exclusive of his wages, is more than enough to meet the family needs on a budget deficit basis? Should more than one member of a household be assigned to work relief? If not, how shall priorities be determined? These are only a few of the matters that a social worker could deal with. However, Mr. Hopkins, it will be recalled, noted with obvious satisfaction that when a man was assigned to WPA, "the social worker drops out of the picture." Later, when Congress reasserted its right to exercise greater supervision over the program, it instituted controls designed to prevent misuse of the program. These controls were administrative in nature and somewhat rigid. Is it unreasonable to think that they were necessitated because of the rather arbitrary separation of relief work from public assistance?

EMERGENCY PROGRAMS FOR FARM PEOPLE

In the chapter on the history of public assistance brief mention was made of certain programs for farm people established as a result of the Emergency Relief Appropriation Act of 1935. They were part of a larger effort to strengthen the agricultural sector of our economy. Strictly speaking, they are outside the main stream of our concern as they did not involve relief in the sense of money payments made to individuals on the basis of need; but in so far as they were a substitute for such assistance they have some pertinence. They are of more than mere historical interest, moreover, because a repetition of the agricultural conditions of the 1930's might well lead to the advocacy of similar measures.

It will be recalled that agriculture was particularly hard hit during the last depression, not only because it had failed to recover from the effects of the previous depression, but also because of the great drought of 1930. The following brief summary of the problems that beset farm people will suggest why the more orthodox methods of assistance, direct relief and work relief, were not a solution for their difficulties:

1. There was a low rate of return from the agricultural enterprise; the price of commodities farmers had to sell was far out of line with the prices of commodities they had to buy: clothing, machinery, processed food, even the price of farm land. Another factor was the decrease in the demand for certain staple crops such as cotton and wheat, on which many farmers depended almost exclusively for their income.

2. The drought ruined many farms in the South and the Far West.

3. It was hard to secure credit. Farmers must depend on credit much more than wage or salary workers; they need it for the conduct of the enterprise from which they derive their living. Farm income, unlike wages or salary, is not received at frequent intervals, but only at certain seasons when the crops are marketed. For most of the year, the farmer must live and must conduct his business on savings, or, more likely, on borrowed funds. A farmer's mortgage on his farm is a business as well as a personal debt. If the mortgage is foreclosed he loses his job as well as his home. Farmers, even tenant farmers, are capitalists, in the sense that they invest their savings, labor, skill, and credit in an enterprise from which they expect to derive a profit. Shortage of cash and a drying up of the sources of credit will cause many farmers to lose their farms, which means their being deprived of gainful employment as well as loss of their investment.

4. Many farms are little more than subsistence homesteads. As of 1940, for example, eight-ninths of our agricultural production came from slightly more than half of the nation's farms. The remaining farms, therefore, produced primarily for home consumption, and cash income from the sale of produce was very small. The factors causing so many farm people to live on a low and precarious standard of living are many: The size of the enterprise is too small to be profitable, and the farmer lacks the capital with which to expand his operations; the soil is unproductive; the farmer lacks technical knowledge to improve his position, and/or he lacks capital needed for improvements.

5. There is, and has been, a high incidence of tenancy. In

1930, for example, 42.4 percent of the nation's farms were rented. Some prosperous farm operators lease land as a matter of business policy, but the majority of tenants are obliged to rent land because they cannot afford to purchase farms. If they cannot pay their rent they lose their jobs as well as their homes. Sharecroppers and farm labor present additional problems which we cannot go into here.

Farm people in need of food, clothing, and the other necessaries of life require assistance just as any other needy group does, but assistance alone is not a solution to their problems since they are not "unemployed." Even farmers who have lost their land are in a situation quite different from that of the jobless wage or salaried worker. The latter, if his living expenses are met, can presumably return to gainful employment when business picks up. But such is not the case with farm people; they need help in retaining or regaining the land and the equipment by which they can support themselves. If nothing more than their immediate personal needs are satisfied they will be reduced to the condition of a landless proletariat, which must choose between flocking to the cities to compete with urban workers for the lowest-paid, unskilled jobs and swelling the ranks of sharecroppers, of migratory workers, or of farm labor groups whose existence, even in times of relative prosperity, is precarious.

Despite the trend toward urbanization, rural people constitute a large and important element of the population. The belief is widely held, moreover, that a rural population which includes a large number of independent and productive farm families is a major stabilizing element in our society. The disruption of our farm economy and of rural institutions and values which would have been inevitable had the effects of the depression in rural areas been permitted to run their course might well have been disastrous to the nation as a whole, as well as to the farm people directly affected. No doubt, it was concern for this problem that prompted the national administration to attempt to deal with the situation on a more fundamental level than by merely providing emergency relief. Some of these efforts were clearly in the economic sphere; others, because of the peculiar nature of the farm enterprise, in which the farm family is both a business and a social unit, took on the characteristics of a social service. These programs will be discussed briefly.

Price Support Programs

The first measure in aid of agriculture was designed to raise farm income by helping farmers to receive a more favorable price for their products. The Agricultural Adjustment Act of 1933 provided for voluntary reduction in acreage in seven specified crops. To prevent famine or excessive prices, however, the reduction applied only to that portion of the crop which had been produced for export, but which, because of the international situation, could not be sold. It was this surplus, thrown on the domestic market, that had depressed prices. The coöperation of the farmers was secured through the payment of direct benefits or by rentals by the Department of Agriculture. When the act was declared unconstitutional in 1936, some of its features were continued under the Soil Conservation Act, and farmers were paid benefits for planting non-marketable, soil-conserving crops. Under the second Agricultural Adjustment Act of 1938, farmers could voluntarily establish marketing quotas, to take effect when there was a surplus above what the domestic and foreign markets could absorb. Loans on various agricultural commodities were made to avert both price collapse and scarcity. The government also purchased various farm products that were surplus, thereby taking them off the market and sustaining the price level. These commodities were distributed to needy families to supplement their assistance grants. The objective of these devices was to restore the relationship between the prices the farmer paid and those that he received that had existed between 1909 and 1914. The government price support program was designed to support this "parity price."

The Tenant Purchase Program

The strength of the agricultural sector of our economy is based to a great extent upon a high incidence of efficiently managed family-sized farms, owned outright, or at least with

a substantial equity, by the operators. It follows that a high rate
of tenancy, of sharecropping, or of farm labor is a sign of weakness. During the depression many farm owners were reduced to
tenancy or to sharecropping, or were forced from the land
entirely. The tenant purchase program of the national government was designed to bring independence and security to people
who normally derived their living from working the land, by
enabling them to own their own farms. Loans on favorable
terms were made for farm purchases. Loans were restricted to
the acquisition of family-sized farms; interest was at 3 percent
and the debt was to be amortized over a period of forty years.
Loans were made upon the recommendation of local committees
of farmers, who were familiar with local agricultural conditions,
with land values, and with the capacity of the individual or
family applying for the loan.

Rural Rehabilitation Loans and Grants

Many farm owners were in a precarious condition, lacking
sufficient resources to supply themselves and their families with
the necessities of life. Many did not have enough cash income to
meet taxes and interest obligations. There were thousands of
farmers who seemed doomed to perpetual dependency or sub-
marginal living because they lacked the capital and the technical
knowledge to make their operations sufficiently productive. The
Rural Rehabilitation program of the Farm Security Administration was established to accomplish two purposes: the relief of
immediate want and assistance in making the farm enterprise
self-sufficient.

Since the farm is both a home and a business it would have
been impracticable to separate the direct relief for the family
from the economic aid designed to make the farming operation
more productive; hence the rural rehabilitation program had
many of the characteristics of a welfare agency. Meriam summarizes the main features of the program as follows:

1. Relief grants made at the outset to carry the family along until
it was again on its own feet; and in some cases renewed from time to
time thereafter in event of illness or death in the family, crop failures,

or human failures where the workers had not succeeded in mastering the new ways or displaying the interest, ingenuity, or "stick-to-itive-ness" necessary for even partial success.

2. Loans to obtain necessary equipment, seed, fertilizer.

3. Adjustment of debts due for taxes and prior loans on land, equipment, or crops to prevent foreclosures, evictions, or seizures of necessary equipment and personal property.

4. In some cases, relocation on land that offered an opportunity for a passable measure of success.

5. In many cases a very considerable measure of education, assistance in planning, and at least general direction if not immediate close supervision.[4]

Although the above program had certain definite relief aspects, it was carried on separately from both the poor law and the emergency unemployment relief programs. Sound administration demanded an unusual combination of qualifications—a blend of social work and agricultural economics. Thus, according to Meriam:

The intimate relationships with the members of the family inherent in the undertaking called for the highest skills of the successful family case worker. Planning and supervising the farm activities called for knowledge and skill in farm management and farm home management. It is perhaps questionable whether the nation had a sufficient number of persons qualified in either of these two fields to have staffed so large an undertaking. It seems unquestionable that it had few individuals who combined the two different types of qualifications that were requisite.[5]

The foregoing programs were the major efforts to improve the conditions of farm people. They have been criticized on several counts. One argument is that the federal government, in its efforts to aid the farmer, perpetuated the very conditions that had depressed agriculture. It is claimed that, from the viewpoint of strict economics, the trouble with agriculture is that there are too many farmers. If there were fewer, those that remained could secure a more adequate income, and there would

[4] Meriam, *op. cit.,* pp. 296–297.
[5] *Ibid.,* p. 319.

be no need for artificially maintained prices. The "New Deal" farm programs, however, made it possible for many people to continue as farmers who otherwise would have been forced out. Government subsidies, in other words, enabled farmers whose operations, for one reason or another, were inefficient to remain in competition with the "efficient" farmers.

While this argument may appear persuasive, there are other factors to be considered. Farming is more than a business; it is a way of life with values that many people believe transcend strict dollars and cents accounting. Had the inexorable laws of competition been given full sway, it would have been the operators of the family-sized farms who would have suffered the most. It is not improbable that the whole pattern of agriculture might have changed to large-scale industrialized farms worked by low-paid, poorly housed farm labor. Even from the point of view of strict agricultural efficiency, large-scale farming has only a slight advantage over the well-managed family-sized farm, and, in the light of many other social and economic factors, its disadvantages counterbalance this margin.[6]

It is difficult enough to get workers to shift from a declining industry (such as coal mining) to other lines of work, especially if moving from one community to another is involved. How much more difficult and how much more damaging would it be to uproot farm people from their accustomed mode of living! It would have been ironic, to say the least, to have let this happen during a period when millions of industrial and service workers were unemployed and there were literally no other jobs to be had. Even in normal times urban communities are able to maintain or increase their populations only because of the migration of young men and women from rural communities. During the depression, when the American people, perhaps for the first time, began to lose faith in their productive capacity, there was a movement in the opposite direction. Many influential people were convinced that industry would never be able to reabsorb all the unemployed and that the solution was a "back to the land"

[6] J. H. Kolb and E. de S. Brunner, *A Study of Rural Society* (Boston: Houghton Mifflin, 1946), pp. 99–103.

movement, based on the belief that those for whom industry no longer had any need might be able to gain at least a subsistence from the soil.

FEDERAL PROGRAMS FOR VETERANS

Federal money payment programs for veterans and their dependents have a long history and may be traced back to pensions paid to survivors of the American Revolution. Since World War I, however, there has been a vast development in such programs. As Eveline Burns points out, a mere summary of the legislation enacted up to the end of 1944 occupies over 180 pages of a Congressional report.[7] Since many persons are receiving income or institutional care as a result of such legislation, and since many more are potentially eligible for benefits, they have a direct bearing on the scope of public assistance. Because of their complexity, these programs constitute a field of study in themselves. We will merely describe their main characteristics.

1. Retirement programs. For personnel of the regular military establishment and for reserve officers.
2. Disability compensation. For veterans of any war who have service-connected disabilities. Compensation may range from $15.75 to $172.50 a month without reference to other income. (Compensation payments to peacetime veterans with service-connected disabilities are limited to 80 percent of these amounts.) If the veteran has a 50 percent disability, special dependents' grants are available. Survivors of veterans whose death was service connected are eligible for benefits (widows, minor children, dependent parents).
3. Disability pensions. Benefits under the pension acts are available to some war veterans who have disabilities not resulting from service, or who have attained a specific age. In addition, pensions are available to dependents of certain deceased war veterans whose deaths are not service connected. As to World War I and II veterans and their dependents, pension payments

[7] Eveline M. Burns, *The American Social Security System* (Boston: Houghton Mifflin, 1949), p. 265.

are limited to persons whose incomes do not exceed specified amounts. For example, a World War II veteran who is permanently and totally disabled from non-service-connected injury or disease may receive a basic monthly pension of $63 (upon attaining age sixty-five or having been rated permanently and totally disabled for a continuous period of ten years, he has his pension increased to $75) provided his annual income is less than $1400, if single, or $2700 if married or having minor children. As another example, a widow and child of a deceased World War II veteran whose death is not traceable to service-incurred injury or disease, but who at the time of death had a service-connected disability, may receive a monthly pension of $60, provided their annual income does not exceed $2700.

4. Readjustment allowance program. Veterans of World War II who have been discharged under conditions other than dishonorable are entitled to certain benefits to enable them to adjust to their return to civilian life. These include unemployment benefits and benefits for self-employed persons with low income. Veterans with at least ninety days of service between September 16, 1940, and July 25, 1947, were entitled to benefits. Such benefits were payable to qualified veterans until two years after their discharge, or after the termination of World War II (July 25, 1947), whichever was later. The program for all veterans ended on July 25, 1952 (except for a very small number who are eligible under the terms of the Voluntary Recruitment Act of 1945, Public Law 190, 79th Congress).

5. Education and training program. The education and training benefits established under Public Law 346 are available to essentially the same group of World War II veterans as are the readjustment allowances. A course of education or training at any approved institution or establishment must have been initiated before July 26, 1951, for those veterans who were discharged from the armed forces prior to July 26, 1947 (termination date of World War II). Persons who were in the service after July 25, 1947, including those who enlisted or reënlisted between October 6, 1945, and October 5, 1946, inclusive, must initiate their courses within four years from the

date of their first discharge from the service after July 25, 1947. Training may not be pursued beyond July 25, 1956, except that for those veterans who enlisted or reënlisted between October 6, 1945, and October 5, 1946, inclusive, all training must be concluded within nine years from the termination of such person's enlistment or reënlistment. The amount of education or training to which the veteran is entitled depends upon the length of service in the armed forces, with a minimum entitlement of one and a maximum of four calendar years. A veteran may not pursue courses of training which are avocational or recreational in character. During the period of education or training (which may be in an educational institution, on the job, or a combination of institutional and farm training) all tuition, supplies, and equipment costs up to a limit of $500 a year are paid by the Veterans' Administration. In addition, a veteran pursuing institutional training receives a subsistence allowance of $75, $105, or $120 a month depending upon the number of his dependents, if his subsistence allowance and compensation earned for productive labor do not exceed $210 per month, if he has no dependents, $270 if he has one dependent, or $290 if he has two or more dependents. A veteran pursuing on-the-job training may receive subsistence allowance at the rate of $65 per month if without dependents and $90 per month with one or more dependents, with the same limitation as to earnings and subsistence allowance. In addition an on-the-job trainee's subsistence allowance plus the wages due from his training establishment may not exceed the wage which he will receive from his trainer upon completion of training. Thus, while the entitlement to education or training is not dependent on the veteran's income, if he is otherwise qualified, the receipt of the subsistence allowance is directly related to the amount of his earnings while taking a course of education or training. Veterans of the Korean conflict who have served in the U.S. government forces and who have been honorably discharged are eligible for training and educational benefits under Public Law 550. In contrast to the so-called "G.I. Bill," benefits under this act are paid as a flat sum to the veteran covering both tuition and subsistence allowance. A single veteran is entitled to $110 a month; veterans with one dependent receive $135 and those with two or more dependents $160 per month, provided they are registered for at least fourteen semester hours.

6. Vocational rehabilitation program. For veterans who have had service-connected disabilities, and who are vocationally handicapped, there is a program of physical rehabilitation, vocational counseling and guidance, training, and placement. Training may be for as long as necessary, without regard to length of military service, but exceeding four years only in extraordinary cases.

7. Loan guarantee program. Veterans who satisfy the same service requirements as for other benefits may have home, farm, or business loans from private lenders guaranteed or insured by the Veterans' Administration. Loans are guaranteed up to 60 percent of the principal, but the guaranteed portion may not exceed $7500 for real-estate or $2000 for non-real-estate loans. There are certain restrictions on the conditions of the loans from private lenders, with regard to interest rate and maturity date.

8. Medical program. Hospitalization, including all medical and surgical services, is available for all veterans. Those with non-service-connected disabilities, however, must state that they are unable to pay for it, and they are admitted to a Veterans' Administration hospital only if there is an available bed. Domiciliary care in a Veterans' Administration home, including medical and dental care, is available under certain conditions to all veterans, provided they are unable to earn a living because of disability and are without adequate means of support.

9. Burial program. This benefit is available in an amount not to exceed $150 for the purpose of defraying funeral and burial expenses of certain veterans. To qualify for this payment, the deceased veteran (1) must have served in the armed forces during a period of war and been discharged other than dishonorably; or (2) must have been discharged for disability in-

curred in line of duty; or (3) must have been receiving compensation for disability at time of death.[8]

An examination of these programs reveals a threefold purpose: to rehabilitate or otherwise recompense veterans whose health and economic potential has been impaired as a result of military service; to equalize with the civilian population the economic opportunities of veterans upon their return to civilian status; and to provide an expression of gratitude to those who have risked their lives in the defense of their country. It will be noted that distinctions in eligibility for benefits are made between peacetime and wartime veterans, and between veterans who have incurred service-connected disabilities and veterans who are not disabled or who have non-service-connected disabilities. While the eligibility of the latter groups for some benefits is conditioned upon economic status, no income test is required, but only their affirmation as to their circumstances. While some programs have a definite time limit, other programs will continue to be a potential resource which will either make public assistance unnecessary or reduce its amount.

In addition to federal veterans' programs, most states also provide benefits and services of one kind or another. These include information and consultation services, veterans' bonuses, loans supplementary to federal loans, additional educational benefits, etc. It will be recalled, moreover, that many states have a special form of public assistance for needy veterans and their families. Many states maintain homes for needy veterans and their wives, or for their widows.

SELECTED REFERENCES

Howard, Donald S., *The WPA and Federal Relief Policy*, New York: Russell Sage, 1943.
Lester, Richard A., "Is Work Relief Economical?" *Social Service Review*, June, 1936.

[8] Factual data taken from the document *Selected Governmental Programs Which Aid the Unemployed and Low-Income Families*, 81st Congress, Joint Committee on the Economic Report.

Linford, Alton A., "Public Works and Fiscal Policy," *Social Service Review,* September, 1944.

McMahon, Millett, and Ogden, *The Administration of Federal Work Relief,* Chicago: Public Administration Service, 1941.

Meriam, Lewis, *Relief and Social Security,* Washington: Brookings, 1946, chaps. 10, 11, 12, and 13.

Security Work and Relief Policies, Washington: National Resources Planning Board, 1942.

Swartz, Philip, "Work Relief in 1950," *Public Welfare,* August–September, 1950.

CHAPTER 14

Social Insurance

Guild of the Holy Cross in St. Lawrence Jewry, London (1370) pays
to members in infirmity by reason of mutilation of limbs or because
of old age 14 pence a week but the brothers so helped must have
paid their quarterage (4 pence a week) for seven years.
—Quoted by Edith Eckert in *Chaucer's World*

INTRODUCTION

The Relation of Insurance to Assistance

The character and extent of public assistance depend upon
the various economic arrangements whereby society enables its
members to support themselves. One such arrangement or institution is social insurance.

We have already pointed out that public assistance is the last
line of defense against want. The first line is, of course, the economic structure through which the individual is enabled to earn
a living. Historically, when this structure failed the individual,
either because the structure itself broke down or because personal handicap prevented him from participating in economically
productive activity, his only recourse, apart from the help of relatives or friends, was poor relief.

Within the last hundred years, however, a new institution has
been interposed between poor relief and gainful work: the institution of social insurance. The concept of insurance is by no
means new, nor, as the quotation heading this chapter testifies, is
its use for achieving social objectives. But insurance sponsored
and administered by government, and financed by legally enforced contributions, is of relatively recent origin. The purpose of

social insurance is to provide some measure of economic security by guaranteeing, under certain specified conditions, and as a result of the various contingencies of life, a minimum income if earning power is curtailed or lost.

The principles and techniques of social insurance constitute an extensive field for study; therefore, we can do no more here than treat briefly of its major concepts and characteristics as found in this country. The reader whose interest is aroused will, we hope, explore this field further.

The rapid extension of social insurance in all parts of the world, especially in industrialized nations, is an indication that the needs of those groups particularly exposed to the hazard of income loss are receiving increased consideration. The popularity of social insurance stems from several factors. There is a growing demand for protection against insecurity resulting from the vagaries of the economic system. While public assistance is a vast improvement over poor relief, there is marked dissatisfaction with a "means test" program as the major bulwark against want when income ceases. More important, perhaps, is the recognition that insurance benefits, when added to existing resources, enable many persons to retain at least some semblance of their customary standard of living.

Many advantages accrue to the person protected by social insurance; in the event of a specific loss of income his benefit is guaranteed; the amount of the benefit may be calculated with a high degree of accuracy; eligibility is usually based upon covered employment and can be determined by reference to certain objective criteria which do not touch upon the more intimate aspects of a person's life. Since "need" is not a factor, one's personal affairs are not investigated; the amount of the benefit is not conditioned upon actual or potential resources; nor is its receipt conditioned upon the beneficiary's changing his behavior to conform to standards set by the administrative agency. Finally, receipt of the benefit is not accompanied by that loss of status which, despite all our fine words and efforts, is too often the lot of the assistance recipient.

The Nature of Social Insurance

To understand social insurance it is first necessary to grasp the principles of insurance and not only to distinguish social insurance from public assistance but also to distinguish social insurance from private insurance.

Insurance is a method whereby men may protect themselves from economic loss resulting from life hazards to which they may be exposed. It is based upon the operation of the law of averages when applied to large numbers. Thus experience has demonstrated that, with respect to a given risk such as property damage, theft, death, or the like, the extent of the loss that will occur during a given period and among a given group can be predicted with increasing precision as the size of the group is increased. Since no one can foretell upon whom the blow will fall, but since the total loss likely to occur can be calculated in advance, men can guard themselves against loss by the payment of a small sum into a central fund from which they can be reimbursed in full or for whatever part of the possible loss they elect to insure. A select committee of the British House of Commons, reporting in 1825, stated the principle of insurance as follows:

Whenever there is a contingency, the cheapest way of providing against it is by uniting with others, so that each man may subject himself to a small deprivation, in order that no man may be subjected to a great loss. He upon whom the contingency does not fall, does not get his money back again, nor does he get for it any visible or tangible benefit; but he gets security against ruin and consequent peace of mind. He, upon whom the contingency does fall, gets all that those, whom fortune has exempted from it, have lost in hard money, and is thus enabled to sustain an event which would otherwise overwhelm him.[1]

Insurance as a private venture is based upon the following elements:

1. *It is voluntary.* The success of the insurance enterprise depends upon the extent to which individuals can be induced to buy protection from a particular carrier.[2]

[1] "Insurance," *Encyclopaedia Britannica* (Chicago: 1948), pp. 452–453.
[2] Workmen's compensation, although social insurance, has certain features

2. *The cost of protection is born individually.* Persons who need protection for themselves or for others (as in the case of employees or relatives) must pay the full cost themselves. Those who do not do so are deprived of such protection.

3. *The risk is calculated.* Not only must the nature of the risk against which insurance is sought be clearly specified but the degree to which the person on whom the policy is written is exposed to that risk must be taken into consideration in determining the amount of the premium. Thus, if a man wishes to insure his household goods against fire, he will have to pay a higher premium if he lives in a nonfireproof dwelling. The solvency of the insurance enterprise's reserve fund is thus protected either by excluding the poor risk or by charging a higher premium.

4. *Full reserves are required.* The reserve fund must be large enough so that all actuarially anticipated claims can be met. The fund must be invested wisely so that the enterprise's capital is not diminished, and so that the interest on the investment can strengthen the fund.

5. *Ownership is divided.* As a private venture, the insurance enterprise may be a proprietary one, that is, owned by stockholders who hope to derive income from the profitable conduct of the business; or it may be a mutual concern in which the policyholders are the owners. Even though the primary purpose may not be to make a profit, the cost of providing protection may include the cost of an extensive sales organization.

6. *It is contractual in nature.* The eventual benefits from private insurance are defined and guaranteed by contract and are equitable. Meriam explains this equitable quality as follows:

> A private insurance contract is said to be equitable when all the members of a class receive the same degree of insurance protection for the same amount of premium paid. It does not mean that all get back the same number of dollars for dollars paid in, for they are buying insurance, but all have the same protection, and all face on taking out the insurance approximately the same hazard. Obviously

---

related to private insurance. Thus, although employers may be required to provide such protection for their workers, most states permit them to place this insurance with private carriers.

voluntary insurance in a competitive society must have this attribute or a close approach to it, because few persons would voluntarily purchase insurance when their risks were much lower than the risks of their fellows. Private insurance companies tended, moreover, in one way or another to offer lower rates to those whose hazards were lower.[3]

Private insurance is one of the most important elements in our business structure. Although it does not contribute directly to production (except in so far as the reserves are invested in productive enterprises), it makes possible a much more effective utilization of capital. If, for example, a businessman were unable to insure his raw materials, his finished product, and his plant against loss from fire, theft, or other contingency, he would have to keep a substantial amount of liquid capital as a reserve against such a loss; otherwise he might be forced into bankruptcy. Because of the protection afforded by insurance, he can apply such capital to more productive purposes.

Private insurance has been able to offer protection against many contingencies that result in economic loss. The necessity of relating the charge for such protection to the degree of individual risk, however, tends to deprive those whose need may be greatest of the benefits of such protection. For this same reason, the hazard to which low-income families are particularly exposed, loss of earning power, is not insurable privately. Policies paying benefits because of retirement, accident, or ill health are not within their reach. Unemployment, moreover, is not considered an insurable risk.

Social insurance has been evolved to overcome this difficulty. Its purpose is to provide a minimum income when, because of old age, accident, ill health, unemployment, death of the family wage earner, and the like, individuals or families are deprived of their normal means of support. It is predicated on the assumption that in our complex society the vast majority cannot protect themselves against the distress resulting from loss of income through insurance, savings or other provisions. Hard work, thrift,

[3] Lewis Meriam, *Relief and Social Security* (Washington: Brookings, 1946), p. 126.

and intelligence are not enough; they must be combined with a readily marketable skill, trade, or profession and a generous helping of good fortune.

It is difficult to generalize about social insurance; not only does it vary from nation to nation with respect to covered risks, financing, and administration, but even in a given nation there may be considerable variation in the pattern of insurance against different risks. The following points, however, are sufficiently characteristic of social insurance to distinguish it from private insurance:

1. *Protection is compulsory.* With respect to a given risk, the employed person (possibly the self-employed person), under certain conditions defined by law, is covered. This automatic coverage of large numbers tends to compensate for the adverse effect of the inclusion of those who are poor risks.

2. *The cost is borne socially.* The insured person is not obliged to bear the full cost of protection; indeed, he may not be required to make any direct contribution. Depending upon the particular plan, the employer, the employee, and the general taxpayer (as represented by the state) may share in varying combination and proportions the cost of this coverage.

3. *The charge is not related to the degree of individual risk.* While the contribution (i.e., premium, pay-roll tax) paid by those participating may be a flat sum for a given period or a percentage of pay roll, it is not varied with the degree of risk to which the covered individual may be exposed.

4. *The benefit may be only loosely related to the total amount of contribution paid in behalf of the insured person.* Although the size of the benefit may be related to earnings, the relationship may be a loose one in that the formula for calculating the benefit may be weighted in favor of the person whose aggregate earnings are lower. Even in systems charging a flat money premium and providing a flat benefit there is some variation because the benefit may increase with the number of dependents.

5. *The right to benefits is more likely to be a legislative right than a contractual right.* The contribution rate (or tax), the benefit formula, and many other essential elements in the plan

are authorized by statute and may be modified by subsequent legislation. Thus, contributions at a given rate do not necessarily guarantee that a benefit of a specific amount will be received; the dollar amount of the benefit may be increased or decreased (more probably the former) as the legislature sees fit to alter the formula.

Social insurance must also be distinguished from employee retirement and pension plans. Private concerns or government in its capacity as employer may institute such programs, but they are part of its employment policy rather than social insurance.

Social insurance, moreover, should not be confused with various non-contributory, non-means test, flat-grant pension programs found in many nations and sometimes advocated for this country.

In assessing a nation's system of social security all income maintenance programs must be taken into consideration—public assistance, social insurance, pension systems, public and private employee retirement plans, labor-management welfare funds— since all involve transfer payments (i.e., redistribution of purchasing power). Whether the total system is a sound one—one that will achieve the desired goal of security—depends upon many factors, especially on the economic consequences of the methods whereby the programs are financed. Will the redistribution of income that is inherent in such programs impede or promote total productivity? A nation's social security system cannot, of itself, guarantee protection against want. As Professor Edwin Witte points out, "The possibilities of providing even a minimum satisfying income to all people and in all contingencies of life depend first of all upon total production." [4]

THE DEVELOPMENT OF SOCIAL INSURANCE IN THE UNITED STATES

A convenient date from which to trace the development of social insurance is 1883, when Germany, under the leadership of

[4] William Haber and Wilber J. Cohen, "What to Expect of Social Security," in *Readings in Social Security* (New York: Prentice-Hall, 1948), p. 63.

Chancellor Bismarck, enacted its compulsory health insurance law—the first of a series of related measures adopted by Germany and other nations to provide protection against loss of income. The concept of social insurance did not emerge fully developed from the mind of Bismarck or his advisers, nor, for that matter, had it originated in the minds of his socialist opponents, who had been campaigning for it for years and whose ideas Bismarck has been accused of purloining. Actually the agitation for social insurance was part of a much wider movement for social security in one form or another. While insurance has come to the fore as, perhaps, the most hopeful device for providing that security, the history of its development is intertwined with a great variety of experimental and transitional programs.

Behind the German legislation of 1883 was a long record of experience, crude, abortive, and limited, to be sure, and lacking in wide public acceptance, but nonetheless of great preparatory value. First of all there was the long tradition of self-help agencies dating back to the guilds and miners' funds of the Middle Ages and including the later mutual aid organizations, "friendly societies," and trade unions which paid sickness, accident, and, perhaps, superannuation benefits from funds built up from the contributions of the membership. The increasing resentment against poor relief, moreover, had led to widespread agitation for noncontributory pensions, paid from general tax funds and available to certain needy groups—especially the aged, and widows with young children. Even when such proposals included some form of "means test" or "income test" they were a great social advance since they were based on a different conception of dependency from that of poor relief and their methods and standards of assistance were more liberal. Concern for the plight of the workingman, injured in the service of his employer, led to measures which placed increasing responsibility upon employers for compensation—on the theory that such injuries were a natural consequence of economic activity and were thus part of the cost of production. The practice of pensioning employees after long and faithful service was not new, but now there developed a movement to regularize such pensions, making them less of a gratuity, less dependent upon the discretion, continued solvency, and good faith of the employer. Thus, guaranteeing of such payments through pension funds was a natural consequence. Finally, there were the expanding and highly successful accomplishments of private insurance, whose techniques of administration, of actuarial science, and of finance provided a useful guide to the planning of insurance protection for those who could not or would not take advantage of voluntary programs.

All of these experiences and movements have contributed to the shaping of social insurance policy. In the seventy years since the passage of the first social insurance law the nations of the world have tried many experiments. The overall pattern of social security varies from nation to nation with respect not only to the risks against which protection is provided but also to the manner in which such protection is afforded.[5] Between social insurance and public assistance may be found various intermediate forms of social assistance. Under this heading come pension programs which may or may not be contributory. They may provide a flat grant or one which varies with the pensioner's income. Thus, under some plans payments are reduced if the pensioner has other income over a certain amount; under other plans the payment may be increased if the pensioner has outside income less than a certain amount. The value of the pensioner's property may or may not be taken into consideration. Such tests of income, however, should not be confused with the "means test" in which the individual's total resources, actual and potential, are evaluated. Sometimes, with respect to a given risk, one program supplements another (i.e., old-age assistance supplements old-age insurance); sometimes one program replaces another. The following comment illustrates this complexity:

The long-term risks of income loss resulting from old age, invalidity (of non-occupational origin), and death of the worker are most commonly met through a system of contributory old-age, invalidity, and

[5] See *Social Security Legislation Throughout the World,* Federal Security Agency, Social Security Administration, Division of Research and Statistics, Bureau Report No. 16 (Washington: 1949), with supplementary information to May, 1953.

survivors' insurance in which benefits are provided without an income test to persons who meet the qualifying requirements. In a number of countries pensions are paid to all aged, disabled, or survivor claimants with insufficient means, provided they meet citizenship or residence requirements. Such pensions subject to income test are the only benefits in Australia, Canada, Denmark, Norway, Spain, and the Union of South Africa. In another group of countries, assistance payments on the basis of need supplement insurance programs; this is the case in Argentina, Belgium, Czechoslovakia, France, Great Britain, the Netherlands, New Zealand, Sweden, Switzerland, the United States, and Uruguay. In Ireland, old-age pensions require an income test, but insurance programs govern payments to invalids and widows and orphans. . . .

Most of the industrialized nations had enacted unemployment insurance legislation by 1939. . . . In Czechoslovakia, France, and Spain the systems formerly in existence have been eliminated in favor of cash assistance or public works and vocational training. New programs include those in Australia (cash benefits subject to an income test rather than insurance). . . .[6]

Since social insurance—indeed, all social security—is of recent origin, it is hardly fair to say that the United States has lagged far behind the nations of Europe. Nevertheless, it was not until this country experienced a depression of catastrophic proportions that the American people were aroused from their complacency and their conviction that poverty and dependence were necessarily of one's own making. Although the American system of social security is relatively new, and is still in its formative stage, the pattern is clear. Controversy may rage over significant details of the system, but there is substantial agreement, even between capital and labor, and between the major political parties, that we are committed to a system in which social insurance will play the major role supplemented by a residual public assistance program. Although pension concepts may be detected in the old-age assistance plans in some states, and though the vociferous advocates of the Townsend and other "share-the-wealth" plans are politically embarrassing to certain legislators, there seems to be

[6] Carl H. Farman, "World Developments in Social Insurance," *Social Security Bulletin*, March, 1950, pp. 3–4.

little likelihood of income-test pension programs being substituted for either public assistance or social insurance.

In Chapter 3 we discussed briefly the origin of social insurance in the United States. In this chapter we will treat of further developments in the sections devoted to discussion of the specific programs.

OLD-AGE AND SURVIVORS' INSURANCE

Old-Age and Survivors' Insurance is a federal program authorized by Title II of the Social Security Act ("Federal Old-Age and Survivors' Insurance Benefits"). The program is administered by the Bureau of Old-Age and Survivors' Insurance of the Social Security Administration, a division of the Department of Health, Education and Welfare. Over five hundred local offices are located in strategic centers of population throughout the United States. The funds collected for the program are managed by a Board of Trustees composed of the Secretary of the Treasury, the Secretary of Labor, and the Commissioner for Social Security.

Since the time of its enactment, Title II of the Social Security Act has undergone drastic amendment: Coverage has been extended to many more persons, new types of benefits have been introduced, the benefit formula has been changed to provide increased benefits. There have also been changes in contribution rates and in the method of financing the program. It is unnecessary to dwell upon these changes; it is sufficient to point out that the program is a dynamic one and that the changes reflect the experience gained in administration, the recognition of the need for extended coverage, and the adjustment of the program to changing economic condition.

Current Old-Age and Survivors' Insurance Provisions

The major provisions of OASI may be considered under the following points: who may draw benefits, who is covered, how eligibility is determined, and how the benefit is computed.

WHO MAY DRAW BENEFITS

The primary beneficiary draws a benefit by virtue of having fulfilled all eligibility requirements in his own right. The amount of the monthly benefit is determined by the benefit formula.

The wife or dependent husband, on reaching the age of sixty-five, is entitled to a benefit equal to one-half that of the primary benefit.

The widow or dependent widower, upon reaching the age of sixty-five, is entitled to a benefit equal to three-fourths of the primary benefit.

The dependent child, if under the age of eighteen, is entitled to a benefit if parent died "fully" or "currently" insured. If there are more than one, each child receives one-half of the primary benefit plus one-quarter of the primary benefit divided by the number of children.

The widow (current) of a worker who dies "fully" or "currently" insured is entitled to a benefit of three-fourths of the primary benefit if she is caring for deceased worker's children under eighteen years of age.

Dependent parents of a worker who died "fully" or "currently" insured are entitled to benefits equal to one-half of the primary benefit, *provided* they were substantially dependent upon him, and provided he left no wife or child who would be eligible for benefits through him.

Lump sum death payment is payable to the widow, widower, or to a person who paid or contributed to the burial expenses of a worker who died "fully" or "currently" insured. Payment is three times the primary benefit.

WHO IS COVERED

All "employees," in the sense that the term is used at common law, are covered, with the following exceptions or stipulations:

Railroad workers (including employees of railroad labor organizations) are excluded. Such workers are covered by a separate system, the Railroad Retirement System. This is a federal program, based upon principles similar to OASI but differing in many significant details. Workers who have had coverage in both systems may add these periods together so as to qualify for benefits under either program.

Government employees (state or local, with the exception of policemen and firemen) can get Social Security under special agreements between the state and the federal government even if they are under a retirement system, provided a majority of the members of the system vote for Social Security coverage. Most employees of the federal government who are not covered by another retirement system can now be covered under Social Security.

Employees of religious, educational, and charitable organizations are excluded unless the employer elects to enter the system and two-thirds of the employees vote to accept it. If this occurs, all employees who voted in favor of it are covered as well as all future employees.

Agricultural laborers, after 1954, will get Social Security credit for their work for each farm operator who pays them $100 or more cash wages in a year.

Domestic help, after 1954, will get Social Security credit for their work for any household employer who pays them $50 or more in cash wages in a calendar quarter.

Certain occupational categories which common law excludes from the employer-employee relationship are specifically covered; these are: full-time life insurance salesmen; full-time traveling or city salesmen (but not house-to-house salesmen); certain agent drivers and commission drivers; and home workers.

All *self-employed* persons are now covered except those whose income is derived from medicine, dentistry, optometry, osteopathy, naturopathy, chiropody, veterinary science, and law. If such professional people are employed, they are, of course, covered.

HOW ELIGIBILITY IS DETERMINED

Eligibility for primary benefits is based upon the length of time the insured worker has been in covered employment. The unit of measurement is the calender quarter. To secure credit for such coverage, earnings must be at least $50 per quarter for an employee and $100 per quarter for a self-employed person. Persons with wage credits in covered employment fall into several categories:

To be *fully and permanently insured,* that is, to be guaranteed a benefit at age sixty-five, the insured person must have forty quarters in covered employment. They need not be consecutive quarters. It is possible, therefore, for a young man to work ten years in covered employment, spend the rest of his working life (which might be twenty years or more) in some non-covered occupation, and yet be guaranteed a benefit at age sixty-five. As coverage is extended to more occupations, there is, of course, less opportunity to work in non-covered employment.

Older workers entering covered employment for the first time, or those whose occupation has just been covered, might be unable to acquire forty quarters of coverage before reaching the age of sixty-five. In their interest a modification has been introduced. Thus the fully insured status may also be acquired by accumulating one quarter of coverage for every two quarters elapsing after 1936 and before age sixty-five (or death, if earlier), provided that such quarters of coverage equal half the quarters after 1950. Thus, a person aged sixty-two in 1950 needs only six quarters of covered employment before becoming eligible for a benefit in 1953.

To be *currently insured* is to have a status which guarantees benefits to survivors. Six quarters of coverage in the thirteen-quarter period consisting of the quarter of death and the twelve preceding quarters is required. The insurance thus resembles paid-up life insurance.

It is important to note that a person who has more than five quarters of coverage but less than forty quarters does not necessarily guarantee benefits to his survivors. Quarters in non-covered employment cancel out quarters in covered employment until forty quarters of coverage have been achieved. For example, should a young man leaving covered employment after ten quarters die at any time during the next eleven quarters, his survivors will be protected because he will have fulfilled the requirement of having been in covered employment for half the number of quarters from his first being covered to the quarter preceding his death. Should he die after that, without having acquired any more quarters of coverage, his survivors will be deprived of benefits.

THE BENEFIT FORMULA

The size of the monthly primary benefit is determined by applying the benefit formula to the average monthly wage in covered employment. The latter can be figured from either 1937 or 1951 (whichever will give the higher payment, if the insured person reached age 22 before 1951 and has six quarters of coverage after 1950) until the time of retirement or death. Beginning in 1955, the first $4200 in annual earnings is used in computing the average monthly wage. Recent revisions in the law made it possible, under specified conditions, to exclude some years of low (or no) income in computing averages.

The formula as revised by the 1954 amendment to the law is: 55 percent of the first $110 of average monthly wages, plus 20 percent of the next $240.

This formula will apply generally to persons who retire in the future. Current beneficiaries will have their benefits increased by means of a special conversion table.

Under the new formula the maximum monthly benefit for a retired worker is $108.50, for a retired worker and his wife $162.80. For a family the maximum benefit is now $200. The family benefit is limited to 80 percent of the wage earner's average wage. The minimum monthly benefit is $30.

In contrast to the earlier benefit formula which was weighted in favor of the worker with low average earnings, the present formula is weighted in favor of the middle-income group.

Although receipt of the primary benefit is not based on need, there are restrictions with respect to earnings. A person between the ages of 65 and 72 is not eligible for any Social Security benefits if he earns more than $2080, regardless of the source of his earnings. A person 72 or over may earn any amount and receive Social Security benefits.

NOTE: The foregoing outline of eligibility requirements merely illustrates the general character of the program. The many fine points of definition and interpretation have been omitted.

The Financing of Old-Age and Survivors' Insurance

At the present time, OASI is financed by a tax on pay rolls shared jointly by employers and employees covered by the law. Employee pay-roll deductions and the employers' contribution are a percentage of annual wages up to a maximum annual wage of $4200. The tax on employees and employers was first fixed by Congress at 1½ percent each. In 1954 this rate was increased to 2 percent; in 1960, it will be increased to 2½ percent; in 1965, to 3 percent; after 1969 the rate is to be 3¼ percent.

The pay-roll taxes collected each year are, at present, more than adequate to pay current benefits.[7] During the first generation of the life of the plan, however, there will be a steady increase in disbursements relative to collections for two reasons: (1) the population is aging, that is, more people are reaching the retirement age of sixty-five and living beyond it, and (2) until the program matures, there will be a proportionate increase each year in the number of persons reaching retirement age and qualifying for benefits.

Individuals who are now over age twenty-one, moreover, will quality for benefits although they will not have spent an entire working lifetime in covered employment; people near retirement age, in fact, can qualify for benefits with as few as six quarters of covered employment.

A central issue in the financing of OASI concerns the calcula-

---

[7] In 1951, although benefits paid amounted to $1,125,464,000, the trust fund increased from $14,735,567,000 in January to $15,539,734 in December. See "Current Operating Statistics," *Social Security Bulletin,* April, 1952, Table 3, p. 16.

tion of a tax rate adequate to maintain the solvency of the system at the time maximum demand is made upon it. The ultimate cost of the system is difficult to determine. Estimates of future costs are affected by many factors. Some of the factors concerning which assumptions must be made are these: how many persons will reach age sixty-five; how many will be eligible for benefits; how many will retire; how long benefits will be paid; how much will be paid as retirement benefits; how much will be paid as supplementary and survivor benefits.

In 1948 the Advisory Council on Social Security estimated that the cost of financing benefits, as then provided for, would in the year 2000 range from a low cost estimate of 4.19 percent of pay roll to a high cost estimate of 8.12 percent of pay roll. Benefits liberalized in accordance with the council's recommendations (most of which were enacted into law in 1950) would entail costs estimated to range from 5.87 percent of pay roll to 9.70 percent of pay roll by the year 2000.

Complicating factors in the financing of OASI are the political and economic implications of a tax rate adequate to meet the ultimate cost of the program. Congress has been understandably reluctant to impose such a tax so long as the reserve fund continues to grow in spite of increased disbursements. The tax on wages is regressive, that is, it bears more heavily on persons with low incomes; since deductions are made on wages up to $4200 annually, workers with earnings less than that amount suffer a proportionately greater loss of purchasing power than workers whose incomes are higher. The tax on pay rolls, to the extent that the employer can shift it to the consumer in the form of higher prices, is also regressive since it is, in a sense, similar to a sales tax.

In the past, proposals have been advanced that government participate in the financing of OASI through the use of general tax funds. This action was recommended by the Advisory Council on Social Security in 1938 and in 1948. In view of the low tax rates prevailing at the time some such arrangement seemed desirable if not inevitable. In 1950, however, Congress decided that the program should be on a completely self-supporting basis and adopted the present tax schedule, which is designed, on the basis of reasonable estimates, to achieve this objective.

The financing of OASI involves technical matters, largely economic in nature, which lie outside the scope of this work. One point, however, must be explained because it has given rise to so much misunderstanding concerning the management of the reserve fund: OASI reserves are invested in government bonds. This has been repeatedly criticized on the grounds that it involves double taxation. The argument is that the money collected in pay-roll taxes is loaned to the government and that all the trust fund has left are government IOU's. When the reserve has to be drawn upon to pay benefits these bonds have to be redeemed by the government, and the only means of redemption is through revenue collected from taxes; hence the American people have to pay twice for OASI protection. The fallacy in this reasoning was exposed in the report of the Advisory Council on Social Security in 1948, thus:

This reserve has been invested in United States Government securities, which in the opinion of the Council represent the proper form of investment for these funds. We do not agree with those who criticize this form of investment on the grounds that the Government spends for general purposes the money received from the sale of securities to that fund. Actually such investment is as reasonable and proper as is the investment by life-insurance companies of their own reserve funds in Government securities. The fact that the Government uses the proceeds received from the sales of securities to pay the cost of the war and its other expenses is entirely legitimate. It no more implies mishandling of moneys received from the sale of United States securities to life-insurance companies, banks or individuals.

The investment of the old-age and survivors' insurance funds in Government securities does not mean that people have been or will be taxed twice for the same benefits, as has been charged. The following example illustrates this point. Suppose some year in the future the outgo under the old-age and survivors' insurance system should exceed payroll tax receipts by $100,000,000. If there were then $5,000,000,000 of United States 2-percent bonds in the trust fund, they would produce interest amounting to $100,000,000 a year. This interest would of course have to be raised by taxation. But suppose that there were no bonds in the trust fund. In that event $100,000,000 to cover the deficit in the old-age and survivors' insurance system would have to be raised by taxation; and in addition another $100,000,000 would have to be raised by taxation to pay the interest on $5,000,000,000 of Government bonds owned by someone else. The bonds would be in other hands because if the Government had not been able to borrow from the Old-age and Survivors' Insurance Trust Fund, it would have to borrow the same amount from other sources. In other words, the ownership of the $5,000,000,000 in bonds by the old-age and survivors' insurance system would prevent the $100,000,000 from having to be raised twice—quite the opposite from the "double taxation" that has been charged.[8]

Adequacy of Benefits

OASI benefits do not vary with individual need; nevertheless, it would be incorrect to say that this program was unconcerned with need. Its very existence testifies to the fact that need exists. The method of insurance, unlike public assistance, however, is designed to meet average need. The question then arises: How large should the benefit (primary, supplementary, and survivors') be on the average? This question cannot be answered in terms of mere dollars and cents because the purchasing power of money varies, whereas the dollar amount of the benefit is, at least in theory, predetermined by earnings and contributions in covered employment.

In private insurance, a policyholder who contracts for an annuity pays a certain premium in return for which he is guaranteed a monthly benefit of x dollars. If, at the time he becomes entitled to his annuity, the value of the dollar has risen he gains; if the value of the dollar has declined, he loses. The risk which is inherent in private insurance would defeat the purpose of social insurance. The only means of overcoming it, however, involves a departure from the principle of proportionality (i.e., the relation of benefits to contributions) and periodic revisions of the benefit

[8] U.S. Congress, Senate, *The Reports of the Advisory Council on Social Security to the Senate Committee on Finance*, Appendix I-A, "The Old-Age and Survivors' Insurance Trust Fund," Document No. 208, 80th Congress, 2nd sess. (Washington: Government Printing Office, 1949), p. 48.

formula so that the purchasing power of the benefit will not fall so low as to defeat the objective of the program.

The necessity for adjustments in the benefit amounts is reflected in the following illustration:

A worker enters covered employment in 1937, expecting to retire in 1949 at age sixty-five. With an average monthly wage of $200, his retirement benefit, according to the formula adopted in 1939, would have amounted to $39.20 a month; his wife would have drawn a "wife's benefit" of $19.60 a month. Their combined monthly benefit, $58.80, would have barely met minimum needs in 1939, and in 1949 would have been utterly inadequate. Yet the average primary benefit in 1949 was only $28.39.

OASI was not designed to afford an ideal standard of life for its beneficiaries, except in so far as insurance benefits are supplemented by outside resources. Few beneficiaries, however, have sufficient outside resources (apart from supplementary public assistance, and help from relatives or friends) to provide a reasonably adequate level of living when combined with their monthly benefits.[9] The benefits payable under the formula prevailing prior to 1950 were so low as to have very little effect on the economic well-being of their recipients. In 1950, however, the formula for computing current and future benefits was drastically revised upward; the average benefit was increased by 77½ percent. In 1952 the average benefit was raised another 12½ percent.

It has been necessary to change the benefit formula from time to time because the formula does not give adequate weight to increased earnings. Although a rise in the price level is generally accompanied by a rise in wages, the average monthly wage (which determines the size of the benefit) is related to total earnings in covered employment, and this is pulled downward by the lower earnings in the earlier years of coverage. Furthermore, the maximum annual earnings which can be credited is limited to $4200 (prior to 1950 it was $3000). In 1949 the Social Security Administration stated the case for raising the maximum annual creditable wage thus:

[9] See *Social Security Bulletin,* especially Edna Wentworth and Margaret L. Stecker, "Resources of Beneficiaries of Old-Age and Survivors' Insurance," November, 1949, pp. 3–12.

When the maximum creditable annual wage was set at $3,000 in 1939, only 3 percent of all workers in covered employment received more than that amount. Of those in covered employment all the year, approximately 5 percent earned over $3,000. At today's wages, about 24 percent of all covered workers, and 37 percent of the workers regularly in covered employment earn more than $3,000; 19 percent of all covered workers and 29 percent of the regularly covered workers earn between $3,000 and $4,800. Because the cost of living has increased about 70 percent since 1939, workers who today earn $4,800 live no better than those who earned $3,000 in 1939. To provide approximately as much protection as was intended when the formula was established, the maximum creditable wage should be increased to $4,800.[10]

Periodic liberalization of the benefit formula and of the size of current benefits complicates the problem of financing a system which, theoretically, should be financed from prior contributions. Since Congress has affirmed that the system must be completely self-supporting, that is, financed solely from pay-roll taxes and interest on the reserve, a tax rate had to be set which was high enough to take care not only of the increased cost of future benefits but also of the increased expenditures for current benefits. Thus, a good part of the benefit of current beneficiaries is being subsidized by the pay-roll taxes of future beneficiaries.

Changes in the benefit schedule in recent years indicate clearly that Congress intends that OASI provide an income sufficient at least to meet subsistence needs—that is, a benefit roughly approximating an old-age assistance grant. The average old-age assistance grant in March, 1953, was $48.86; the average old-age retirement benefit during the same month was $49.94.[11]

UNEMPLOYMENT COMPENSATION

Unemployment is a hazard which, strictly speaking, is uninsurable because of its unpredictability. The risk is such that—quite aside from structural differences—a program designed to pay benefits because of unemployment must differ in many essential respects from a retirement and survivorship program such as

[10] Social Security Administration, *Annual Report*, 1949, p. 40.
[11] "Selected Current Statistics," *Social Security Bulletin*, June, 1953, p. 2.

OASI. Some workers covered by unemployment compensation may never need to draw benefits; others may qualify on numerous occasions during their working life. Since there is no way of foretelling how long unemployment will last, it is obviously impossible to guarantee benefits for such a period; they must be limited in duration. Unemployment compensation is restricted to persons who are involuntarily out of work but who are able and willing to work. Those who quit their jobs without good cause, or because they are unable to work, are not eligible for benefits.

Unemployment compensation, unlike OASI, is essentially a state program. It is administered by the states under state law. Like public assistance, however, it has come into being largely because of inducement by the federal government. The inducement is in the form of a 90 percent rebate on a 3 percent federal tax on pay rolls of employers of eight or more persons, if the taxable employers are covered by a state unemployment compensation plan. It was inevitable that every state would enact a law conforming with the minimum federal requirements, for otherwise employers would have to pay a tax from which no one in the state would derive benefit. The 10 percent of the tax retained by the federal government is used to make grants to the states for financing the administration of the program.

What is the purpose of unemployment compensation? Despite the fact that the program has been in operation for seventeen years, and that the theory of unemployment compensation had been discussed for many years prior thereto, there is still considerable difference of opinion. The report "Issues in Social Security" suggests that "the most generally accepted view is that UC is justified primarily as a method for providing benefits needed to maintain unemployed workers and their families." These benefits, however, are limited in amount and duration. Another view is that it has the primary objective of stabilizing employment. This is reflected in the provisions in state law for a tax reduction for employers with good employment records—an incentive for employers to regularize their employment of labor. Still another view is that, at least in part, UC is a device for maintaining purchasing power. Thus, unemployed workers and their families are enabled

to continue buying needed goods and services, thereby preventing, or at least retarding, the decline in demand which might
otherwise result in further unemployment.

Professor Domenico Gagliardo comments succinctly on this
point:

What then is unemployment compensation designed to do? As a
first approach to an answer it may be said that unemployment compensation is designed to distribute part of the money losses that are
suffered by workers because of unemployment. Not all unemployment
is paid for, and what is compensated is at less than the full amount
lost, especially for the better paid workers. The duration of benefits
in even the most liberal system is not long enough to care for extended unemployment. In short it may be said that unemployment
compensation is designed to distribute in part the loss suffered from
erratic unemployment and to absorb the first blow of depressional
unemployment. There is reason to believe that seasonal unemployment results in a disproportionate amount of payments made. As
presently designed, the relief of prolonged unemployment falls altogether outside its scope.[12]

Because of the great variety in state laws with respect to such
matters as coverage, eligibility, amount, and duration of benefits,
it will be necessary to limit discussion to the more general features of unemployment compensation legislation, with only brief
reference to significant differences.

Title III of the Social Security Act, "Grants to States for Unemployment Compensation Administration," deals only with certain broad aspects of administration and with the conditions
under which states qualify for funds to administer the program.
The provisions of Title VIII, "Taxes with Respect to Employment," are now contained in and superseded by Sub-chapter A of
Chapter 9 of the Internal Revenue Code. Here we find the heart
of the federal unemployment compensation legislation—the conditions under which employers in a given state are allowed to offset
the federal tax on pay rolls because of approved state unemployment compensation plans. As in public assistance, considerable

[12] Domenico Gagliardo, *American Social Insurance* (New York: Harper,
1949), p. 231.

latitude is permitted. States may be more liberal than the federal minimum but they cannot be more restrictive.

Coverage

Employment that must be covered includes any service of whatever nature performed within the United States by an employee of an employer of eight or more persons within twenty or more weeks in a calendar year except:

1. Agricultural labor.
2. Domestic service in a private home.
3. Service performed by an individual in the employ of his son, daughter, or spouse, and the service performed by a child under the age of twenty-one in the employ of his father or mother.
4. Service performed in the employ of a state, or a political subdivision thereof, or an instrumentality of one or more states or political subdivision.
5. Service performed in the employ of a corporation, community chest, fund, or foundation organized and operated exclusively for religious, charitable, scientific, literary, or educational purposes, or for the prevention of cruelty to children or animals, no part of the net earnings of which inures to the benefit of any private shareholder or individual.
6. Casual labor not in the course of the employer's regular business.

Merchant seamen were excluded until 1946. Railroad workers were included until Congress established a national railroad unemployment insurance system in 1939.

In general, the state legislation contains the same exclusions as the federal law except for the "size-of-firm" limitations. As of December, 1949, only twenty-one states restricted coverage to employees of firms employing eight or more workers. The other twenty-nine states covered employees in firms of one, three, four, or six employees; in seventeen of the states the coverage was for "one or more workers." [13] The Advisory Council on Social Security

[13] Ruth Reticker, "Trends in Unemployment Insurance Coverage and Benefits Legislation," *Social Security Bulletin*, December, 1949, p. 11.

has recommended that the "size-of-firm" limitation be eliminated from federal legislation, but it had not been.

The Benefit Structure

Among the most important questions that must be answered before a program of unemployment compensation can be established are these: What portion of an unemployed person's wage loss should be compensated? What should be the amount of the weekly benefit, and how long its duration? How should an unemployed person qualify for benefits? Who is an "unemployed" person under the terms of the law? For the most part, the federal act is silent on these points and the states have answered them variously. In this and the following section we shall attempt to explain the basis on which the states have sought to work out the problems confronting them.

Usually an unemployed person becomes eligible for benefits of a certain amount and for a specified period of time because, during a prior period, he had specified minimum earnings in covered employment. The twelve-month period during which unemployment benefits are available by virtue of prior coverage is known as the "benefit year." The twelve-month period during which earnings in covered employment qualify a worker for subsequent benefits is known as the "base year." The benefit year may begin for all workers on a specified date, usually April 1, or it may begin when each worker files his claim for benefits. There is a three months' interval or quarter between the beginning of the benefit year and the end of the base year. Thus, if the benefit year begins April 1, the base year is the preceding calendar year. This lag is necessitated by administrative considerations, such as the reporting of wages and taxes by the employers.

One of the objectives of the original state laws was to pay benefits of approximately 50 percent of full-time weekly wages. Since taxes are paid, and base period earnings are computed, on only the first $3000 of annual wages, and since there are statutory minimum and maximum limits to the benefits paid, only the lower-paid workers are compensated at a rate even approaching 50 percent. The fact that wage levels have increased in recent

years while the figure for maximum creditable wages has remained stationary makes the relationship between weekly benefits and prior weekly wages even less realistic. Dependency
benefits, payable in eleven states, also affect this relationship.

Although states differ widely in the method of computing
benefits, the latter are always related in some way to prior earnings. While unemployment is usually measured and compensated
in units of seven days, technical difficulties in the reporting of
essential data by employers make it difficult to measure covered
employment in terms of weekly earnings; hence, quarterly earnings are used. The base period earnings requirement varies from
state to state. It may be a flat amount, say $200; it may be a
minimum amount plus minimum earnings in two or more
quarters; it may be a sum equal to a multiple (usually thirty
times) of the weekly benefit, combined with other requirements
such as specified minimum earnings in at least one quarter.

The weekly benefit is usually computed by dividing the earnings in the quarter of highest earnings in the base period by a
fraction (ranging from one-twentieth to one-twenty-sixth). Most
states pay benefits for partial unemployment through some form
of proration. Weeks of unemployment or of employment in non-
covered work during the base period may reduce the size of the
benefit.

The theory of relating benefits to the amount and continuity
of prior earnings is based upon the presumed desirability of
having benefits reflect the different levels of living represented
by different earnings, in order to determine whether the applicant
is a bona-fide member of the labor market, and of maintaining
incentives to work by having a substantial differential between
earnings and benefits. The generally low benefits fulfill the last
need, but for that very reason, i.e., the narrow spread between
minimum and maximum benefits, the first requirement is not
fulfilled.

The duration of benefits is as important a consideration as the
weekly benefit amount. The usual way of setting limits to the
number of weekly benefits is to specify that they shall not exceed
a specific multiple, usually from twenty to twenty-six, and shall

not exceed a maximum amount, usually one-fourth, one-third, one-half, or two-thirds of base period wages. As of July, 1952, maximum potential duration varied from sixteen to twenty-six and one-half weeks. Nineteen states with a majority of the covered workers have twenty-six or twenty-six and one-half weeks' duration. Only eight states with 7 percent of the covered population provide less than $400; fifteen states with 55 percent of the covered population afford maximum annual benefits of $600–$700. These maxima do not include additional sums for dependency benefits. In the eleven states that pay such benefits, the maxima range from $312 to $936.

The minimum weekly benefit ranged in July, 1952, from $3 to $15, while the maximum ranges from $20 to $30. These sums do not include dependency allowances. In some states, the maximum potential benefits for the lowest-wage claimant qualifying for benefits are greater than the maximum basis benefits payable to any claimant in other states.

The Waiting Period

All but two states require a waiting period without benefit between the filing of a claim and acceptance for benefits. In all other states except Colorado and Montana the waiting period is one week. The main purpose of the waiting period is to conserve funds. Many workers are reëmployed within a week after losing their jobs, and it is assumed that in most instances they will have sufficient resources to tide them over that period. The benefit outlay and the administrative cost of processing single benefit claims would add greatly to the burden of financing the program.

In addition to the waiting period, eligible claimants must wait a further period before the receipt of benefits. Processing difficulties may delay the payment of the first benefit even further.

Most states pay benefits weekly, but, at the end of the fiscal year 1949, fifteen states, including the large states of Illinois, Missouri, New Jersey, and Texas, were paying all compensable claims on a biweekly basis, and twelve other states were paying part of their claims biweekly.

Qualifications and Disqualifications

Eligibility for benefits is based upon a number of requirements other than earnings in covered employment. Failure to fulfill these requirements may result in denial or postponement of benefits, reduction in the number of *potential* weekly benefits, or even cancellation of benefit *rights.*

The major eligibility requirement is "involuntary unemployment" and ability and willingness to work. A worker may leave a job and be considered "involuntarily unemployed" provided he left the job for "good cause." The latter term is subject to varying interpretations in the different states. It is often interpreted to mean "causes attributable to the employer." Consequently, if a worker leaves a job because of transportation or housing difficulties or for urgent family reasons, he or she may be disqualified. Workers who are discharged for gross misconduct are also disqualified.

The unemployment compensation beneficiary must demonstrate his attachment to the labor market by registering and regularly reporting at the local office of the state employment service. There is an increasing trend in state legislation to include the requirement that the beneficiary be "actively seeking work." While sound in principle, this provision is largely meaningless in practice, since the employment service is not in a position to evaluate what "actively" means in a particular case.

Beneficiaries who are unable to accept "suitable work" for reasons of health lose their benefits. One modification, introduced in Vermont in 1949, is that in such cases benefits will not be discontinued so long as no work, suitable but for the disability, is offered and refused.

The "suitable work" provision is one of the most difficult provisions to administer. In general, a beneficiary is expected to accept work which his past experience and training qualify him to perform, which will compensate him at a rate roughly comparable to his previous earnings, and which does not impose drastic personal hardships, e.g., moving to another part of the country. Not only are these factors interpreted differently in the various states, but they must be related to each beneficiary's personal situation. Thus, there is a much greater element of discretion involved in the administration of unemployment compensation than in OASI. The employment interviewers have to appraise the individual situation in a way much more reminiscent of public assistance.

The federal act stipulates that no one can be denied benefits for refusing a job if it is available because of a strike, lockout, or other labor dispute; if the wages, hours, or working conditions are substantially less favorable than those prevailing for similar work in the community; or if, in order to get the job, the worker must join a company union or sign a "yellow dog" contract (i.e., give up membership in a union or promise not to join a bona-fide union). Workers who are unemployed as a result of a labor dispute do not lose benefits but have them postponed.

The whole question of "policing" the administration of unemployment compensation is too complex to be discussed here. It is sufficient to point out that vigilance is necessary to insure that only eligible claimants receive benefits. Two examples will suffice. First, we have the case of the New York City workers who, at the close of their "season," applied for benefits and then took winter vacations in Florida, banking on the fact that neither in New York nor in Miami would there be much likelihood of "suitable" job referrals. The second illustration comes from a personnel director:

Here is a diemaker, employed for several weeks of temporary work in a General Motors plant in Detroit. This particular job is completed, but at the time of layoff he is informed that another motor company needs diemakers. We have been asked to refer to them any such employees who become available. Soon we receive word from the Michigan Unemployment Compensation Commission that the individual has applied for benefits.

Did he apply for work at the other company? No! The papers are full of ads for diemakers. Did he call at any of those plants? No! Did he make any effort to seek work? No! We protested the payment of benefits to the individual. Our protest was sustained, and benefits were denied.[14]

Workers who are denied claims have the right of appeal. Employers may also appeal, but they do so relatively infrequently. The total number of annual appeals has never been high, although there has been an increase in recent years.

The Financing of Unemployment Compensation

The federal act does not prohibit employee contributions, and though nine states have introduced this requirement, only two still retain it. The Advisory Council on Social Security recommended that the federal act be amended to provide for employee participation but the recommendation was not acted upon. The council believed that, as a matter of principle, at least part of the cost of benefits should be borne by the beneficiaries. It also thought that such participation would increase employee interest in sound administration and would strengthen labor's position in making known its views to state legislators.

The 90 percent offset on the federal tax on pay rolls need not be paid in full toward the financing of the state unemployment compensation plan. All states have "experience rating" provisions which make it possible for employers with good employment records to reduce the amount of their tax. In 1951, therefore, the average rate of contribution in the United States was 1.7 percent of taxable pay rolls instead of 2.7 percent, and in one state the rate was only 0.4 percent.

Although all states have now adopted some form of experience rating, it is still a subject of considerable controversy. Organized labor is opposed to it, the Social Security Administration does not favor it, and the Advisory Council on Social Security has proposed changes in the financing of the program that would eliminate it. Businessmen generally favor it, at least under the present arrangements for financing which place the full burden on employers.

The main idea behind experience rating is that a great deal

[14] George A. Jacoby, "The Significance of Employer Interest," *American Economic Security,* April–May, 1949, p. 38.

of unemployment can be prevented if employers will make efforts to stabilize their labor force. Experience rating provides an incentive for such efforts, since individual employers are thereby enabled to secure reductions in their tax rates if they regularize their employment of labor, and thus reduce the number of compensable job separations. Another factor is that, since their tax rates will be affected by the number of compensable separations (or rather, the amount of benefits paid out to their former employees), their interest in coöperating with the unemployment compensation authorities, so that only eligible claimants receive benefits, will be maintained.

Very probably, many employers look upon experience rating more from the viewpoint of money-saving than of employment stabilization. Although the latter is the more plausible justification in actuality, its efficacy in stabilizing employment is doubtful. While a certain amount of economic activity can be regularized, taken as a whole, it is not subject to such manipulation. Some enterprises are by their very nature stable, e.g., banks and insurance firms; other enterprises are by nature seasonal (the pre-Christmas business of department stores is a case in point); still others are subject to various other fluctuations beyond their control. While many industries may point with satisfaction to their achievements in stabilization, such achievements often affect only a small part of their total operations.

It seems hardly fair to favor certain employers, and thus penalize others, when the degree of employment regularity is largely inherent in the nature of the activity and not subject to their deliberate control. Meriam mentions further difficulties:

> One objection to experience rating is that it may cause employers to seek to attain too high a degree of employment stability. They may hesitate to expand and employ more persons when expansion is possible, for fear they will have to let the new people go when work slackens and either pay them from the individual employer's fund or pay higher contributions into the pooled fund. Stability of employment may not be a virtue if it results in a lessened aggregate of employment over a considerable period. Experience rating and individual employer's funds tend to make the employer's ideal a relatively small force of carefully selected, highly efficient employees continuously

employed. Such a system adds further weight to the fact, present in many enterprises, that carefully selected, highly skilled employees give lowest labor costs per unit of output. It also may encourage the introduction of labor-saving machines to facilitate adjustment of output to demand without changing the size of the force. It may likewise lead to meeting peak demands by lengthening the work week rather than by hiring more employees. An employer may prefer to pay overtime, even penalizing overtime to his highly selected permanent staff —"members of the organization" where morale is high—than to incur obligations to pay unemployment benefits to temporary workers, especially in enterprises where the inexperienced workers give relatively high wage costs per unit of product and sometimes high spoilage charges.[15]

Since tax reductions are related to reductions in compensable unemployment (rather than actual unemployment), employers have an incentive to challenge the individual claimant's right to benefits, and to advocate state unemployment compensation legislation that is restrictive with respect to the length of the waiting period, disqualifications, and other factors that make eligibility for benefits difficult.

States differ greatly in the manner in which they apply merit rating provisions. These provisions (there are at least five broad types) are too complex to be discussed here. It is sufficient to point out that each plan seeks to relate the individual employer's tax rate to the benefits paid his former workers, and each establishes standards for measuring employment. Tax rates are also related to the condition of the reserve fund so that if the latter is low there may be no reductions despite an employer's immediate past experience.

Experience rating results in the following fiscal anomaly: When business is prosperous and both employment levels and employers' profits are high, the tax rate is reduced; when business is slack and employment as well as profits fall off, the tax rate is increased. Assuming, however, that the maximum rate of 2.7 percent is not too great a burden on employers even in bad years, this situation is not necessarily unsound so long as the

[15] Meriam, *op. cit.*, pp. 226–227.

contributions in prosperous years, even at greatly reduced rates, are sufficient to maintain the reserve fund at a high level.

The reserve funds of the several states vary with respect to the degree to which they can meet possible claims. One writer on the subject comments thus:

It is estimated that 58.7 percent of all covered workers employed during an average month in 1947 could be paid benefits for the maximum duration provided under most recently enacted State laws out of funds available on June 30, 1948. Funds in five States were sufficient to pay benefits for the maximum duration to all employed covered workers in the State. . . . Thirty-seven other States had reserves large enough to pay benefits for maximum duration to at least half their workers. Massachusetts was at the bottom of the scale with a reserve sufficient to pay such benefits to only 24.3 percent of the employed covered workers. The variations among States reflect differences in the State laws as well as in the size of reserves and coverage.[16]

In 1948 the Advisory Council recommended that the federal unemployment tax should be payable at a rate of 0.75 percent for both employees and employers. They should each be allowed to credit 80 percent of this tax to contributions paid to a state unemployment fund. No additional credit should be allowed for experience rating. This would have made the combined rate for employers and employees 1.2 percent, which was the average employer contribution in 1948. This change might well have reconciled many employers to the abandonment of experience rating. It was not enacted.

The states do not manage their reserve funds. The pay-roll taxes collected by the states are turned over to the federal Secretary of the Treasury, who is responsible for the management of the Unemployment Trust Fund. Separate accounts are kept for the several states, and sums available from their balances are returned for the purpose of paying benefits.

Space does not permit discussion of several important controversial issues, such as the extension of coverage and whether or

[16] Nathan Ginsberg, "Status of Unemployment Insurance Reserves," *Social Security Bulletin,* December, 1948, p. 14.

not the unemployment compensation, including the employment service, should be administered by the federal government.

WORKMEN'S COMPENSATION

Protection against loss from industrially connected accident and disease is the oldest form of social insurance in the United States. It is wholly outside the Social Security Act and is based entirely upon state legislation except, in so far as the federal government provides such protection for its own employees, for harbor workers and longshoremen.[17] A distinctive feature of workmen's compensation is the extent to which this risk is insured by private carrier. In 1948, for example, 62.4 percent of the total amount paid out in claims was paid by private carriers. Even where state insurance funds operate more or less in competition with private carriers, they do so along strict actuarial lines.

The movement for workmen's compensation began as an effort to make employers assume responsibility for the compensation of workmen injured in their employ. Interest in the subject seems to have arisen as a consequence of the changes in our economic structure, especially the increasing size of industrial enterprises, and the increasing rate of injuries resulting from large-scale manufacturing, transportation, and extractive industry.

Under common law, injured workmen, at least in theory, were entitled to damages. However, not only was litigation costly and time consuming, but the injured workman who hoped to return to his former job would think twice before bringing suit against his employer. More important, perhaps, was the fact that employers had three common-law defenses against suits for damages. If the employer could establish that the injury had resulted from the carelessness of the worker, or that the negligence of a fellow worker had contributed to the cause of the injury, or if he could show that the worker, being aware of the risks involved in the occupation, had nevertheless willingly accepted employment, he could not be held liable. In view of the employers' ability to command greater legal talent and to finance appeals, it was seldom, indeed, that they could not absolve themselves of all responsibility.

[17] The term "state" applies to Hawaii, Alaska, Puerto Rico.

In 1902 Maryland passed a rudimentary workmen's compensation law which was declared unconstitutional two years later because it deprived individuals of the right to a jury trial, and because it gave judicial powers to the insurance commissioner. During the next ten years several states explored the possibility of legislation. The New York and Montana laws were also declared unconstitutional. In 1908, however, the federal government enacted compensation legislation extending protection to several classes of federal employees. In 1913 New York amended its constitution to permit compensation legislation, which was declared constitutional by a decision rendered in 1917. In the meantime, many other states had followed suit—five laws being passed in 1911, eight in 1913, and four in 1914. The movement has now spread to all states.

Variation in state workmen's compensation legislation is even greater than in unemployment compensation. While we can do no more here than point out the major characteristics and differences, it must be noted that, in order to evaluate the program in a given state, we need answers to questions such as: By what method is protection afforded? How extensive is coverage? What is the nature and duration of benefits? How effectively are claims processed? To what extent is there failure to comply with the law?

Coverage

Variations in state programs make it difficult to determine the number of persons covered by workmen's compensation. It was estimated that in 1948 three out of four civilian wage and salary workers were protected against employment injuries.[18] The estimated number has risen from roughly 25,000,000 in 1940 to 34,000,000–35,000,000 in 1948.

Most states exempt employers of agricultural, domestic, and casual labor. Some states restrict coverage to hazardous employment only; however, in a few instances the list of "hazardous" occupations is so extensive as to provide almost complete

[18] Dorothy McCamman, "Workmen's Compensation: Coverage, Premiums, and Payments," *Social Security Bulletin*, July, 1950, p. 6.

coverage. In the majority of states there is some "size of firm" limitation. In most instances employers of fewer than three or of five are excluded; in some states the minimum runs as high as ten, eleven, or fifteen.

All states provide for money payments for industrially connected accidents or death, but only three-fourths of the laws provide for payments for even a few occupational diseases. The latter are equally divided between states that cover all occupational diseases and those that cover only specified diseases.

A peculiarity of workmen's compensation is that, in more than half the states, covered employers and employees are permitted the option of staying out of the system. Employers who choose to "elect out," however, are usually denied the three traditional defenses at common law: "assumption of risk," "contributory negligence," and "the fellow-servant doctrine." [19] Employees who "elect out" may have damage awards scaled down, to the extent that their contributory negligence can be established.

Most states permit employers to insure with private carriers. Of the eighteen states with state insurance funds only seven require that they be used exclusively. The great majority of states permit employers to be "self-insurers" if they can present proof of ability to carry their own risks.

Distinction between workmen's compensation and employers' liability insurance must be noted; the latter, while protecting the employer from losses resulting from injury claims, does not guarantee benefits to the injured workman. The carrier may contest his claim in court.

Benefits

There are several different theories underlying workmen's compensation; we may say that in general, however, it is based on the social and economic desirability of a simple, convenient, and inexpensive method for reimbursing the injured or ill worker for medical care, rehabilitation, and at least part of his wage loss. It also involves the payment of benefits to the dependent of a deceased worker for at least part of the loss of his support.

[19] For a discussion of these defenses, see Gagliardo, *op. cit.*, p. 370.

The amount and duration of benefits vary, not only with respect to the individual situation, but also in accordance with state legislation. Eligible claimants fall into four broad categories: the temporarily but totally disabled (the most common occurrence); the permanently but partially disabled; the permanently and totally disabled; and the dependents of deceased workers.

Although medical payments are provided for in all laws (forty-two of which require the furnishing of prosthetic appliances), only twenty-five states provide for substantially full medical care. In the other states there are limits to the amounts required to be paid. There is considerable variation among the states in their emphasis upon rehabilitation. All states provide services available under the terms of the federal Vocational Rehabilitation Act, while fifteen states have, in addition, special funds for the rehabilitation (including maintenance) of persons who have been industrially disabled. The quality of medical care is uneven. In some jurisdictions "contract practice" prevails; that is, the treatment of industrial injuries and diseases is turned over to a specified physician or hospital for a fixed fee.

Benefits to compensate for wage loss during the period of incapacitation, or for loss of earning power resulting from the disability, vary. Most jurisdictions have established schedules setting forth the number of weeks during which compensation shall be paid for specific injuries. In some states, and in the federal program for civilian employees, life benefits are paid to persons who are totally and permanently disabled. In the other jurisdictions there are limits to the total amount and the duration of benefits. The latter may range from 260 to 1000 weeks, the former from $5000 to $12,000. In some states the weekly benefits may vary with the number of dependents. Permanent partial disability usually involves a period of total disability (the "healing period"), which is taken into consideration in determining total benefits. There is little uniformity in the payment of death benefits. In some states benefits are paid to the widow for life, or until remarriage; children receive payments until they reach a specified age. Other states set limits to the duration and total amount of such benefits.

There is little uniformity, too, in the pattern of weekly benefit amounts. Death benefits and total permanent disability benefits may range from 50 percent to 70 percent of weekly wages, with a maximum of $18 to $20. Benefit schedules have not kept pace with the change in cost of living. The higher-paid workers, moreover, do not fare as well as those whose weekly wages had been lower, owing to the maximum limits on weekly benefits.

Only one state has no waiting period. In the other states this period may range from one to ten days. Its purpose is to reduce costs by eliminating claims for minor injuries. The waiting period applies only to compensation; medical and hospital care is provided immediately. Many states provide that, if the period of disability extends beyond a specified time, payment of compensation is retroactive to the date of injury.

Administration

In all but six states there are specialized agencies or commissions to administer the provisions of the state law. In view of the often complex and delicate nature of claims, it is surprising to find that as many as six states have left to the courts the task of determining whether the rights and duties established by law have been satisfied.

Efficient administration of compensation legislation involves the determination of such matters as whether or not the injured person is covered by the law; whether the employer has complied with the law in providing insurance protection or "self-insurance"; the nature and extent of the injury; computation of the amount of benefits; and determination of the kind of medical aid and rehabilitation required. Issues involving matters of health, employability, and percentage loss of earning power due to injuries are highly technical, difficult to determine, and subject to considerable difference of opinion. The possibility of more or less conscious malingering has to be weighed against the possibility that the insurers wish to skimp on the cost of benefits and medical care.

The process of establishing eligibility for compensation is, therefore, more complicated than for most other types of social insurance, partly because of the nature of the risk—the fact that entitlement is dependent upon so many highly individual elements—but partly also because of the method of protection, since private insurance companies, no matter how seriously they take their responsibility for providing compensation, have a natural interest in conserving their funds by paying benefits only where the evidence clearly requires it. Thus, injured workers, or their survivors, may have to press claims under circumstances in which they are at a disadvantage.

In states with workmen's compensation authorities, various arrangements have been worked out to provide at least some supervision of claims and awards. From the point of view of insuring full compliance with the intent of the law, it would undoubtedly be desirable to require hearings, formal or informal, presided over by a representative of the compensation authority, who would adjudicate claims. This procedure has not been found to be practicable. The administrative cost and the wage loss of workers attending such hearings have been too great, so that states that have used the hearings procedure have generally restricted it to cases that appear to be compensable.

A more common practice is for the insurer and the injured worker to come to terms through some form of agreement or direct settlement, subject to later review by the compensation authority. This is not entirely satisfactory, as the worker may be at a disadvantage in negotiating with the employer or insurance company. The written reports of the negotiations, moreover, may not be sufficiently detailed to enable the authority to determine whether or not the worker has had the opportunity, or the ability, to present his situation in the most favorable terms.

Workmen's compensation is the one form of social insurance that insures against a contingency which is largely preventable. Since protection is provided, for the most part, through private insurance companies or state funds operating in competition with them, the profit motive provides a powerful incentive to efforts to reduce the incidence of claims through safety education and the development of safety devices. The relation of premium rates to the accident or industrial disease rate in different firms transmits this motive to employers. Perhaps this pattern of private insurance has resulted in greater emphasis upon prevention than upon the payment of prompt, adequate, and equitable benefits. Even if so, if one assesses the value of the program in terms of the well-being of *all* covered workers, this might be better than if the emphasis had been reversed.

SOME UNFINISHED BUSINESS

The Advisory Council on Social Security, in its 1948 report to the Senate, recommended that insurance be provided for the totally and permanently disabled. Such a program would protect persons who are attached to the labor market in very much the same fashion as OASI provides protection, except that there would be no dependency benefits. The program would be correlated with workmen's compensation so that there would be no overlapping of benefits. Congress rejected this proposal and instead set up an assistance category for the totally and permanently disabled. Whether or not one approves of this Congressional substitution, in all likelihood a few years' experience with an assistance category of this nature will result in the development of procedures and controls with respect to the determination of what constitutes total and permanent disability, so that eventually an insurance program may be established without fear of its getting out of hand. The Railroad Retirement system pays benefits to persons who are permanently and totally disabled, or whose disability prevents them from working in their regular occupation.

Some progress is being made in providing protection against non-industrially connected temporary disability or illness. At present four states (Rhode Island, California, New Jersey, and New York) and the Railroad Unemployment Compensation system offer such protection. Benefits are available only to persons who are attached to the labor market. The program is integrated with the unemployment compensation program except in New York, where it is administered by the Workmen's Compensation

Board. An interesting contrast in financing is that in the railroad system the employers supply the funds, whereas in the state programs it is the employees who pay for their own protection.

Health insurance is undoubtedly the most controversial form of insurance that has been proposed. Because of its complexity we cannot discuss it here.[20] It should be noted, however, that, even though the establishment of a program of health insurance may be desirable, it may first, perhaps, be necessary to (1) expand medical facilities so that they could meet the demand upon them were such a program to be established and (2) provide greater insurance protection against the loss of income due to ill health or accident.

No single program of social insurance can be evaluated in isolation. It must be studied not only in relation to all the other insurances but also in relation to other welfare programs such as assistance and industry pension plans. They all involve transfer payments. A particular type of program, examined in isolation, may appear to be desirable but, when related to other programs, may prove to be unsound. As Eveline Burns points out: "To an overwhelming extent, therefore, the costs of social welfare must be considered from two major angles: how great a drain do they represent on our total economic resources, and how great a measure of income redistribution will our country stand for." [21]

SELECTED REFERENCES

Burns, Eveline M., *The American Social Security System,* Boston: Houghton Mifflin, 1949.

Gagliardo, Domenico, *American Social Insurance,* New York: Harper, 1949.

Haber, William, and Cohen, Wilber J., *Readings in Social Security,* New York: Prentice-Hall, 1948.

[20] A comprehensive report, *Building America's Health,* was published by the President's Commission on the Health Needs of the Nation in December, 1952.

[21] Eveline M. Burns, "How Much Social Welfare Can America Afford?" *Bulletin of the New York School of Social Work,* July, 1949.

Index

Abbott, Edith, 60, 72–74, 95–98, 222–223
Ability, fund raising, 118–119
sufficient, 225–229
Administration, local, see Local agencies
Advisory Council on Social Security, 363–365, 370–371, 376, 379, 386
Aged, assistance for, see Old-age assistance
homes for, 136–138
Agencies, see Local agencies; Voluntary agencies
Aggression, 273–274
Agricultural Adjustment Acts, 337
Agriculture, see Farming
Agriculture, Department of, 172, 337
Aid to dependent children, see Children
Aid to the blind, see Blind
Aid to the disabled, see Disabled
Alabama, 106
Alaska, 293
Alcohol, 183
Allowance in support of wages, 150–152, 186, 267
Almsgiving, 23–24, 141
Almshouses, 22, 23, 28, 35–37, 39–40, 43, 46, 130
American Association for Labor Legislation, 53
American Association of Social Workers, 74, 123, 184
American Asylum for the Deaf and Dumb, 43
American Medical Association, 129
American Public Health Association, 131 n., 162, 172 n.
American Public Welfare Association, 118, 123, 130–131

outline for assistance workers, 247–249
report on assistance standards, 167–186
Appointment, local agency, 310, 318–319
Argentina, 356
Arizona, 188
Arkansas, 106, 187
Armstrong, Barbara N., 8–9
Aronson, Albert H., 309–310
Asia, 9, 158
Assertions, in investigation, 253–254
Assistance, right to, 95–103
Assistance standards, and minimum standard of living, 186–187
clothing, 173, 182–183
food, 172, 178–180
grant, size of, 187–192
payment method, 170, 175–178
personal incidentals, 173–174, 183–186
shelter, 172–173, 181–182
Assistance worker, 224–225
and individual, see Human relations
investigation, see Investigation
knowledge and skills, 240–250
supervisor, see Supervisor
training, see Training
Associated Press, 106
Association for Improving the Conditions of the Poor, 48
Assumption of risk, 382
Auctioning off, 35, 38, 150
Australia, 356
Automobiles, 163, 183

Ball, Robert, 102
Baltimore, Md., 51, 287
Banks, 266